Front row left to right: Antoni Kuklinski, Niles Hansen, André Raynauld, François Perroux, Benjamin Higgins, Donald J. Savoie and Fernand Martin.
Second row left to right: Lloyd Rodwin, John Friedmann, John Vanderkamp, James Melvin, Kingsley Haynes, Raymond Courbis, William Alonso and Harry Richardson.

REGIONAL ECONOMIC DEVELOPMENT

Other titles by Benjamin Higgins

Canada's financial system in war. New York: National Bureau of Economic Research.

Canada's trade policy in the second development decade. With Jean Downing Higgins. Montreal: Private Planning Association.

Economic development of a small planet. With Jean Downing Higgins. New York: W. W. Norton.

Economic development: problems, principles, policies. New York: W. W. Norton.

Indonesia: the Crisis of the Millstones. With Jean Downing Higgins. New York: Van Nostrand.

Indonesia's economic stabilization and development in Latin America. New York: Institute for Pacific Relations.

Japan and southeast Asia. With Jean Downing Higgins. New York: Harcourt Brace.

Lombard Street in war and reconstruction. New York: National Bureau of Economic Research.

Public investment and full employment. Montreal: International Labour Office.

Stanvac in Indonesia. With other contributors. Washington DC: National Planning Association.

Social aspects of economic development in Latin America. Paris: UNESCO.

The rise – and fall? of Montreal. Moncton: Canadian Institute for Research on Regional Development.

United Nations and US Foreign Economic Policy. New York: Richard D. Irwin.

Urban Housing in Papua New Guinea. Port Moresby: Institute of National Affairs.

What do economists know? Melbourne: Melbourne University Press.

Other titles by Donald J. Savoie

Essais sur le développement régional. Edited with André Raynauld. Montreal: Les Presses Universitaires de Montréal.

Federal-Provincial Collaboration: The Canada-New Brunswick General Development Agreement. Montreal: McGill-Queen's University Press.

The Canadian Economy: a regional perspective. Editor. Toronto: Methuen.

Regional economic development: Canada's search for solutions. Toronto: University of Toronto Press.

REGIONAL ECONOMIC DEVELOPMENT

Essays in honour of
François Perroux

EDITED BY
Benjamin Higgins and Donald J. Savoie

Institut canadien de recherche sur le développement régional

Boston
UNWIN HYMAN
London   Sydney   Wellington

© Institut canadien de recherche sur le développement régional 1988

This book is copyright under the Berne Convention. No reproduction without permission. All rights reserved.

Allen & Unwin, Inc.,
8 Winchester Place, Winchester, Mass. 01890, USA

Published by the Academic Division of
Unwin Hyman Ltd
15/17 Broadwick Street, London W1V 1FP

Allen & Unwin (Australia) Ltd,
8 Napier Street, North Sydney, NSW 2060, Australia

Allen & Unwin (New Zealand) Ltd in association with the
Port Nicholson Press Ltd,
60 Cambridge Terrace, Wellington, New Zealand

First published in 1988

Library of Congress Cataloging in Publication Data

Regional economic development.

Papers presented at a conference held during the summer of 1985 at Grand Pré, Nova Scotia, Canada, sponsored by the Canadian Institute for Research on Regional Development.
Includes bibliographies and index.
  1. Economic development.
  2. Regional economics.
  I. Perroux, François, 1903– .
  II. Perroux, François, 1903– .
  III. Higgins, Benjamin Howard, 1912– .
  IV. Savoie, Donald J. V. Université de Moncton. Canadian Institute for Research on Regional Development.
  HD75.R44   1987   338.9   87–16749
ISBN 0–04–338155–3 (alk. paper)

British Library Cataloguing in Publication Data

Regional economic development: essays in honour of François Perroux.
  1. Regional economics
  2. Economic development
  I. Higgins, Benjamin
  II. Savoie, Donald J.
  III. Perroux, François
  330.9   HT391.3
ISBN 0–04–338155–3

Typeset in 10 on 12 point Zapf by Oxford Print Associates Ltd, Oxford
and printed in Great Britain by Biddles of Guildford

Preface

This book had its origins in a conference sponsored by the Canadian Institute for Research on Regional Development at Grand Pré, Nova Scotia, Canada. The conference brought together a group of distinguished Canadian and international scholars for four days in the summer of 1985. The purpose of the conference was not to produce a "proceedings" which would merely group together a series of papers. Nor is this volume the usual festschrift, each author contributing a chapter on a subject of his own choosing. Rather, each participant was invited to write on a particular topic, and the conference was held *in camera*, with the intention of producing an integrated book on a distinct subject, coordinated whole consisting of a series of connected chapters.

The Grand Pré Conference was the first major conference organized by the Canadian Institute for Research on Regional Development. The Institute felt it was important to explore fully existing theories of and approaches to regional development and to take stock of current thinking in the field before launching major research initiatives on possible new approaches. What better opportunity to do this than by inviting scholars from around the world who, over the past 20 years, have distinguished themselves by contributing in a significant fashion to our understanding of regional development problems and approaches?

Among all scholars of regional development, one in particular has stood out during this period. François Perroux is in many ways the father of regional development theory. His contributions to two important concepts in economics – time and space – have been substantial. His essay on growth poles gave rise to countless other essays and scholarly work, and to a variety of government programs for regional development here in Canada and in many other countries. Paul Streeten, past president of the American Economists Association, described François Perroux as "a giant figure, of Nobel prize stature, among political economists." He adds that Perroux's "notion of growth poles and of the dominant economy have helped to bring about paradigm changes, by incorporating variables such as power into the analysis."

It is thus only fitting that the Institute's first major conference would be held in honour of François Perroux. We also had the pleasure of his company at the conference. At the age of 84, he participated in a spirited fashion in the conference's deliberations, and also gave the keynote address, which is Chapter 2 of this book. The reader will note that Mr Perroux retains the capacity to write original and thought-provoking essays.

The conference gave me personally a sense of *l'ironie de l'histoire*, and I cannot refrain myself from highlighting it here. The hotel where the conference was held overlooks Grand Pré. There, some 230 years ago, British soldiers expelled an Acadian settlement and scattered the inhabitants on boats for a variety of destinations, most of them unknown. My ancestors on both my father and mother's side were inhabitants of Grand Pré at the time, and they too were expelled from the region. I wonder if my troubled ancestors, unsure of their future, and looking back at their community which was being so brutally destroyed as they were sailing away, ever considered that some day one of their descendants would return to Grand Pré in the capacity I did. For I was there as head of a research institute, organizing a conference in Grand Pré to which scholars of some of the leading universities of the English-speaking world came to present papers in honour of a French economist, François Perroux.

The Institute received support from several quarters throughout this project. Our first debt is to the participants at the conference, who brought considerable insight to the complexities of regional development theory and practices. In particular, Benjamin Higgins and André Raynauld deserve special thanks for co-chairing the conference. Benjamin Higgins also played a vital role in the preparation of the conference. My final debt is to Ginette Benoit and Jacqueline Robichaud for typing and retyping the manuscript and for grappling superbly with the difficult task of typing the conference deliberations and to Mrs Duc for her excellent work on François Perroux's bibliography. The deliberations form the basis for the concluding chapter of this book. Louise Robichaud was very instrumental in overlooking the various stages in preparing the manuscript for publication. I want to say a special thank you to her.

Donald J. Savoie
Moncton

Contents

Preface

List of contributors   *page*

Introduction: the economics and politics of regional development

  Benjamin Higgins and Donald J. Savoie   1
  Progress in regional development programming and regional
  theory development   4
  Part I: Perroux   13
  Part II: Methods and approaches   15
  Part III: Canadian experiences   20
  Part IV: Experience in other countries   25
  References   27

PART I: PERROUX

1 François Perroux

  Benjamin Higgins   31

  1.1 Perroux's general theory and social philosophy   33
  1.2 Perroux, Keynes, Schumpeter   37
  1.3 Growth poles   41
  References   46

2 The pole of development's new place in a general theory of economic activity

  François Perroux   48

  A Economic analysis   48
  2.1 The pole of development and the general theory of the economy   48
  2.2 Present-day dynamics and the poles of development   51
  B Economic policy and poles of development   54
  2.3 Responses to criticisms of the development pole concept   58
  C An application   61
  2.4 Transnational firms, leading sectors, development poles
       in less-developed countries   61
  2.5 Towards a general theory of growth-inducing units   67
  Appendix A   73
  Notes   75
  References   76

3   Peregrinations of an economist and the choice of his route
    François Perroux   77

    3.1   Peregrinations and acquisitions   78
    3.2   Choosing one's path   82
    3.3   From extratemporal equilibrium to the temporary
          exhaustion of the drive for change   84
    3.4   From exhaustion of the drive for change to dynamization   86
    3.5   From dynamization to regulation   88
    Notes   90
    References   90

4   Growth pole theory and strategy reconsidered: domination,
    linkages, and distribution
    Karen R. Polenske   91

    4.1   Historical context   92
    4.2   Comparison of the growth pole theory and strategy
          with alternatives   95
    4.3   Conclusion   108
    References   108

PART II: METHODS AND APPROACHES

5   The politics of place: toward a political economy of
    territorial planning
    John Friedmann and Yvon Forest   115

    5.1   The classical paradigm: a critique   116
    5.2   The politics of place: the case of Quebec Province   120
    5.3   Propositions concerning the politics of place   124
    5.4   Implications for the practice of regional planning   126
    Notes   128
    References   129

6   Population and regional development
    William Alonso   131

    6.1   Large regional models, denometrics, and group differences
          within populations   132
    6.2   Migration, regional policy, and the new economic
          fundamentalism   135
    6.3   Magic, regional development and population quality   138

7   A review of techniques for regional policy analysis
    Harry Richardson   142

    7.1   Economic base models   143

	7.2	Input–output models	144
	7.3	Shift–share	146
	7.4	Gravity models	147
	7.5	Cost–benefit analysis	148
	7.6	Structural econometric models	149
	7.7	Time-series forecasting models	151
	7.8	Demoeconomic models	152
	7.9	Integrated multiregional models	154
	7.10	Qualitative impact models	156
	7.11	Growth poles	157
	7.12	Aggregate growth vs. interregional equity	159
	7.13	Concluding observations	161
	Notes		163
	References		164

8 A neoclassical approach to regional economics

Thomas J. Courchene and James R. Melvin   169

	8.1	Introduction	169
	8.2	The representative consumer	171
	8.3	Different consumers within a region	176
	8.4	Preference differences in the traditional model	177
	8.5	An interregional model with differences in preference	180
	8.6	An interregional model with endowment differences	182
	8.7	The natural rate of interregional disparities	186
	8.8	Conclusions	188
	Notes		189
	References		189

PART III: CANADIAN EXPERIENCES

9 Regional development and efficiency of the national economy

Benjamin Higgins   193

	9.1	The concept of "efficiency"	194
	9.2	Market failure	195
	9.3	The mechanism of the market	196
	9.4	Things the market leaves out	201
	9.5	Philosophical underpinnings	202
	9.6	Interactions of regional and national development	204
	9.7	Conclusion	222
	Notes		222
	References		223

10 Regional development in a federal state

André Raynauld   225

	10.1	The political process in a federal state	225
	10.2	Regional transfers of resources in Canada	229

	Appendix: factors contributing to income disparities – standardization procedure	240
	Notes	241
	References	242

11 The influence of unemployment insurance benefits upon the social cost of labor in lagging regions

Fernand Martin — 244

11.1	The problem	244
11.2	The definition of the social cost of labor	245
11.3	Types of unemployment	247
11.4	The effects of unemployment insurance benefits upon the employment rate: the theory	248
11.5	Welfare implications of UIB	254
11.6	Empirical measurement of the impact of UIB upon the unemployment rate in Canada	256
11.7	The extent of the underevaluation of the SCL in Canadian cost–benefit studies	259
11.8	Conclusion	262
	Appendix: partial distribution of components of total unemployment rate, various periods, Canada and some provinces	260
	Notes	262
	References	266

12 Regional disparities: a model with some econometric results for Canada

John Vanderkamp — 269

12.1	Introduction	269
12.2	The model	272
12.3	Data	278
12.4	Empirical results	280
12.5	Implications and simulations	283
12.6	Concluding comments	290
	Appendix: definition of variables	292
	Notes	295
	References	296

PART IV: EXPERIENCE IN OTHER COUNTRIES

13 Some lessons and implications of the World Bank's experience in urban development

Lloyd Rodwin — 299

13.1	The system of international aid	300
13.2	International learning and the training of national bureaucracies	301
13.3	The nature of the urban and regional programs	303

	13.4 Why the Bank changed its views in urban policies and programs	306
	13.5 Learning by doing?	307
	13.6 Ideological and pragmatic critiques	309
	13.7 Organizational behavior and implementation	311
	13.8 Concluding observations on growth theory and World Bank practice	314
	Notes	316
	References	316
14	Small and medium-size cities in development	
	Niles Hansen	318
	14.1 City size and city functions: the static setting	318
	14.2 City size and city functions: the hierarchical diffusion paradigm	319
	14.3 Patterns of urban change	323
	14.4 Technology and decentralization	324
	14.5 Adaptation to a changing spatial division of labor	326
	References	328
15	Evaluating capital grants for regional development	
	Kingsley E. Haynes and Tony Dignan	330
	A Introduction	330
	15.1 Microlevel effectiveness of regional policies	331
	15.2 Macrolevel effectiveness	338
	15.3 Mesolevel effectiveness	339
	B Regional policy: dual perspectives	343
	15.4 The United Kingdom	343
	15.5 Irish industrial policy for regional development	354
	Notes	372
	References	373
Conclusions		
	Benjamin Higgins and Donald J. Savoie	375
	Growth poles	377
	Optimal size of cities	380
	Regional disparities and government intervention	380
	Notes	384
	References	384
	Appendix: The main publications of François Perroux	385
	Index	411

List of contributors

William Alonso, Harvard University
Thomas J. Courchene, Department of Economics, University of Western Ontario, London, Canada
Tony Dignan, School of Public and Environmental Affairs, University of Indiana
Yvon Forest, University of California, Los Angeles
John Friedmann, University of California, Los Angeles
Niles Hansen, Department of Economics, University of Texas
Kingsley E. Haynes, School of Public and Environmental Affairs, University of Indiana
Benjamin Higgins, National Center for Development Studies, Australian National University; and Canadian Institute for Research on Regional Development, Université de Moncton
Fernand Martin, Professor of economics, Université de Montréal
James R. Melvin, Department of Economics, University of Western Ontario, London, Canada
François Perroux, Honorary Professor at the College of France, Paris. President of the Scientific Council of the ISMEA, Paris
Karen R. Polenske, Professor of regional political economy and planning, Massachusetts Institute of Technology
André Raynauld, Professor of economics, Université de Montreal
Harry Richardson, Department of Economics, State University of New York, Albany, and Department of Economics and School of Urban and Regional Planning, University of Southern California, Los Angeles
Lloyd Rodwin, Ford International Professor, Massachusetts Institute of Technology
Donald J. Savoie, Executive Director of the Canadian Institute for Research on Regional Development; and Department of Public Administration, Université de Moncton
John Vanderkamp, College of Social Science, University of Guelph

Introduction: the economics and politics of regional development

BENJAMIN HIGGINS and DONALD J. SAVOIE

The time is ripe for a reexamination of regional development theories and approaches. Substantial amounts of public funds have been spent throughout the Western industrialized world under the regional development banner over the past 25 years. In the developing world, few indeed are the countries which have not launched regional development programs as major components of their national development strategies. A growing number of academics throughout the world are taking an active interest in regional development issues and problems, attempting to shed new light on them and seeking possible solutions.

Yet regional development programs are increasingly under attack. Concern over inflation and mounting public debts, and consequent restraint on spending, are forcing governments to hang question marks over the continuing relevance of regional programs. In most industrialized countries regional development programs fall in the discretionary spending category, and are invariably candidates for cuts when the government treasury is looking for ways to economize.

But attacks on regional development programs go beyond issues of government restraint. There are of course neoclassical economists (e.g., Courchene 1978) who argue that we should let the market deal with regional disparities. Government programs for regional development, they suggest, often have the opposite effect of what was intended, and can make slow-growth regions dependent on transfer payments. Equally important is that a growing number of economists and public policy specialists who have long favored government intervention for promoting regional development are now rejecting centrally, and in some instances all, government-planned and -implemented programs. They point to alternate measures such as government-funded but locally planned initiatives (see, e.g., Savoie 1986). In some cases, it is argued that governments should merely provide start-up funding and leave everything else to locally organized agencies.

In short, there are today few voices being heard in favor of continuation of existing policies and programs for regional development. Thus industrialized nations in particular are – or will soon be – plunged into debates on the politics of regional development. New proposals for redesigning policies and programs will be promoted, and controversy will surface. Political debates over regional development invariably encompass larger issues of national identity and the appropriate role of government in the national economy.

Here in Canada the regional development policies of the last 15 years are under fire from academic economists, other social scientists, federal and provincial politicians, and the general public. The recently released *Royal Commission on the Economic Union and Development Prospects for Canada* (1985, p. 215) recommended, among other things, far-reaching changes to Ottawa's approach to regional development. The federal government in turn has made it known that it wishes to overhaul Canada's regional development policy.

Yet there are several strong arguments for paying particular attention to the regional structure of a national economy, and all of them are expressed somewhere or other in this volume. Among those most frequently put forward are the following:

(a) Regional disparities create social and political problems that must be addressed in any democratic society, and especially so, perhaps, in countries with a federal constitution where "regions" and the gaps among them correspond fairly closely to states or provinces.

(b) National economies are aggregations of regional economies, which vary widely in the degree of integration among them. In some countries, some regions are more closely integrated with the world economy than with other regions in the same national economy. Regions are an integral part of the structure of the national economy, and national economic systems cannot be understood, nor effective policies formulated nor plans made, without understanding the regional structure.

(c) Accelerating growth of the national economy as a whole requires an attack on the problems of retarded regions.

(d) All countries face urban problems of increasing severity and complexity. Interactions between cities and regions are a fundamental aspect of these urban problems, and of regional and national social and economic problems as well.

(e) Some kinds of resource management – natural and human – are best studied and executed at the regional level, because the package of resources involved are best defined in terms of space. Examples are river valleys, mining and forest areas, metropolitan regions, drainage systems, transport systems, recreation areas, parks, and so forth.

(f) Improving the methodology of the social sciences, and improving policy and planning based upon these sciences, requires study of the principal actors where they are, on the spot; and this is best done at the community and regional level.

No matter which of these aspects of regional analysis, policy, and planning is being addressed, there are certain questions which are frequently raised in the literature, and which were raised again in one form or another at the conference. These include:

(a) Under what conditions is it legitimate to describe an economic or social malady as "regional?"

(b) Where there are distinctly "regional" problems, under what circumstances do they require government intervention of one kind or another, and when should they be "left to the market?"

(c) What is the current status and "state of the art" of regional economics, regional science, and regional analysis more generally?

(d) What is the role of economics in regional analysis, as distinct from sociology, anthropology, political science, geography, physical planning, and so on?

(e) What is the current status of growth pole/development pole doctrine?

These are not of course the only questions that arise frequently in discussions of regional development, but they are typical, and they reflect three characteristics of the field in the mid-1980s: there is a good deal of uncertainty and disagreement both as to scope and method and as to specific doctrine; the field has nonetheless achieved a high level of sophistication in a rather short time; it is thoroughly implanted as an aspect of economic and social policy in industrialized and developing countries alike, and as such is not likely to disappear in the near future.

It is in this context of controversy and uncertainty that some of the leading scholars of regional development were invited to contribute to this book. Its purpose is to take stock of where we have been in the regional development field and to see if new approaches may offer potential for future efforts.

Progress in regional development programming and regional theory development

It was not until the 1950s that academics and government began to look at economic development from a regional perspective. There was very little that went under this heading before, but several factors now gave rise to a rapidly growing interest in regional development.

Certainly one of the most important of these was the improvement in mass communications which brought developments in highly developed regions to the consciousness of residents in traditionally slow-growth regions. From the 1950s onward, wars were declared on a host of perceived public policy problems, including regional disparities. As a result of this activity and the propaganda of politicians, regional equity in national economic development became an important part of the political agenda of many countries.

This trend was particularly evident in countries with a federal system of government. Federal–state or federal–provincial relations have contributed to the notion of an equitable regional distribution of the economic benefits of federalism, and have ensured that economic debates were not simply concerned with the functional efficiency of national economic policies. Thus, while improvement in mass communications made residents of slow-growth regions aware of uneven growth in the national economy, federalism has created a framework that has served to promote debates on regional economic interests.

Governments responded with a host of programs and initiatives. In Canada, the federal government established in 1957 a fiscal equalization program intended to reduce disparities among regions, to achieve a national standard in public services, and to equalize provincial government revenues. A few years later, Ottawa introduced a program to rebuild the depressed rural economy. The program initially had a wide spatial application but was later revised to limit its geographical applicability to the most economically depressed rural areas of the country. Efforts to strengthen these areas included measures such as industrial development services and research, and the provision of industrial development infrastructure such as industrial parks. Special incentives to selected business enterprises in the form of grants and interest-free loans were also introduced. In addition, assistance was provided to residents to relocate to selected centers that offered better employment opportunities. A series of other regional development initiatives followed which were on the whole designed to bring improved physical infrastructure to the underdeveloped regions of the country. A special agency, the Atlantic Development Board, was established and given a development fund to administer. The fund was essentially employed to assist in the provision or improvement of Atlantic Canada's basic economic infrastructure. Over half the fund, which totalled $186 million, was spent on highway construction and water and sewerage systems (Careless 1977).

In Western Europe, preoccupation with rebuilding national economies at war's end effectively precluded any sustained regional development effort until the 1950s. However, national economic miracles in the immediate postwar era gave rise to some concern over regional balance in national economic development. This concern was reinforced by those who argued that greater regional balances made sense in national economic efficiency terms because of inflationary demand pressures from rapidly growing regions.

From the 1950s onward, every member country of the European Economic Community developed a variety of incentive programs to spur development in slow-growth areas. Physical infrastructure programs and manpower training programs were also introduced. In some countries, government corporations were charged with a mandate to invest in slow-growth regions. Jobs to people rather than people to jobs became the objective pursued by the majority of governments in Europe.

In the United States, problems of regional development have not been as widespread, as difficult, and as persistent as they have been in Canada and Europe. To be sure, there have been problem regions at various times in the United States, but by and large the problems have not been cumulative or even chronic. Regions that were economically depressed at one time become leading regions at another time – witness the southeast region. Benjamin Higgins observes that "it almost seems as if Adam Smith's invisible hand operates in a special way, at the local and regional level, just for Americans." He adds that since regional problems in the United States have been rather "undramatic," policies and programs for regional development have been equally so (Higgins 1981, p. 4).

Perhaps as a result of the above, regional programs in the United States historically have had a distinguishing characteristic: they have operated not from a specific regional designation but more from an established set of conditions under which regions can qualify. The conditions have been low income, high unemployment, and outmigration.

There have been notable exceptions – one being the Tennessee Valley Authority (TVA). Initially established to control the floods resulting from land erosion and to distribute hydroelectric power and fertilizers, it subsequently became a model for multipurpose regional development in many parts of the world. TVA was successful in that it introduced a host of socio-economic development initiatives such as reforestation, energy development, and basic improvements in social and recreational conditions in the area (see, e.g., Freeman 1985). Another case was the Appalachia Regional Commission, which was established in 1965 and which had features similar to those of the TVA.

Philosophies or regional development theories were also being defined to provide frameworks for regional development activities. François Perroux's work, followed by those of Walter Isard, Gunnar Myrdal, Albert Hirschman, Jacques Boudeville, John Friedmann, William Alonso, Lloyd Rodwin, Harry Richardson, and Niles Hansen, among others, contributed to the development of an important regional planning literature. From Walter Isard's work emerged a school of regional science. Geographers, sociologists, demographers, and economists have under this new discipline attempted to explain the location of industry and the zones of trade, industry, and agriculture around urban areas. Complex input–output models were devised, involving such considerations as transport and labor costs, size of establishments, weight loss in manufacturing, and so on.

The above led to broad theories of industrial location, but government policymakers found them of little value in defining new initiatives for regional development. They were searching for a framework to guide the formulation of such initiatives to find solutions to actual regional problems. In short, governments wanted guidance on the kind of programs and on the type of initiatives they ought to put in place to promote regional development.

Many turned to François Perroux's work on growth poles (Perroux 1969). Perhaps the most-quoted sentence in the study of regional development is Perroux's observation that "Growth does not appear everywhere and all at once; it reveals itself in certain points or poles, with different degrees of intensity; it speads through diverse channels." From a regional development perspective, then, efforts must be made to strengthen these focal points in slow-growth regions and start a process of self-sustained economic growth.

The concept, in the opinion of many government officials, held promise. For one thing, it had the potential for giving rise to a "no-cost" regional development policy. Past efforts to deal with economically depressed rural areas, whether in northern New Brunswick in Canada, or the Appalachian Mountains in the United States, had proven costly, with no apparent progress being made. By concentrating efforts on selected growth centers, employment opportunities would be created which would not only lead to other opportunities, but would also mop up surplus labor from surrounding rural areas. Regional development efforts, it was felt, would now lead to self-sustaining economic activity and it would not, as in the past, constitute an on-going drain on the treasury.

In Canada, past efforts of the late 1950s and early 1960s at promoting development and economic adjustment in economically depressed rural areas gave way to a comprehensive regional development strategy based essentially on the growth pole concept. A new department – the Department of Regional Economic Expansion (DREE) – was established; it embraced, as its principal program instrument, the growth pole approach. Twenty-three areas across Canada were designated as special growth areas. Federal–provincial agreements were signed in support of these areas so that projects could be launched whether they were under federal or provincial jurisdictions (Careless 1977).

These Special Area Agreements sponsored a great variety of projects. They included highways, water systems, industrial parks, tourist attractions, servicing of industrial land, sewer systems, and schools. Financing arrangements were also varied, the most generous being federal financing of 50% of the cost of certain projects plus a loan for part or all of the remainder. In the case of highway construction, Ottawa paid up to 100% of the cost.

A quick survey of the various Special Area Agreements reveals that the great majority of projects sponsored were indeed of the infrastructure type. In Newfoundland, a new industrial park was built in Saint John's, as were new water and sewer systems, a new arterial highway, and a new high school. Similarly, in other Special Areas, nearly all of the DREE funds were allocated to new water and sewer systems, roads, industrial parks, and schools. The pattern established in Newfoundland was followed elsewhere. The Halifax–Dartmouth area, for example, saw some 65 projects exclusively for roads, sewer and water systems, and school construction.

Special Area Agreements also supported a host of diverse initiatives right across the country. In some instances, new access roads were built to new industrial parks, as was the case in Newfoundland, or to new tourist facilities, as in Quebec. In other instances, an engineering building was built for Memorial University in Saint John's, while a seminary was rebuilt in Quebec City. New water and sewer facilities were constructed in the Pas area in Manitoba, in the Lesser Slave Lake area in Alberta, in Lévis, Québec, and in Saint John, New Brunswick, among others.

In the United States, the Economic Development Administration (EDA) launched as part of President Johnson's "Great Society," was based, or so government officials thought, on the growth pole concept (Hansen 1978, pp. 15–21). EDA was established under the Public Works and Economic Development Act of 1965, and counties with high unemployment, low incomes, or both were encouraged to organize "economic development districts" comprising several such counties or redevelopment areas. To qualify for assistance under the Act, each district was required to designate one or more "growth centers." These centers in turn were expected to generate spread efforts to their hinterlands.

In the United Kingdom, France, and Spain, regional development has been motivated mainly by a desire to offset the tendency towards conglomeration in the neighborhood of London, Paris, Barcelona, and Madrid and to decentralize industrialization and urbanization. In comparison to Australia, Canada, and the United States, these are rather small countries, and regional problems and potential do not appear in the same form. Also they have unitary constitutions, so that regional policy is not confused with debates over taxing powers, revenue sharing, social security, and so forth.

Japan's most recent approach to regional development is called the Technopolis Plan. It involves the cooperation of private enterprise, government, and universities to establish high-tech industrial complexes in relatively small towns in retarded regions of Japan. "Regions" are defined for this purpose as the 47 prefectures, and are therefore small areas as compared to the 5 regions of Canada or to the Australian states. From 11 to 19 prefectures are to be designated for the application of the plan. These must lie outside the congested Tokyo–Nagoya–Osaka axis, but must have access to good transport and communications facilities, universities and research institutions with scientific and engineering facilities, and pleasant urban centers capable of attracting the managers, scientists, and engineers on which such hi-tech industries are based. The plan is based both on the growing desire of Japanese to escape the pressures of big-city living and the presence of unused initiative and vitality in smaller centers. The plan provides a wide range of incentives to push enterprise from the largest centers and pull them to smaller ones. In Japan the policy will probably work because of the extraordinary degree of cooperation throughout Japanese society, sometimes expressed in the concept of "Japan Inc."

Not long after governments introduced measures ostensibly based on the growth pole approach, the concept fell into disfavor among many government officials. For one thing, the approach posed a number of political problems. Politicians representing areas that did not qualify under the approach repeatedly argued for their regions to be included. This was especially true of politicians representing economically depressed rural areas. How could a regional development strategy, they asked, ignore their areas and concentrate exclusively on urban areas, where growth should take place without assistance?

Other government officials grew impatient with the approach. Some had looked to the growth pole approach as a panacea, as an instant solution to regional problems. The Canadian government, for instance, had set the doing away of regional disparities as one of its principal goals in 1969. This objective, the government had declared, would be realized through the growth pole approach.

But there was another, more serious problem. The approach when applied in practice was invariably confused, and often far removed from the original statement of the theory by François Perroux. For instance, Perroux was careful to point out that firms sharing the same economic space may be on opposite sides of the globe in geographic terms. Policy makers and many economists ignored this point. By and large, they discarded the pure theory of Perroux and converted it into something different. In the end, practically all policies and initiatives regarding urban growth and regional development were accepted as applications of the growth pole approach. The approach was applied, for example, to urban centers ranging in size from a few thousands to several millions.

With the growth pole approach rejected in a number of the jurisdictions which had at first embraced it, the search was on for another panacea. A number of economists and policy analysts attempted to apply well-known economic theories to the study of regional disparities. Attempts were made, for instance, to apply trade theory. Though developed to deal with the movements of goods and money between nations, the theory has also been adopted to explain the movement between regions within the same nation. Application of this theory at the regional level implies that each region is treated as a nation. The theory suggests that a region will maximize its economic potential by concentrating its efforts on its economic strengths. If, for example, a region is high in capital and short on labor, then it seeks to promote the kind of economic activity which requires a great deal of capital but limited labor. A by-product of this theory is the notion of a region's "comparative advantage."

In short, the trade approach, when applied regionally, would see regions specialize in their areas of strength and comparative advantage. With each region building from its strength, one would then see market forces making the necessary adjustments in terms of surplus labor.

The regional comparative advantage approach has been particularly popular among policy makers in recent years. Like the growth pole approach, it represents, potentially at least, a no-cost regional development policy. It also holds commonsense appeal. Regions will grow and specialize according to what they can do best, and governments will not waste funds attempting to reproduce the industrial structure of highly developed regions in all slow-growth areas. In addition, the approach held promise in terms of bringing forward self-sustaining economic activity.

By the late 1970s many governments with policies for regional development pointed to the regional comparative advantage approach as their guide for defining new initiatives. Canada and several European countries tied their regional programming to this approach. In Canada alone, a series of intergovernmental agreements involving over $5 billion of public funds were based ostensibly on regional comparative advantage (Savoie 1986). But as was the case with the growth pole approach, the regional comparative advantage approach was only evident because it was highlighted in annual reports, in speeches, and in pamphlets describing the programs.

In practice, however, regional development initiatives in Canada and in European countries in recent years have been noteworthy mainly because of their diversity. Regional development programs in many ways have become the catch-all for the government departments with miscellaneous activities. Initiatives have been supported that would force one to stretch the definition of the regional comparative advantage approach to the point where any type of proposal can be supported.

In Canada, initiatives under the regional development banner include the construction of a marina for pleasure boat owners, golf courses, a water treatment system for a large urban area, road constructions, and a host of other initiatives far too numerous to list here. In Europe, regional development programming has been described as a "smorgasbord of national techniques," with well over 50 instruments in use supporting a host of initiatives (McAllister 1982). Some of these include control and disincentive mechanisms and regional allocation of public purchasing. How these measures fit the principle of pursuing a regional comparative advantage approach is far from clear.

In addition, in all countries having specific regional development programs, a multitude of regional subsidies are offered. Subsidies are offered to attract firms, often unrelated to the region's existing resources or manufacturing structure. Moreover, subsidies to bring firms to a given region are in fact an admission that the regional comparative approach is not being followed. If the subsidies are not a windfall profit for the firm, they obviously must be based on the need to overcome the region's comparative disadvantage.

Evaluations of the effectiveness of regional development initiatives have at best been inconclusive. In Britain, a review of regional subsidies concluded with an observation that about all that can be said is that there is a *feeling* that "things would have been much worse" for slow-growth regions if the subsidies had not been available. In Canada, practically every evaluation – and they have been many – of regional subsidies has presented a different version of their effectiveness in the locational decisions of firms. They range from a lukewarm endorsement of regional subsidies to a highly negative assessment of their usefulness.

With regard to other regional development initiatives, evaluations are either nonexistent or also inconclusive. The one theme that surfaces time and again in efforts to assess regional development programming is that evaluation is very difficult, if not impossible. For one thing, policies and programs have been reviewed and updated at such frequent intervals that it is hardly possible for anyone to assess their impacts on a regional economy. For another, most regional development efforts have been so small in the total order of things that it is exceedingly difficult to evaluate their importance even in a small regional economy. Many suggest that the foreign exchange value of the national currency, together with national fiscal and monetary policies, plays a far bigger role in regional economies than a government's regional development efforts.

Perhaps more important still is that, by and large, governments in Europe and North America have attempted to promote regional development by "trying this and that." Theoretical frameworks for defining measures have been singled out by governments but, it appears, only for the benefit of annual reports or ministerial declarations and speeches. When one looks at the actual initiatives, and then at the theoretical frameworks which were supposedly there to underpin their development, one is left wondering how the two could possibly be linked. Evaluating initiatives based on a "this and that" approach is only possible on a project-by-project basis.

Thus about all that can be said about efforts at promoting regional development is to echo the British view that "things could have been much worse" for slow-growth regions if not for these efforts – hardly a ringing endorsement. Mounting concern over growing national debts, and over the ability of national economies to perform in an increasingly volatile and competitive international setting, will invariably put pressure on governments to take a close look at their spending for regional development. In fact, one suspects that regional development programs in recent years have been sustained by commitment at the political level. Politicians from slow-growth regions are clinging to regional development programs for fear that the economy of the region they represent will deteriorate further after losing ground in relation to their national economies in recent years. It also goes without saying that politicians representing slow-growth regions know full well that the electorate back home would react strongly if special programs for their regions were to be cut. We must say, however, that if there were ever any strong support for special regional development measures among permanent government officials, it seems to have waned considerably in recent years.

That said, political and popular support for regional development initiatives will not disappear simply because many permanent government officials no longer see merit in them, nor because economists are pointing to the need to strengthen the national economy. In the words of a leading neoclassical economist, governments will intervene and will not "stand idly by and allow the unfettered market to call the adjustment tune". (Courchene 1981).

The objective of this book is to assist in the process of defining new approaches to regional development. The book is divided into five parts. The first part, on Perroux and his work, is followed by a discussion of methods and approaches. Part III deals with experiences of regional development in Canada, and the last part on regional development experiences elsewhere. The concluding chapter presents an overview of the regional development experience based on discussion at the conference as well as the content of the papers.

To complete this Introduction, the rest of the present chapter is devoted to a review of the material in the other parts of the book so as to present the various contributions in the overall perspective.

Part I: Perroux

This first part of the volume is concerned with the work of François Perroux. It begins with a new paper by Perroux himself, which is an elaboration of his Keynote Address to the Grand Pré conference. It proceeds to a revised version of an already published, but too little known, paper, in which he tells something of the influences that shaped his thinking early in his career, and outlines the intellectual process that led him to his current system of thought. The third chapter in this part presents a critical evaluation of Perroux's theory of growth poles by Karen Polenske.

The editors of this volume take particular pride and pleasure in presenting this definitive treatment by Perroux of growth poles as a major factor in a general theory of economic activity. We feel that it is of major importance in the history of thought in the field of regional economics, and indeed of economics in general. It brings out with crystal clarity what for many of us was hidden or only mistily visible in Perroux's early work, although it was always there: that the growth pole concept is the core of a general theory of development. It also illustrates the *manner* in which the concept can be made operational, which turns out to be quite different from the manner in which it has been applied in actual development planning and policy, as a generator of spread effects to some defined peripheral geographic region. Perroux makes it quite clear in this paper that he never had in mind any such simplistic notion; growth poles, and development poles, which are differently defined, are key components of a complex system of interactions and feedbacks in irreversible time and in economic space. A development pole is much more than an instrument of regional policy, and may or may not operate in "banal" territorial space.

The paper also continues Perroux's running attack on the neoclassical system. He quotes with approval Oscar Morgenstern's dictum that there is no path from the Walrasian system to reality. He goes further, contending that in a system which operates at the sectoral and regional level (with varying degrees of overlap between sectors and regions) a simple macroeconomic analysis can be very misleading. Also, where an economic system is dominated by large units that alternately fight and cooperate with each other, there is no determinate outcome of economic activity, let alone equilibrium, and talk of "rational expectations" is meaningless.

Perroux's theory is in fact a good deal more "general" then Keynes's general theory. Keynes paid virtually no attention to space as such, apart from a nod in the direction of international trade; Perroux's theory deals simultaneously with activity in (irreversible) time and in space. Moreover, Perroux's actors are more varied and more realistic. Their behavior can differ from sector to sector, from region to region, and from time to time. In Perroux's highly dynamic economy, regional balance never occurs and should not occur. Thus regional "balance" cannot be a policy objective. Rather, the objective of regional policy should be optimal *differences* in per capita income, occupational structure, and rate of growth. A national economy is best treated as a system of poles of unequal power, rather than as a system of competing firms of equal bargaining power, and the relative position of various poles, sectors, and regions is subject to constant change. Yet Perroux recognizes the possibility of "unbearable disequilibria," when regional disparities become so great that the growth of GNP declines. Ultimately the way to deal with such problems is through multilevel planning. It is to be hoped that Professor Perroux will see fit to expand this paper to book length. But even if he does not, the paper itself provides clear guidelines for his "cluster of followers" to pursue.

The first part of Perroux's new paper presents an argument against general equilibrium theory of the Walrasian type, which is essentially neoclassical micro and macro analysis, and introduces the notion of growth poles in a framework where structured subsets in the economy are linked with each other by asymmetrical relations.

The second part of the paper deals with the practical aspects of the growth pole notion, that is, the usefulness of the notion in development planning. In doing so, an analysis is presented of the conditions under which a big unit, a transnational enterprise for example, becomes a motor of development in a less-developed country. Throughout this section, the author emphasizes the importance of propulsive effects emanating from certain centers of economic activity to other places called "subcenters." Those effects are created through four main channels, which can be analytically defined and expressed in statistical and econometric terms: these are the investment effects, the production effects, the income effects, and the balance of trade effects.

Perroux warns that attempts to use the concept of growth pole in order to seek an equilibrium of the balances of transfers between regions are not always justified. The choice of the industries that must be given priority should be made on the basis of what their anticipated complementarity will be with the existing industries.

Karen Polenske compares growth pole theory and strategy with alternative approaches, mainly dependency theory and the 'new international economic order' strategy. The comparison deals with three aspects: domination, economic linkages, and distribution of wealth. The author first sets the Perroux growth pole theory in its historical context of the 1940s and 1950s, a period of massive reconstruction in Europe. Four factors are listed as having a profound influence on the birth and formulation of Perroux's theory: the need to rebuild the European economy; the declining colonial relationships of France to Africa and other countries; the writing of Schumpeter on innovations and business cycles; and finally, Perroux's participation in France's postwar industrial planning.

The issue of domination is seen as central to both the growth pole and dependency literature. Growth pole theorists see the domination of some firms as being beneficial to all parties, while dependency theorists argue that the capitalists exercise needlessly far too much power.

Growth pole theorists are concerned mainly with interindustry linkages and the identification of propulsive and lagging sectors. Dependency theorists study linkages in a much broader social context. They focus on the international flows of goods and services and their impact within a core–periphery context.

According to growth pole strategists, investment in propulsive industries generates widespread growth and increased income through backward and forward linkages. They argue that when this fails to occur, the fault lies with a defective political economic structure and not with the growth strategy. Dependency theorists believe, on the other hand, that disparities between developed and underdeveloped countries will continue to widen unless some form of new international economic order is implemented for the specific purpose of providing lagging nations with increased income.

Part II: Methods and approaches

The second part of this volume gives us a picture of the state of the art of regional analysis, policy formulation, and planning. In terms of scope and method, and to some extent of basic ideology as well, the essays in this section cover a broad spectrum – from John Friedmann, through William Alonso and Harry Richardson, to Tom Courchene and James Melvin. They illustrate once again the yeasty state of the field of regional development, and the keenness of the debates among its practitioners. Yet in the aggregate they demonstrate something that is more interesting and more important: despite the absence of a widely accepted general theory of regional development or a large body of received doctrine, there is nonetheless a body of knowledge that serves very well in practice for the conduct of penetrating regional analysis, for the prescription of regional policies, and for the assembly of regional plans. The breadth of experience and depth of sophistication behind these essays is apparent.

For those who have moved at least some of the way from a "physics" approach to a "biological" approach, this superficially paradoxical situation will come as no great surprise. For the nature of regional analysis is such that it forces those specializing in the field to take a hard look at the regions with which they are concerned, their structure and functioning, and their maladies. As a result they are often in a position to make a diagnosis and prescribe treatment for individual regions, without having an agreed general theory as a foundation for their practice. This fact too should come as no surprise. It would bode ill for life expectancy if medical practitioners had always to wait for universal agreement on a "general theory of health" before treating the specific maladies of individual cases. Fortunately we know enough about the anatomy, physiology, biology, biochemistry, and neurology of cities and regions to diagnose their maladies and prescribe treatment case by case. It should also be remembered that in North America, Western Europe, and Australasia there is a much longer experience with physical planning for cities and regions than with other kinds of economic and social planning, and a considerable store of knowledge of cities and regions has been accumulated as a result.

We begin this part with John Friedmann's essay because it is broadest gauged and closest to the views and approach expressed by Professor

Perroux in Part I. Tillers in the regional development field are accustomed by now to having their flow of adrenalin stimulated by John Friedmann's writing, and this joint essay with Yvon Forest is certainly no exception. Their willingness to step outside the bounds of conventional economic analysis is the key to this stimulation. They argue that regional planning should in future make room for what they label "the politics of place." Politics of place, they suggest, come into being essentially because of the failure by state and capital to provide for livelihood.

Regional problems, they insist, have become matters of politics not simply questions of resource allocation as in the past. The debates go beyond questions of regional disparities to issue of regional identity and regional survival. Implicit in this shift is an emphasis on the social, cultural, and historical attributes of a given region.

No longer should we look at a region from a simple functional perspective as defined by the central government for the convenience of administrators and analysts; this functional perspective and accompanying policies also failed to establish spatial equilibrium. The rise of large multinationals pitted one nation against another in attempts to provide for a benign economic climate to attract the footloose economic activities of these multinational firms. With governments adopting neoliberal economic policies, regional policy and planning were tossed aside.

The authors point to Quebec as a case in point of the new politics of place. The Quebec regional movement had as its objective the politicization of space. It grew on an adverse relationship with the central government and had as its leadership an important part of the region's intellectual and cultural elite. As in other regional movements, several stages elapsed between the development of a regional consciousness and the formal institutionalization of the movement.

The politics of place hold important implications for regional planning. For one thing, a new kind of planning process is required. The regional population, or the client, is involved in the planning process to a much higher degree than in the past. It becomes increasingly important to rely on the self-organizing capacity of the regional population. The new planning process should also look to regional resources and to alternate work organization to stimulate development. New forms of people-centered organization such as worker cooperatives are also encouraged.

William Alonso's chapter on demographic aspects of regional development is perhaps a little closer to conventional economic analysis of regional development, but he too incorporates big chunks of sociology, social psychology, and anthropology in his essay. He argues that both academics and government officials in the regional development field have not given sufficient attention to the population factor. In employing the term "population factor," he goes beyond demographic dynamics to include age, attitude, education, and so on, all of which affect a population's capacity to contribute to regional development.

In a striking and illustrative comparison, he equates past efforts with the cargo cult among the natives of the Pacific islands. These natives busily laid out what they believed was the necessary infrastructure to attract the big silver bird – cargo airplane – they had seen land at a nearby American air force base. Similarly, he suggests, governments have given the necessary infrastructure in the form of industrial parks and new roads among other things to slow-growth regions to attract economic development, believing that if these facilities can attract economic development in highly developed urban centers, they should be able to do the same for peripheral and even rural areas. All the while the local population, its quality, and the role it can play in promoting development is virtually ignored. Just as the natives were unable to attract the big silver bird, the facilities built in slow-growth areas have never been able to attract the manufacturing firms they were designed for. By concentrating on the population factor, Alonso paves the way for suggestions for new approaches to regional development. Questions are asked in terms of the people living in the designated regions – what is their culture, their institution, their environment? To illustrate his point further, he suggests, for example, that the transformation currently taking place in the Quebec population will likely have important long term implications for that province's economic development. He not only singles out the dramatic decline in population growth (i.e., the fertility of the French-speaking Quebec population), but also the career shift of educated Québécois from the public to the private sector. What this suggests is that public policy planning for regional economic development should focus more on the population factor and less on duplicating the industrial infrastructures found in highly developed regions in all slow-growth regions.

With Harry Richardson we move into a different arena of discussion. His essay is a sober appraisal of tools available for regional analysis by one who has both added to the toolkit himself and struggled to apply tools designed by others. The significance of this chapter is not so much in the specific evaluation of various techniques, but in the fact that such a hard-nosed, clear-eyed, and clinical appraisal can be made at all. The fact that it can is testimony to the progress that has been made in the field since World War II, despite continuing debates and differences in approach – or, indeed, possibly because of them.

Harry Richardson reviews the usefulness of a number of techniques used in regional analysis. The author points to the difficulty in evaluating the regional impact of policy decisions, to the need to further document some techniques already in use, and also to the need to develop more sophisticated models.

The 12 techniques reviewed can be grouped into four categories. The first category comprises the economic base models, gravity models, and shift-share analysis. In spite of a few recent attempts to revitalize these techniques, they seem to hold little promise in policy impact evaluation. A second group of four techniques still find applications in regional analysis: cost–benefit analysis, input–output models, time series forecasting models, and structural econometric models. These techniques are found to be useful in a number of cases providing that the researchers are fully aware of their limitations. At present, this set of techniques remains the most widely used in regional analysis. In the author's view, input–output models remain for the present superior to alternative techniques for measurement of economic impacts.

The third group includes growth pole models and aggregate growth versus interregional equity models. Both these models are difficult to apply, he reports, largely because they are so comprehensive that they are operationally almost impossible to evaluate.

Finally, the fourth set brings together three models which have been recently devised to overcome the difficulties associated with previous techniques: the demoeconomic model, the integrated multiregional model, and the quality impact model. All three attempt to include social factors into their structure. As these models are new, they are as yet largely untested. The author points to the integrated multiregional model as the most promising.

The Courchene–Melvin paper that concludes this part is in one sense the most conservative of the four. It illustrates neoclassical analysis at its best, and in so doing makes a notable contribution to the theory of international and interregional trade as well as to regional economics. It also demonstrates that neoclassical tools can be used to deal with cases of market failure, whether due to the innate structure of markets or to misguided government intervention. Their concept of the "natural level of regional disparities," roughly analogous to Milton Friedman's concept of the "natural rate of unemployment," is a useful and challenging addition to the debate on regional economic policy. So is their argument that factor mobility is not always a cure for regional gaps, and that disparities which are the result of differences in factor endowment or preferences should *not* be corrected by interregional transfers. After careful consideration of the implications of this analysis, it doesn't seem so "conservative" after all.

On many points, they find themselves in sympathy with Perroux, despite the latter's generally critical attitude toward neoclassical theory. They readily admit, as Perroux has argued time and again, that simplifying assumptions to general equilibrium models pose difficulties for policy-makers. They go on to point out, however, that simplifying assumptions also mask important issues that must be understood in attempts to define regional development policy. This paper seeks to assist in this process.

They challenge one central theme of Professor Perroux's research – the claim that the neoclassical general equilibrium approach is sterile and simplistic and clouds important underlying issues. Two specific criticisms are taken up: the model excludes structures and structure subsets, and it has never succeeded in proposing an identical theory for application to both international exchanges and domestic exchanges. While the authors agree that much of the general equilibrium analysis does suffer from these deficiencies, they suggest that the problem does not lie in the methodology itself but in its application.

The major theme of the paper is that specifically identifying regions which differ in some substantial ways allows an analysis of the interaction among the regions and their joint interaction with the rest of the world. In the main example explored in the paper, the differentiation between regions is made on the basis of preferences, therefore relaxing the assumption that all individuals have identical preferences.

In doing so, five specific themes are dealt with:

(a) the disaggregation of the consumption side of the model
(b) the introduction of a region by extending the model to include distance
(c) the examination of a case where consumers with different preferences work and consume in distinctly different regions
(d) the examination of a case where the economy consists of several regions with different endowments, and where these regions can trade both with the rest of the world and with each other
(e) the expectation of interregional equality and the natural rate of interregional disparities.

The paper is especially interesting from a policy viewpoint since the effect of tariff policy is introduced in the discussion. It is recognized that tariffs push consumers to greater interaction within the country where the tariffs are applied; consumers, however, bear the cost, specifically those individuals who live closer to the border and who will have to pay a higher transportation cost. Tariffs therefore create disparities in the welfare of consumers. The paper also discusses the distinction between tariffs and taxes, with respect to the effects of the latter on the welfare of consumers, assuming consumers have different preferences. A discussion of the effect of tariffs on factor mobility is also presented, stressing the possibility of migration occurring from a region disadvantaged by the tariffs to a region favoured by tariffs as an attempt on the part of the consumer to reestablish his former level of consumption.

Part III: Canadian experiences

Canada is one of the most highly regionalized of the "industrialized market economies" (IMEs). Despite recent signs of a tendency towards convergence, regional disparities remain large for a country at Canada's general level of economic and social development. These continuing regional gaps reflect deep-seated elements of the structure of the Canadian economy. In a country with a federal constitution, where the population is keenly aware of regional differences, the gaps cannot be ignored. Canadian politicians have realized this fact intuitively ever since confederation, and national economic policy has been to some extent "regionalized" from the beginning. The new federal government, and the provincial governments as well, are committed to bringing about improvements in regional development policy. In this respect, they are in tune with the temper of the electorate. The regional development policies of the last 15 years are under fire from academic economists, other social scientists, federal and provincial politicians, and the general public. The time is ripe for a general overhaul of Canada's regional development policy; and with its massive mandate for change, and strong support from disadvantaged regions (such as Quebec and New Brunswick) which have traditionally voted Liberal, the Mulroney government is poised for an innovative attack on regional problems.

Because of Canada's peculiar combination of geography, history, and constitution, it has been natural for Canadians to think of "regional" policy in terms of the nine or ten provinces or groupings of them. These are, however, very large regions with a good deal of economic and social diversity within them. Many of the difficulties and defects of Canadian regional policy spring from the attempt to define it in terms of the five major regions.

There has probably never been a time since confederation when the people of all regions were content with the regional impact of national policies. Currently there is a flood of complaint and criticism regarding the operations of DREE and DRIE. In Quebec and the Atlantic Provinces, the dissatisfaction expressed sometimes takes the form of protesting that government programs have not been big enough, or effective enough, to bring significant reduction in regional gaps. Other critics, especially among academic economists, take the position that the combination of industrial incentives, public investment in infrastructure, revenue sharing, and other transfer payments, designed to generate greater equality among regions with regard to incomes, employment and unemployment, and standards of public service, in fact have the opposite effect: they misallocate resources, reduce mobility of both labor and capital, and delay adjustment to change. Others still are prepared to admit that the regional development programs and policies have brought some improvement in economic and social conditions to the disadvantaged regions of Canada, but maintain that these gains have been bought at the cost of a reduction in "efficiency" of the national economy. At best, they argue, there is a trade-off between faster growth of national income as a whole and further efforts to reduce regional disparities through the sort of devices that have been applied in the last decade or two.

For these reasons, Part III, dealing with various aspects of Canadian experience with regional development, holds a special interest for anyone concerned with Canadian economics and politics. It begins with an essay by Benjamin Higgins which effectively forms a bridge between Part II and Part III. Like Part II, it is concerned with questions of scope and method, and with new approaches to regional analysis, policy, and planning. To that extent its arguments are applicable to any country. However, its illustrations come mainly from Canada, its policy applications are made mainly to Canada, and even some of the general ideas are derived from Canadian experience.

In a sense, this essay also provides a link between Part III and Part I, since it resembles the essays by François Perroux in three important respects: (a) It expresses a conviction that regional economics should not be treated as a "branch" of general economic theory, standing a bit aside from the main body of doctrine, but as an essential part of any complete and realistic general theory. National economies, and even the world economy, can be thoroughly understood only if regional structures, the nature and functioning of the various regional economies comprising national economies, their interactions among themselves and with the national and world economies, are carefully analyzed. (b) The essay brings together components of a more general theory, which has been evolving for many years, and is still incomplete. (c) This theory is designed to offer an alternative to both the neoclassical and the neo-Marxist theories, which will provide a better basis for policy and planning.

The central argument of the essay is that one cannot really speak of "regional development" and "efficiency of the national economy" as though they were two distinct objectives between which societies with limited resources must make marginal choices. Regional development is a key component of any policy or program for raising the efficiency of the entire national economy.

The argument is conducted in terms of five basic propositions:

(a) "Regional development" and "efficiency of the national economy" are aspects of the social welfare of every nation which cannot be measured, or even ranked, in any market.

(b) Levels and rates of growth of per capita income at the national level are inversely correlated with the magnitudes of regional disparities.

(c) Trade-off curves between unemployment and inflation tend to be at the national level. The greater the magnitude of regional disparities within the nation, the more unfavorable trade-off curves tend to be at the national level.

(d) Regions with slow rates of growth tend to have more violent economic fluctuations than regions with rapid rates of growth; migration from stagnant to dynamic regions will tend to prolong booms and make recessions shorter and shallower in the dynamic regions, and to lengthen and deepen depressions in stagnant ones, thus aggravating regional disparities.

(e) For these reasons, well-construed regional development policies and programs can diminish regional disparities and enhance the efficiency of the national economy at the same time; regional development and national efficiency should be regarded as complementary rather than a trade-off.

The second chapter in this part deals with problems of regional development in countries with federal constitutions, and especially in Canada. André Raynauld is in a unique position to deal with this topic. He was already deeply involved in problems of regional development as Director of the Economic Research Station of the Royal Commission on Bilingualism and Biculturalism and as Director of the Centre for Research Development at the University of Montreal. During his period as its chairman, the Economic Council of Canada devoted much of its resources and energies to this field. Later as the opposition Finance Minister in the Quebec National Assembly he participated at first hand in the complex politics of regional development policy, both at the provincial and at the federal levels. His essay reflects this wealth and variety of experience.

Professor Raynauld states that the purpose of this paper is to examine the rationale and impact of government policy in regional development. In the first section he analyzes the federal state essential as a market, and shows that the methodology of neoclassical economics can be effectively applied to the analysis of political behavior. Within this framework he treats intergovernmental transactions as a form of trade, and derives social welfare implications for the centralization or decentralization of government activities. Contending that "governments nowadays have the power and the resources to build or destroy regions," he proceeds to give a picture of regional disparities in Canada in terms of unemployment, and in terms of income subdivided into earned income, income from investment, and income from transfer payments. He provides a detailed account of the factors involved in regional differences in per capita income in Canada, and in the trends in these differences. He then analyzes in similar detail the net fiscal benefits to the various provinces of federal government taxation and spending, and asks a very important question: Can the regional differences be rationalized in terms of efficiency, equity, or "political market considerations?" For efficiency the answer is clearly "No". For equity the results are not very convincing either. That leaves the political market as the explanation; but since the results of intergovernmental trading in the political market are determinate, we are left with the impression of a rather haphazard government policy in this regard.

Fernand Martin's chapter also reflects deep involvement with Canadian regional development policy and planning, as well as decades of reflection at the theoretical level on the same topic. He was a member of the Special Task Force which was set up to recommend a site for Montreal's new international airport in the light of its impact on the pattern of urban and regional development; he was later a member of the three-man team (together with Benjamin Higgins and André Raynauld) commissioned by DREE to prepare a strategic plan for the development of Quebec; he has advised the Office of Planning and Development of Quebec; and in recent years he has undertaken a series of assignments for DREE and DRIE, both to prepare systems of evaluations of projects and to make evaluations of actual projects.

In his essay, Professor Martin discusses the problem of evaluating the true cost of establishing firms in lagging regions and the difficulty in determining the relationship between unemployment insurance benefits and the social cost of labor in these regions. The author hypothesizes that the methods presently used underestimate the social cost of labor when the welfare function is taken at the national level and, consequently, too many activities are sent to lagging regions.

The author describes the difficulties of measuring labor supply and demand within the neoclassical and Keynesian paradigms. He also discusses the effects of unemployment insurance benefits upon the rate of unemployment and describes a number of econometric models that have been put forth to deal with the question. The author also demonstrates that, theoretically, unemployment insurance benefits can generate a degree of unemployment and a number of annoying side effects. Finally, the author demonstrates the relationship between unemployment insurance benefits and the unemployment rate within the Canadian context and decries the existence of "perverse interpenetration between measures favoring equity and measures to bring about social efficiency." He concludes on the need to devise more equitable methods to help the unemployed.

With the paper by John Vanderkamp we move into a somewhat different sphere of analysis. Here we see the contemporary econometrician practising his art to address two specific questions of regional analysis: Why do regional disparities exist and persist? What is the relationship of interregional migration to regional disparities? Some of his results are not very firm, and some that are firmer he describes as "surprising." He finds some support for the Myrdal thesis regarding cumulative causation: emigration from a disadvantaged region may increase unemployment there, immigration into a dynamic region may reduce unemployment in the region.

He describes a number of theoretical issues that arose in the construction of the model he uses to address these questions, such as migration as an adjustment mechanism to wage disparities and labor demand and supply, and time lags in migration adjustment. The model has three principal components: supply, demand, and wage adjustments, with the emphasis placed on change and adjustment of these variables. A set of five equations determines the set of endogenous variables: net outmigration, potential labor supply, wages, employment, and employment change. Other variables, such as government transfer payments, are considered exogenous. The data extends back to the 1930s.

Testing of the model indicated the need to redefine a number of the parameters, and brought out the role and impact of sets of economic and social shocks. The model's coefficients were not very significant statistically, although the signs of these values were largely as had been predicted from theoretical considerations. The model is only modestly successful in predicting regional disparities, and migration is only moderately responsive to wage differentials. Most shocks have a primary impact on unemployment but little effect on wage disparities. The author concludes that the Myrdal's "cumulative causation" has contributed to the persistence of regional disparities. Migration has not acted as an effective adjustment mechanism to the labor supply and demand market.

Part IV: Experience in other countries

In most areas of public policy, one is able to learn a great deal about how well one's country is doing by comparing its efforts with those of other countries. This is particularly true in the regional development field. One can look at how other approaches are formulated and implemented, and can assess the magnitude of the regional development efforts of one's own country against the backdrop of the efforts in other countries. A comparative review can also point the way to new solutions or to revisions to current approaches. When a particular policy field is confronted with a widespread rejection of past efforts and a plea for new directions, as is currently the case for regional development policy in many countries, the need to compare notes is obvious. It is from this perspective that scholars were invited to contribute to this part.

In this part, we take a look at experience in other parts of the world. In the first chapter Lloyd Rodwin considers World Bank operations in the field of urban and regional development, in many of which he has shared. Next Niles Hansen looks at the changing role of small and medium-size cities. Kingsley Haynes reviews experience with capital grants for regional development in the United Kingdom and Ireland.

Rodwin explains the motives which led the Bank into the urban development field in 1972, its approaches, and its experiences over the past decade. He also points out the difficulties in trying to promote development in TWC through the simple transfer of concepts and planning procedures established in developed countries.

The paper points out that the urban development program takes up only 4% of the World Bank's funding, but it nevertheless represents a major shift in the Bank's outlook on development aid. The Bank felt that such a shift would promote wider distribution of the economic returns from its investments. The new policy steered the agency towards large integrated urban land use planning, but just short of overall comprehensive regional planning. The paper reviews the criticisms of the programs from both non-interventionists and interventionists. Rodwin concludes that the Bank sees institutional and managerial reforms as the principal long-term solution to the economic development of Third World countries.

Niles Hansen evaluates the role of small and medium-size cities in the development of economic systems in the context of recent technological innovation. His chapter examines the relationship between city size and city function in advanced economies. The author shows that the spatial setting of these small and medium cities is a dominant factor in determining their functions. The paper states that most cities of these size categories are called upon to expand the functions they provide.

The paper then examines the relevance of the hierarchical diffusion model in today's economy. The author finds that even though the model was useful in accounting for the rapid growth of the larger metropolitan centers in the 1960s and early 1970s, for theoretical as well as empirical reasons, it cannot be employed in describing the urban growth patterns of today.

Finally, from an examination of the most recent data and literature available, the author shows that the present urban growth patterns are largely related to the influence of new technology. As a consequence "small and medium-size cities are no longer condemned to be 'mere lower order' central places or passive recipients of older technologies." The growth and development of these smaller centers will be more related to the dynamic nature of their internal economic systems than to their hierarchical position within the urban system.

Haynes and Dignan start their paper by pointing out that while a good many countries have used capital grants to influence the location of industry, the manner in which this policy has been implemented has varied a good deal from one country to another. Even the objectives differ from country to country, and from time to time in the same country. The paper presents a comparative analysis of capital grant policy in the United Kingdom and Ireland. First, however, it provides a theoretical framework for evaluating the effectiveness of capital grants policy. At the microlevel the analysis is cast in terms of the impact of such policies on a firm's "location-choice behavior." An elaborate mathematical model is provided for the conduct of this analysis. The authors then move on to analysis of macrolevel effectiveness, and provide another model for that. They also provide data for EEC countries on the types of incentives utilized to influence choice of location, on maximum levels of assistance available in each country, and on total population in assisted areas.

The rest of the paper is devoted to a detailed account of the policies pursued in the United Kingdom and Ireland regarding industrial location since World War II. This account includes an econometric model for testing the effectiveness of these policies. They present some evidence that, apart from their influence on choice of location, the capital grants led to some substitution of capital for labor. For Ireland they find that exports constitute the bulk of sales by assisted firms. For foreign-based firms, the sales are often to affiliates. Thus, downstream spread effects are felt outside the country. More than half the inputs were imported, so that the upstream spread effects were felt mainly in other countries too. New industry accounts for a significant proportion of output, exports, and employment, but these were widely dispersed throughout the country rather than being concentrated in disadvantaged regions. The paper includes a statistical summary presenting a wealth of information about the two programs.

References

Careless, A. 1977. *Initiative and response: the adaptation of Canadian federalism to regional economic development.* Montreal: McGill-Queen's University Press.

Courchene, T. J. 1978. Avenues of adjustment: the transfer system and regional disparities. In *Canadian confederation at the crossroads: the search for a federal–provincial balance,* 145–86. Vancouver: Fraser Institute.

Courchene, T. J. 1981. A market perspective on regional disparities. *Canadian Public Policy* **7** (4), Autumn, 513.

Freeman, S. D. 1985. The nine lives of TVA. *Environment* **27** (3), April, 7–11.

Hansen, N. M. 1978. *Location preference, migration, and regional growth.* New York: Praeger.

Higgins, B. 1981. *Regional development planning: the state of the art in North America.* Nagoya, Japan: United Nations Centre for Regional Development (November).

McAllister, I. 1982. *Regional development and the European Community: a Canadian perspective.* Montreal: Institute for Research on Public Policy.

Perroux, F. 1969. *L'Économie au XXe siècle.* Paris: Presses universitaires de France.

Regional Industrial Development, December 1983, p.9. Presented to Parliament by the Secretary of State for Trade and Industry by Command of Her Majesty the Queen. London: Her Majesty's Stationery Office.

Royal Commission on the Economic Union and Development Prospects for Canada 1985. *Report,* vol. 3. Ottawa: Ministry of Supply and Services.

Savoie, D. J. 1986. *Regional economic development: Canada's search for solutions.* Toronto: University of Toronto Press.

PART I

Perroux

1

François Perroux

BENJAMIN HIGGINS

I remember vividly my first meeting with François Perroux, although I am quite certain he does not. It was at the London School of Economics, over 50 years ago. I was in the office of Lionel Robbins, my thesis supervisor, when Perroux came to the door. Both Perroux and Robbins were tall and of striking appearance, and I felt very small in both wisdom and stature beside these two giants. Perroux said in English, which he spoke considerably less well then than he does now, that he had used his time well while waiting for his appointment with Robbins in visiting the School's magnificent library. Robbins replied, "Vous parlez de la librairie ou de la bibliothèque?" – a legitimate question, since in addition to the splendid library at the LSE, there was in the narrow winding street behind it the famous Economists' Bookshop, surely one of the best specialized bookshops to be found anywhere in the world. Since that first meeting, I have been with François Perroux in Paris, Geneva, Cambridge, Massachusetts, Montreal, Quebec City and Ottawa. Over the years we have become fast friends, despite occasional disagreement on minor issues of economics.

Robbins' replying in French to Perroux's remarks in English brings to mind another characteristic of the LSE at that time, one that is germane to any discussion of Perroux's status in the economics profession. The School had no formal language requirements for higher degrees, but it was taken for granted that graduate students, and even undergraduates, would read any language in which there existed an important literature related to the student's work. The better departments of economics in the United States required reading knowledge of two languages for the Ph.D. These requirements were not just formal hurdles. Professional economists and graduate students really did read books and journals in languages other than their own, even when their own was English.

This admirable practice began to disappear after World War II, partly as a result of the isolation from the main stream of the Keynesian Revolution in France, Germany, and Italy until well after the war, partly because of the domination of the debate by British and American economists. A whole generation of anglophone economists discovered that they could get by without making the effort to read other languages. Among the unfortunate consequences of this new trend is the fact that Perroux's esteemed position among those who have kept up with the French literature is not replicated amongst those economists who have not done so. There exist today younger British, American, Canadian, and Australian economists who, if they know of François Perroux at all, know him only as the father of the "growth pole" concept, and are quite unaware of the depth and breadth of his contribution to economic thought. It is worthy of note that Perroux has honorary doctorates from distinguished universities in France, Germany, Spain, Portugal, Brazil, and Uruguay, but none from an anglophone University.

Yet Perroux is truly one of the giants among economists of his generation. Donald Savoie, in his Preface to this volume, quotes Paul Streeten as referring to Perroux as "a giant figure, of Nobel Prize stature." Paul Streeten is certainly not alone in this view. Perroux has been nominated for the Nobel Prize several times; and if the Committee ever breaks out of the circle of Scandinavians, British, American, and Dutch economists, writing mainly in English, in which they have been trapped thus far, Perroux would surely be one of those at the top of the list. He has been Professor at the Collège de France and Directeur d'Études at the École Pratique des Hautes Études at the Sorbonne since 1955. He is founder of the Institut des Sciences Économiques Appliquées and editor of the prestigious journal *Économie appliquée*. He has also been Director of both the Institut des Sciences Mathématiques et Economiques Appliquées and of the Institut d'Études de Développement Économique et Social. It is not for nothing that Perroux's associates in Paris normally address him as "maître."

It is mainly because, ironically, Perroux's name and work are less well known to some anglophone social scientists than may be the names of some of the other contributors to this volume that this foreword is written. The other reason, of course, is that it gives me a much appreciated opportunity to pay a personal tribute to my old friend François Perroux.

As this book went to press, we received a letter informing us of the death of François Perroux on April 25th 1987. This sad news was not altogether unexpected, Perroux was in frail health at the time of the Grand Pré workshop two years ago.

Unless there exists a manuscript of which we are unaware, his death means that Perroux's chapters in this volume are the last major statement of his theory, and it also means that he died with his work unfinished. In one sense, that statement holds for every great economist, yet in another sense the statement is more true of Perroux than of most economists.

The two great economists with whom Perroux is compared, Keynes and Schumpeter, both died some twenty years younger than Perroux, but they left behind them the completed structure of their general theories. No doubt both would have continued to enrich the literature of economics had they lived longer, but almost certainly they would have continued to work within an existing framework. Not so with Perroux. He was still struggling to fill in the gaps in his general theory; the structure was incomplete. What is more tragic, he knew it.

For my own part, a deep regret is that François Perroux died before being awarded the Nobel Prize that he so richly deserved.

1.1 Perroux's general theory and social philosophy

Perroux's writings cover 60 extremely prolific years and a very wide range of subject matter, as the bibliography appended to this volume shows. To summarize his main ideas and to trace the evolution of his thought throughout six decades would require a long book in itself. (Bocage (1985) gives an excellent survey.) In order to obtain a picture of the depth and breadth of his thought in shorter compass, let us look instead at a recent article of his, "Au-Delà du Welfare State" (Beyond the welfare state – Perroux 1984) which provides a good deal of insight into his current thinking and philosophy, and which was distributed to the participants in advance of the Grand Pré conference for that reason.

In typical Perroux fashion, the article goes straight to the attack. The opening sentence states, "Of all the difficulties in the theoretical analysis of the welfare state, the most massive and the least perceived springs from the very bringing together of these two terms, defined without rigor." He considers the concept of "state," starting with Max Weber. The concept is hard enough to pin down, he says, but it does not gain in clarity when it is considered as an entity charged with favoring "welfare," a "notion almost impossible to grasp."

Perroux then moves on to J. R. Hicks, who called welfare "badly named," without saying what it is. As used by the welfare economists, "welfare" is a sort of banal good fortune (*bonheur*) supposedly accessible to all, but which does not exclude widespread and persistent unemployment, nor poverty, nor even pockets of destitution (*misère*) in advanced capitalist countries, adding up to what Tibor Scitovsky called "the Joyless Economy."

Perroux then distinguishes two currents of thought regarding the conciliation of individual rationality with the collective rationality of the economy:

(a) From the Vienna School to Marshall, Pareto, and his disciples, which tries to reconcile individual utility with collective advantage, through the market.

(b) From Condorcet to Kenneth Arrow, in terms of the Grand Agent, the major decider who chooses, from an ordered series of variables and relationships, the combination best for the collectivity, under the constraint of a certain respect for individual choice.

Referring to the work of Wicksell, Pigou, Hicks, and Pareto, Perroux dismisses the first stream, because of its static framework, its logical flaws, and the gap between "trivial textbook geometry" and the real world. He finds the second stream more promising, and comments on the writings of Abraham Bergson, I.M.D. Little, and Kenneth Arrow. Arrow, he says, has given the most profound reply to the question, "Is it *possible* to derive a purely formal collective choice from the individual choices themselves?" Arrow's answer, as is well known, is a resounding "No!" even if we assume that all *individuals* are capable of ordering their preferences. Perroux goes on to say that "the market" is an institution created and regulated by *society*; there are as many markets as there are societies; and he quotes approvingly Kenneth Boulding's *The economics of love and fear*. To reduce the economy to adjustments of prices and quantities without considering the social framework and the dynamism of supply and demand "is simply unacceptable".

Perroux distinguishes between "équilibrage," deliberate acts of equilibration by Agents capable of modifying their environment to their advantage, and "équilibrations," trial and error adjustments (*tâtonnements*) in a *disequilibrium* situation, which lead eventually to a provisional stabilization because the energy in the system approaches zero ($\Delta \phi_e \simeq 0$). (It is this kind of thinking that leads Perroux to prefer the mathematics of thermodynamics to the mathematics of mechanics for economic analysis. Like Marshall, Pigou, and Keynes, Perroux reproduces far less mathematics than he knows in his publications.) These concepts, he says, bear no relationship to Walras–Paretian equilibrium, and radically transform the viewpoint from which "welfare" is conceived. Societies are dominated by differing and unequal Active Agents, engaged in struggles–competition, in conflict–cooperation, with projects which are not spontaneously compatible, and which require regulation of a sort which is not achieved by the functioning of a free market.

And so the question is, can contemporary Western societies begin to move toward *social* rationality, with rational plans (*projets*) from the standpoint of an economy which is logical and scientific in its intent? Can Western society humanize itself? To do so we must move toward a different kind of individualism, one that recognizes the importance of social groups with differing interests and differing degrees of power. Perroux reminds us that the Classical school, from Adam Smith to John Stuart Mill, understood very well that society is composed of groups with *conflicting* interests. The individual is not a "robot of price." Rather, he or she is an "open system," as the biologists would have it, receiving and emitting forces and effects. Analysis in terms of individuals as closed systems is unsustainable. But once reestablished in its *classical* scope, scientific economics can deal with *organization* designed to order the conflict–cooperation of the active social groups so as to benefit the entire collectivity under consideration. Organizations are hierarchical everywhere. Analyzing their conflicts–cooperation calls for systems analysis and games theory.

We need to acknowledge, beyond the paradigm of exchange, the paradigm of organization. For market exchange, the ideal process is the contract; but for organization, the best instrument is status; that is, a lasting hierarchical order attributing to individuals, as members of a group, a function and a role in the whole. On the basis of this distinction, one can demonstrate that power conflicts are unavoidable in any society, both with respect to the contract and with respect to status; that the concept of social contract contains a logical impasse but nonetheless is a normative requirement; that the ideal of economic solidarity can be thought of as a doctrine of compromise, an economic law of distribution, or as a moral imperative. The conflicts among private power groups in the political sphere show that the game is one of redefining roles within the *Cité* (city, in the sense of defined society). We would commit a grievous error in opposing solidarity linked to status, and to a redistribution of costs and of roles by means of contractual negotiations.

At this point, naturally, Perroux turns to Jean-Jacques Rousseau; indeed, to the "two Rousseaux." The natural tendency of the individual is to escape the social order, to make his vital choices as though he recognizes no competent authority with regard to them. But in fact the individual is bound by society. Mankind, supposedly "free," is everywhere in chains from birth. The relationship of the individual to the society in which he lives is more than a "contract"; it is a social *pact*, involving the total commitment of the citizen to the "Cité."

Perroux concludes in any case, that "solidarity" is what we must strive for, even if we never attain it. The final paragraphs of this article have a distinctly existentialist ring. "Solidarity is no more linked to the contractual style or the status style than any other inaccessible objective, or any other goal made impossible by the mediocrity of expectations and empirical prognostications." Returning more specifically to the concept of the welfare state, he ends his article with these three conclusions:

(a) The standard general theory of equilibrium is not pertinent. We must substitute for the Invisible Hand a conscious strategy of collective advantage.
(b) This collective advantage cannot be measured or realized by reference to a spontaneous combination of values derived from the market; it is precisely a matter of transcending the market.
(c) The techniques of contract and of solidarity have limited effects without a Collective Plan (*Projet*) formed and accepted (*consenti*, agreed to) in the conflicts and cooperation of the society, with a view to a universal development of the Human Resource.

This short summary of an already short article tells a good deal about François Perroux. It shows the breadth and depth of his scholarship; his knowledge of the literature from before Adam Smith to the latest issues of the leading journals; his willingness to transgress the borders of what is normally considered economics and invade other fields of knowledge. It reveals his human compassion, his concern for mankind the world over, and his view of economics as an instrument for improving the level of human welfare. It reflects his basic liberalism, but it also shows his feeling that human society needs to be ordered and managed if the desired results are to be achieved. It is a good example of his running battle with neoclassical economics, of which his theory of polarization and the related concept of development poles is a significant part. It illustrates his rejection of the concept of a basic harmony of interests in society, especially as it relates to the operation of the market. It underlines his emphasis on the role of power, and the importance of interest groups as well as individuals. He also rejects, however, the Marxist concept of *class* conflict, and makes room in his analysis for cooperation as well as conflict and competition among social groups. (I have never thought to ask Perroux how much he has been influenced directly by Marx, but I suspect not much. Perhaps he derived those elements of his theory that resemble Marx indirectly through Schumpeter, or simply from his own observation.) It is worth reiterating Charles Kindelberger's point that Perroux's concept of "dominance" is a theory of leadership, not of exploitation (Kindelberger 1978). Perroux seems to have a rather kaleidoscopic view of the world; economies and societies are pulled and pushed in various directions by ever-changing constellations of Leading Actors, with constant groupings and regroupings through (irreversible) time, so that the distribution of power is constantly changing too. Moreover, the patterns and the changes in them differ from society to society at any one time, as well as from time to time in any one society. It is a complicated theory; no wonder it is sometimes hard to follow, as the passages above also illustrate.

1.2 Perroux, Keynes, Schumpeter

In order to situate Perroux's general theory more precisely within the spectrum of contemporary economic thought, let us compare it to the theories of two other twentieth-century giants, Keynes and Schumpeter. Schumpeter had a great deal of direct influence on Perroux's thinking, Keynes considerably less. Let us therefore begin with Keynes.

Keynes

At the end of his book on ten great economists, Schumpeter says, "I am not going to grade the *General Theory* as if it were a student's examination book" (Schumpeter 1951). Any evaluation of Keynes's work must start from the recognition that Keynes was by far the most influential economist of his time. My purpose is not at all to rank these three economists, but to bring out the differences among them where general theory is concerned, so as to enhance understanding of Perroux.

The first thing that must be said of Keynes's *General Theory* is that it introduced no really new variables into the system of analysis. All the major variables had been in the literature, somewhere, before; some of them for a long time. Analysis of fluctuations and growth had concentrated for some time on relationships among savings, investment, the flow of money, the demand for cash balances, interest rates, expected profits, risk and uncertainty. As the discussion raged after publication of the *General Theory*, it gradually became apparent that the Stockholm School had been on a more fruitful track in dealing with these things than Keynes was. What Keynes accomplished was a highly ingenious *rearrangement*, simplification, synthesis, and systematization of the interactions among these variables.

Second, the Keynesian system relies heavily on axioms or tautologies. The equality of savings and investment as Keynes defined these is one; the multiplier is another. Where principles based on behavioral assumptions are introduced, such as liquidity preference or the investment function, the theory ceases to be truly general. It is culture-bound, tied to time and space, essentially to the world that Keynes knew in Western Europe and America during his own lifetime.

Third, it does not really advance much beyond comparative statics. It contains no real theory of development. It is much more concerned with the mechanism with which economies react to events or shocks from outside the system than with what makes an economy grow. It retains the basic neoclassical assumption that growth is "normal" in a capitalist society, and concentrates on how to make that growth "steady," with acceptable rates of unemployment and inflation.

Fourth, it did not survive, as a basis for policy formulation, the relatively simple institutional changes which changed the economy he knew from one with *alternating* inflation and unemployment to one of *simultaneous*, and even simultaneously increasing, unemployment and inflation. From the Keynesian model alone, one cannot derive policy prescriptions for reducing unemployment and inflation together.

Fifth, there is beneath Keynes's theory the neoclassical assumption of a basic harmony of interests of various social groups within a society. The economy must be managed, at least with respect to the rate of growth of the money supply. But once that is done the market will bring increasing welfare for all groups. The unequal distribution of *power* among social groups and among nations plays no real role in Keynes's general theory.

Sixth, Keynes took no account of space beyond the neoclassical theory of international and interregional trade. Indeed in his general theory he took little enough notice even of those, apart from the "foreign trade multiplier," which was another tautology.

One has only to compare the dreadful confusion in most of the literature on "business cycles" before the appearance of the *General Theory* with the comparative clarity after it to appreciate the stunning magnitude of Keynes's contribution. Nonetheless, we are now – many of us, at any rate – trapped in it, together with the rest of the neoclassical system. We might be better off today if one of the other "giants" had managed to convincingly systematize his theory first. Working entirely within the Keynesian framework, we have no solutions to today's economic problems.

Schumpeter's analytical framework is of an entirely different genre. It is much broader in scope than the Keynesian system, a theory of interlocking cycles and growth, incorporating social change, almost a theory of history. At the core of the theory is a sociological phenomenon, the "social climate." Innovation, the exercise of entrepreneurship, is the mainspring of economic and social progress, but how much innovation there is depends upon how favorable the social climate is for the exercise of entrepreneurship. Schumpeter worried a good deal about the impact of Keynes, of his Harvard colleague Alvin Hansen, and the Roosevelt New Deal. He feared that so abrupt and drastic changes in the rules of the enterprise game and in the allocation of decision-making power would kill the spirit of enterprise and sound the death knell of capitalism, at least the capitalism that he had known and so much admired.

Because of his emphasis on entrepreneurship, Schumpeter also had a very different view of monopoly from that of his more purely neoclassical colleagues. For them monopoly was the Sinner who prevented the market from working as perfectly as it could and should. For Schumpeter, monopoly was the necessary bait that would lure entrepreneurs into taking the risks of innovation. Schumpeter had little admiration for mere scientists, engineers, and inventors. There were plenty of tinkers around to produce gadgets. His admiration went to the true innovator, the captain of industry, who brought together the land, labor, capital, and management to turn the gadgets into burgeoning enterprises. He did not think of monopolies as a necessary evil; he didn't think of them as evil at all. His entrepreneurs were, rather, delicate and rare creatures, an endangered species who needed nurturing with juicy monopolies to keep them going. Anyhow, a successful innovation always gave rise to a "cluster of followers," who quickly competed away monopoly profits. Then a new innovation was needed to keep the economic system expanding. Schumpeter didn't much mind landed aristocrats; they gave the captains of industry something to aspire to. The ultimate drive of the entrepreneurs was not merely to get rich, but to rise on the social scale, "to found a family."

Schumpeter incorporated a good deal of Marx in his analytical framework. He thought in terms of power, of social groups, and of social change. Like Marx, he thought that capitalism would eventually disappear, not because of its failures, however, but because its very successes would arouse antagonism to it. Unlike Marx, Schumpeter was saddened rather than gladdened by this conclusion.

Schumpeter had within his system all the variables of the Keynesian system, although combined in somewhat different ways and with somewhat different emphases. Variations in the money supply were as crucial to his theory of three interlocking cycles (Kitchin, Juglar, Kondratieff) as they were to Keynes's general theory; but Schumpeter linked the money supply to the process of innovation. Schumpeter also recognized explicitly that a vigorous capitalist system entails failures of enterprises as well as profitable successes. Schumpeter's system has a good many more variables than Keynes's, and is harder to reduce to a few simple equations and to quantify. Perhaps for these reasons, Schumpeter's own "cluster of followers" was a good deal smaller than Keynes's.

Perroux took over the whole of the Schumpeterian system and put it into space. Schumpeter paid little more attention to space than did Keynes, although there is an implicit theory of location in some of Schumpeter's historical discussions. When I say "took over," I do not mean that Perroux simply started from the Schumpeter model and added to it. I mean that he was in general agreement with Schumpeter's analysis and did not find it necessary to drop from his own theory any of the major variables that were in Schumpeter's. Above all, Perroux as well as Schumpeter emphasized entrepreneurship and innovation as the driving force in the economy and in society. Perroux's propulsive enterprises are, above all, innovating enterprises; his growth poles and development poles are sources and diffusers of innovation. But Perroux added the fundamental observation that these propulsive enterprises are at any point of time concentrated in particular *places*, leading to domination of some places and dependence of others. The "backwash effects," negative propulsive effects, tantamount to Schumpeter's failures of enterprises in the normal course of development, are also put into space; the failures too tend to be concentrated in particular *places*. As Schumpeter thought temporary monopolies were part of the normal development process, Perroux thinks polarization is a normal part of it.

Putting events into space in this sort of fashion makes a great deal of difference in the evaluation of a market economy and a democratic, capitalist society. For spaces are inhabited by particular groups of people, with particular interests. Resources of all kinds are not spread evenly through space. Intense concern for the fishing industry will not be found among the peoples of regions with no large bodies of water. And when fishermen are Basques, or Gaspésiens, or Acadiens, with a language and culture different from that of the majority in the country as a whole, the distribution of economic activity in space can be a threat to the very survival of the nation. Also, consideration of space in this form means that it is ludicrous to retain the assumption of instantaneous and costless mobility of all factors of production, underlying much of the neoclassical theory of regional development. One must incorporate into that theory barriers to movement, not only of people but of fixed capital as well. From basically harmonious individual choices of the neoclassical theory one is driven to Perroux's formulation in terms of Leading Actors, social groups as well as individuals, conflict and cooperation as well as competition.

Perroux's theory bears too little resemblance to that of Keynes to permit direct and useful comparison. Let us, however, make a schematic comparison of Perroux with Schumpeter.

Economic Development

	Schumpeter	*Perroux*
Progress due to:	Innovation	Innovation
Made by:	Entrepreneurs	Propulsive enterprises
Situated:	?	In growth/development poles
Leading to:	(1) Monopoly	(1) Polarization: dominance/dependence
	(2) Cluster of followers: (a) monetary expansion (b) failures of firms	(2) Propulsive effects: (a) spread effects (b) backwash effects (c) upstream (d) downstream

It is apparent that the Perroux system, which incorporates all the variables of the Schumpeter system and space as well, has – potentially – more explanatory power than the Schumpeter system and much more than the Keynesian system. Having said that, however, it is necessary to add that the "Perrouxian Revolution" is still less complete than the Keynesian Revolution. Some of the equations remain to be written in the Perrouxian system, more remain to be quantified. But once these tasks are accomplished, the Perrouxian system will be a more useful basis for planning and policy than either the Keynesian or the Schumpeterian systems.

Keynes was luckier in his "cluster of followers" than Perroux has been. One reason for that was that Keynes's act was easier to follow than Perroux's. But that is not all that has been involved. The growth pole fad, the pressure to disaggregate national economies as a basis for policy and planning, the worldwide trend toward disaggregation in space, came too soon from the standpoint of the state of evolution of the theory. The theory was not ready for immediate application. The result was that those disciples of Perroux who found themselves in a position of having to come up with regionalized development plans within a limited time frame invented a theory totally different from that of Perroux, and applied that theory instead.

1.3 Growth poles

Let us then turn to the subject for which Perroux is best known, growth poles and development poles. Karen Polenske's chapter in this volume (Ch. 4) deals specifically with this subject, and I do not wish to repeat here her exposition of Perroux's growth pole doctrine, nor her comparison of Perroux's concept of dominance/dependence with the doctrines of the dependency school. I should like, however, to relate Perroux's growth pole theory to his more general theory. (In doing so, I shall inevitably draw on two of my earlier papers (1981, 1983) on Perroux's work.)

In order to understand Perroux's system, it is essential to know what his growth pole theory is *not*; so many people have written about and applied what they *thought* was Perroux's growth pole concept, without having bothered to find out what he really said, that a few words here may be appropriate.

The growth pole doctrine is, to begin with, a theory of *polarization*. Economic development does not spread itself evenly throughout space. The mainspring of economic development is technological progress or innovation, and innovation tends to be concentrated in particular enterprises, the propulsive industries. These firms tends to be clustered in particular places. These centers of concentrated innovative activity are often cities, but in principle they could be areas of high-technology agriculture (plantations, wheat belts, corn belts) or mining. Any constellation of propulsive enterprises is a growth pole.

The growth poles will generate spread effects, but there is no telling a priori where these will be felt. Certainly there is no assurance that they will be felt in the immediately surrounding peripheral geographic region, which Perroux dismisses as "banal" space. They may not even be felt in the same country as the propulsive enterprises. Perroux's "economic space" is a highly abstract affair, a "field of forces." While insisting that polarization is a fact of life in contemporary economic and social development, Perroux's treatment of the ways in which growth poles and development poles are formed and function is highly theoretical, to the point of being on occasion difficult to follow. Consider the following series of statements of Perroux, mostly from Chapter 2 of this volume:

"The growth pole is a set that has the capacity to induce the growth of another set; the pole of development is a set that has the capacity to engender a dialectic of economic and social structures whose effect is to increase the complexity of the whole and to expand its multidimensional return." In this context "growth = a lasting increase in the dimensional indicator of a set." Growth operates in and through privileged points. Development "springs up" and "ends in" privileged points. Development poles cannot be considered in isolation; they are an integral part of development analysis. Space is a "field of forces," and there are "as many spaces as there are structures of abstract relations which define an object" (Perroux 1950). The active units (Actors) in an economy *create* their own abstract spaces of decision and operations, generating propulsive effects that in certain combinations can engender the multidimensional development of the economic whole. The dynamics of development are thus closely linked with the theory of spaces, structures, and active units. No present-day dynamics can be worked out without taking account of development poles. Propulsive effects can be expressed by quantified matrices *without* locations as well as by matrices specifying locations.

In order to understand Perroux's theory of growth poles and development poles, it is essential to understand that it is just one facet, although an important one, of his running battle with the neoclassical system.

Neoclassical economics implies that the market will bring, among other pleasant things, an essential harmony in the distribution of economic activity through space, a kind of Pareto optimum of spatial equilibrium. It was precisely this comfortable conclusion that Perroux denied, contending that the natural tendency was towards polarization, dominance, and dependence, which was likely to become cumulative. Here Perroux's theory bore some resemblance to Harrod's (1948) theory of growth, with its cumulative movements away from equilibrium once equilibrium is disturbed, or Myrdal's (1957) concept of cumulative causation.

Perroux has a general theory of development, one that he has been working on for decades and still has not completed. The most complete statement is probably his 1975 book (Perroux 1975). But the most recent and perhaps the best statement of this general theory is his chapter in this volume. It is not an easy general theory, and in some ways is more unfamiliar in concept, terminology, and mathematics than was Keynes's *General Theory* when it first appeared. The new paper is made all the more difficult by the fact that it really is an outline of a book. At any rate it makes it clear that for Perroux the concept of growth poles is only one part of a much bigger and much more complex system. In his theory, growth poles are concentrations in space of propulsive industries, generating effects in the form of "fields of force" to a global "economic space." Perroux was quite emphatic that he was not talking about spread effects in "banal" geographic space, let alone increases in income and employment in the immediately surrounding region of some urban center selected as a growth pole. Yet it is in this form that the concept was applied by disciples of Perroux who found themselves in the position of having to put together regional and national development plans.

Perroux's own theory was imperfectly understood and still more imperfectly applied. But applied it certainly was. Many more governments have stated officially that they were pursuing a growth pole strategy, at least in the urban and regional aspects of their development policy, than have claimed to be guided by any other philosophy, apart from laissez-faire; it became the guiding principle for regional planning in France, Belgium, Italy and Quebec as early as 1960, and in the decade that followed spread to Spain, the United States, Japan, Latin America, Africa, and Asia.

As initially presented by Perroux, the theory was too complex, too abstract, and too nonoperational to be used as a basis for planning. Indeed to apply the pure theory of Perroux would require global planning, if we take into account Perroux's more recent insistence on planning transmission lines and receptors as well as generators of growth. Perroux's economic space, in which spread effects are felt, is global. He argues, for example, that Latin America's true growth poles still lie in Europe and, to some degree, in the United States. Such a concept is useless for regional planning which is confined to a single country. As a consequence, economists who found themselves involved in practical regional planning simply discarded the pure theory of Perroux. They converted it into a totally different theory which treated growth poles as urban centers, and spread effects as being generated in a particular geographic space, namely the region adjacent to the urban center itself. Once this happy doctrine is accepted, it is possible to imagine that by pushing and pulling new enterprises (mostly industrial enterprises) into urban centers of retarded regions, it is possible to reduce regional disparities, decentralize urbanization and industrialization, and accelerate national development all at once. It did not take long for this pleasant version of the growth pole doctrine to spread to developing countries and to be applied there as well.

It is here, of course, that the mistake was made. There are, to be sure, conditions under which industrial investment in a city will lead to increased income and employment in its peripheral region. In general, these conditions are that the industries in the city are natural-resource based, and that the natural resources required are found in the peripheral region. When the concept of growth poles was first introduced, it should be remembered, many industries in Western European cities were still natural-resource based, and many cities were based primarily on these industries. For such urban centers, the simplified theory of growth poles may hold. But there are many situations in which this theory – let us label it the Boudeville version because of Boudeville's major role in spreading this "revisionist" version of the original Perroux doctrine – simply does not hold at all. (For those unacquainted with Boudeville's work, the best introductions might be Boudeville (1976, 1977); Kuklinski (1981) gives an extensive bibliography.) One of the situations in which this theory does not hold is in the case of the propulsive region, in which it is the expansion of economic activities in the hinterland which generates growth of its urban center, rather than vice versa. Another is where the urban center is too small and too unsophisticated in its economic activities to generate significant spread effects of any kind, as in the case of a small town with a cannery or some jaggery mills. A third is where industries are natural-resource based, but the natural resources are found outside the peripheral region. And the fourth, most common among major metropolitan centers today, is the situation in which the propulsive enterprises in the city are based not on natural resources but on human resources. In such cases, industry consists of scientifically oriented manufacturing and quaternary services; there is no link to the peripheral region at all, because the enterprises operate in a worldwide economic space. The Boudeville version, however, simply took no account of these cases, which are certainly in the majority, until it had become abundantly clear that the application of this simple version of the theory was not working. In effect, the adherents to this theory behaved as though growth pole theory and economic base theory were essentially the same. We learned in time the falsity of this premise. We found that it was indeed possible, although not easy, to lure new enterprises into urban centers designated as growth poles in retarded regions. Snaring them required a combination of investment in infrastructure, relocation of government enterprises, and incentives to private enterprise. But in most cases the hoped-for and expected spread effects to the rest of the region did not appear.

Before we learned this bitter lesson, however, and once the door was opened to Boudeville's revisionism, all manner of policies regarding urban growth and regional development were justified as application of the growth pole doctrine. The urban centers labeled "growth poles" ranged in population from many millions to a few thousand. In Japan growth poles were vast industrial complexes requiring hundreds of millions of dollars of investment in each. In Mauritania the small, sleepy town of Kaedi on the Senegal River, with about 10,000 population, was treated as a growth pole that could generate spread effects to the countryside. Such effects would come from the linking of the stable, grain-growing agriculture of the Senegal River Valley with the semi-nomadic livestock cultivation of the Sahel, using grain surpluses (when there were any) to fatten livestock in feedlots before slaughtering them in Kaedi's small but very modern abbatoir. The Economic Development Administration in the United States worked with growth centers as small as 500 people, mere villages in remote hill country consisting of exhausted mines and marginal farmland.

It is a long march from Perroux's own theory to giving a capital grant to Volvo to make Halifax into a development pole, generating propulsive effects, in the form of higher employment and incomes, throughout the

Atlantic Provinces. Indeed, Perroux is quite specific that it is "untenable to reduce the theory of development poles to a mere instrument of regional policy". One cannot implant any old kind of productive activity anywhere one wishes, in any kind of environment. A rational policy involves both the choice of the motor and the management of the environment. Moreover, Perroux continues, "Clearly, the market, full as it is of monopolies and various imperfections, is not up to these two tasks." In today's mixed economy, communication between public and private sectors is constant; the ideal solution to its problems is offered by the multilevel planning of (Janos) Kornai (of Hungary) and Liptak.

Statements such as these, together with Perroux's related theory of dominance/dependence, which is well analyzed in Karen Polenske's chapter below, make Perroux sound as though he were a radical political economist. But while Perroux is a heretic in relation to his more purely neoclassical colleagues, in politics he probably would be placed slightly right of center in the French political spectrum. He is conservative enough, at any rate, to have run into severe difficulties during the left-wing student riots in Paris in 1968, including the loss of his editorship of the Journal *Tiers monde* of which he was the founder. Perroux was certainly interested in politics at both the national and the international levels. Like Keynes, he wrote a good many "essays in persuasion," as the bibliography appended to this volume shows. He has limited faith in the free market, and believes that dynamic capitalist economies need some degree of planning and management. Nonetheless, his political philosophy remains basically liberal.

Professor Ducarmel Bocage states at the end of his book on Perroux, "Professor Perroux is one of the greatest and most original thinkers of our time" (Bocage 1985). In his well-known book on *The Growth of Economic Thought*, Professor Henry W. Spiegel characterizes Perroux as "the only living economist who developed a theoretical system rivaling conventional equilibrium analysis" (Spiegel 1971).

But the best way to understand and evaluate Perroux's ideas is to read what he has written himself. For those who do not read French easily, there is enough of his work available in English to absorb the main thrust of his thought. And among the very best of his writings in English are his contributions to this volume.

References

Bocage, D. 1985. *General economic theory of François Perroux.* New York and London: University Press of America.
Boudeville, J. 1976. *French regional polarization and planning.* Paris: Pion.

Boudeville, J. 1977. Functional regional analysis: an elementary exposition on some selected topics. In *University of Toronto Lectures*, J. H. P. Paelinck and A. Sailez (eds). Paris: Association de Science Régionale de Langue Française.
Harrod, R. 1948. *Towards a dynamic economics*. London: Macmillan.
Higgins, B. 1981. Growth poles: do they exist? In *Polarized development and regional policies*, A. Kuklinski (ed.), 19–36. The Hague, Paris, and New York: Mouton.
Higgins, B. 1983. From growth poles to systems of interaction in space. *Growth and Change* **14** (4), 3–13.
Kindelberger, C. P. 1978. Dominance and leadership in the international economy. In *Homage à François Perroux*, 283–91. Grenoble: P.U.G.
Kuklinksi, A. (ed.) 1981. *Polarized development and regional policies: tribute to Jacques Boudeville*. The Hague, Paris and New York: Mouton.
Myrdal, G. 1957. *Economic theory and underdeveloped regions*. London: Duckworth.
Perroux, F. 1950. Economic spaces: theory and applications. *Quarterly Journal of Economics* **64** (1), 90–7.
Perroux, F. 1975. *Unités actives et mathématiques nouvelles*. Paris: Dunod.
Perroux, F. 1984. Au-delà du Welfare State: Une société pleinement économique. *Économie appliquée* **37** (1), 99–121.
Schumpeter, J. 1951. *Ten great economists from Marx to Keynes*. London: Allen & Unwin.
Spiegel, H. W. 1971. *The growth of economic thought*. Englewood Cliffs: Prentice Hall.

2

The pole of development's new place in a general theory of economic activity

FRANÇOIS PERROUX

A Economic analysis

2.1 The pole of development and the general theory of the economy

The elements of the pole of development concept consist of a few elements which can be found in two papers I gave at Harvard in 1954. One of the papers concerned economic spaces; polarized space, space considered as a structure, and space considered as the content of a plan. The second lecture dealt with macrodecisions (macrounits seen as complex units) and introduced the concept of a hierarchy of subsets composing a set. My paper on the concept of growth poles appeared shortly after.

In sharp contrast with the brevity of these first texts, a considerable literature has evolved around the concept of growth pole (pole of development) in France and elsewhere in a variety of political contexts around the world.

Professor Nemvinov, at a conference in Paris, mentioned its being used in models for the opening up of Siberia. In Canada, in-depth studies for regional planning have been based on the same concept. A report by Marjolin Duquesne de la Villele describes it at length without bothering to acknowledge the original source. A Spanish law on regionalization mentions the term "polos de desarrolio," though its interpretation is questionable. The BariTaronto contribution has provoked a lively polemic whose reverberations are still being felt.

In the French context, the work of Davin and Paelinck, and especially the ample and profound contribution of Jacques Boudeville, the researches and analyses led by Joseph Lajugie and his team (Pierre Delfaud, Claude Lacour), so significant in their scope and complexity, all attest to the considerable interest shown in the concept, in the new point of view implied by it, and in the analytical developments it commands. In the United States, this line of thought has attracted the attention of Niles M. Hansen, and quite recently, John Friedmann and Clyde Weaver have published a volume *Territory and Function*, where the French school is well represented. As for the application of the concept in the Latin countries of Europe and America, we could devote a whole book to recording its bibliography and studying its influence.

This immediate and enduring acceptance was also accompanied, as usual, by simplifications, and by abusive and polemical interpretations generated by vested interests.

The object of the present study is to clarify the debate and to place the concept back within the general theory where its meaning and explicative virtue lie.

Let me first be specific about a point that is more than terminological. While elaborating my first studies, I went from the concept of "growth pole" to that of "pole of development." Let me here draw the distinction that will become increasingly clear as my argument proceeds: the *growth pole* is a set that has the capacity to induce the growth of another set ("growth" being defined as a lasting increase in the dimensional indicator); the *pole of development* is a set that has the capacity to engender a dialectic of economic and social structures whose effect is to increase the complexity of the whole and to expand its multidimensional return.

The facts refer to two different representations of economic evolution. One is the balanced *growth* that many models have popularized; aggregate investment is its motor. The rate of balanced growth is situated at the level where the savings and investments curves intersect, and the stability of this position is assumed, in my opinion, without adequate proof. The picture is simple and is suitable for a set ruled by perfect competition. Questions about the addable quality of the prices used to evaluate the total product, or about the meaning, for the agents concerned, of an increase in production or of the rate of production growth, are avoided; and no reference is made to the social structure, or to a less summary distribution than the division into total product and total wages.

The picture of evolution by way of *development* is something quite different: it allows the parts and the structured and economically significant subsets to combine; production is analyzed, and is shown to be made up of industries and agricultures, new and established industries, industries with a high or a low rate of growth, and so on. The current observation is that in an industrialized and developed country, certain of these sectors (in the most general sense), in the medium and long runs, depend on the configuration of the "motor" and the "moved" sectors, and of its effects on the size and structure of the aggregate product. Similarly, the population is made up of active groups (classes, functions) that exercise their activity in the name of less active groups.

This brief parallel suggests that the concept of *pole of development* cannot be considered in isolation from the general theoretical interpretation to which it belongs. On the contrary, it is an integral part of the analysis of development, as distinct from growth. Moreover, what growth and development have in common is that, at the level of observation, not a single example of evolution was ever found where the constituent elements and the results are equally distributed in a set. Growth operates in and through privileged points. Development "springs up" and "ends in" privileged points.

Another distinction justifies my choice of subject. Although an enormous amount of descriptive, critical, and analytical literature has been written on the concept of "pole of development," there is very little explicit and purposeful discussion of the *general economic theory* that serves as its framework. Today, the choice seems to be between *general equilibrium theory* of the Walrasian type, and the *theory of the generalized "equilibrium"* of active units.

The first of these – general equilibrium theory – forms the basis for the spatial conceptions of a number of authors, from Loesch to Walter Isard. Spatial interdependence is constructed in the homogeneous space of the perfect competition model. The displacement of an economic unit can then be likened to a **substitution** of factors of production. After the displacement, A factors substitute themselves for B factors that are qualitatively different. The movement is justified by the prices and costs that confront the firms' chief executives. The law of price places and displaces the factors: that the agents may have their own power to change this law is ruled out of the question.

By contrast, the general theory of active units assumes axiomatically that, given certain conditions, the agents (actors) have the capacity to change their environment. It describes the successions of activities and events in *irreversible time*. It constructs *balancing* (the action of equilibrating) and *equilibrations* (real groupings around a terminal position), and it only sees the general equilibrium of instantaneous equality of supply and demand at all levels – an arbitrary mental construct, devoid of all operational capacity and burdened with grave internal contradictions. It is the general theory of active units that makes coherent the theories of domestic and foreign exchange, of regional planning and the strategy of nations, along with the theories of *abstract* economic spaces and territorial spaces.

The theory of poles corresponds with the theory of economic spaces which is itself included in the theory of active units. Because the active units *create* their own, abstract spaces of decision and operation, it is possible to construct centers that exercise propulsive effects that, in certain combinations, engender the multidimensional development of the economic whole. The actual dynamics of development is thus closely linked with the theory of spaces, structures, and active units.

The maturation of the new general theory of economy has proceeded gradually, lending power and scope to the analysis of development and its poles. Partial models remain inadequate when they are not tied to a general theory of the operation of the whole system.

The object of the present outline is to show that: (a) there is no dynamic model that can be constructed which is applicable to today's world without taking into account poles of development; and (b) no *economic policy* applicable to a large (e.g., national) set can be formulated without methodical coupling of the poles with their planned environment.

This analysis in itself already refutes the superficial objections raised against the concept of poles of development. I shall however meet these criticisms directly before presenting a conclusion.

2.2 Present-day dynamics and the poles of development

The Walrasian theory of the standard general equilibrium poses known obstacles to the construction of a coherent and operational economic dynamics. It sees equilibrium as instantaneous and static; the system never quits its equilibrium position except under the action of an exogenous factor. For this reason, endogenous causes of change are minimized. Furthermore, in this strictly mechanistic equilibrium, individuals are reduced to the status of *robots* whose actions are determined by price. Lifted from mechanics and physics, the Walrasian equilibrium describes the movements of objects by price and their stoppage at the point of equilibrium: in accordance with an inspiration derived from thermodynamics, it deems it improper to describe the actions and reactions of the agents in irreversible time.

In my opinion, modern dynamics may be deduced from the theory of active units. Each individual carries energy for change, usually in the form of expansion energy. It is a function of the individual's personal coefficient, his position in the social networks, and the extent of his means. Essentially, *to act* means to change one's own material and human environment. Individuals are to some degree unequal, depending on the case considered. They are agents and not passive beings who submit to their milieu.

Under given conditions and at a given time, the units upon which the agent exercises his decision have very unequal capacity to modify their environments, because of differences in size and structure. Today, the great oligopolistic units are outstanding *strategically active units*. Such oligopolies and economic and financial groups have their own capacity to increase their share of the market by manipulating prices, flows, and information. They are much more than *price-makers* in this regard. Besides, by their fixed and committed capital strategy and by their ability to establish powerful organizations, they create durable, structural spaces within economic and territorial systems. To some extent, they impose *their* space on the less efficient or less powerful firms and decision-makers. This structural hold can be seen at work within a country and between countries. It is one of the most characteristic features of the contemporary economy.

A preliminary approach to a system's energy for change may be made through an indicator: the *anticipated profit*. Provided, of course, that the different levels of competition are taken into consideration: that of the large (oligopolies and groups) and that of the medium and small firms. It can be said that the conflict-laden alliances of the large firms and their anticipations of profit exert, at given nodes in a network, a determinant effect on the possibilities of medium and small companies realizing and predicting their own profits. In this situation, the drying-up of the system's energy is tied to the co-satisfaction or exhaustion of the large firms, and not at all to the co-satisfaction of all the units of the whole system under consideration.

A kind of pause (*Ruhestand*) in the system is linked to a deceleration of the effects of the system's energy for change ($\Delta\phi_e \simeq 0$). This moment of rest has nothing to do with the uniqueness, stability, and optimality of the standard equilibrium. Thus reinterpreted, the image of the economic system is one of *economic* space and *territorial* space created by agents according to their degree of efficiency and their powers. The most powerful are *economic space-makers*. Unequal agents making decisions about unequal units and unequal structured subsets (industries) exercise asymmetric effects upon one another, the most favourable of which (from the point of view of development) being *propulsive effects*.

These propulsive effects can of course be observed and analyzed at the level of the parts of the system (let us call them sectors); hence, they radically alter the conditions of macroeconomic analysis. Thus, disequilibrium is no longer corrected by changes in total savings and total investments; it is the *sectoral* flows or savings and investments that, if they are equal, form the equilibrium or, if unequal, restore it. The quasi-mechanical actions via interest are excluded. Evolution of the sectors, as regards their contents and relations, is in the medium run.

Could these changes conceivably be correctly anticipated by entrepreneurs and public authorities? Since the law of profit does not reconcile contradictory aspirations, it is hard to imagine a hypothetical controller who would be able to make them mutually compatible, without delay or error. The aggregate climate is one of *pseudo-equilibria* of large monopolistic and oligopolistic active units whose *conflictual cooperations* exert their action on the whole economy.

The picture of large units acting strategically on a less active remainder of the economy is not arbitrary. It reflects observable facts. Furthermore, it is the highly probable sequel of the destabilization of price systems that evolves as soon as one considers unequal units in irreversible time, even in conditions nearest to perfect competition – that is in imperfect competition with no monopolistic element and without oligopoly. Equilibria created under such conditions result in units that do not have exactly the same rate and volume of profit. These privileged units can, by simple observation of the current economic rationality, engage themselves in strengthening their relative position. Thus the transition is made to the possibility of monopolistic or oligopolistic formations. This trend is inherent in all observable evolutions in industrialized countries.

In these countries, innumerable propulsion effects can be observed between unequal (simple or complex) units, brought about by the *flow of goods and services*, by *transfers of productivity*, and by the *investment flow*. For every pole of development born of these propulsive effects, one can draw three matrices that describe the *three modalities* of propulsion quantitatively.

Thus, an operative scheme of evolution in irreversible time reintroduces the discontinuities, the ruptures, the non-linear movements that observation imposes on us. A certain stability, which might be called monopolistic (and that is of course economically judged only after scrutiny), results from the manifest and tacit alliances between the Great decision-makers in the fields of production, credit, and finance who eventually agree on common lines of resistance and offensive.

The *points of development by propulsive effect* may be found anywhere in a dynamics of industrialized and developed countries (for a concrete example, see Robineau 1978). Conventionally, it is decided that for given conditions and in a given period, the term "pole of development" is reserved for action centers that have the maximum intensity and reach. It cannot be repeated often enough that the attention is focussed primarily on *economic spaces* before it reaches *geographical spaces*; that quantitative expression can use matrices without location as well as matrices referring to location. In a word, it would be untenable to reduce the theory of poles of development to a mere instrument of regional policy, very important though the latter might be; in this domain, one can always conduct the analysis by applying imaginary abstract economic spaces to territorial spaces.

Today's dynamics of the medium and long runs utilizes several types of analysis drawn from the new theory of development – for instance:

(a) The distinction between primary and secondary poles, the latter created by the first or instigated by them, by liaison between existing poles; these procedures, in certain conditions, give rise to a region of development.
(b) The tracing of transportation lines that, by *liaison effects*, at the extremities and laterally, become *axes of development*.
(c) Propulsive complementarities between industries and activities that generate *junction effects* between techniques.
(d) The impact of poles, over very long distances, generating reverberations in local development.

Without difficulty, one can build a whole corpus of conceptual tools, formalizations, and models such as have already produced an ample harvest of established data applicable to policy questions. Contrary to hasty and superficial statements, it can be said that the pole of development is situated within an already articulated and coherent general theory.

Thus, the concept is indispensable to a rational economic policy for the management of industries and of territories.

B Economic policy and poles of development

To define an economic policy, one must never start from a whole where development is evenly distributed. A nation that has been industrialized for a long time is made up of economically *active* and surplus-producing regions, and regions that are relatively *less active* and deficit-producing. Even if we had (which we don't) good statistics of interregional exchanges of raw materials, of interregional accounts, there would be no justification for seeking an equilibrium of the balances of transfers of resources between regions: it would halt the propulsive effects that active regions (régions motrices) exercise on the others.

Thus, the objective is a combination of the relative rates of growth and development for each region so as to maximize the aggregate net product while attaining the desired structure of the national economy.

This aggregate effect presupposes the elimination of *unbearable disequilibria*. For a national aggregate made up of two regions, A and B, unbearable disequilibria exist when the growth rate in A is high enough to impose so low a growth rate in B, that the growth rate of the aggregate declines, or the vital level of consumption in the population of B is threatened.

The most interesting but least quantifiable point is seen in developed countries with a democratic regime where there is a free flow of information. Region A has a high growth rate, region B a low rate; the people in B *deem* that this difference, well justified though it might be on the economic plane, is "unbearable" in the name of "national solidarity." In a parliamentary democracy, these psychological and social reactions influence the public authorities. The eventually irrational argument caused by inadequately digested information plays a role between regions and between nations.

The statistical descriptions of regions constitute the basis for all decisions of economic policy and of regional planning. Let me say that they can be correctly interpreted only if at least account is taken of the propulsive effects of external origin from which they benefit: there exists no region, in fact, that has grown and developed as a closed vessel.

If this is the case, one must conclude that, in looking to the future too, the distinction must be drawn between territorial development and development through poles (internal or external to a given territory). This means that regional economics must be extended to include small, specific models that will adequately bring into relief the polarizations inside and outside the regions.

Transportation and communication programs and plans have a crucial role to play here. They establish connections among existing poles; thus, the transportation route becomes, under certain conditions, an *axis of development*. Set against a relatively empty space, the transportation network predetermines, in large measure, the privileged forms and sites of development for a given level of technology.

Internationally, the pooling of a pole of development (energy, for example) is meant to serve all interested parties, in theory. The historical experience does not warrant excessive optimism in this regard. The egotism of the state that controls the territory on which the pole is implanted puts obstacles in the way of a common sharing of its effects and its results.

The whole preceding analysis reveals the error commonly made by public opinion on the subject of the pole of development. The picture conveyed by everyday language is that of the implantation of a production apparatus within a territorial space, followed by the spreading of exchanges. The briefest reflection upon this idea shows that just any kind of productive unit cannot be implanted in any kind of environment with the hope of generating development effects. A rational policy, in developing countries as well as in long-developed ones, involves the *choice of the motor* and the *management of the environment* in which it is to exert its propulsive effects.

Clearly, the market, full as it is of monopolies and various imperfections, is not up to these two tasks. An authority concerned with the collective interest should make as precise an assessment as possible of the actual state of a large aggregate (for example, the nation), and from there deduce what the best choice is for the motor and for the management of its milieu.

The choice of the industries whose creation or extension is to be given priority must be made on the basis of what their anticipated *complementary* effects will be on existing industries, and on the effects that voluntary *substitution* of renovated industries will have on established industries or on part of them. This choice must be made while taking into account the competition in the world market.

From the start, putting these innovations to work involves numerous executive decisions for the channeling of inputs and the delivery of outputs. Once the installation is completed as part of the overall process of growth and development, the structuring of cadres and workers, the assembly of scientific and technical information, the influencing of users and consumers, and other activities essential to the success of the operation can be undertaken.

In the mixed economy prevailing today, communication between private and public decisions is constant. Without it, information that is essential for analysis of fundamental options would be inadequate: one such option, for example, would concern the degree of commitment to external or internal development desirable for the whole national economy; another example is the choice between an industrialization policy that stimulates and values agriculture or one that debases and absorbs it.

The national economy is an evolving structure that changes profoundly in the long run, but which entails relative stability in the medium run. Fixed, capital assets committed to specific uses and, no less, the complex organization of the contemporary economy, have a coefficient of inertia. The extension of the public sector and the widening scope of the mixed economy further distances the national economy from the flexibility assumed in neoclassical models. Prices alone are not enough to determine structures; public authorities should strive to direct choices in internal and external growth industries that will develop the export capacity without sacrificing the domestic market. These nodes, these subsets capable of propulsive effects, are at the origin of the development of the whole provided that the distribution of the product and revenue are managed correctly.

The market as it is, and prices as they are formed in it under the pressure of monopolies, are clearly not enough to obtain complex desired results. Development is a form of evolution that can serve either the oligopolies and other economic and financial groups, or the whole of the population. The second option calls for an orientation and arbitration in favor of the collective interest.

The phenomenon is quite obvious in the *relations between industry and agriculture*, and between individual *industrial and agricultural enterprises*. Technologies, organization, the financial power of industry generally give it the means to dominate agriculture and put it in its service. Harmonious development requires a reversal of this asymmetric relationship and assumes that industry should, in a sense, be at the service of agriculture, moving it without absorbing it. This strategy includes choices relating to the nature and products of agriculture, to the transmission of the positive effects of investment and information for the benefit of populations. In this case too, a choice must be made between development for the oligopolies and dominant groups, and development for the benefit of all.

In brief, the pole of development could harbor *dangerous ambiguities*, unless precise qualifications are made.

This last observation introduces the question of the location of investments and enterprises as it is formulated in terms of the new dynamics. The question splits into two: (a) how, under what pressures, and by what means has the location of economic activities occurred, since the beginnings of Western industrialization; and (b) how can the location of enterprises or groups of enterprises be conceptualized today, in the light of the new analyses?

As regards the first question the observer who is liberated from the routines of traditional interpretations is struck by the part played, both within a single industrialized country and in the relations between countries at different levels of development, by the large private and public mixed enterprises and the great public organizations. During the English hegemony of the nineteenth century, these great units manipulated costs and prices for imports and exports. They systematically operated "enclave economies" where local developments were unrelated to the surplus product and productivity procured by dominant units for the dominant power. In view of these strategies (which have by no means disappeared from the world scene), neoclassical statements about relative supplies of factors and relative costs in perfect competition appear as more or less unconsciously deluding conceptualizations and reconstructions that tend to self-justification of the system.

How much did comparative costs at the beginning of the twentieth century owe to nearly perfect competition, and how much to the pressures of the large mixed and public units?

Given today's structures, it is untenable to maintain that the market *as it now stands* should allocate resources nationally or internationally and that it should determine the site of their territorial implantation.

As to the second question the *ideal* solution for the location of new units is offered, in pure theory, by the multilevel planning of Kornai and Liptak. The parts of a large whole draw up their plans for the optimum utilization of their resources; the authority controlling the whole ensures the compatibility of these plans through the circulation of information. The most advanced nations lag far behind the degree of centralization on which regional programs are based, and in their political system may be farther still from the vigor and flexibility required in order to efficiently coordinate regional plans that have been rationally worked out. Private firms and public authorities have at their disposal descriptive inventories of sectors and regions that, joined to *models of development* proper, could help quantify the *objectives* chosen by the final criterion of the collective good.

If carefully followed, the synthesis I have just presented is a good enough reply to the objections and criticisms leveled against the concept of pole of development. Opponents more often than not forget one vital thing: that it is not an isolated concept but an aspect, and a key aspect, of a general theory and of a policy of development. It is, however, appropriate at this point that I consider and assess the main criticisms.

2.3 Responses to criticisms of the development pole concept

Does the pole of development exist?

Let me repeat that there never has been a historical case of economic evolution where one does not observe clustering, cumulative, and propulsive effects that generate development. History has handed down its verdict: there is no other way of development. In these circumstances, one should perhaps avoid asking, without detailed specifications, this question that is so apt to strike and confuse uninformed spirits: does the pole of development exist?

When a pole of development establishes itself, it more often than not borrows the resources it needs from a space different from the site of its implantation. It "empties" this space, relatively speaking, while it assumes shape; in the second phase, it exerts its actions in its own space and in other spaces, near or far.

Following the *attraction phase*, the *expansion phase* manifests itself through the flow of goods, of investments, and of information. Examples of this phenomenon are widely varied and innumerable, and they concern rapidly growing firms. To stop the description after the *first* phase is tantamount to comparing what is "lost" on one side and "gained" on the other. If an exact and quantitative reasoning is preferred, one would have to accurately evaluate the transfers of resources and their varied effects in the space that produces them and the surplus of production in the space that receives them – something which one generally does not want to do.

Even before considering the second phase (without which the phenomenon is *truncated*), it must be observed that the attraction of resources by the pole may concern fresh additional resources seeking employment; that it can decongest another region in regard to one of its resources (labor, for instance), and that *from the beginning* of the operation, productivity in the receiving space is generally increased.

The essential point is to be quite specific about *the period* one is dealing with and to remember the two phases of clustering (densification) and expansion. Historical experience indicates that this inevitable dual process procures positive results – especially if it is directed and planned, which is frequently the case for the far-reaching poles.

Can the pole of development be formalized?

Formalization *is already here* as far as the propulsion effect is concerned, both in commonly used techniques of expression in matrix form and graphs, and in the extended use of *cost–benefit analysis* as applied to very large aggregates. The medium run complementarity effects (not to be confused with the Keynesian multiplicator) are drawn up for investments, for products, and are derived from distribution of income coefficients. That the models in question are subject to uncertainty in irreversible time, and that they have not mastered the risk factor is a feature they share with *all* mathematical and econometric models: no specialist doubts it.

The pole of development does not offer an instrument for choosing locations (of investments, or production units)

I am tempted to say that the interminable discussions about whether enterprises or industries should be located according to the *source* (raw materials, energy) or according to the *demand* seem somewhat outdated, given contemporary techniques that, in the case of a large firm, open up a wide range of options comprising both types of location on the world scale. The theory of poles of development in a fixed and planned environment certainly allows the choice of location to be referred to a larger number of important data than is the case in traditional discussions about general options. I maintain plainly that the most modern method of representing the national economy is to draw up the picture of a network of actual and potential poles of development (industries, regions). The study of the whole saves private and public decision-makers from failures of perspective and favors rational locations.

The criticisms I have just reviewed are not convincing. But there are other reasons for the resistance to the concept of pole development and to the development theory to which it is attached. I shall not dwell too long on the role of vested interests. Established industries define their strategy over a long period: they have every reason to oppose the constitution of powerful regions and centers of development that will ultimately become competitors able to "take off" with the latest techniques unburdened by the dead weight of assets invested long before.

On quite another level, the equilibrium of perfect competition and growth in a state of equilibrium owe their success to simplicity and habit.

Finally, communication from one discipline to another is not easy. The geographer clings to *location*, the economist to *delocation* linked to industry and to contemporary techniques. Economic space can legitimately disorient the geographer who is professionally attached to territorial space.

Viewing the problem as a whole, we can, I think, look forward to a growing interest in the theory of development and of poles of development. The main industrial poles of development are gaining in size, in complexity, and in the scope of their influence. The contrast between less-developed countries and industrialized countries brings into relief the difference between the development of territorially fixed populations and the growth of poles (oil-industry centers, for instance) that have no immediate application in their geographical vicinity. The planning necessary for poles implanted in developing countries is no longer in question. Those who, a few years ago, were asking for a distinction to be drawn between the people's right to exercise control over their territory and the people's right to exercise control over their poles, were bringing out a distinction that has become a burning issue.

The pole of development in the general theory of development, intimately linked to that of active units and of the most up-to-date dynamics, remains a fundamental concept of rigorous and operational analysis.

C An application

2.4 Transnational firms, leading sectors, development poles in less-developed countries

The concept of growth centers, which was conceived around 1947, has subsequently not only been developed by those who first promoted it, clarified in monographs and applied studies and incorporated into the general analysis of the so-called *"active"* units able to change their environment – it has also been assimilated and enriched in a number of directions.

Today, the concept of growth poles seems to be: (a) an aid to a correct interpretation of economic history; (b) an analytical tool for development planning; and (c) the basis of a general theory of development related to asymmetrical and irreversible effects, during a period, exerted by the *growth inducing units*.

My purpose here is to try to demonstrate this, in a first approximation. I should therefore like (a) to analyze the conditions under which a big unit, for example a transnational one, becomes a motor of development in a less-developed country, and (b) to offer a more general framework of development based on growth-inducing units and industries.

Let us concentrate on the relationships between a big US transnational firm, and a developing country, where this firm acts on its own behalf or through a subsidiary or an associated company.

We count as developing countries those in the $200–499 group or in the $500–1499 average income per capita group. We aim at one of those countries: for example India, Nigeria, Paraguay or Egypt. The country selected should, of course, at a second glance, be characterized by the structural conditions of its identity and evolution, as well as by per capita income.

The economic relations between big firms and developing countries will be sketched in order to bring out some essential features. The sketch can subsequently be filled in and enriched by reference to the chosen country.

We shall not immediately map out the flows of goods, investment, information; and shall in fact consider that these flows are *still to be realized*. This extremely simplified interpretation should give us a grid to interpret a concrete situation, and an orientation allowing the selection of priorities for a development plan.[1] After drawing the basic diagram (Fig. 2.1), we shall analyze the choice of channels and the choice of means.

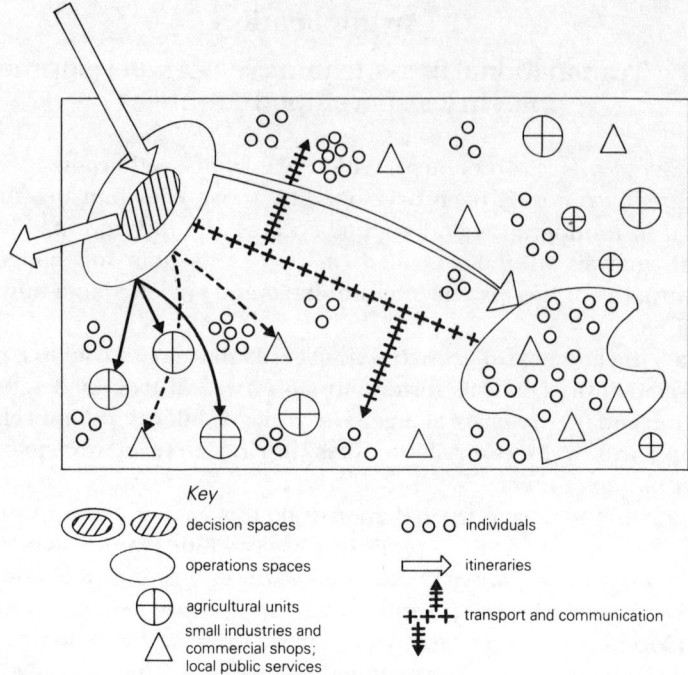

Figure 2.1 Territory T.

The basic diagram

Given a territorial space T with physical dimensions, which allow for distance, inputs, and outputs whose economic meaning and size result from the fact that T contains elements (individuals, agents) which carry on production and consume energy. Within space T, we apply a big firm's *decision space* – its capital and labor forces – and its *operation spaces* (commerce of goods, supply and demand of investment, supply and demand of information; Perroux 1975).

These operation spaces are extensible with or without distortions, until the medium of their expansion is saturated, after a certain lapse of time. It is, for the moment, quite irrelevant to take into consideration whether or not the firm is transnational. The unit we are considering is in any case large in comparison with the economic dimensions of the small units in the territorial space: local industries, local trades, and agricultural units. This difference in size always coincides with a difference in the kind of activities pursued. Moreover the individuals concerned are never evenly distributed throughout the territory; they are widely dispersed in certain regions and conglomerate in others when in contact with local industry, trade, or local public services.

The orientation of *rationally desirable* flows between units and individuals will be represented by a *diagram of channels*.

Choice of channels The choice of channels or itineraries is governed by a very crucial option which commits the future and creates dynamic complementarities.

It is assumed that the big firm has flows of trade with the exterior. Its traffic with the recipient country obeys the laws of profit maximization; under the constraint of solvency, it develops, as far as possible, towards the *agglomerated areas* where economic activities are denser and income relatively higher. If nothing comes to correct this inherent tendency of big corporations, the relative development of the agglomerated areas will continue from period to period, without ever necessarily allowing the rest of the population to benefit from the development process.

Let us imagine a means of transportation (communication) joining the big firm to the agglomerated area. This will stimulate and develop economic activity at the extremities of the line, widen the small units' horizons in the agglomerated area; and will increase the big firm's clientele. Historically, these effects have been detected many times.

If for any given reason, agents from either side of the main channel obtain or promote the building of secondary routes, similar effects will occur laterally: the transportation axis tends to become a development axis. This sequence of events has also been observed on many occasions throughout long periods.

Constructing a route for transportation, for example, depends mainly on the big firm's and the governing public authority's decision.

Let us indicate the essential point if we wish to develop the entire population and not just that of the agglomerated area. We must add to the channel which goes from the big firm towards the agglomerated area, where a solvent clientele is to be found. Other channels we may call conventionally "intentional development channels," because they are conceived with a view to promoting new development lines. These channels would lead from the big firms towards the small industrial and agricultural units.

This diagram places in opposition: A development which will mainly benefit the big firm and the agglomerated area, and a development which will benefit the whole population. The big firm has extensive and intensive relations with the exterior: with its head office if it is a subsidiary, or with its main partner if it is an associated company; therefore, we shall say that in order to develop the entire population on the whole territory, we must define and then implement interior exchange channels.

In the conditions described by this diagram, along these channels, there will inevitably appear influences, dominances and eventually, partial dominations. Influences are asymmetrical actions exerted by the big firm upon other units, which can either accept or reject them. Dominances take place when the small entities can hardly resist the asymmetrical action of the big firm. Partial dominations will occur when the big firm simply dictates to the small units some aspects of their behavior.

The choice of channels indicates the options that must be defined before even elaborating a development plan, if there is to be one. This strategy can be rational only if it takes into account the transportation routes and the communication channels in general between people and places, and if it puts into effect a will to spread economic activity to the whole country. In other words: from a development point of view, a strategy can only be evaluated with reference to its multidimensional effects on the whole population and not solely by its consequences in terms of the commercial economy, or in terms of increases in real average income.

Certainly, the center (i.e., the big firm) will receive feedbacks from its periphery. These effects may differ according to the operationally defined (short, medium or long term).

Obviously, these feedbacks are not excluded from our scheme. On the contrary, it is they on which we count, since development is a dialectic triggered off and maintained among structured sets producing reciprocal effects of mutual propulsion.

The same dialectic on a more general level is precisely the enticement of the production device by the population and vice versa.

Choice of means This choice ranges between two extreme possibilities: either a spontaneous benevolent agreement of the big firm, or a constraining pressure upon it by a political power. The effectiveness of these extremes seems quite uncertain nowadays. Let us therefore consider the intermediate cases, which are:

(a) the rational consent of the big firm to direction by the authorities; and

(b) methodical negotiation between the firm and the authorities.

(a) Without giving up its strategy of private profit, the big firm may consider it to be in its own interest to participate in the development of the people on whose territory it is implanted. The firm considers eventually that this action may avoid threats from the developing population. When one takes into account the possibility of widespread dissemination of information on its activities, the firm could be judged, often severely, by the population undergoing economic and cultural development. On the other hand, let us not quite exclude the hypothesis that the firm may grow conscious of its moral responsibilities, which create a public service in the shape of a private enterprise. (The conscience of the king; Adolf Berle).

(b) As for negotiations, these can take place in an atmosphere of commercial bargaining, where the local entities, appropriately grouped, negotiate on a strictly professional level with the big firm. Or, on the other hand, social groups (such as trade unions) associated with the public authorities can intervene and obtain progressive compromises from the big firm through a combination of polite objections and forceful oppositions.

Apart from its main objective, this analysis should help correct some of the most common errors which burden the interpretation of development poles. It is not difficult to distinguish the poles of development which improve the structures of a developing country and which raise the standard of living of the whole population, from the development of the poles by private firms which produces a well-paying clientele and cumulative benefits for the implanted industry.

Beyond this distinction we can repeat that a development pole can be either territorialized or nonterritorialized. (This localization is explained by Figs. 2.2 and 2.3.) Either there will be a group of firms that exert driving influences upon other sectors, inducing growth and structural changes, by occasional or typical enticing actions, or we shall be able to identify a zone of development with territorial matchings located in a geographical space and that induces similar effects, if its relations with its environment are conveniently organized.

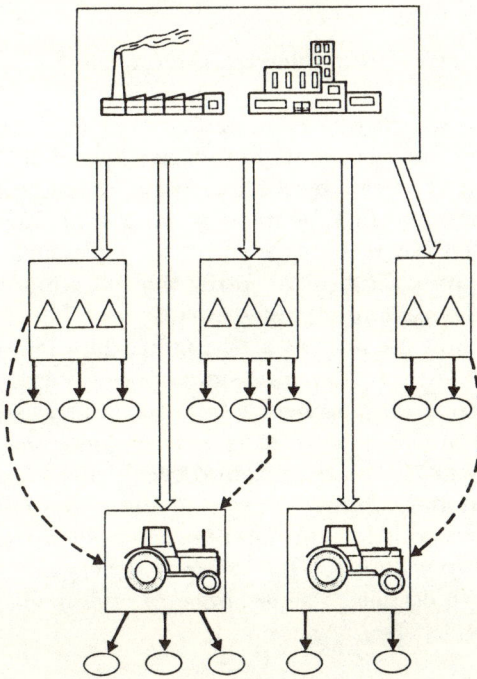

Figure 2.2 Itineraries, nonterritorialized.

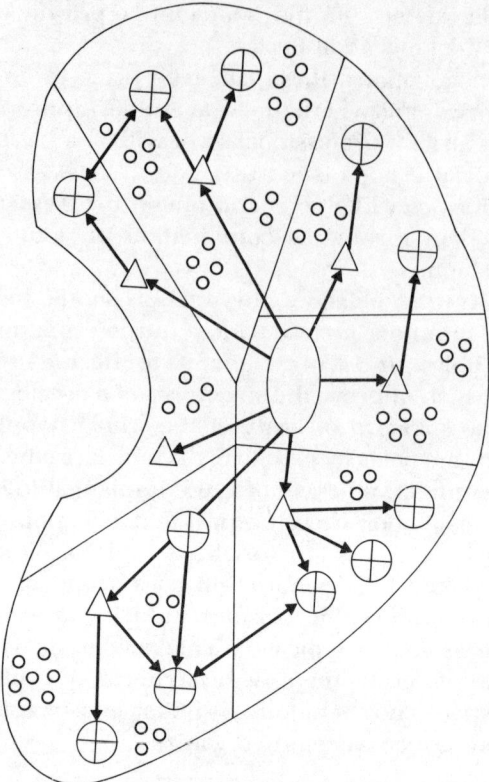

Figure 2.3 Itineraries, territorialized.

Finally, it is wise to take into account the time factor and the sequence of periods. Growth and development in a given place occur jointly, first through grouping of means by the increasing spatial concentration of men and machines, and then by the spreading of radiated effects. After the systole, the diastole, if the environment is suitable.

My friend Benjamin Higgins asked me the following direct question not long ago: "Do development poles exist?"

I hope he will allow me to answer by another question which requires a straightforward answer: "Do you know of an example, anywhere on earth, of growth and development where these processes have taken place without the presence and effects of development centers, whether territorialized or not?" We are forced to accept that *there is no more evenly distributed development than there is homothetic growth.* In order to build a "reasoned history" of the economic evolution as well as for an exact interpretation of the unequal development of different countries today, we do need a general theory of *growth-inducing units.*

2.5 Towards a general theory of growth-inducing units

Growth-inducing units

Let us begin with some concrete examples. A large, developing enterprise increases its demand or its supply for raw materials. One enterprise provides another with a machine that enables it to eliminate a bottleneck that would otherwise prevent it from supplying a growing demand. A large concern erects a plant in a region and thereby so transforms the region that it comes to be named after the firm; an enterprise communicates new manufacturing techniques to another firm which it has selected as a subcontractor; an enterprise introduces new techniques that are for practical purposes imitated by its competitors. The list of examples could be extended without difficulty.

To generalize: *the dynamic enterprise exerts an induction effect upon another enterprise in a given environment for a more or less short or long period*. The induction effect, which may be either accidental or typical in nature, breaks down into two components that frequently combine with each other: (a) *a dimension effect* – that is, the increase of demand on B by A, or the possibility provided by A to B of increasing its supply; and (b) *an innovation effect* or (productivity): the capacity provided by A to B or induced by A to B to introduce an innovation which for a given quantity of factors of production yields the same quantity of product at a lower price and of better quality.

Concretely, in the organic development of economic life it will be of advantage to consider an economic entity as made up of propelling units and propelled units, of *active* agents and *less active* (or passive) agents.

To bring about the favorable transformation of an economic milieu it will be necessary – putting it very briefly – to increase the number and thrust of the active, dynamic elements, and to stimulate the diffusion of their influences throughout the economic and social entities that are acted upon. The hope is then that these latter will in turn acquire a growth-inducing dynamism of their own. These effects are exerted between simple units (firms) or between complex units (organized groups of firms, usually having a certain hierarchical structure). This brings us from the growth-inducing *unit* to the growth-inducing *industry*.

Growth-inducing industries

Even in the *developed* countries, statistics show that there is a group of industries which may be termed *growth industries*. These have a higher than average rate of growth of product, a higher than average rate of growth of productivity, and a rapidly increasing share in the industry as a whole.

In the developed countries, this group includes: (a) entirely new industries, for instance, all those based on nuclear power, electronics and certain aspects of plastics and chemicals; and (b) modern industries, those that constitute the basic framework of the modern production device – iron and steel, metal manufactures, engineering, electrical equipment, motorcars, and aircraft.

In contrast, the traditional industries such as textiles, leather, forestry and wood products and agriculture, have a relatively low growth rate.

Nowadays all industries make innovations. The first two categories of industries exert a powerful effect on the traditional group and on the pace of renewal of the entire economy. This renewal rate is one of the chief assets in the competitive struggle beween nations.

It need hardly be said that countries differ greatly in structural composition with respect to these three categories of industries. The less-developed countries differ with respect to level of industrialization, and none of them possesses the entire range of industries that would be needed to permit an organic combination of the three above-mentioned categories.

It would therefore be to the advantage of a number of countries to combine their investments, both in expansion and in the establishment of new plants, in order jointly to achieve the capacity for sound renewal of their product capacity, once they have filled the gaps in the existing capacity.

In the case both of entirely new industries and of far-reaching modernization of their modern *as well as* of their traditional industries, they will necessarily turn to the more developed countries for a time, but the design of their industrial structure must eventually incorporate the growth-inducing centers provided by the innovation-bearing industries which are among the most powerful driving forces of progress alongside industries of the other category.

For the present, multinational investment must indispensably be referred to an *industrialization model* that defines explicitly and coherently the role of each of the sectors, instead of abandoning them to the confusion inherent in "global" or "overall" approaches, or in mere lists of specific projects or of regional improvements schemes.

It follows that it is essential, both in the design and in the execution of *development* poles and of *integration* poles, to keep constantly in mind *a general interpretation of the concept of industrialization*; this principle becomes even clearer as we pursue the analysis.

In the developed countries of Europe, industry gives the lead to agriculture. There is a clearly marked direction of flow of innovation, from the urban-industrial to the rural-agricultural centers. This is the case with the main new products (fertilizers, herbicides, and insecticides) and the main new machines (tractors, bulldozers and motors).

The same may be true of ways of life and consumption patterns. In the less-developed countries, because agriculture accounts for a major share of savings and export earnings, it is easy to forget that industry continues to exert its own growth-inducing effects. It supplies the means for modification of physical and intellectual infrastructures, provides agriculture with its chemical products and machinery, processes agricultural raw materials, and preserves and packages food products. By these indirect means, industry introduces innovations into agriculture.

With respect to the economy as a whole, there are certain systems of industry combinations – prominent among which is the system: power + iron and steel + metal manufactures + engineering – that have the virtue of generating new industrial units and providing the entire industrial sector with the capacity for renewal.

This analysis opens up perspectives with regard to growth-inducing combinations of industries. Their various components are not all located, or are not necessarily located, within the same countries; moreover, when these components have to be created, they cannot all be created in each country.

For this reason, multinational investments carried out under properly formulated programs designed to foster simultaneously the industrialization, the development, and the relative self-reliance of the regions concerned, can lead to the establishment of two types of combinations of industries: (a) Industrial complexes, around common centers for the extraction of raw materials, power generation, and distribution and technological research; and (b) agro-industrial complexes, for on-the-spot processing of agricultural products, either for export or for domestic consumption.

Numerous combinations are both conceivable and practicable which, even prior to the creation of new units, are capable of increasing the relative participation of local interests in the local subsidiaries of large foreign firms and of orienting the policy of these latter toward local processing and usage.

Poles, areas and axes of development

The establishment of foreign-tied mining or raw materials producing enterprises inadequately integrated into the domestic economy is a common feature of the less-developed countries. These countries furnish striking examples of markedly polarized urban areas (such as the capital cities and their conurbations, and the ports) and at the same time of vast "empty" or very backward regions.

An approved multinational investment program within a development plan seeks eventually to remedy the present state of affairs while retaining, however, the principle of the grouping and concentration of economic resources which is essential to stimulate economically beneficial diffusion effects.

An understanding of development poles, polarized development areas and development axes is essential in order to be able both to choose among multinational investments and to calculate their effects.

Development poles A growth or development pole is a growth-inducing unit coupled with its surrounding environment. In an environment that is already well knit and vigorous, thanks to active individuals, the establishment of a new enterprise generates wide and varied agglomeration and complementarity effects.

Growth and development are far from synonymous. Since *growth* means a sustained increase in the dimension index for an economic entity (for example, gross product), a growth pole is the dynamic unit that raises the economic "size" index of an area or of a country. *Development* is the sum of the changes in social patterns and mentalities through which the production device is coupled with the population: the latter acquires the capacity to utilize the production device to achieve what is considered to be a satisfactory growth rate, and the production device supplies a product that serves the population instead of being "alien" to it.

This dialectic of production device and population is the *essence* of development that pinpoints the radical difference between a growth pole and a development pole.

Areas and axes of integration The distinction drawn by Latin American economists between the concept *integration pole* and *development pole* deserves attention. It introduces us, in a specific form and along the lines of modern analysis, to the difficulties and prospects of integrating the developed as well as the less-developed countries; it also helps us to understand certain aspects of the integration of Europe.

While not every development pole is an integration pole, every pole of integration is a pole of development. An oil industry pole in southern Patagonia does not, or need not necessarily, bring about integration between Argentina and another Latin American country; on the other hand, a hydroelectric integration pole on the frontier between Paraguay and Brazil will very likely lead to the development of several parts of each of those countries.

It is immediately clear that more precision is needed. What is to be understood by integration, whether in the context of a *pole of integration* or an *area of integration*?

Integration pole   For a pole to constitute the nucleus of widespread and integrated development, two conditions must be fulfilled: (a) *connections* must be established between the pole and the regional or national economies, and (b) *institutions* should exist that make possible, at least progressively over time, the distribution of the incremental product in the form of additional incomes from which the population will obtain a surplus for local consumption and saving.

From the foregoing, it is clear that there are fundamental differences both in policy terms and analytically between the *development of the poles* and the *development poles themselves*.

Development areas   When several development poles are mutually interlinked and exert reciprocal induction effects upon each other and upon their environment, a *development area* is created.

Development axes   In contrast to transport axes, which are the transportation links between two units or groups of units, *development axes* are systems of development poles, the emergence and proliferation of which are favored by physical or nonphysical communications axes.

Four basic effects of poles of development and polarized areas

Whatever method is used to distinguish between them, the effects of development poles and development areas come down to four, which can be characterized by reference to an initial investment. The initial investment is assumed to be growth-inducing; in other words, capable, *under given conditions*, of generating other (induced) investments. The growth-inducing investment, so understood, generates four effects which can be analytically defined and expressed in statistical and econometric terms just like any other quantity in the national accounts.

(a)   *Investment effects.* The total investment in a system or subsystem is the sum of the *growth-inducing investment* and of the *induced investments*; the period of physical implementation and time taken to achieve the anticipated effect (for example, the appearance of the product) are to be explicitly stated.

(b) *Production effects.* Every investment affected by a *coefficient of efficiency*, the approximate expression of which is the inverse of the capital coefficient, yields a product. The total incremental product is the sum of the products obtained from the initial induced investments. These induction mechanisms clearly bear no relationship to the economic content of the Keynesian multiplier, which expresses the mobilization by an incremental monetary flow of idle resources; what we are concerned with in the present case is *complementarity mechanism* that can be expressed entirely in real terms.

(c) *Income effects.* The incremental *wages* and the incremental *profits* generated by the incremental product can be obtained by applying to the latter, the *appropriate coefficients*, which vary according to sector and over time. Similarly, the application of this incremental income of the coefficients of propensity to consume gives the savings generated by these incremental wages and profits.

(d) *Balance of trade effects.* The incremental product *increases the total product.* By applying two coefficients to this increase, the additional imports and exports can be obtained, and hence, by reference to an initial position, the *net effect on the balance of trade.*

It is thus possible, given adequate statistics, to describe or to predict approximately the internal and external effects of a *set of development poles* or *development areas.*

The *region* or country can no longer be regarded as a single unit, a homogeneous entity. To do so would be quite non-sensical in some cases. It is a *complex* of *polarized subaggregates*, of *development poles, each exerting its effects on the development milieu.*

To summarize in a few words the main lesson of this exposition, I would like to suggest that a more rigorous and operational analysis tends to serve both science and the collective advantage of the population: it is developing away from neoclassical micro- and macro-analysis and taking into consideration structured subsets linked with each other by asymmetrical and active relations. It paves the way for a kind of mesoeconomics acceptable to the historian as well as to the modern economist.

Appendix A

A.1 Environment and land policies

Land improvement policy (e.g., irrigation):
(a) Transport:

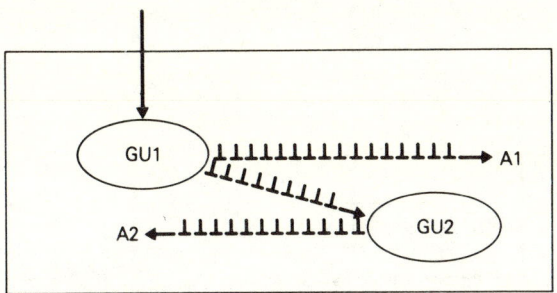

(b) Operations for environment policies:

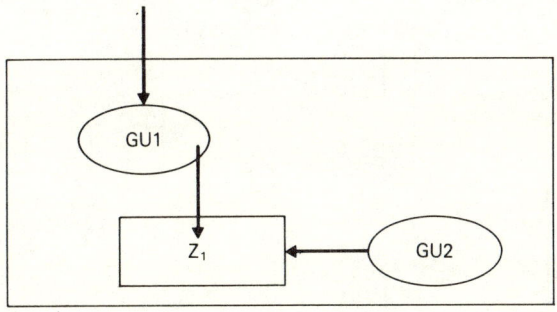

(c) Formation

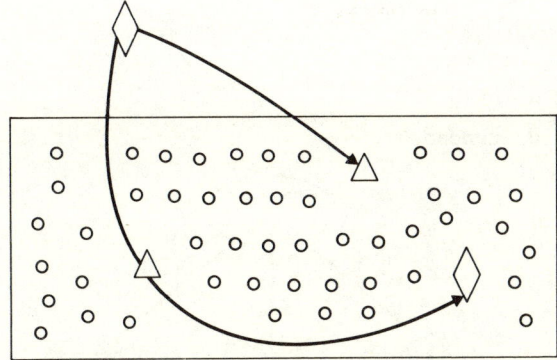

Propagation of know-how
○ individuals
△ population capable of receiving know-how communication
◇ units for education and know-how diffusion

A.2 Technical articulations of units

(a) Actions and reaction – feedback:

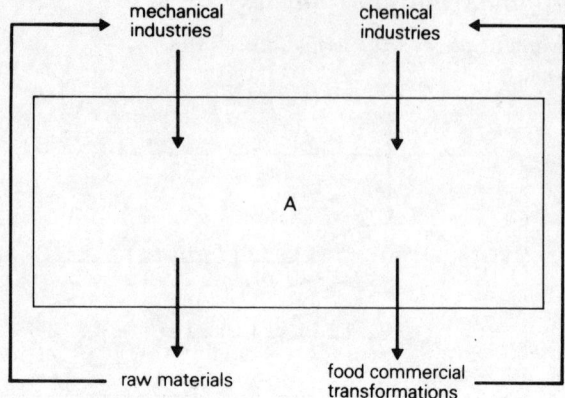

(b) Regulations:

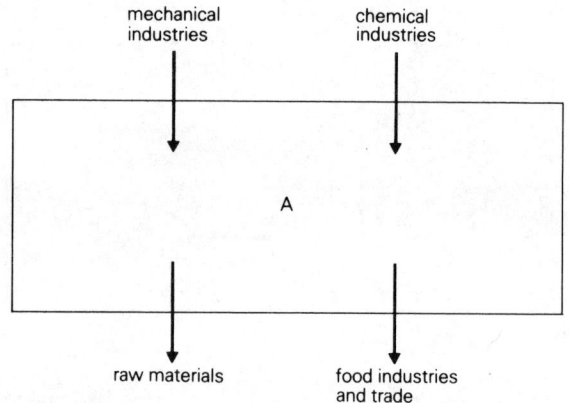

A.3 Integration of units

(a) Structural ascendancies:

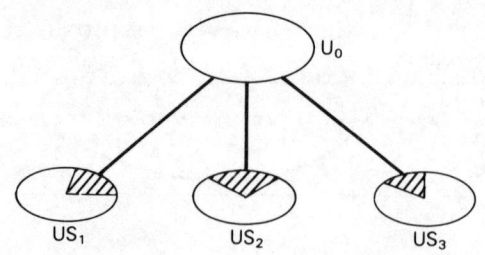

(b) Formation of a complex unit:

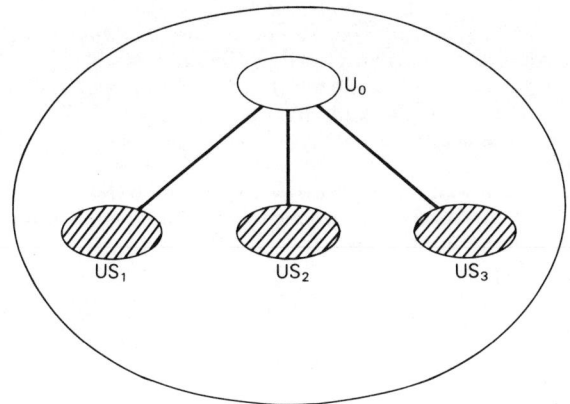

A.4 Export push development

(a) Circuit – export industries and currency:

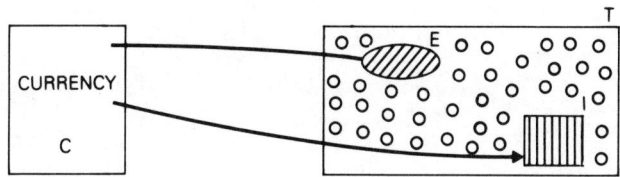

(b) Diffusion of propulsive actions to agriculture:

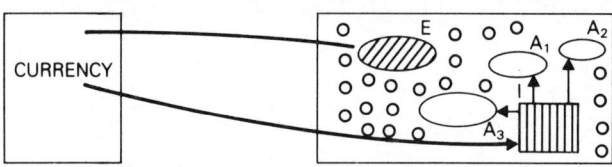

Notes

1 For concrete reference amidst many others, cf. Robineau (1978).

References

Kornai, J. 1971. *Anti-Equilibrium: on economics systems theory and the tasks of research*. London & Amsterdam: North Holland.

Livingstone, I. (ed.) 1974. Notes on the concept of growth poles. *Economic policy for development*. London: Penguin.

Perroux, F. 1955. Note sur la notion de pôle de croissance. *Economie appliquée*, 1–2. Paris: ISEA.

Perroux, F. 1975. *Unités actives et mathématiques nouvelles*. Paris: Dunod.

Robineau, P. 1978. Industrialization, the motor of the economy, Algeria. *Le Monde diplomatique*, June.

3

Peregrinations of an economist and the choice of his route

FRANÇOIS PERROUX

I would be tempted to date my birth certificate as an economist "Vienna, 1934," the date I arrived there as a Rockefeller fellow accompanied by my young wife. But that would be ungrateful to my first French masters.

At the University of Lyons, René Gonnard conferred on the Chair for the History of Economic Doctrines an exceptional lustre, combining a personal approach with an acute analysis of his predecessors. In addition to this homage, I owe him a debt of undying gratitude. Words are powerless to describe a young man's feelings when his intellectual ambitions and capacity are brought out by a mentor who treats him as his son.

Etienne Antonelli took an interest, which was exceptional in those days in France, in Léon Walras's mathematical economics and its sociological setting. He foreshadowed the confrontation between pure economics and socio-economics which is still proving fruitful.

Thanks to one of the first French mathematicians to be deeply interested in relativity, M. Eyrault, I had the privilege of teaching in an Institute for Financial Science which he directed.

Long before I worked in the French capital (1937–8), I was exchanging views with a great master, Albert Aftalion, who was to become my friend.

I therefore rapidly obtained a grounding in the abstract and rigorous aspects of general theory and was well prepared for the refined casuistry of the Viennese.

3.1 Peregrinations and acquisitions

There was an ardent pursuit of research in the seminars of Ludwig von Mises whom a certain ostracism kept at a distance from the University. These meetings, sponsored by the Chamber of Commerce, were thronged by an international audience attracted by his books and gripped by his lectures. Madame Berger Lieser, an incomparable promoter, organized subtle discussion on the famous foundations of interest, production capital, and financial capital, and on the relations between interest rates and wage rates. Philosophers, historians, epistemologists, and senior civil servants subjected the constructions of the famous Viennese to a vigilant criticism. Friedrich von Hayek, Joseph Schumpeter, Gottfried von Haberler, and Fritz Machlup were already in other countries. As well as von Mises, one could meet R. von Strigl and, on the opposite side, Oskar Morgenstern, who was already fascinated by higher mathematics, closely concerned with economic forecasting (*Wirtschaftsprognose*), and dubious as regards marginal utility and the general interpretation derived from it. With all respect to his memory, I would venture to suggest that Hans Mayer, with his blond Jove-like beard, whose lectures were well received and who was mad keen on hunting chamois from peak to peak, was perhaps as an economist content with less elevated pursuits.

As to the complex and profound personality of Othmar Spann, it would call for a lengthy study which, as it happens, has been vigorously carried out by Vallarché. Spann, a sociologist and philosopher, was far removed, thanks to his *Universalismus*, from the prevailing intellectualist positivism. His ardent temperament impelled him to make a thorough study of the relations between social formations and economics. He never succumbed to the temptations of the national socialism which was then beginning to ravage the German world. Catholic by upbringing, and having drunk at the wellsprings of the old idealistic and romantic Germany, he belonged to a different spiritual universe. Violently attacked by the Viennese liberals, he deserved sympathetic attention which he did not always receive, and he suffered from this isolation. When they invaded Vienna, the national socialists threw him into a concentration camp, where he suffered terribly and almost lost his sight. His memory and his work deserve respect.

Any genuine economic thinking is bound to tackle the equilibrium of interdependence. The Viennese school constructed its theory in a spirit which in many ways was contrary to that of the Lausanne school. It made a distinction, not without justification and using its own analytical instruments, between a halt in the flow of goods and the decisions of economic agents which by their interaction adjust supply and demand.

As it took as its starting point the agent (*Wirtschaftssubjekt*) and the subjective theory of marginal utility (*Grenznutzenlehre*), the result could not be otherwise.

The differences between real taxes (*Echttaxen*) and those which are merely apparent made it possible, with refinements which are still fruitful, to arrive at zones of indeterminateness and at thresholds. This also meant, even when one did not admit it, opening the irritating debate on the rigorous and meaningful definition of what is called "normal" profit. I recall lively discussions between Ludwig von Mises and our common friend, Hugh Gaitskell, who was one day to become chancellor of the exchequer and who at that time was modestly pursuing his studies in advanced economics side by side with us.

Whereas von Mises stigmatized the inevitable unemployment caused by the excess of the supply of labor over the demand or pointed out the long list of disequilibria and compensations which were unavoidable in the abstract, the future leader of the Labour party stressed the margin for manoeuvre by acting on profit. Even before the great proliferation of analyses of imperfect or monopolistic competition, this kind of discussion could take one very far. "What can you expect?" insinuated von Mises with a feigned indulgence, the sincerity of which was not quite above reproach. "He is bent on a socialist career." The truth was not quite so simple.

It was not just "naked economics" (utterly opposed to the spirit of the German historical schools) that one learned in Vienna. One was given lessons in an elevated, delicate and all-pervading culture. These were the days when it was possible to follow a course by Sigmund Freud, whose psychoanalytical explorations were transmuted into a teaching calculated to arouse immediate enthusiasm. We would listen to the famous historian, Dobsch; then, having enjoyed the subtle messages transmitted by the imperial palaces, the Stefankirche, the Votivkirche and the sumptuous galleries of the Kunsthistorisches Museum, sometimes we were privileged to round off a wonderful day of cultural delights by listening to Lotte Lehmann singing *Fidelio* at the Opera.

None of us has forgotten the parties organized by the admirers of Ludwig von Mises at which Felix Kaufman, a living memory with a musical voice, sang in several languages the series of Lieder of the seminar since its foundation.[1]

"You're leaving for Berlin. So you'll meet Werner Sombart. He's now got to his tenth definition of Socialism..." Such was the *viaticum* of Ludwig von Mises. At my first visit to the author of *Der moderne Kapitalismus*, he greeted me with the words: "You're coming from Vienna. You must have known my enemy von Mises there..."

In Germany at that time, to be truthful, there was very little to glean. H. von Stackelberg and Erich Schneider came later. It was from Fritz Neumark, my old friend, who gave the best lessons in financial science and general economics, and in listening to them one could immerse oneself in lofty European German culture. I was also interested in the works of Carl Schmitt on the philosophic foundations of politics. I subsequently got to know the profound moral greatness of the man, whom I call my friend, when he courageously snatched one of my students from the clutches of the Nazi police.

How fruitful was that stay in Rome where I followed some lectures by Luigi Amoroso, and where I became familiar with that extraordinary mathematician, statistician, sociologist, and economist, Corrado Gini, and where I also formed irrevocable friendships with Ugo Papi, Giovanni Demaria, and later Giuseppe Palomba. I am not forgetting Alberto de Stefani or Lello Gangemi who awakened my interest in special points of public finance, thanks to our joint admiration for De Viti de Marco.

It will be obvious that the assimilation of Pareto's thought via Maffeo Pantaleoni, Barone, and their main disciples provides an analytical framework and food for methodological reflection which leaves its mark on whoever benefits from it, especially, perhaps, if he refuses to accept it too docilely.

My wife and I were on the point of steering a course for the United States when war broke out. The "manoeuvres" in Lorraine and the different diversions of the occupation period had little connection with abstract economics. Since I had to lecture all the same, I took advantage of the opportunity to take up again in detail the Austrian-style equilibrium by preparing a book on *Value* (Perroux 1943), and to compare it, in seminars at the École des Hautes Études of the Sorbonne, with the versions of equilibrium propounded by Gunnar Myrdal, Knut Wicksell, and of course Léon Walras.

Over and above this, there was the Institut de Sciences Économiques Appliquées, founded in 1944 with the French Resistance and of which one of the first protectors was Lord Keynes himself. These were splendid moments, despite the harshness of the time. We worked there in company with the American doctor, Sanders, and the famous Soviet biologist, Serve Chakhotin, a disciple of Pavlov. Pierre Uri and I proceeded to make a detailed study of the Keynes and White plans, with our eye on the future. I had founded, with François Divisia and René Roy, a Group of Mathematics Applied to Economics, which was assiduously promoted by Maurice Allais, G. Dubourdieu, Jacques Dumontier, and G. Lutfalla.

On Liberation, René Pleven gave me the task of studying national accounts in England, and we embarked with some other members of the Institute on a Liberty ship.

At last we were free to enjoy those personal encounters which we had so long yearned for during the terrible years of the occupation. At Oxford, we were welcomed by Thomas Balogh, Paul Streeten, Burchardt and Steindel; at Cambridge, by Professor Joan Robinson. We were received not far from Manchester, in the gracious dwelling generously thrown open to us by Sir John and Ursula Hicks – in London we worked with Richard Stone. Everywhere in that great country, which had so recently surmounted glorious trials, we resumed contact with English thought.

Relations were established between the London School of Economics, the famous universities, and our Paris centers where Sir Roy Harrod, Sir John Hicks, Joan Robinson, and Friedrich von Hayek, at that time a professor at LSE, Sir Dennis Robertson, and many another expounded their last works.

Edward Chamberlin from Harvard, after a first visit which followed close on one by Mr Kalecki from Oxford, became a frequent guest and a permanent associate of the ISMEA. It was owing to his friendship and to that of Joseph Schumpeter, to whose work I had devoted a book, that I was invited in 1947 to lecture at Harvard. These lectures are the basis of a long series of my own research efforts and of those which they have inspired.

The first of these dealt with *economic spaces* and presented the three concepts which I regard as fundamental: structured space, polarized space, and plan space. The other was concerned with *macro units* and *macro decisions*. It contained the seed of complex units and of hierarchized subsets. It was valuable being able at that time to meet, at the Littauer Centre, W. Leontief, Walter Isard, and Gerschenkron, and, at MIT, Paul Samuelson, who submitted to ISMEA the algebraic form of the HO model.

We all knew the potential advances inherent in J. M. Keynes's macro-economic theory, which was gradually adapted, quantified, and steered in the direction of the breakdown of aggregates and of meso-economics ... To introduce asymmetry into economic theory means going beyond the static equilibrium of perfect competition and preparing a radical change of perspective in order to understand interdependence.

3.2 Choosing one's path

The recent review in *Les Recherches économiques de Louvain* (1978) of a *Homage* which was generously devoted to my research[2] credits me with a general concept of economic life in line with the contemporary trend in science and completely different from the "neoclassical vision." It will be noted that this concept admits of an irreversible time, time scales, probabilized spaces, evolutive structuring, and disequilibrium analyses.

The choice of my path in fact demanded these substantial interlinking changes *"at the expense of the tranquil certainties of other ages"* (ibid.). The concepts, particular models, and theorems which I proposed (ibid.) and which "have stimulated a whole school of researchers to go beyond the mechanics models" flowed from a central intuition and foreshadowed an attempt at the recasting of the theory of interdependence which I undertake in my book *Active units and new mathematics, a revision of the theory of equilibrium* (Perroux 1975) which will be completed by a *Dynamics of active units*, the object of my research at the Collège de France for 20 years (1955–75).

Partial approaches to interdependence in a whole

In a course delivered in 1947 at Balliol College in Oxford, "An outline of a theory of the dominant economy,"[3] I concentrated on the asymmetric effects exercised by the United States on world trade. But I was very careful to emphasize that this analytical outline was also in its essence applicable to a firm or an economic subset.

I linked the asymmetry to three parameters: the dimension, the nature of the activities, and the negotiating strength. I have not changed my mind. The changes in the state of the world have profoundly transformed the conditions in which they are present and also their consequences, but have not erased their analytical interest.

The word "domination" was rather clumsy and somewhat sweeping. It gave the impression that one unit completely substitutes its decision for another's. This is precisely the case where the analysis loses its interest, since we are then in the presence of one and the same unit. I labored this distinction, but to absolutely no avail. The unusual terminology chosen in order to avoid the confusions inherent in the word "imperialism" made people think that I accepted the thesis. Although from the start I introduced precise distinctions, I had to make the point very strongly and explicitly for people to avoid confusing (a) influence, (b) dominance and (c) partial domination. Since then, a very large number of works have formalized these asymmetries by topological representations and by graphs.

In thorough studies in other countries and in France on general equilibrium, I have often repeated (and appropriated) two affirmations which have been far too little reflected upon. One is by Vilfredo Pareto at a celebration in his honor: "I saw the concrete aspect and was unable to get through to it!" (*Vedevo la realtà e non potevo coglierla!*). The other is by Oskar Morgenstern, to whom we owe so much and who has been so unfairly treated: "There is no road leading from L. Walras to reality."

This is something which should make us realize the distance between the determination of a mathematical system and the "determination" of an observable system, and, no less so, to try to identify the prefabricated obstacles impeding the passage from the conditions on which the famous theorems (of existence, uniqueness, stability, and optimality) determine each other[4] to a description of the activity which can simplify it without destroying it.

The critical and fundamental intuition which has since then always guided me has led me to carry out special research which is illuminated by one and the same hypothesis. The conflicts–cooperations, the battles–assistance, components of any relation between agents – the macro units or complex units, economic spaces, influences, dominances, the effects of propulsion, the real propensities to work and change (innovation), the growth-inducing points of training (poles of development, whether spatialized or not), the propellent firms or regions – all these concepts, carefully tried out with the help of numerous observations, will perhaps now be admitted as proceeding from a methodical search for asymmetry in particularized forms and conditions. This same research leads us, in the field of distribution, to take into explicit consideration the social *roles* and *on the other hand* to analyze at the present time the *income discussed* on the levels of primary distribution and redistribution (so inappropriately termed).

A recasting of the theory of interdependence was maturing in the course of this special research. A first overall exposé was presented in my *Active units*. Better than anyone else, I know *all that still has to be done*, and I am doing all I can to fill in the gaps. But it will perhaps be understood after these remarks that I cannot uncritically accept the verdicts which reduce my contribution to a simple criticism or which congratulate me on penetrating views lacking a comprehensive logic, or which, in a polemical spirit, decree that my position is not operational. What is not operational, but not in the slightest, is the standard equilibrium, repeated without the subtlety and the scrupulousness of the founders, because it *destroys* the reality of the agent and of his activity on pretext of simplifying it, whether this is expressed uncritically in the current handbooks, or whether it conceals its weaknesses in quantitative models which, be they macro or mesoeconomic, play with *hand-restructured* blocks or sub-blocks which are incompatible with the standard equilibrium if it is interpreted strictly.

3.3 From extratemporal equilibrium to the temporary exhaustion of the drive for change

The standard Walras–Pareto equilibrium, whatever form it assumes, applies to micro "doubles" (*sosias*) so "small" and so numerous in the homogeneous space of perfect competition that none is in a position to oppose that *Diktat* of the price system and to modify the objects and agents surrounding it. Lagrange's mathematics confer on this view a coherence borrowed and indeed plagiarized from classical mechanics. These presuppositions and their consequences are being subjected to some sharp criticism that tends to become general.

We are not going against the stream of advanced research when we start from the agent with an energy capable of transforming his surroundings but which is temporarily exhausted if it reaches its own goal, if it comes up against a physical obstacle, or meets with opposition from the partner. By deciding on the goods and services which are at its direct disposal (*space of decision*), it projects and brings into play *operational spaces* (purchases–sales, investment, information).

These spaces are extensible, and under limiting conditions make it possible to define temporary equilibria in given periods. The whole proposition is amenable to topological formalization as a prolongation of that of G. Debreu and of K. J. Arrow. The method gives a new lease of life and enriches the current models of monopoly, differentiated competition (R. Triffin), or aggressive or peaceful oligopolies and economic and financial groups. It admits of the representation of subsets articulated hierarchically.

This method is, in one sense, a return to A. Cournot inasmuch as it sees in any economic action a component of free choice and a component of power relations, and also offers an image of the relations between the *parts* (structured subsets)[5] which "hold together," to repeat the very words of A. Cournot, in quite a different way from perfect competition prices. In line with the teaching of the general systems, each part, each structured subset, has a *dimension*, receives a *place* in a network of relations, and constitutes a locus of actions and of *retroactions*.

The concept of economic space as a whole formed of hierarchically articulated parts has decisive consequences for general equilibrium. Let there be a small number of large units with a structure and given activities; let us call them the Large ones, in trade relations with a large number of the Small ones, also characterized in these two ways. Let the Large and the Small ones be placed in a vertical structure, from the first transformation to the final consumer. The Large ones can impose constraints on the Small ones. The cosatisfaction of the Large ones or the cessation of their oligopolic struggle to avoid loss may be concomitant, to a large extent, with the dissatisfaction of the Small ones or of a part of them. For reasons of structure, the banking oligopolies, the financial groupings of large businesses, are at a certain time in a position (as a result of the concentration of supply and demand, their superior capacity of information, and their technical superiority) to exercise an asymmetric action on the small units and individuals. In the field of international relations, too, the provocative question can be equally fittingly raised, given the very large concentration of foreign trade: "Commerce between Big Firms *or* commerce between 'nations'?" Between "nations," that is to say, between sets of small units and of individuals whose behavior depends on costs and relative prices, and, alone, is the basis of the substitution theorems on which the whole economic logic of the open economy depends.

A number of other cases of asymmetric relations between structured economic areas can be observed and are integrated into the reworked model of *general* interdependence (using "general" in the sense of "concerning the whole"), but not a *uniform* one (that is to say, translated by the same reversible relations in each point of the homogeneous economic space).

I have said enough to bring out the opposition between the *fictitious equilibrium* and two *equilibria of observable situations*.

The fictitious equilibrium, it should be repeated again and again, does not describe any "observable state"; it is a grid for reading off positions, "a transparent plate with points of reference" through which we can look at economic activity. The grid, the points of reference in the transparent plate, draw attention to the existence, the uniqueness, the stability and the optimality of a *point* of equilibrium, of a *price* for which all the supply is equal to all the demand at the micro-, meso-, and macroeconomic levels. No doubt. The question remains whether the choice of the form of the grid or of the points of reference of the transparent plate does not conceal the very substance of economic life which is the activity, the action of the agents, who are endowed with memory and plans, differing one from the other and unequal among themselves for given operations in a given period.

There is a radical opposition, as *regards the essence or the substance* of what is observed and constructed, between the general equilibrium of things (Ec); and the general balancing of activities ($E'a$).

In Ec, goods are moved by the neutral forces of the price system, assimilated to physical forces. Outside time and space, a stoppage of the flow is privileged on the basis of the maximization theorems linked to perfect competition. If we are to achieve that, the agent "must be" as if "he did not exist." He is reduced to a symbol of passiveness. Supply and demand are always equal to each other in each case by virtue of *one* price, as *impossible* as the perfectly homogeneous space to which it corresponds and the agent with no activity. This equalization dictates the cessation of the flow. *Ec* is the stoppage of the flow of the goods, and is translated by recourse to a type of mechanics specific to physical phenomena.

In $E'a$, agents with a drive for change, equipped with units differing in dimension and structure, engage in operations which are or are not compatible with each other. In the whole formed by the articulation of structured parts, the interactions of dissimilar and unequal agents give rise to equilibrations, very real *tâtonnements* (as opposed to the famous Walrasian *tâtonnement*).

The equilibria eventually achieved presuppose, first of all, the intercompatibility of the structures. The equilization of demand and supply at *one* price has in itself no economic significance except when it is characterized by a relation to the interactions of activities. The temporary exhaustion of the drive for change in the system is characterized by a deceleration of the flow which forces the analysis to define the conditions of metastability, price hierarchy, and levels and degrees of cosatisfaction at the moment at which the *net* energy of the system is approximately equal to zero ($d0c \simeq 0$). Its construction implies methodical borrowings from thermodynamics and recourse to topological forms. It should be obvious that uncertainty, risk, conflict, and information are not properties of inert objects, but on the contrary are inherent in man and his activity. Hence, economics fails to function when, in order to "determine" itself fallaciously, it confines itself to describing the movements of inert objects which a reified man registers passively.

$E'a$ is not, strictly speaking, a generalization of *Ec*: it is a balancing of activities (in the sense of a balancing action) different *in kind* from the mechanical equilibrium of objects and exercised in irreversible time. It does not deserve to be called "encompassing" except as regards the variables which it considers in addition to those of standard equilibrium (the information of the agents) and as regards the types of relations which it admits (equilibrations and regulations).

3.4 From exhaustion of the drive for change to dynamization

It is the balancing of activities ($E'a$) which enables us to arrive at a rigorous dynamization and coherence of the system.

This is so for a decisive reason. All economic dynamism has its source in man – that is, in the agent; it derives its value from the interaction of activities, unfolds in irreversible time, and is maintained or eventually gains in intensity and in quality which can only be appreciated in relation to the human being.

The great statistical works on growth, whose merits cannot be overvalued, have sought to find regularities among aggregates and subaggregates, between blocks and sub-blocks of variables supposed to be linked causally by quantitative relations. Working from insufficient materials and statistical mixtures which are in no way analytical quantities, the method was, in advance, exposed to very restrictive limitations. To which must be added those stemming from the moving ten-year averages and from the paradoxical recourse to the Cobb–Douglas function and its constant returns, where evolution has to be described on the basis of modern industrialization.

In parallel, we have been acquainted with subtly elaborated models of *equilibrium growth* which, as is noted by their creators and competent exponents, add little to what statics tell us.

Research during the last 30 years is thus in sharp contrast to the ambitious, significant and fruitful dynamics of the first "classics," the Physiocrats, Turgot, Adam Smith, and his immediate successors. All of them base their interpretation of long-term evolutions on activities, on the active operations of men and their social groups operating in relations of conflict–cooperation, in ambivalent mixtures of struggles and collaboration.

We are harking back to this impressive tradition if we insert any study of relations between quantified aggregates in such dynamic frameworks where the economic factor finds its coordinates in a social system. Population, technique, the rules of the game, cannot be reduced to relations between prices and quantities. It is as well to consider them, to start with, as exogenous factors, and then be free to see to what extent these groups of variables can be endogenized, inserted in the equations of the "economic" functioning of the whole.

The typical model of this functioning is the one which links a propulsive subset to a static one, the rate of growth and the change of structure of the latter being a function of these variables for the former. Clearly, qualifications and specifications are essential for the construction of the particular models of propulsive firms, propulsive industries, and propulsive regions.[6]

The evolution, when tested against the observable reality which is studied by this method, puts the cycle and its trend back into the periods of development, distinguishes between cyclical contraction and structural crisis, and connects economic dynamics with the dynamism of social groups.

As it happens, carefully defined mathematics supports the reworking of the dynamics by appropriate formalizations such as Lyupanov's "stability," R. Thom's point of catastrophe, and the models of sequential and organizational games.

Thus, we discover the prospects of an integration in the same analytical body of the metastatics of the balancings of active units and of the moving equilibrium of a reelaborated dynamics.

3.5 From dynamization to regulation

In the economic whole considered, the decision-makers maintain and upvalue the structure of their units, whether simple or complex, and enter in both cases into a conflict–cooperation relation, acting in both cases through regulations and partial equilibrations. In certain conditions, the result is a tendency to the metastability of the structures and of the functioning, subject to exogenous actions. The degree of this metastability, at various levels, depends on the information and the activity of the agents.

Another point is that history does not record any case of large sets, or "nations," able to dispense with the activity of units called public ones which try to effect a regulation of the whole, with the welfare of the community in mind. It is not on the basis of objects, of collective goods, of merit goods, that this regulation can be correctly interpreted, but as the permanent interaction of activities whose plans have neither the same scope nor the same time horizon or even the same means.

There is not, on the one hand, a "private" subsystem which can be completely isolated under the law of the pure market and, on the other, public agents who engage in sporadic and successive interventions. The market is molded by the society in which it functions and by the evolving social structures which underlie the overall structures of production, consumption, and distribution. Their relatively slow transformation is effected in the conflict–cooperation in the organizational games of the social groups. The latter act to obtain their maximum profit and to change the rules of the social game to their advantage.

If this is really so, it is only to be expected that the welfare theories deduced from competitive statics should reveal their weakness. The consumers' surpluses and the Paretian compensations were ill suited, both because they referred back to perfect competition and because they were congenitally linked to statics.

The three famous conditions of economic policy laid down by A. C. Pigou – maximization of the overall product, reduction of fluctuations, and income equality – have not stood up any better to historical experience. To the first there has been added in recent times the optimum product structure accepted by the population. As to the second, a distinction is made between cycles and structural crises. As for the third, if the reduction of unjustified economic inequalities remains a considerably more fruitful perspective than the general reference to equity, it has become fairly clear that it is the search for a socially optimal inequality which is really important. What is involved is the very form of society, and it is the dynamism of the social progress of the various hierarchized groups which enables us to hope for acceptable approximations to the least possible inequality. The main means of achieving it are concerted and contractual economics accompanied by widely disseminated economic information and training of the organized social participants.

It is only in this perspective that we can regard as meaningful both the balance among the three flows – buying and selling, constrained deductions, and transfers of solidarity – and, on the other hand, the first attempts to effect a really collective economic computation which would set out to assess the surpluses and losses imputable to well-defined social subsets.

Have I recognized the huge debt which I have contracted towards my predecessors and towards all those who have been for me incomparable fellow researchers? Justified, at least in these few pages, the choice of my path? I hope so, without being convinced that I have. It is difficult to record in so brief a compass half a century of investigations and to convey to the indulgent reader my sincere regret at not having been able to do better. At least I can bear witness that economic knowledge, gradually organized, checked and purified by science, economics carried out in a scientific spirit, is worthy, because of the importance of the issues at stake and of its earliest conquests, of the devotion to it of a whole lifetime.

(Slightly revised version of an article under the same title in *Banca Nazionale del Lavoro Quarterly Review*, no. 133 – June 1980.)

Notes

1 There still echo in my ear the lines:

> When a Frenchman loses his way in Vienna,
> He retains, whatever happens,
> Many a charming memory:
> Noble gardens, distinguished palaces,
> A story of form and line,
> And the graciousness of the moment...
>
> As regards the Wienerschule,
> Like a knight it arms him
> With the "Ist es denkbar?" and with the charm
> Of the a priori method...

2 Presses Universitaires, Grenoble, 1978.
3 Cf. Transnational Corporations and World Order. In *Readings in International Political Economy*, G. Modelski (ed.), 135–54. New York: W. H. Freeman.
4 Very imperfectly even in the mathematical order.
5 And not the *elements*.
6 Cf. 1967. *Le progres economique, Economies et Societes*, Paris: ISMEA; and 1956. *Prises de vues sur la croissance de l'economie francaise, 1820–1914*, London: IARIW.

References

Perroux, F. 1943. *La Valeur*. Paris: PUF.
Perroux, F. 1975. *Active units and new mathematics, a revision of the theory of equilibrium*. Paris: Dunod.
Recherches économiques de Louvain. **44** (4), (1978). Institut des sciences économiques, Université Catholique de Louvain.

4
Growth pole theory and strategy reconsidered: domination, linkages, and distribution

KAREN R. POLENSKE

The purpose in writing this paper is to provide a critical review of the relevance and usefulness of the concept of growth pole for regional economic analyses and planning. At first, it seemed a useless enterprise to add still another review of the growth pole literature to the vast number that already exist. These include reviews by Conroy (1973), Coraggio (1973), Darwent (1969), Gaile (1978), Hansen (1981), Hermansen (1972), Higgins (1978), Klaassen (1972), Lasuen (1972), Moseley (1974), Parr (1973), Richardson and Richardson (1975), Thomas (1972), and a great many others. Even as far back as 1969, Darwent included 155 growth pole references in his review. By 1974, Moseley listed 296 references in the bibliography to his book *Growth centres in spatial planning*, prefaced by a statement (or understatement) that "this is not a comprehensive bibliography." He referred readers to Davy (1973) and Storey (1972) for more extensive readings on the growth pole concept.

Usually, however, the existing reviews and studies of growth poles lack at least four important components. First, few analysts provide the historical context for Perroux's work. Second, most of the reviews do not cover current development theories and strategies. They were written in the early 1970s when current views of development, such as the dependency concept, were just being formulated. Only a small number of analysts, therefore, deal with the contradictions that a growth pole strategy can create for regional development, and the growth pole strategy of development is usually not compared with other development strategies (such as basic needs, self-reliance, the New International Economic Order, etc.) that have been proposed partially in response to the dependency theory of development. Third, most of the analysts do not relate the discussion of growth poles to a multiregional or multinational setting. They only use a single-region or single-city setting to analyze and evaluate the implementation of the growth pole development strategy. Thus, the discussion of the growth pole concepts and strategies is not usually grounded in a political economy setting encompassing an entire nation. Fourth, relevant measures have not been devised to determine whether or not the growth pole strategy has succeeded; consequently, most analysts do not arrive at clear conclusions as to the actual consequences of the strategy.

Needless to say, even the perusal of a major portion of what appeared to be the most relevant literature proved to be a monumental task. Not all of the material reviewed is included in the bibliography to this article; rather, only the literature that was either quoted directly or used extensively in preparing the critique is included. Most of the literature reviewed here was written in English. Of course, many articles and books about the growth pole concept have been written in Spanish, French, Polish, and other languages, but generally translations into English are either nonexistent or are unavailable in the Cambridge libraries; so a comprehensive review was almost impossible to do. Fortunately, this reviewer was able to borrow some material from her colleagues.

To be able to review the growth pole literature within the limitations of a single paper, it was necessary to focus on only three issues: domination, linkages, and distribution. These issues are raised over and over in the literature, yet they have not been addressed in a systematic way. This focus will be used to help explain why Perroux concentrated on the growth of industries rather than the growth of regions. A brief historical context is presented first.

4.1 Historical context

The growth pole concepts are compared in this paper with alternative theories and strategies of development. To do this, it is useful to set Perroux's work in historical context. Although Perroux mentioned the term "pole" and "center" in an article in 1950, it was not until his 1955 article that he presented a thorough discussion of the concept. By 1961, he devoted the entire second part of his book *L'Économie du XXe siècle* to growth poles (*Les Pôles de croissance*), with the second chapter of that part of the book repeating his 1955 article on "La Notion de pôle de croissance." As a number of previous reviewers, such as Darwent (1969) and Hermansen (1972), have noted, Perroux never made a clear distinction between a growth pole and a growth center. Some of the reasons why he did not do so are discussed later.

Perroux's 1950 article provides some important insights into his views on the political economy of capitalist development. He said that establishments of each firm are "geographically dispersed," and "bounds of organization of varying strength" are formed among them (1950, p. 94). He indicated that it was more important to concentrate on the economic spaces than on the banal (defined by points, lines, surfaces, and volumes) spaces of the firm. In this regard, he defined economic space by three concepts: by a plan, by a field of forces, and by homogeneous aggregates. It was in terms of the second type of economic space, the field of forces, that Perroux first mentioned [growth] centers (poles) and explained why the firm, rather than the region, should be the focus of analysis.

> As a field of forces, economic space consists of centres (or poles or foci) from which centrifugal forces emanate and to which centripetal forces are attracted (1950, p. 95)... The topographical zone of influence of Michelin in France is inscribed in a region, but its economic zone of influence, like that of all large firms, defies cartography. (1950, p. 96).

Four important factors should be noted in terms of his work on growth poles.

The first major factor concerns the French economy in the 1940s and 1950s. The aftermath of World War II was still being felt throughout France and Europe during the late 1940s and the 1950s as reconstruction and recovery from the war took place. The Marshall Plan was implemented in April 1948, and during the next four years over $12.5 million of aid would be poured into Europe and Japan by the United States under that Plan, representing 5% of the gross national product (GNP) of the receiving countries and 2% of the GNP of the United States (Anell & Nygren 1980, pp. 44–5). There was a great need for investment in Europe in basic industries. As Higgins notes, Western Europe

> was still dominated by "propulsive enterprises" based on exploitation of natural resources – iron and steel, heavy chemicals, textiles, pulp and paper, etc. (Higgins 1978, p. 238).

Higgins also mentions the influence on Perroux of other factors, such as the relatively primitive communications networks, the reliance on railroads for interurban transport, and peripheral regions where coal and iron mines or forests existed, regions that were indeed benefited by the expansion of steel mills or paper mills in nearby towns. Even as late as 1965, only 67% of the population of France lived in urban areas (Moseley 1974, p. 44).

The second major factor that influenced Perroux's thinking was the then current view of economic development. France's orientation was still to its colonies throughout the world, but they were in fact becoming independent. In writing about domination, Perroux made specific reference to the colonial relationships of France to African and other countries (Perroux 1958, 1961). Literature on economic development was relatively scarce in the late 1940s and early 1950s compared with today. As an example, when the third edition of *Economics* was published in 1955, Samuelson for the first time included a chapter on economic development; neither his first nor his second edition, published in 1948 and 1951, respectively, had contained this chapter. Perroux was well aware of the then current development literature. Throughout his 1961 text, he refers to the now-classic development literature of Western development economists, such as writings by Chenery, Domar, Harrod, Hirschman, Myrdal, Nurkse, Rosenstein-Rodan, Rostow, Tinbergen, and Watanabe. He was influenced by and, in turn, influenced many of these and later development economists. He was also very much aware of the Marxist literature. His knowledge of Marxist theory and writers is well documented in many of his publications, but especially in the book *Masse et classe* (Perroux 1972). If the English translations of Perroux's books had been widely distributed, he would probably be known more for his theories of development than for his theory of growth poles.

The writings of Schumpeter were the third major factor that greatly influenced Perroux. Innovation plays a key role in all of Perroux's writings on the capitalist system. The influence of Schumpeter can be partially seen by the 254-page book Perroux published in 1965 on the economic thoughts of Schumpeter. Also, he continually refers to Schumpeter in his 1961 text on the economy of the twentieth century, explicitly referencing Schumpeter 15 times in the text. Many of Perroux's ideas concerning innovations and business cycles are based upon concepts advanced by Schumpeter in his *Theory of economic development* (1941) and other writings. Perroux seems to have developed the growth pole concept partly to help explain the long and short cycles of economic development and growth.

The fourth major factor that must have influenced Perroux was the growth of planning throughout the socialist and European countries. He was concerned with the concepts of planning and the role of innovations and the large corporation in the development process. In 1962, he wrote a treatise on the Fourth Plan, in which he raises the question: "Can a decentralized economy of the capitalist type really be planned?"

(Perroux 1962, p. 108). He also noted that monopolies engendered both the negative effects of high profits and the positive effects of innovations, which he did not believe could be sorted out through the plan (p. 22). He was very active in the development of the French national accounts, and input–output accounts comprised part of that accounting system. The input–output accounts were used in the formulation of the indicative planning upon which France embarked in the late 1940s (Hansen 1968). Perroux recognized the interregional interdependencies that were developing in the European countries, and he was concerned with the effect interregional trade had on the terms of trade with the developing countries.

In each of Perroux's writings cited earlier, he implicitly or explicitly discusses the issues of domination, linkages, and distribution, thus providing important insights into his views on the political economy of capitalist development. It is therefore in terms of these three issues that his work on growth poles will be compared with that of some other development theorists.

4.2 Comparison of the growth pole theory and strategy with alternatives

As noted in the introduction to this paper, the literature on growth pole theory is extensive. It is therefore surprising that few comparisons are made in the existing literature between the growth pole theory and strategy and some of the leading theories and strategies of the left. Corragio (1973) is one of the few analysts to present a critique (in the readily available literature) from a radical perspective. He places considerable emphasis on Perroux's "idea of domination as an unavoidable reality" (Corragio 1973, p. 296; it should be noted that he cites the 1964 edition of *L'Économie du XXe siècle* while I had access only to the 1961 edition.) During the 1970s, one of the leading theories of development was the dependency theory. In addition, alternatives to the prevailing capitalist strategies of development were proposed. These included the strategies of self-reliance, the New International Economic Order (NIEO), and basic needs. The comparison in this paper will have to be restricted to the dependency theory and the NIEO strategy of development. They appear to differ significantly from the growth pole theory and strategy in terms of the three key issues (domination, linkages, and distribution) mentioned earlier. Because they have been described, discussed, and critiqued in numerous articles and books, the purpose here is only to summarize the main features from the literature pertinent to a comparison with the growth pole theory and strategy.

Domination

The issue of domination (in terms of firms, cities, regions, and nations) pervades both the literature on growth poles and that on dependency. The perspective of the two schools of development theory is, of course, vastly different. While the growth pole theorists maintain that the domination of certain firms is a positive factor in the development process required to help the mass of the population, the dependency theorists argue that domination leads to expropriation of the surplus product not for use by the masses, but for use by the capitalists. Each argument will be summarized, and a critique will be presented.

Perroux's growth pole theory Perroux maintained that the initial investments by dominant firms and dominant nations would generate income, expand effective demand, and create new markets for the increased production by the Third World producers (Perroux 1961, pp. 49–51). Although many development economists failed to foresee the emerging transformation of an explicit colonial relationship into an implicit one, dominated by huge multinational firms, Perroux discussed in detail how the mass of the population would benefit from this relationship created by dominant (oligopolistic) forms. In his earlier book *Le Capitalisme*, he specially mentioned that the logic of pure domination and pure profit leads the capitalist system to function "for the benefit of the masses," rather than leading to the exploitation of the masses as argued in the leftist literature, which he referred to as "Marxist propaganda" (1958, pp. 66–7). He maintained that the capitalist system had forces that restricted the "cumulative effects of exploitation" (1958, p. 67). His argument was that the Marxists' analysis of the theory of domination in terms of imperialism involved only the use of "emotional vocabulary," whereas the analysis should be conducted with "scientific neutrality" (1961, pp. 46–51). He also argued that the analysis of the world economy must be undertaken in terms of the market forces and that the role of innovation was critical to the augmentation of production as global demand expands. Thus, as Coraggio states, Perroux assumed that growth poles would "become the decision-making centres of the world capitalist system" (Coraggio 1973, p. 290).

Almost all of Perroux's 595-page book *L'Économie du XXe siècle* is devoted to an elucidation of the growth pole concept in terms of the role played by innovations in the dominant firms, and by the dominant nations, in transmitting growth throughout an (international) economy. (This transmission process will be discussed later under the issue of linkages). In the first chapter, he mentions the adverse terms of trade between what he called the less-developed (*sous-développés*) countries, which were the colonies, and the advanced capitalist countries, which dominated the colonies (1961, p. 51), and he refers to the 1945 book by Hirschman, *National power and the structure of foreign trade*, to document his argument concerning the terms of trade. The entire fourth chapter of Perroux's 1961 book is devoted to a discussion of the issue of domination. He seems to have been aware of the now current arguments that growth poles may lead to dependency relations, and he explicitly describes in that chapter the dual economy in terms of "un moderne et l'autre archaïque" (1961, p. 156). The references cited earlier contain several places where he indicated his opposition to a European nation, a European market, and the liberal block. Instead, he wanted to strive essentially for free international trade. Thus, his analysis focused on the firm, actually on the dominant firm, as it interacted in the international, rather than the national or regional, setting.

Even as late as 1968, Perroux continued to support the "delocalization of the analysis." For him, the capitalist world would necessarily be divided into the dominated and the dominators, and the nations of the international economy must give way to a "system of dominant poles" (Coraggio 1973, p. 298). But, as mentioned earlier, he maintained that this division would benefit everyone. His reasoning was that because dominant firms are very efficient, can make effective use of innovations, and can achieve greater increases in output than nondominant firms, a high rate of growth in per capita income could be achieved, and the gains would accrue eventually to everyone through the multiplier effect. The discussion of his views on linkages given in the next sections helps to show how he felt this benefit would occur. First, however, the contrasting views of the dependency theorists on the issue of dominance are presented.

Dependency theorists One of the early studies of the causes of underdevelopment and of the role that dominant capitalist countries played was conducted by Paul Baran and described in *The political economy of growth* (1957). He states there that the "economic development in underdeveloped countries is profoundly inimical to the dominant interests in the advanced capitalist countries" (Baran 1957, p. 28). He goes on to indicate how capital generated in the Third World would be expropriated in large amounts by the foreign capitalists who made the investments. Thus, he predicted that the dominant firms would be organized in such a way as to drain both capital (in the form of profits) and raw materials from the producers in the Third World. Baran's theory was supported by studies made by other analysts, such as the work in the 1950s by Raul Prebisch and Hans Singer (now referred to as the Prebisch–Singer thesis), who maintained that the terms of trade were adverse for most developing counties. They claimed that because these developing countries, such as those in Latin America, relied only upon the exports of primary products, the terms of trade fluctuated widely in the short run and deteriorated in the long run. A concerted effort was made in the 1950s by Prebisch and other analysts at the Economic Commission for Latin America (ECLA) to document the deterioration in the terms of trade and the insufficiencies of technical progress in manufacturing. During this period, an entire school of analysts, called the structuralists, was formed, with many of the analysts later becoming dependency theorists. For interesting discussions of the different dependency theorists, the reader is referred to the papers by Bienefeld, Evans, Palma, and Seers in the book edited by Seers (1981).

The initial reaction of the neoclassical economists to this deterioration in the terms of trade was to stress that monetarist policies could help alleviate the inflation as well as the foreign exchange shortages that were confronting countries in Latin America and elsewhere. Partially as a response to the worsening terms of trade, the structuralists advocated changing the structure of production in the periphery through state intervention, exchange controls, increased wages to augment effective demand, and import substitution. Usually, however, none of the policies was sufficient to reverse the trend in the terms of trade. Concerning import substitution, for example, Seers said that "while these policies reduced the imports of certain finished goods, such as consumer durables, they required increased imports of capital equipment, intermediate products, raw materials, and fuels" (Seers 1981, p. 14).

In other words, according to Seers, import substitution led to new forms of dependence. Thus began the transformation of many of the analysts of the structuralist school into dependency theorists as it became apparent that changes in the structure of production may be necessary, but certainly are not sufficient, conditions to augment the rate of economic growth. Instead, they maintained that emphasis needs to be placed on altering the underlying social relations of production.

Dependency has been analyzed both in terms of international dependencies and internal dependencies, called by Walton "internal colonialism" (Walton 1975). Because it provides the best contrast with Perroux's views of dominance, only the international dependency relationship will be discussed in this paper. The discussion of dependency theory and the related unequal exchange theory by analysts such as Amin (1977), Becker (1982), Bodenheimer (1970), Cardoso and Faletto (1979), Chilchote (1974), dos Santos (1970), Emmanuel (1972), Evans (1979), Frank (1977), Ray (1973), Seers (1981), Shaw and Grieve (1977), Wallerstein (1974), and others is based upon the concept that the world economy is divided into a core of dominant nations and a periphery of dependent ones. The relationship between "core" and "periphery" (concepts that Friedman (1967, fr. 50, p. 68) claims were 'first introduced to systematic regional analysis' by him in 1966) can be summarized as follows.

All countries in the world economy, with the socialist countries usually excluded, are viewed as being divided into two groups. The First World, or industrialized countries, form one group, and the Third World countries form the second group. Within each of these two groups of countries, there is a core and a periphery. The periphery is viewed as being composed of subsistance agriculture and small-scale rural industry, both of which have low productivity, with the marginal productivity of labor being zero, or sometimes even negative. The sectors in the periphery, such as subsistence agriculture, provide a constant oversupply of laborers, who create a strong downward pressure on wage rates in the modern sector of the core. This leads to a low effective demand in the Third World countries, so that expansion of markets for manufactured products of their own countries cannot generally occur, nor are new markets easy to create.

The industrialized countries have historically imported raw materials from the Third World, paying low prices for the imports, while exporting manufactured goods, especially capital equipment, to the Third World countries (partly resulting from import-substitution policies). The capital equipment has often been used to construct infrastructure conducive to the production and transportation of the raw materials to be exported, but not necessarily to the production and distribution of commodities for people living in the periphery. The dependency theorists state that one result of this pattern of trade in raw materials and manufactured goods has been the serious deterioration in the terms of trade between the industrialized countries and the Third World countries cited earlier. According to Todaro, the terms of trade of nonoil-producing Third World countries continuously deteriorated between 1972 and 1982, rising slightly in 1983 and 1984. "In fact, during the 1980s, the terms of trade for these nations fell to their lowest level in 25 years" (Todaro 1985, p. 372). Nondependency analysts, such as Higgins (1981, pp. 138–9) maintain that the opposite has happened, namely, that the terms of trade for major industrialized market economies have become worse, while those for the developing countries (except for the least developed) all made gains. Several analysts have tried, not altogether successfully, to counter the adverse terms of trade argument by showing that there is a cyclical movement in the terms of trade. The "facts" concerning the terms of trade vary depending upon several variables, including the time period chosen, the base year used, the countries included or excluded from each group, and the statistical source(s) from which the data are obtained.

The core in the Third World countries is thus seen as being directly linked with the core in the industrialized countries. Both cores drain profits and resources (land, labor, and capital) from their own peripheries, and the core in the industrialized countries also drains profits and resources from the periphery of the Third World countries, thus augmenting its ability to be dominant. Implicit within the dependency theory, therefore, is a rejection of Perroux's rationality for the establishment of growth poles. In contrast to Perroux's views on how the social and cultural relations must be transformed as the dominant firms and nations become more prevalent, dependency theorists stress these relationships to show how it is precisely this capitalist development by dominant firms that drains capital from the periphery for the benefit of the core. In Perroux's view, the domination of particular firms is a necessary element of the development process if the largest possible rate of growth of the gross national product is to be achieved. He emphasized that dominant firms could achieve significant economies of scale and foster innovative activity far more readily than smaller firms and that both factors help a firm to achieve substantial increases in output. The benefits of this increased output are dispersed throughout the economy through the multiplier effects. For the dependency theorists, the income accruing through the domination by these firms benefits only the capitalist class. The way in which this factor affects the views of both sides on the issue of distribution will be discussed later. But first, it is necessary to discuss how each views the role of linkages.

Linkages

Linkages are interpreted in many different ways in the development literature. The most frequent interpretation is in terms of interindustrial linkages, as shown through input–output tables, but reference is also made to interregional and international linkages. Also, as noted in the introduction to this paper, most growth pole analysts have concentrated only on regional, rather than multiregional or multinational, growth. (Perroux is one of the few exceptions.) On the other hand, dependency theorists have had the exact opposite concentration, with primary emphasis being given to the growth of the international economy. Attention here will be focused on the way in which both schools of thought view the question of interindustrial, interregional, and international linkages. Because the political factors underlying both schools of thought have been covered in the section on domination, the economic factors will be stressed in this section.

Growth pole theory Most growth pole analysts concentrate only on the interindustry linkages. Although Perroux's primary focus is on these linkages, he constantly refers to the position of the firm in the international economy. Two main types of linkages are discussed: backward and forward. A backward linkage is defined as the ratio of purchased intermediate inputs to the total value of production; a forward linkage is defined as the ratio of interindustry demand to total demand. According to Perroux, the propulsive firm (*firme motrice*) plays the key role in development in that it has an propulsive effect (*effet d'entraînement*), while other firms will experience growth if they react (*la firme entraînée*) to the propulsive firm. The question then becomes one of determining which industries are propulsive.

One answer was given by Hirschman, who stressed the importance of determining the propulsive sectors in the economy through the use of backward and forward linkage indices. He devotes an entire chapter of his book *The strategy of economic development* to their definition and use in development planning (Hirschman 1958, ch. 6). Backward linkage effects are considered by him to be the most important because they are demand-induced, while forward linkage effects arise only in terms of output utilization (p. 101). To provide quantitative measures to the concepts, he cited calculations from Chenery and Watanabe's then unpublished manuscript (pp. 106-7). They had developed backward and forward linkage indices for 28 sectors, using data from input-output tables for Italy, Japan, and the United States. Of the 28 sectors, 9 were classified as having both high backward and forward linkages, 10 as having a high backward and a low forward, 6 as having a high forward and a low backward, and 4 as having both low backward and forward linkages. Hirschman stated that these linkages (which he also called interdependence ratios) "are very rough indexes of the potential linkage effects that might be introduced into nonindustrial economies by specific industrial sectors" (p. 108). He also tries to show how the backward linkage effect can be used as a base for a model of capital formation, and he notes that the inverse tables, rather than just the direct coefficient tables, may be required to define the total (direct and indirect) linkage effect, thus providing a more refined measure of the backward linkage effect (p. 113).

Analysts who have used the linkage concepts have developed an entire set of literature of their own that is far too extensive to review here. The causal relationship that Hirschman tried to establish between unbalanced growth and economic development has, for example, been challenged by Yotopoulos and Nugent (1973, 1976). In their first article, they analyzed 11 countries (6 industrialized and 5 nonindustrialized), using input–ouput tables for 18 sectors and for 6 sectors. They concluded that there is

> considerable similarity in the structure of linkages between DC's [developed countries] and LDC's [less developed countries], although not surprisingly the indices are generally higher in the DC's than in the LDC's (Yotopoulos & Nugent 1973, pp. 162–3).

Their study was challenged by four different analysts (Laumas, Boucher, Riedel, and Jones), each of whom presented an alternative indicator. Yotopoulos and Nugent responded to the four in the same journal (May 1976), maintaining that their indirect linkage index is the most appropriate of the five. They also questioned whether the use of any of the alternative indices would have changed their conclusions (1976, p. 343). This rather technical side of defining and testing the linkage indices in quantitative terms is still not conclusive. Although this part of the linkage literature tends to be very technical, one of the principal aims of the analysts is to determine whether or not there is any correlation between firms (sectors) with strong backward and forward linkages and the rate of economic growth.

Other literature on linkages deals more directly with the growth pole theory. Some of the analysts focus on the macro (global) linkage effects, while others concentrate on the micro (firm) effects. Davin (1964, pp. 61–2) and Paelinck (1963, pp. 201–5) classify principal growth poles and derived growth poles according to variations in their economic structures. Moore (1972) uses the growth pole framework to classify "products, processes, and the technical and legal linkages between industrial plants" (Moore 1972, p. 253).

Overall, however, growth pole analysts have been interested in looking at linkages in order to determine multiplier effects of particular investment programs. Part of the reason for the intense interest in the development of the most appropriate linkage indicator is the fact that it is used to help development planners choose the firm (sector) in which to invest. The rationale is that investments in firms (sectors) with high backward and forward linkages will generate a greater multiplier impact than investments in firms (sectors) with low backward and forward linkages.

So far in the discussion of linkages, the focus has been on the interindustrial linkages that can be calculated from input–output tables. Growth pole analysts have concentrated their attention on the linkages between firms producing goods and services only for current consumption. Thus, their emphasis has been on interindustrial linkages either in a national or a regional setting. With the exception of Perroux, almost all the growth pole analysts have been concerned with only a very narrow aspect of the overall linkage issue. Perroux viewed the linkages not only in terms of the interindustry linkages, but also in the broader international framework. In his 1961 book, for example, he discusses the flows of capital that will be necessary for development to occur. Dependency analysts have also looked at the issue of linkages from an even broader perspective, which will now be discussed.

Dependency theorists' views Dependency theorists look at the overall social relations of production in a nation or in the world and consider the linkage phenomenon within this broader context. Because of this perspective, most of the dependency analysts discuss the links between the core and the periphery in terms of the flows of capital and labor as well as the flows of goods and services. They emphasize both the physical and the financial capital flows. Their focus is on the international flows of the goods, services, capital, and labor. Thus, for example, Amin refers to the need for a new international division of labor in his discussion of a self-reliant strategy for development in the nonaligned countries (Amin 1978–9, p. 480).

The discussion of the dependency relations by Szentes (1976) will be used here to illustrate the broad perspective on linkages of the Marxist component of the dependency school. He distinguishes four types of dependencies: (a) direct economic dependence, (b) trade dependence, (c) financial dependence, and (d) technical dependence. The international and interregional linkages play an important role in the development of his discussion of these four types of dependence. He interprets direct economic dependence as the case in which the key sectors are controlled by foreign monopoly capital. In this case, the linkages become the ways in which capital, labor, and resources flow between the dependent and the nondependent nations. Because not all inputs can be produced domestically and because the size of the market in the dependent countries is small, Szentes maintains that the interindustry linkages also help to foster trade dependence. Thus, the dependent countries require foreign trade both to supply inputs to local manufacturers and to provide a market for the sale of the locally produced goods, many of which cannot be sold locally because of the limited effective demand. According to Szentes, financial dependence provides yet another link between the core and the periphery, because in many countries the banking and credit systems are under foreign control. The international financial linkages control the flow of capital to and from the dependent countries. Finally, technical dependence is defined by Szentes to mean the import of technology and of experts. Whereas Perroux wants to establish dominant firms to take advantage of technical capabilities in the industrialized world, Szentes maintains that such firms create technical dependence of the Third World owing to the "industrial investment policy of international oligopolies." He states that the advanced capitalist countries "see to it that the production of new plants does not embrace the whole cycle of processing" (1976, p. 187). Much of Szentes' reasoning on the manufacturing processing cycle is supported by studies being made by the product life-cycle theorists, such as Vernon (1966), Wells (1972), and Norton and Rees (1979).

It is later in his book that Szentes develops some of these dependency arguments in terms of linkages. He says that the interindustry relations and linkage effects in the Third World cannot be enlarged in those nations because they are "missing links in the chain of the vertical structure of social production" (p. 239). Thus, as industries change from labor-intensive to capital-intensive techniques, the import-orientation is intensified because of the lack of local technical skills, local capital, etc. The main thrust of the dependency analysts' arguments is that the linkages between the core and the periphery do exist and are very pervasive. They affect the social relations of production in each country. As the development of the advanced capitalist countries progresses, there is an increased drainage of income from the periphery to the core. The effect this has on the distribution of income is discussed in the next section of this paper.

Distribution

Growth pole and dependency theorists have been shown above to have opposing viewpoints on the benefits and disadvantages of large, propulsive, dominant firms and of the international, interregional, and interindustrial linkages created by these firms. They also develop opposing strategies to take account of the effect these factors have on distribution.

Growth pole strategy As noted earlier, Perroux maintained that investment centered on dominant firms was a necessary condition to obtain sufficient growth to benefit the masses. The spreading of these benefits, he said, would occur the fastest if investment were devoted to the dominant firms that had the greatest backward and forward linkages. He argued that if a country implemented this growth-pole strategy of development, the investment would generate increased output (employment and income) not only in the initial firm, but because of the strong backward and forward linkages, a multiplier effect would transmit these increases to other firms as well.

Detailed studies by Kuznets (1964) and Williamson (1965) indicated that inequalities were decreasing, while Leontief et al. (1977), Tinbergen (1976), and others have documented the lack of progress in reducing income inequalities. To explain some of the contradictory evidence, some analysts refer to Williamson's findings that

> rising regional income disparities and increasing North–South dualism is typical of early development stages, while regional convergence and a disappearance of severe North–South problems is typical of the more mature stages of national growth and development (Williamson 1965, p. 44).

The growth-pole strategy was seen by many development planners to be a way to assure that inequalities would lessen over time.

According to Gaile, by the late 1970s, the growth pole strategy of development had been "implemented, provided for, or seriously discussed" in at least 28 countries. These included Austria, Belgium, Bolivia, Brazil, Bulgaria, Canada, Chile, Columbia, Cuba, France, Ghana, Great Britain, India, Ireland, Italy, Kenya, Libya, Malaysia, Nigeria, Peru, Poland, Russia, Spain, Sweden, Tanzania, the United States, Venezuela, and Yugoslavia (Gaile 1978, pp. 2–4). The number of countries in which it has been implemented, or, at least, seriously discussed, is far greater than Gaile implies. According to Higgins, however,

> the strategy applied was seldom the one that Perroux favoured. Far from strengthening and encouraging existing growth poles, the strategy has been one of trying to create growth poles in *retarded*, disadvantaged regions, hoping for spread effects from the chosen pole to its own geographical regions ... In my view, it is very important to make it clear that "the failure of the growth-pole strategy" was not the failure of the *Perroux* theory, but failure of a distorted version applied by his disciples, mainly Boudeville (Higgins 1985, p. 3).

Even with so many efforts to augment per capita income, there has been little effect on the technical progress in the Third World. Technical progress either has not penetrated to the Third World to the extent envisioned by Perroux, or it has not been diffused to the periphery of the countries in cases where some penetration has occurred. As noted by Seers (1981), structures of production in the Third World remain, for the most part, primitive, with little diversification.

Two recent studies, one by Leontief and his associates (1977) and the other under the direction of Tinbergen (1976), have led to increasing concern about the present course of development and to disputes over the types of effort required to alter present levels of per capita income and inequalities within and between countries. According to the study of the world economy by Leontief and his associates, agricultural output in the Third World would have to increase by 5% per year, manufacturing output by a range of a low of 6% for some African countries to a high of 14% for the oil-producing countries (Leontief et al. 1977, pp. 4, 8). The Leontief group also maintained that "far-reaching international changes of a social, political, and institutional character" would have to occur in the developing countries and "significant changes" would be necessary in the world economic order (Leontief et al. 1977, p. 11), indicating that technological changes must be accompanied by important changes in the political economy of the nations and of the world. A study had been conducted in the preceding year under the direction of Jan Tinbergen. In that study, one of the conclusions was that per capita income inequalities may not be substantially reduced even with the 5% target (Tinbergen et al. 1976, p. 103).

Some analysts argue that the reason for the lack of progress is that the growth pole strategy either has not been implemented in sufficient countries or has not been implemented in the appropriate way. Other analysts argue that an entirely different strategy is required. Several alternative strategies of development have been proposed as a means of reducing income inequalities. They include the new international economic order, self-reliance, and basic needs. Because of the limitations of this short paper, only the first strategy will be discussed here, although, as will be seen, it can be considered part of one more loosely structured alternative that includes the strategy of self-reliance.

New International Economic Order Strategy The request for a New International Economic Order (NIEO) can be dated to 1964 when Raul Prebisch as director of the United Nations Economic Commission for Latin America (ECLA) called for a new economic order at the first United Nations Conference on Trade and Development (UNCTAD) meeting in Geneva. Sometimes the origin is traced back to the 1955 meeting in Bandung, Indonesia, of the Afro-Asian Meeting of the Nonaligned Nations. In any case, very little specific action resulted, although these nonaligned nations kept meeting once every year or two to define their positions more clearly. Finally, in 1974, two resolutions, 3201 (S-VI) and 3202 (S-VI), were passed at the Sixth Session of the UN General Assembly providing for the Declaration and Programme of Action on the Establishment of a New International Economic Order. These resolutions seem to have provided some concrete foundation for action.

According to Frank, part of the reason for the present "crescendo" of activity around the NIEO is that the "old economic order has disadvantaged the Vast Majority" (Frank 1980, p. 265). He lists as causes of its initial failure four wrong assumptions that were made about development during the 1960s and 1970s. First, it was assumed, he says, that trade barriers would be reduced, but they were not. Second, it was assumed that multinational firms would make a positive contribution to development, but the activity of these corporations was not appropriately assessed. Third, it was assumed that the multinational firms would change the pattern of development to favor the Third World, but the patterns of development imposed by the corporations was inappropriate for development of the Third World economies. Fourth, it was assumed that the income gaps within developing countries would decline, but increases in the gross national product in the developing countries augmented income disparities in these countries. In terms of the fourth point, it has already been noted, for example, that the detailed studies by Kuznets (1964) and Williamson (1965) indicated that inequalities would eventually decrease, while, more recently, Leontief et al. (1977) and Tinbergen (1976) have presented far more pessimistic conclusions.

Both Frank (1980, pp. 269–70) and Amin (1978–9, pp. 477–9) cite the formation of the Organization of Petroleum Exporting Countries (OPEC) in 1973 as providing a boost for the proponents of the NIEO in that the "Third World countries became aware, not of their rights, but of their power" (Amin, 1978–9, p. 478). At one end of the spectrum of nonaligned countries are those that are oil-rich, while at the other end of the spectrum are the very poor (mostly) African and Asian countries. The initial 75 to 77 nonaligned countries that supported the establishment of an NIEO have been expanded now to include more than 120 countries.

The exact nature of the NIEO strategy of development has yet to be set forth in detail. Amin, however, indicates why it is important to reform the present international division of labor, which "confines the developing countries to the exports of primary (agricultural and mineral) commodities" (Amin 1978–9, p. 479). He maintains that the products of the Third World manufacturing sectors are limited to the domestic market, which lacks sufficient effective demand because of the low wages paid to the laborers, and that this limitation can be overcome partly by restructuring the international division of labor. Amin not only stresses the need for restructuring of the international division of labor, but states very emphatically that "the NIEO cannot be implemented" unless a self-reliant development strategy is pursued by the Third World countries (Amin, 1978–9, p. 480). According to him, the implementation of such a strategy may require a "delinking" of the NIEO from the current international division of labor by augmenting the commodity and monetary transactions between Third World countries, by transferring Third World technologies within the Third World, rather than accepting technologies from the advanced capitalist countries, and by using other means to unify the economic power base of the Third World countries.

4.3 Conclusion

The contrasting views of growth pole and dependency theorists and of those analysts proposing selected alternative strategies of development have been presented in terms of three critical issues: domination, linkages, and distribution. Throughout this paper, it has been shown that essentially the same factual evidence is being used by both sides to support their opposing points of view. Perroux maintains that domination and interindustrial linkages are necessary, but not sufficient, conditions for rapid economic growth; at the same time, increases in the rate of economic growth are required for improved income distribution. Dependency theorists maintain that domination and linkages not only limit the increases in per capita income, but also augment the gap between the rich and the poor, both within and between countries. A thorough quantitative analysis to support either set of arguments is missing, but would be an important, even though difficult, task to undertake.

References

Amin, S. 1977. *Imperialism and unequal development.* New York: Monthly Review Press.
Amin, S. 1978–9. New International Economic Order and Strategy for the Use of Financial Surpluses of Developing Countries. *Alternatives* **4**, 477–85.
Anell, L. & B. Nygren 1980. *Developing countries and the world economic order.* New York: Methuen.
Baran, P. A. 1957. *The political economy of growth.* New York: Modern Reader Paperbooks.
Becker, B. K. 1982. The political use of territory: a Third-World perspective. Rio de Janeiro: Federal University.
Bodenheimer, S. 1970. Dependency and imperialism. *Politics and Society*, 327–58.
Boudeville, J. R. 1966. *Problems of regional economic planning.* Edinburgh: Edinburgh University Press.
von Boventer, E. 1975. Regional growth theory. *Urban Studies* **12**, 1–29.
Cardoso, F. H. & E. Faletto 1979. *Dependency and development in Latin America.* Berkeley, Calif.: University of California Press.
Chilcote, R. H., 1974. Dependency: a critical synthesis of the literature. *Latin American Perspective* **1** (1), 4–29.
Conroy, M. E. 1973. Rejection of growth centre strategy in Latin American regional development planning. *Land Economics* **49** (4), 371–80.
Coraggio, J. L. 1973. Towards a revision of the growth pole theory. *Viertel Jahres Berichte: Probleme der Entwicklungslander* **53**, 289–308.
Darwent, D. F. 1969. Growth poles and growth centres in regional planning – a review. *Environment and Planning* **1**, 5–32.
Davin, L. E. 1964. *Économie régionale et croissance.* Paris: Éditions Genin.

Davy, B. W. 1973. *Annotated bibliography on growth centres*, Exchange Bibliography no. 374–5. Monticello, Ill.; Council of Planning Librarians.
dos Santos, T. 1970. The structure of dependence. *American Economic Review* **60** (2), 231–6.
Emmanuel, A. 1972. *Unequal exchange: a study of the imperialism of trade.* With additional comments by Charles Bettelheim. Translated from the French by Brian Pearce. New York: Monthly Review Press.
Evans, P. 1979. *Dependent development.* Princeton, N.J.: Princeton University Press.
Frank, A. G. 1977. Dependence is dean, long live dependence and the class struggle: an answer to critics. *World Development* **5** (4), 355–70.
Frank, A. G. 1980. *Crisis: in the world economy.* New York: Holmes & Meier Publishers.
Frank, A. G. 1981. *Crisis: in the Third World.* New York: Holmes & Meier Publishers.
Friedmann, J. R. 1966. *Regional development policy: a case study of Venezuela.* Cambridge, Mass.: The MIT Press.
Friedmann, J. R. 1967. *A general theory of polarized development.* Santiago, Chile: The Ford Foundation Urban and Regional Advisory Program in Chile.
Gaile, G. L. 1978. The concept of growth centres. Storrs, Conn.: Department of Geography, University of Connecticut.
Galtung, J. 1978–9. The new international economic order and the basic needs approach. *Alternatives* **4**, 455–76.
Hansen, N. M. 1968. *French regional planning.* Bloomington, Ind.: Indiana University Press.
Hansen, N. M. (ed.) 1972. *Growth centers in regional economic development.* New York: The Free Press.
Hansen, N. M. 1981. Development from above: the centre-down development paradigm. In *Development from above or below?* W. B. Stohr & D. R. Fraser Taylor (eds.), 15–38. New York: John Wiley.
Hermansen, T. 1972. Development poles and development centres in national and regional development: elements of a theoretical framework. In *Growth poles and growth centres in regional planning*, A. Kuklinksi (ed.), vol. 5. The Hague, The Netherlands: Mouton.
Higgins, B. 1978. Development poles: do they exist?. In *Growth pole strategy and regional development policy*, F-C. Lo & K. Salih (eds.), 229–42. New York: Pergamon Press.
Higgins, B. 1983. From growth poles to systems of interactions in space. In *Growth and Change* **14** (4), 3–13.
Higgins, B. 1985. Personal communication. (July 10).
Higgins, B. & N. T. Dung 1981. Dualism, dependency, and continuing underdevelopment. In *Changing perception of development problems*, R. P. Misra & M. Honjo (eds.) 123–76. Hong Kong: Maruzen Investment.
Hirschman, A. O. 1945. *National power and the structure of foreign trade.* Berkeley, Calif.: University of California Press.
Hirschman, A. O. 1958. *The strategy of economic development.* New Haven, Conn.: Yale University Press.
Holland, S. 1976a. *Capital versus the regions.* London: Macmillan. (Also published in 1977 by St Martins Press, New York.)
Holland, S. 1976b. *The regional problem.* London: Macmillan. (Also published in 1977 by St Martin's Press, New York.)

Klaassen, L. H. 1972. Growth poles in economic theory and policy. In *Growth poles and regional policies*, A. Kuklinksi & R. Petrella (eds.), 1–40. The Hague: Mouton.

Kuklinksi, A. (ed.) 1972. *Growth poles and growth centres in regional planning.* Regional Planning Series, vol. 5. The Hague: Mouton.

Kulinski, A. (ed.) 1974. *Regional information and regional planning.* Regional Planning Series, vol. 6. The Hague: Mouton.

Kuklinski, A. (ed.) 1975. *Regional Disaggregation of National Policies and Plans.* Regional Planning Series, vol. 8. The Hague: Mouton.

Kuklinksi, A. (ed.) 1981. *Polarized Development and Regional Policies: Tribute to Jacques Boudeville*, vol. 11. The Hague: Mouton.

Kuklinski, A. & R. Petrella (eds.) 1972. *Growth poles and regional policies.* The Hague: Mouton.

Kuznets, S. 1964. Quantitative aspects of the economic growth of nations, IX, level and structure of foreign trade: comparisons for recent years. *Economic Development and Cultural Change* **13** (2), 1–106.

Lasuen, J. R. 1973. Urbanization and development – the temporal interaction between geographical and sectoral clusters. *Urban Studies* **10**, 163–88.

Leontief, W., A. P. Carter & P. A. Petri 1977. *The future of the world economy.* New York: Oxford University Press.

Lo, F-C. & K. Salih (eds.) 1978. *Growth pole strategy and regional development policy.* Oxford: Pergamon Press.

MacDonald, J. S. 1979. Planning implementation and social policy: an evaluation of ciudad guayana 1965 and 1975. *Progress in planning* **11**, 1–211.

Massey, D. 1979. In what sense a regional problem? *Regional studies* **13**, 233–43.

Moore, C. W. 1972. Industrial linkage development paths in growth poles: a research methodology. *Environment and Planning* **4**, 253–71.

Moseley, M. J. 1974. *Growth centres in spatial planning.* New York: Pergamon Press.

Munoz, H. (ed.) 1981. *From dependency to development.* Boulder, Col.: Westview Press.

Myrdal, G. 1957. *Economic theory and underdeveloped regions.* London: Methuen.

Nichols, V. 1969. Growth poles: an evaluation of their propulsive effect. *Environment and planning* **1**, 193–208.

Norton, R. D. & J. Rees 1979. The product cycle and the spatial decentralization of American manufacturing. *Regional Studies* **13**, 141–51.

Paar, J. B. 1973. Growth poles, regional development, and central place theory. *Papers of the Regional Science Association* **31**, 173–212.

Paelinck, J. 1963. La teoria del desarrollo regional polarizado. *Revista de Economia Latino-Americana*, no. 9, 177–229.

Perroux, F. 1950. Economic space, theory and applications. *Quarterly Journal of Economics* **64**, 90–2.

Perroux, F. 1955. Notes sur la notion de 'pôle de croissance'. *Économie appliquée* **7**, 307–20.

Perroux, F. 1958. *Le Capitalisme.* Paris: Presses universitaires de France.

Perroux, F. 1961. *L'Économie du XXe siècle.* Paris: Presses universitaires de France.

Perroux, F. 1962. *Le IVe plan français: 1962–1965.* Paris: Presses universitaires de France.

Perroux, F. 1972. *Masse et classe.* Paris: Casterman.

Pred, A. 1976. The interurban transmission of growth in advanced economies: empirical findings versus regional-planning assumptions. *Regional Studies* **10**, 151–71.

Ray, D. 1973. The dependency model of Latin American underdevelopment: three basic fallacies. *Journal of Interamerican Studies and World Affairs* **15**, 4–20.
Richardson, H. W. 1976. Growth pole spillovers: the dynamics of backwash and spread. *Regional Studies* **10**, 1–9.
Richardson, H. W. & M. Richardson 1975. The relevance of growth center strategies to Latin America. *Economic Geography* **51**; 1, 163–83.
Samuelson, P. 1955. *Economics*. New York: McGraw–Hill.
Schumpeter, J. A. 1941. *The theory of economic development*. Cambridge, Mass.: Harvard University Press.
Seers, D. (ed.) 1981. *Dependency theory: a critical reassessment*. London: Frances Pinter.
Shaw, T. M. & M. Grieve 1977. Dependence or development: international and internal inequalities in Africa. *Development and Changes*, **no. 8**, 377–408.
Stohr, W. B. & D. R. Fraser Taylor (eds.) 1981. *Development from above or below? the dialects of regional planning in developing countries*. New York: John Wiley.
Storey, K. J. 1972. Growth poles and growth centres: a selected bibliography. Department of Geography, Memorial University of Newfoundland.
Szentes, T. 1976. *The political economy of under-development*, 3rd edn. Budapest: Publishing House of the Hungarian Academy of Sciences, Akademiai Kiado.
Thoman, R. S. (ed.) 1974. *Methodology and case studies*, vol. 1. Proceedings of the Commision on Regional Aspects of Development of the International Geographical Union. Meeting held in Vitora, ES Brazil, April 12–15, 1971. Canada: Allister Typesetting and Graphics.
Thomas, M. D. 1972. The regional problem, structural change, and growth pole theory. In *Growth poles and growth centres in regional planning*, Antoni R. Kuklinski (ed.), 69–102. The Hague: Mouton.
Tinbergen, J. 1976. *Reshaping the International Order: Report to the Club of Rome*. Anthony J. Dolman (ed.): Jan van Ettinger, director, 1st edition, New York: Dutton.
Todaro, M. P. 1985. *Economic development in the Third World*, 3rd edn. New York: Longman.
Vernon, R. 1966. International investment and international trade in the product cycle. *Quarterly Journal of Economics* **80**: 2, 190–207.
Wallerstein, I. 1974. Dependence in an interdependent world: the limited possibilities of a transformation within the capitalist world economy. *African Studies Review* **17**: 1, 1–26.
Walton, J. 1975. Internal colonialism: problems of definition and measurement. In *Latin American Urban Research*, vol. 5, *Urbanization and inequality: the political economy of urban and rural development in Latin America*, A. Cornelius & M. Trueblood (eds.), 29–50. Beverly Hills, Calif.: Sage.
Wells, L. T, Jr. (ed.), 1972. *The product life cycle and international trade*. Cambridge, Mass. Graduate School of Business Administration, Harvard University.
Williamson, J. G. 1965. Regional inequality and the process of national development: a description of patterns. *Economic Development and Cultural Change* **13**, 3–45.
Yotopoulos, P. A. & J. B. Nugent 1973. A balanced-growth version of the linkage hypothesis. *Quarterly Journal of Economics* **87** (2), 157–71.
Yotopoulos, P. A. & J. B. Nugent 1976. A balanced-growth version of the linkage hypothesis: response. *Quarterly Journal of Economics* **90** (2), 334–43.

PART II
Methods and approaches

5

The politics of place: toward a political economy of territorial planning

JOHN FRIEDMANN and YVON FOREST

In the sense of centrally directed resource allocation, planning has lost favor in Western capitalist countries. There are exceptions, of course. Fiscal–monetary planning has remained as strong as ever. And, at least in the United States, military planning has moved to the top of the agenda. But planning for civilian, social purposes to promote equity and welfare, has fallen into ill repute. The reasons for this change of view are chiefly ideological. Market forces are seen as the more "natural" way of resolving social problems. At the same time, a certain disenchantment with technocratic planning has set in, and must be held at least partially responsible for the current love-feast with laissez-faire economics.

One of the victims of this change is regional planning. These days, one hears very little about regional inequalities as a problem of public concern. And despite some sparring between "sunset" and "sunrise" regions, discussion of regional policies has all but ceased. Academics, of course, less subject to the vagaries of political fashion, have continued to address these issues. Although the language has changed – we are now more likely to speak of industrial and spatial "restructuring" – regional planning discourse continues to be as lively as ever. One reason for this may be momentum. Journals and teaching programs exist. The subject of regional economics and related policy questions is as interesting now as it has ever been. Another and possibly more important reason is that the regional question has become politicized. The concern today is less with central resource allocation by the state than with questions of regional autonomy and an "endogenous" development.

Among academics of regional planning, a subtle but significant shift has taken place away from a predominant concern with economic questions to a politics of place (Sandercock 1985). There are debates over how to preserve regional identity, how to advance sociocultural regional objectives in face of "global capital," and how to gain a greater measure of regional control over the forces of social and economic change (Rokkan & Urwin 1982).

This new set of debates calls for an expanded model of regional planning. We may call it the political economy model. In this model, the shift is away from an emphasis on functional regions to regions that are historically defined; from an emphasis on state and corporate action to one in which a politically mobilized regional population becomes the main protagonist; from an emphasis on reactive to proactive planning; from long-term spatial equilibrium to spatial conflict and struggle; and from an objective of simple economic growth to one of complex growth and development as an expression of regional priorities.

Speaking politically, the question at issue is the terms on which a regional economy becomes incorporated into the system of global economic relations. Subject purely to market forces, historically formed regions are constantly at risk of losing their identity. They become subordinated to the "logic" of global capital. It is only when regions are politically mobilized that they can begin to offer resistance to market forces and promote their social and cultural distinctiveness as a life space for their population.

This is not merely theoretical speculation. It is a concrete fact of a territorial politics that can be observed in many parts of the world, including North America.

In the remainder of this essay, we propose to (a) undertake a critique of the classical paradigm of regional planning, (b) provide evidence of a territorial politics with reference to the historical case of Quebec, (c) suggest a set of propositions for research into the political economy of territorialism, and (d) spell out some implications of the political economy model for the practice of regional planning.

5.1 The classical paradigm: a critique

A quite unprecedented period of economic growth ensued in the two decades following World War II. It was a heady period led, in the Western world, by a tremendous upsurge of consumer demand. The two preceding decades had been lean years: the Crash had come in 1929 and the Great War erupted a decade later. National states had grown powerful and shouldered new roles. In the forties and fifties, the welfare state was invented to spread demand more evenly among the population and provide a minimum of security against the vagaries of the market. Keynes had provided some useful tools for countercyclical planning at the national level, and full employment policies were devised and carried out. In the Third World, attention focused on the arts of nation-building, economic growth, and modernization. W. W. Rostow's theory of the "stages of economic growth" became a popular handbook of development planners (Rostow 1961).

With publication of the now classic works by François Perroux (1950), Walter Isard (1956), Gunnar Myrdal (1957), and Albert O. Hirschman (1958), the regional planning literature received a big boost during the early postwar period. All four writers were deeply concerned with government policies to guide the new industrialization efforts in both the First World and the Third. Jacques Boudeville (1961) and John Friedmann (1966) added a needed dimension to this discussion. But despite these authors' rejection of a self-correcting market model for guiding regional investment allocations, the basic language of neo-classical economics persisted. Like the others, their central concern was with national economic growth and its regional distribution. Growth poles emerged as the central planning doctrine (Hansen, 1972).

In contrast with the regionalism of the 1930s, post-war planning doctrine stressed a functional concept of region. Regions existed for the convenience of administrators and analysts (Friedmann & Stuckey, 1973). Criteria for their delimitation were defined by the authority of the central state. As might be expected, growth regions were identified with the hierarchy of cities. The dominant region of the period was the metropolis (Friedmann 1956, 1972).

The regional planning paradigm that emerged was based on certain key assumptions which still determine much classical thinking about development. It is important for us to highlight these assumptions in order to contrast them, later on, with a model based on a very different set of first beliefs. Four assumptions are central to the classical paradigm:

(a) *Atomism.* In accord with the marginalist assumptions of neoclassical economics, the classical paradigm of regional planning is primarily concerned with units of capital (firms) and labor. It thus abstracts from the cultural-historical reality of socio-spatial formations. This becomes especially clear when its principal value dimensions are considered. The primary value to be served is allocative efficiency, which is followed by economic growth (measured in terms of aggregative income and rates of change), and relative time preference (time discount rates, or interest). A correlative place preference (which might presumably be the regional economist's way of speaking about people's attachment to place) was never explicitly introduced, and the appropriate vocabulary was conspicuous by its absence.

(b) *Statism.* Classical regional planning doctrine articulates the perspective of an actor who stands outside a given region. In its prescriptive form, it reduces regional populations to the condition of an object of exogenous actions by capital and by the state. It is a bureaucratic paradigm, with prescriptive force "from the top down."

(c) *Nationalism.* The classical doctrine of regional planning accepts the national economy as the largest relevant system for analysis. Regions are viewed as subsystems of the national economy, and the major objectives of regional policy tend to be formulated so as to contribute to national goals and, in the longer term, to spatial equilibrium and system integration. Doctrine fails to consider the possibility of regions as having their own political objectives different in emphasis from those of the nation or, for that matter, as integrated into a global division of labor.

(d) *Capitalism.* Classical planning doctrine reflects the "logic" of capital as the hegemonic force in market economies. A leading assumption is that the unfettered operation of the market tends to allocate resources optimally, even though small corrections may be necessary from time to time, to deal with "market imperfections." The planning paradigm posits a trade-off between efficiency and equity, the implication being that long-term, systemwide efficiency for achieving high rates of economic growth requires short-term inequalities across regions and social classes. As a model – particularly in its current neoliberal formulation – it prefers income transfers to capital ("subsidies") over those to labor ("welfare"), and claims that only short-lived interventions of the state in market processes are necessary to achieve economic objectives.

For a variety of reasons, policy applications of this paradigm did not meet with spectacular success (Holland 1975). Because of the rise and fall of technologies and industries and the changing conditions of location in a dynamic economy, spatial equilibrium was, in principle, unattainable. Enormous multinational corporations appeared on the horizon and began the herculean task of global market integration. Capital was freed from its traditional locations and able to bring even nation states to their knees by the simple device of threatening to move to some other, more benign business climate. In desperation, it would seem, even the most powerful of the industrialized countries adopted neoliberal policies for the specific purpose of decontrolling the economy and getting the state out of the business of planning capital allocations. Regional policy and planning became a victim of supply-side economics.

All this is history. What history neglects to tell us, however, is the failure of regional planning doctrine to incorporate a political dimension and, more particularly, the dimension of a "politics of place". With its origin in the social mobilization of regional populations, a politics of place seeks to achieve a greater degree of mastery over the traditional life space of local, including regional, populations. In his brilliant book, *The year 2000*, Raymond Williams reminds us of regions that are faced with "capital restructuring." In these regions, where the state has conspicuously failed to protect local interests, a politics of place may be expected to emerge as a form of self-defense.

> Communities which at simpler levels had relatively balanced forms of livelihood found themselves, often without notice, penetrated or made marginal, to the point where many of their own people became 'redundant' and were available for transfer to new centres of production . . . Typically, moreover, people were moved in and out on short-run calculations of profit and convenience, to be left stranded later, in worked-out mining valleys or abandoned textile towns, in old dockyard and shipbuilding areas, in the inner cities themselves, as trade and production moved on in their own interests (Williams 1983, 185).

Our purpose is to make room for a politics of place in regional planning. Although classical doctrine has been extensively criticized from a perspective of political economy (Massey 1974, 1984; Holland 1975; Markusen 1978, forthcoming; Bluestone & Harrison 1982), a fully developed *alternative* doctrine has not yet appeared. One reason for this is the critics' ambiguity about the state as a potential actor. On our part, we strongly wish to affirm a view of regional planning which allows for socially mobilized regional populations to emerge as agents in shaping their own life space. To my knowledge, only Pierre Clavel has so far cogently argued this position (1983).

Before proceeding with our task, we wish to provide some details about what may well be considered a paradigmatic case for a politics of place.

5.2 The politics of place: the case of Quebec Province[1]

Formerly a colony of France, the territory of Quebec Province became, after the military conquest of 1760, a British colony, and in 1867, a province of the Canadian Confederation. Early French-speaking colonists were never assimilated into the dominant culture. To strengthen its hand in its dealings with the rebellious American colonies after the conquest, the British Crown granted the Québécois considerable political and cultural autonomy. Subsequently, the preoccupation of the English settlers with opening the Western frontier, combined with the low spatial mobility of the francophone population, inhibited the blending of the two groups and the formation of a single national culture.

The early ethnic differentiation of the Canadian space, combined with the existence of separate colonial administrations for the other parts of English-speaking Canada, led the fathers of the 1867 confederation to opt for a decentralized union in which ample powers were to be retained by the several provinces, while the federal government was granted only limited jurisdiction. As a result, the francophone population, concentrated in the province of Quebec where they formed the ethnic majority, inherited state institutions that would protect and help perpetuate its distinctive character. Outside their own province, Canadian francophones were greatly outnumbered, both by anglophones (by the late nineteenth century) and later by the other ethnic groups that had arrived in the course of several waves of immigration during the twentieth century. Although the dream of a French Canada "from coast to coast" – that is, the development of large French-speaking settlements throughout Canada – persisted until the 1920s, out of Quebec francophones were a minority with little protection for their culture and language. Only in their own province did francophone Canadians feel completely "at home."[2]

Until the first third of this century, this ethno-territorial allegiance posed little threat to Canadian unity. The federal state was still weak and, in its dealing with the provinces, relatively powerless. Strong ethno-regional differences could be easily accommodated within the confederation. Two series of events gradually changed this state of affairs and contributed to the politicization of regional space: the development and centralization of power at the federal level, and the cultural division of labor created by the "industrialization by invitation" of the Quebec regional economy.

During the 1930s, the federal state began to expand its powers of intervention in order to alleviate massive unemployment and assist the provinces, many of which were faced with virtual bankruptcy. The federal government thus intervened in matters that until then had been considered provincial in the main, and began to conceptualize a national space that would conform to the practice of national planning. In the course of World War II, the federal state apparatus expanded still further and was strengthened by Canada's recognition as an international power of some note. The immediate postwar period was one of rapid industrialization. In parallel with other Western governments, the federal state carried out national policies for economic growth and welfare that led to still further centralization of decision-making power in Ottawa.

The provinces were not uniformly happy with this sequence of events. In Quebec, the Duplessis government, elected (and reelected) on a provincial autonomy platform from 1944 to 1959, contended that the survival of francophone culture and Canada's interethnic harmony depended on continued adherence to the decentralized pattern of power sanctioned by the confederative pact. Quebec's resistance to further centralization was reinforced by the fact that until the mid-1960s, the federal state was run as a unilingual anglophone government from whose higher circles of power francophones were virtually excluded. Given this context, any reinforcement of the federal state (or reduction in provincial powers) was perceived by existing francophone elites as a threat to their own position and provoked what many regarded as the somewhat paranoid rejection by the Duplessis government of all federal programs, however well intentioned, that seemed to encroach on provincial prerogatives. This confrontation between Quebec and Ottawa marks the beginning of a long round of ethnopolitical conflict between two states, which came to see themselves as representing each a different national identity and set of interests.

Before passing on to consider other critical moments of this political struggle, we need to present the second series of events that fueled francophone discontent and helped create a popular basis for a secessionist movement in Quebec. A large rural demographic surplus, a low wage structure, and large reserves of natural resources stimulated two rounds of industrialization in the periods centered on the two world wars. Formerly an agrarian society dominated by professional and religious elites, francophone Quebec lacked an indigenous entrepreneurial bourgeoisie. An Anglo-Canadian bourgeoisie had long established a stronghold on the business and commercial activities of the province, and industrialization involved principally American and English-based companies.

These conditions articulated a class division along ethnic lines. For the thousands of French-speaking farmers' sons and daughters who migrated to the cities, the subordination of one ethnic group by another became more visible, for in the factories where they worked, the bosses were "English" and so was the language in which orders were customarily given. For the educated few, access to command positions in the new industrial order was inhibited both by ethnic discrimination and by lack of capital. And for the provincial trade union and workers' movements, especially during the fifties and sixties, the rising consciousness of class and ethnic exploitation often focused on the same "adversary."

The politicization of regional space by ethnic-territorial movements had as its objective the elimination of the two major sources of oppression: a federal (central) state that, until the 1960s, was run by and for the anglophone majority; and a cultural division of labor in the modern industrial sector.[3] From the 1940s to the present, various ethnopolitical options were proposed and debated within and outside party politics. But a significant shift of strategy – from defensive to offensive – occurred in the early sixties, when a dramatic change in the nature of the francophone political and social leadership took place.

Provincial Prime Minister Duplessis had adopted the defensive strategy of protecting the established constitutional powers of the province against encroachments of the central state. The ruling parties of the sixties and seventies, on the other hand, consistently sought to expand these powers and to develop the interventionist tools of the provincial state. The turning point was Duplessis's death in 1959, the change of ruling party in the following year, and the beginning of a long-awaited round of social, cultural, and political modernization of the province's institutions. This period, generally referred to as the Quiet Revolution (1960–5), was marked by four convergent phenomena: (a) the capture of state power and the exercise of social hegemony by an urban-based, technocratic, and pro-union francophone elite, (b) the secularization of civil society, (c) the modernization of the provincial state apparatus and a marked shift toward state intervention in economic life, and (d) the formulation of an aggressive nationalism which involved a redefinition of francophone collective, territorial identity.

A new generation of ethnic entrepreneurs emerged to replace the high clergy whose support of the Union Nationale had been essential under Duplessis. Recruited from among the urban middle classes whose promotion to economic power in the private sector was inhibited by the English-speaking bourgeoisie, this group of young intellectuals decided to use the state as their institutional base for developing a modern economic sector under francophone control. They proceeded to articulate a double identification which proclaimed their own class interest to be at one with the interest of the French-speaking "nation" and a Quebec nation to be at one with the provincial state. This grand scheme for ethnic emancipation through a state-induced development gained the political support of the trade unions, the petty bourgeoisie, and, of course, the nascent middle sectors who had invented it. Under the successive provincial administrations of the Liberal party (1960–6) and the Union Nationale (1966–70), provincial public expenditures per capita increased by three times, and a host of new public enterprises was established.

But these ethnic entrepreneurs soon found themselves in direct conflict with the real "national" state, the Canadian federal government. The agenda of socio-economic development and reform they had in mind required not only a freer hand for the provincial administration but a significantly larger share of federal revenues as well. The question of relations with the Canadian state thus became the crucial issue. As Milner wrote (1977, p. 112), "Once the Quebec state apparatus became the primary institution of the Quebec nation, the question of political independence and therefore separation from Canada became central."

In 1967–8, Quebec's political class divided on the "national question" and produced the two broad options that in the course of the next twelve years would dominate the political debate: a reformed federalism, or secession and political independence. The Liberal party, which had led the march of the Quiet Revolution, refused to support the separatist option that one of its most prominent leaders, René Lévesque, submitted to the party's convention in 1967. Thus rebuffed, Lévesque quit the Liberals to form his own party where he was soon joined by several other associations supporting independence. In the following year, this coalition became the Parti Québécois which, until recently, openly advocated the political separation of Quebec from Canada and the establishment of an economic association with the remaining members of the confederation. The other parties, led by the Liberals and Union Nationale, in turn proposed one or another version of a revamped federalism that would leave Quebec in the union but renegotiate, in favor of Quebec, the existing provincial–federal distribution of powers.

In a sense, both groups argued for the strengthening of the provincial state. Despite difference in the desired degree of empowerment, and in the tactical means to obtain it, the broad similarity of objectives reflects the widespread consensus that existed at the time for some sort of "politics of place" and for the pursuit of greater regional autonomy. Although non-separatist parties ruled the province until 1976, when for the first time, the Parti Québécois was elected to office, each administration furthered the development of the provincial state and issued policies and programs in relative independence from Ottawa. The tendency to practice what Pierre Clavel calls "opposition planning" became, of course, stronger during the Parti Québécois administration when the provincial and federal levels of government engaged in a costly battle to win the allegiance of the province's francophone voters prior to the 1980 referendum on the national question.

5.3 Propositions concerning the politics of place

The foregoing history of territorial movements in Quebec Province suggests a series of propositions about such movements that may serve as the starting point for a serious research effort into the political economy of regionalism. Although the Quebec case should not be taken as prototypical, it does suggest a number of general hypotheses for exploitation.

(a) Regions as identifiable parts of larger wholes called nations can often be defined in terms of their cultural and historically formed identity. As such, they may also be viewed as centers of collective action. The relevant actors here are regionally based social movements which seek greater freedom of cultural expression, greater political autonomy for their "homeland," and the defense of their "life space" against the threats of encroachment by outside capital.

(b) Regional movements have as an object the politicization of national space; they thrive on an adversary relationship between an "oppressor" state and regionally mobilized populations.

(c) The leadership of regional movements will tend to be recruited primarily from among intellectual and cultural elites that find themselves blocked in their aspirations for influence and power. These elites will attempt to articulate and synthesize the dissatisfactions of a cross-section of their society of reference. For much of their history, regional movements are essentially populist, trans-class movements with shifting alliances. Nevertheless, class antagonisms are never entirely submerged and, during different phases of the movement, different class fractions may aspire to its leadership.

(d) In terms of their social and economic agenda, contemporary regional movements typically seek endogenous forms of development – a development "from within." They tend to stress the revitalization of cultural forms of expression, the full and equitable use of regional resources, and political autonomy in setting priorities for investment.

(e) National states may adopt different strategies via-à-vis a regional movement. They may attempt to ignore it, to destroy it, to coopt it, or to accommodate to it. Regardless of outcome, however, regional social movements will tend to persist as a historical expression of territorially based cultural diversity.

(f) Contemporary regional movements typically pass through several phases that may be characterized, chronologically, as follows:

   (i) Building a regional consciousness and sense of collective identity.
   (ii) Social mobilization around an agenda of increased political (territorial) autonomy and self-reliant socio-economic development.
   (iii) If the movement is successful, and its agenda has become institutionalized, social mobilization will tend to "cool off," even as the regional economy comes to be more fully articulated with the dominant structures of the national and world economies. Newly gained political power, however, will tend to be used to set a distinctive agenda for territorial development and to use central bureaucratic planning as an instrument of intervention. But if the movement is repressed by the state and fails to reach its objectives, it is likely to go "underground," perhaps to resurface at some future time.
   (iv) With the institutionalization of the movement and its accommodation to its economic and political environment, class conflict will reemerge as a major form of social dynamics in the region, and the region itself may undergo a process of further spatial differentiation and uneven development.

These hypotheses trace what we might call the natural history of regional movements. They fail, however, to explain why regional movements arise in some areas and not in others. In the United States, for instance, the evidence for regional movement is scarce. Does this mean that the United States has no culturally defined regions? Does the existing federal system adequately reflect regional interests? Or is the Americanization process so effective that America's population has failed to identify itself with specific locales? These questions, and many others like them, fascinating as they are, remain on the agenda, and not only in the United States. They cannot be treated in the present paper.

5.4 Implications for the practice of regional planning

Regional planning has traditionally been seen as a form of direct intervention in market processes by the state. Since the 1930s, such planning has been concerned primarily with national policies for the spatial allocation of resources and for plans and programs to promote the development of specific regions through corporate entities such as river basin authorities. In both cases, planning was seen as a bureaucratic device for achieving national objectives under the direct control of central state power. Regional planning was political only in the sense that it had to be articulated with power-holders in the regions affected. This frequently involved processes of social cooptation (Selznick 1949), whereby either national planners were "captured" by regional economic interests, or the latter were "bought off" by the national institution.

In recent years, however, under the new market dispensation, such planning has dramatically declined. In advanced capitalist countries, the focus of attention has shifted to large metropolitan areas that function as world centers of accumulation and control (Friedmann & Wolff 1982, Friedmann, 1986).

This shift in focal attention, however, has been accompanied in many countries by the resurgence of an intense regional politics, or *politics of place*, rooted in social movements of the type we have discussed. This new politics is abetted in part by the state's inability to successfully defend regional populations from the ravages of an anarchic market, from the devastating effects of the current phase of capital restructuring, and from the extraordinary concentration of resources in the principal centers of global accumulation.

It originates in regions that characteristically are not among the poorest of a given country. Contrary to assertions in classical planning doctrine, regional inequality is not the *primium mobile* of regional politics. When we look for contemporary examples of such a politics, we find old industrial regions threatened by current restructuring (such as the Basque Country and Catalonia in Spain, Switzerland's Jura region, Wallonia in Belgium, and Wales in the United Kingdom); regions of recent industrialization or new mineral wealth hoping for a breakthrough into the global economy on regional terms (such as Flanders (Belgium), Quebec (Canada), Scotland (United Kingdom), and, in the United States, Puerto Rico) and regions that are the life space of severely oppressed ethnic populations in otherwise prosperous countries (such as Palestinians in the Israeli-occupied West Bank, the black people of South Africa, Aborigines in Australia, and Native Americans in both Canada and the United States).[4]

Neoclassical in inspiration, regional planning doctrine has so far ignored a politics of place. Instead it talks of the mobility of capital (money) and labor. But the mobility of capital turns out to be far greater than that of men and women, and when capital moves away from a region leaving a redundant labor force behind, a regional problem is posed. The traditional way of coping with this situation is to petition the national government for help. But in recent years, governments have not been responsive to such calls. In a decision between the interests of capital and people, states tends to lean in the direction of the former. They will argue the case for moving people to the sites of the new economic growth, a policy that will leave everyone "better off" in the end.

Such arguments ignore the social costs that moving people to jobs entails. Not everybody who loses a job can be reemployed elsewhere. More importantly, the social fabric of a community is destroyed if too many people are forced to abandon their homes or are left dependent on welfare. People's savings and investments are forfeited. What was once a flourishing town becomes yet another gully in the "rust belt." Along with their homes, people's hopes are destroyed. The disaster is multifaceted.

What sort of planning, then, can be proposed for regions where a politics of place has relevance? The old economistic model proves to be of little use to us. Its trump card, in practice, was investment in growth poles and growth centers but, for the most part, growth poles didn't work. The planners' client was the state; their ally, capital. In contrast to this model, what might the planners' role be in a politics of place, where people themselves are mobilized for action?

Admittedly, we still lack experience here; even more, we lack knowledge of the relevant experience. Some knowledge based on the specific case of Quebec will soon become available (Forest, forthcoming), but for the rest, we have to put together a picture of a possible planning based, for the most part, on "creative imagination." Here, then, are a few pointers for a planning allied to a politics of place and territorial movements.

(a) Where the state is no longer the principal actor, a new kind of planning process is required, based on social learning (Friedmann 1973, 1985a). In social learning, the basic relationship here between planner and client is one of dialogue. The style is participatory and experimental.

(b) Territorial movements are engaged in a political struggle, and planning must become politically engaged. It must become, in Pierre Clavel's words, "opposition planning," (Clavel 1983). In opposition planning, planners are less involved in policy analysis and design than in inventing, bargaining, and negotiating solutions.

(c) In a politics of place, what is fundamentally at stake is people's livelihood (Williams 1983). This is an embracing concept that includes qualitative as well as quantitative aspects. It looks to alternative work organization where capital is unable to provide the necessary jobs, is as mindful of cultural developments as it is of regional production, and values regional resources, including those of landscape and environment, because it looks to the development of a territorial base in perpetuity. Importantly, it is also a politics of resource redistribution to provide the collective facilities without which the self-production of life is impossible.

(d) In the politics of place, planning looks to an endogenous development (Friedmann 1985b). That means a primary, though not exclusive, reliance on regional resources, and particularly on the resources of civil society, that is to say, on the self-organizing capacity of people (Carnoy & Shearer 1980; Williams 1983; Dahl 1985). Territorially oriented planning emphasizes such still-novel forms of people-centered organization as production cooperatives (Oakeshott 1978).

These are some general indicators of direction. When, as in Quebec, the territorial movement accedes to power, the situation changes once again. Planning then returns to being predominantly statist, and popular movements are less likely to flourish for a while. The politics of place, however, is more powerful than even an interventionist state. It comes into being primarily because of a failure by state and capital to provide adequately for people's livelihood. And that may be the case even where the state, as in Quebec Province, is a regional state.

Notes

1 This section is based, in part, on the following literature: Fortin 1980; Guindon 1964; Hamelin et al. 1976; Heintzman 1983; Latouche 1974; Milner 1977; Monière 1977; Postgate & McRoberts 1976; and Quinn 1979.
2 Ancient francophone settlements have survived in the Maritime Provinces (the Acadians), Ontario and Manitoba, and have enjoyed a significant cultural revival since the federal policy of bilingualism–biculturalism in the late 1960s established parity between the two languages.
3 J. L. Granatstein, in his book on the federal bureaucracy (1982), notes that very few francophones had been hired to fill power positions in the central bureaucracy before the late 1950s. Another, more famous political figure, former Canadian Prime Minister Pierre Elliott Trudeau has long decried the

underrepresentation of francophones in federal institutions, and what he called the unilingual-anglophone image of the Canadian government (Trudeau 1968).

4 The politics of place is especially strong in many of the multiethnic states of the Third World. For the most part a creation of the post World War II era, these states are still relatively weak and do not enjoy the kind of institutional legitimacy that older states do. The result is that most regional conflicts in the periphery of world capitalism quickly degenerate into physical violence and war. Dramatic examples include: East Pakistan (now Bangladesh), Indonesia (West Irian), Iran (Kurdistan), the Philippines, Sudan, Ethiopia, Namibia, Nigeria (Biafra), Sri Lanka and India (Punjab). The case of the Central American countries (El Salvador, Nicaragua, Guatemala) might also be mentioned in this connection. These states are, in effect, regions within the far-flung American empire, and their efforts at declaring themselves independent of US power have embroiled them in a prolonged armed conflict with the United States and its regional allies.

References

Bluestone, B. & B. Harrison 1982. *The deindustrialization of America*. New York: Basic Books.
Boudeville, J. R. 1961. *Les espaces économiques*. Paris: Presses universitaires de France.
Carnoy, M. & D. Shearer 1980. *Economic democracy: the challenge of the 1980s*. White Plains, N.Y.: M. E. Sharpe.
Clavel, P. 1983. *Opposition planning in Wales and Appalachia*. Philadelphia: Temple University Press.
Dahl, R. 1985. *A preface to economic democracy*. Berkeley: University of California Press.
Forest, Y. forthcoming. Ph.D. dissertation, University of California, Los Angeles.
Fortin, G. 1980. Les transformations du pouvoir, 1960–1980. In ASCALF (Colloque 1979), *La transformation du pouvoir au Québec*. Laval: Editions coopérative Albert Saint-Martin.
Friedmann, J. 1956. The concept of a planning region. *Land Economics* 32, 1–13.
Friedmann, J. 1966. *Regional development policy: a case study of Venezuela*. Cambridge, Mass.: MIT Press.
Friedmann, J. 1972. A general theory of polarized development. In Hansen (1972).
Friedmann, J. 1973. *Retracking America: a theory of transactive planning*. Garden City, N.Y.: Doubleday/Anchor; reprinted, with new preface, by Rodale Press, 1981.
Friedmann, J. 1985a. *Planning in the public domain: critique and reconstruction* (manuscript).
Friedmann, J. 1985b. Auto-développement ou auto-dépendance. In *Redéploiment industriel et planification régionale*, M. Boisvert & P. Hamel (eds.), 289–300. Montréal: Faculté de l'aménagement. (Orig. in English, 1982.)
Friedmann, J. 1986. The world city hypothesis, forthcoming in *Development and Change* 17: 1 (January), 69–83.
Friedmann, J. & B. Stuckey 1973. The territorial basis of national transportation planning. In *Perspectives on regional transportation planning*, J. S. De Salvo (ed.), Lexington, Mass.: Lexington Books.

Friedmann, J. & G. Wolff 1982. World city formation: an agenda for research and action. *International Journal for Urban and Regional Research* **6**, 309–44.

Granatstein, J. L. 1982. *The Ottawa men: the civil service mandarins, 1935–1957*. Toronto: Oxford University Press.

Guindon, H. 1964. Social unrest, social class and Quebec's bureaucratic revolution. *Queen's Quarterly* **71**: 2 (Spring), 150–62.

Hamelin, Jean et al. 1976. *Histoire du Québec*, publié sous la direction de Jean Hamelin. Montréal: Edouard Privet.

Hansen, N. M. (ed.) 1972. *Growth centers in regional economic development*. New York: Free Press.

Heintzman, R. 1983. The political culture of Quebec, 1840–1960. *Canadian Journal of Political Science* **16** (1) (March), 3–59.

Hirschman, A. O. 1958. *The strategy of economic development*. New Haven: Yale University Press.

Holland, S. 1975. *Capital versus the regions*. London: Macmillan.

Isard, W. 1956. *Location and space economy*. Cambridge, Mass.: MIT Press.

Latouche, D. 1974. La vrai (sic) nature de la Révolution Tranquille. *Canadian Journal of Political Science* **7** (3) (September), 525–36.

Markusen, A. R. 1978. Regionalism and the capitalist state: the case of the United States. *Kapitalstate* **7**, 39–62.

Markusen, A. R. forthcoming, *The politics of regions*. Totowa, N. J.: Rowman & Allenheld.

Massey, D. B. 1974. *Towards a critique of industrial location theory*. London: Centre for Environmental Studies.

Massey, D. B. 1984. *Spatial divisions of labour: social structures and the geography of production*. London: Macmillan.

Milner, H. 1977. The decline and fall of the Quebec liberal regime: contradictions in the modern Quebec State. In *The Canadian state: political economy and political power*, Leo Panitch (ed.), 101–32. Toronto: University of Toronto Press.

Monière, D. 1977. *Le Développement des idéologies au Québec des origines à nos jours*. Montréal: Editions Québec-Amérique.

Myrdal, G. 1957. *Economic theory and underdeveloped regions*. London: Duckworth.

Oakeshott, R. 1978. *The case for workers' co-ops*. London: Routledge & Kegan Paul.

Perroux, F. 1950. Economic space: theory and applications. *Quarterly Journal of Economics* **64**, 90–7.

Postgate, D. & K. McRoberts 1976. *Quebec, social change and political crisis*. Toronto: McClelland & Steward.

Quinn, H. F. 1979. *The Union Nationale: Quebec nationalism from Duplessis to Levesque*. Toronto: University of Toronto Press.

Rokkan, S. & D. W. Urwin (eds.) 1982. *The politics of territorial identity: studies in European regionalism*. Beverly Hills, Calif.: Sage Publications.

Rostow, W. W. 1961. *The stages of economic growth: a non-communist manifesto*. Cambridge, Mass.: Harvard University Press.

Sandercock, L. 1985. The importance of place and a politics of place: from Wollongong to Bondi Beach. Paper presented to the Place and Place-Making Conference, Melbourne, June 1985.

Selznick, P. 1949. *TVA and the grass roots: a study in the sociology of formal organization*. Berkeley: University of California Press.

Trudeau, P. E. 1968. *Federalism and the French Canadians*. Toronto: Macmillan.

Williams, R. 1983. *The year 2000*. New York: Pantheon.

6

Population and regional development

WILLIAM ALONSO

Modern academic thinking on regional development, and the welter of policies which have reflected it in the past decades, has proceeded primarily from an economic perspective. Although it has taken many forms, it is economic in the sense of focusing on the processes of material production and exchange under rather restrictive assumptions, which usually remain implicit. Recent thinking about regional development, at least in the mainstream, has not paid much attention to culture, institutions, historical processes, international relations, or – and this is the subject of this essay – the population factor. By the population factor I do not mean merely the demographic dynamics of a region, although these are usually simplified down to caricatures in most models of regional development. I mean as well the international differentiation of populations by age, by ethnicity, by sex, by attitude and education, and by any other ways which affect their capacity to contribute differentially to regional development. Most modern approaches to regional policy, especially those which are academically based, slight the population factor. They deal with people as a generic entity, without considering their intrinsic differentiations and dynamics. I think this is a weakness in our approaches, both for intellectual and policy purposes.

In this essay I shall sketch three aspects of the population factor which seem to me important for regional development. These are the non-homogeneity of populations, the nature of migration, and the quality of populations. I shall not attempt to offer, because I cannot, ways in which these could be introduced into the existing models of regional development, especially into the more formal ones. More can be done than has been done in this respect, but my raising these issues here is in the hope that they may be increasingly and more effectively incorporated into the consideration of policy as complements, not substitutes, to the dominant models.

6.1 Large regional models, demometrics, and group differences within populations

There is a surprisingly large number of models in North America which try to predict local and regional economies and populations into the distant future. Some are privately and some are publicly produced, and some are privately produced for public clients. Most of them are, when the feathers and rhinestones are stripped off, crude extrapolations; but many are quite complex mathematical-statistical machines, based on admittedly simplified adaptations of theory and different one from another, but apparently representing various points along the production frontier of what today is possible in such modeling.

I had a chance, a half-dozen years ago, to review in detail most of the major models which existed at that time. They tended to fall into the poles of being purely demographic or purely economic. The purely demographic ones, such as the illustrative projections produced by the US Bureau of the Census, merely extrapolated by applying some current rate (such as survivorship or migration) or a modification of it to existing populations; even the extraordinarily detailed demometric models of Andrei Rogers and his associates at IIASA (International Institute for Advanced Systems Analysis) are, in the end, simple Markovian models in which the transition rates are independent among rows. Thus, in such models it makes no difference for the number of people going from A to B how many other people from other origins are also going to B, or how many people are leaving B. Neither does it make any difference what is happening to the economy of A, or B, or anywhere else.

At the other extreme there are the models which, with greater or lesser elaboration, try to forecast the economic activity of a region or a set of regions, either unconditionally or conditionally as in certain policy models. In the pure case of such models, which are (whatever the bells and whistles) variants of the economic base model, regional population simply adjusts to the regional economy. In these models the population is most often derived by calculating the aggregate number of workers needed according to the projected regional economy and then multiplying this by an estimated ratio of population to workers. It is assumed that the region's net migration will be just such as to produce this result. In interregional models it often happens that the aggregate of regional populations obtained in this way is not consistent with a credible projection of the national population. In this case some iterative procedures are introduced, with no appreciable basis in theory, to force the aggregate of regional populations to conform to a national total. A few models are hybrids, in that a demographic model is developed in parallel to an economic model, but even in these the reconciliation of the two for consistency is done by numerical brute force of iteration without either much theory or parametrization of the implied behavior. There is, simply put, no explicit theory of the migratory behavior, or of the rates of labor force participation, which would underly the adjustments.

These economic models, in brief, are pull or labor-demand driven models, with scant if any consideration given to the dynamics of labor supply. By contrast the purely demographic models are push- or supply-driven, with no consideration given to labor demand.

It is clear that in the real world there will be an interaction of supply and demand through their elasticities. One may go further and say that these elasticities are unlikely to be universal parameters, like Plank's constant, but rather will vary over time and from place to place. For instance, one would expect that when labor markets are tight jobs will chase people more avidly than when the economy is slack, and that the opposite will hold for people chasing jobs. And, from an extensive literature on migration, we may expect that the migration behavior of one region will differ from that of another according to their populations' educational level, age composition, proportion of recent immigrants, and ethnicity, among other variables. Yet, to my knowledge, except for age in a few cases, none of these variables are expressed in the models. Thus, while on the economic side there is always some and sometimes a great deal of industrial disaggregation, the demographic side is treated at an extreme level of aggregation.

I will offer here some illustrations of the importance of population differentiation for regional modeling in general and for policy-oriented modeling in particular.

Consider, first, the common assumption that a region's population (and hence labor force) adjustments will be made through a combination of migration and natural increase. In many models this is stated explicitly as an identity which, in its reduced form amounts to

change in labor force = (participation rate) × (change in population)
                    = (participation rate) × (natural increase + net migration)

This clearly is a poor approximation, for the participation rate of migrants is highly unlikely to be the same as that of natural increase. In most cases, the gain or loss to the labor force per migrant will be high and immediate, since migration is concentrated in the prime ages of labor force participation. The new births of natural increase, on the other hand, will not enter the labor force for twenty or so years, while under today's life expectancies most of those dying will have left the labor force some years earlier. For the purpose at hand, therefore, a better measure than natural increase would be the difference between, say, the 20–24 and the 60–64-year-old cohorts. This may differ significantly from natural increase because of past migration and differences and changes in fertility. Thus, within our lifetimes, Quebec's fertility has gone from very high to very low, while in the United States the oscillations of fertility of the baby boom and bust differed markedly among states.

To my knowledge, most regional models have not paid much attention either to the possible changes in the labor force participation rate, which is the other argument in the above equation. This seems a doubtful procedure, given the remarkable changes which have been occurring. In the United States, for instance, the overall participation rate rose from 59.4% in 1960 to 64.6% in 1984; this 8.8% rise in the overall participation rate of the population consists of a drop of 8.2% in the rate for men and a rise of 43.0% in the rate for women during this period. Using a single participation rate (even if trended or otherwise temporally adjusted) seems a dangerous simplification when its components are so variable.

Sex is only one of the forms of differentiation within the population, of course. Others include age, race and ethnicity, language, general and job-specific human capital, and legal status of immigrants. Many failures can be documented resulting from policies based on undifferentiated aggregate labor demand as the key variable without recognition of important variations on the supply side. For instance, there have been cases (as in the Mezzogiorno and in the American Southwest) where efforts were made to attract high-skill high-wage industries to regions with high unemployment but low skill levels. When and if such industries arrived, they tended to import their workers, while any multiplier-related benefits for the original inhabitants were vitiated by local inflation and the disruption of such local economic activity as small retail and petty industry. In other cases, such as currently in the Pacific Northwest, an effort is being made to compensate for the decline of the traditional logging industry by developing tourism. While in a depressed region it is probably better to have tourism than not to have it, it seems highly unlikely that this will provide much employment for unemployed loggers.

I am quite aware that it is impossible to incorporate the full complexity of population structure and characteristics into formal models, although more is possible than is done. My point is, rather, that the models, both as formal instruments and in the type of thinking they foster, are rather blunt instruments; policy would be better served if their limitations were more clearly recognized, and their undoubted usefulness were supplemented by greater awareness of the context in specific cases. Particularly for programs guided by equity objectives, use of an undifferentiated population is likely to confuse (to use Louis Winnick's phrase) "place prosperity" for "people prosperity"; that is to say, that even when they succeed in generating regional development, they may miss the populations they set out to help.

6.2 Migration, regional policy, and the new economic fundamentalism

Traditional approaches to regional planning are being challenged in Canada, the United States, and in several other of the developed countries by a fresh conviction that almost any attempt at policy intervention will be not only ineffective but also counterproductive. This across the board criticism is based on a faith that market processes will produce results which are efficient and, in the long run, equitable. Is there unemployment in a region? Let its people move to where the jobs are. Are wages low here? Capital will move in to take advantage of cheap labor, productivity will rise, and in time wages will rise to the levels prevailing elsewhere. In short, this challenge to traditional planning is based on a belief in the invisible hand, where the sectoral and the geographic mobility of the factors of production will bring about, at least within a nation-state, that best of all possible worlds where equity and efficiency are both maximized. This non-interventionist criticism of regional planning (and of almost any other public action) I shall call "the new economic fundamentalism."

It is not my purpose in this essay to take issue with or support the new fundamentalism as a general proposition. Rather I want to look at the mobility of one particular factor, labor, and its implications for regional policy.

The standard economic literature on migration has usually relied on the idea that people move from one place to another because it is to their advantage to do so. The particular forms of this calculation vary from one author to another, but basically they hold that, other things being equal, the move is made for material advantage. Thus, the typical econometric investigation of migration will look for its independent variables at wage differentials (perhaps adjusted by cost of living), at unemployment, at the cost of moving, and perhaps at some others such as local climate. The overwhelming evidence from all these studies is consistent with the basic notion that economic reasons are important for migration, although they are not the only ones.

This general finding of the social science literature is consistent with the new economic fundamentalism's view of market processes: if jobs are scarce and wages low in one place and abundant and high in another, people will vote with their feet going one way (and presumably capital by transfers the other way) eventually bringing the system into an optimizing equilibrium. But the new fundamentalism generally subscribes to a further tenet, which is that, at least in relatively free economies such as those of the United States and Canada, current prices are the best available approximation to market prices, in spite of externally imposed distortions. This view has, in the past dozen years, produced a lively literature on "urban disamenities" which has had some importance for cost–benefit evaluation of programs of environmental improvement, crime reduction, and the like, and which seems to me to raise interesting questions for regional policy in general.

The "urban disamenities" theory goes thus: We live in societies in which it is very easy to move, and we presume that economic man will move to maximize the value of his human capital and other endowments. Under a regime of free mobility, the market will insure that comparable people at different locations will receive the same returns to their labor and human capital.

But in fact we observe not only that comparable people receive different monetary returns at different locations, but that differences in monetary income persist after adjustment is made for such obvious considerations as cost of living and unemployment. How can this be? The fundamentalist view says, in effect, that real income *must* be everywhere the same (or nearly so); therefore, the remaining observed differences in monetary income (after adjustment for cost of living, etc.) must be a measure of shadow wages for non-monetary income or costs in the form of public goods or bads which the worker experiences at that location. For the sake of illustration, one might say that price-adjusted wages in a large city are higher than in a smaller city because industry needs to pay extra compensation (disamenity premiums) to attract workers who have to put up with more congestion, crime, and pollution. Following this logic, some scholars have regressed the differences in price-adjusted wages for comparable labor at various locations against "bads" (such as congestion, pollution, and crime) and "goods" (such as good climate, symphony orchestras and winning baseball teams) to estimate the hedonic prices of these environmental factors. These prices have then been used to calculate the value of modifying such public goods or bads in cost–benefit analysis of such programs as crime suppression. This set of concepts and techniques is interesting if problematic, but such cost–benefit applications are not the concern in this essay.

What is interesting for our purposes is what acceptance of the "disamenities" theory would imply for migration and for regional policy. If the material rewards were everywhere the same for comparable labor, workers would have no economic reason for moving. There might be considerable migration, but it would be based on non-economic motives, such as life-stage moves associated with marriage, fleeing of in-laws, family reunion, retirement, and so on. There might also be economically based migration for individual career advancement, but such moves would cancel out overall. In normal times migration would then be, in economic terms, essentially random noise, and its efficiency (one half of the sum of absolute regional net migrations divided by total gross migrations) would be effectively zero. Econometric studies which tried to explain migration patterns in terms of money-wage differentials would fail to produce significant coefficients because of the omission of the compensatory environmental or shadow-wage variables. Equity-oriented policies aimed at reducing differences in price-adjusted wages would be not only inefficient but indeed regressive because they would increase rather than reduce income inequality.

But the fact is that the empirical literature on migration shows that differences in money wages, even after adjustments, are statistically significant variables for explaining migration streams. This means that, although money wages may not represent real incomes exactly, they capture enough of real income differences to serve as proxies. More to the point this means that real incomes are not everywhere the same, or even nearly so, contrary to the fundamentalist tenet that the system is sufficiently near to equilibrium that current prices (including shadow prices) are the best approximation to those which would obtain under a totally free market.

How can it be that differences in real wages continue to exist in an advanced society, where there is ample information and freedom of movement? Having rejected on the evidence the proposition that the differences in real wages is merely an illusion produced by the omission of non-money income, we have to come to terms with their reality. The fundamentalist position would fall back to arguing that such differences as may exist are either lags in adjustment to exogenous shocks, or the result of misguided policies, or both, so that the policy solution is to stand aside and let the market take its course. This would result, according to this view, not only in greater efficiency but also by definition in greater equality since real incomes would converge.

By contrast, various other strains of thinking about regional planning and the economic geography of nations emphasize the limits of market mechanisms, holding that either they take unendurably long to deliver on their promise, or that perverse situations frequently cause it to produce perverse results. In such views intervention is needed either to bring about directly some desired results, or to help the market break out of vicious circles so that it can go on with its work.

In my view the existence and persistence of substantial geographic real wage differentials indicates that the new fundamentalism cannot be totally right in this area of policy, that something – whatever it may be – has prevented the cybernetics of the market from functioning as the fundamentalists believe it should. Therefore, I believe there are grounds for believing that certain forms of policy intervention might be useful for equity and for efficiency, and for rejecting a blanket recommendation that the best policy would be not to intervene at all. On the other hand, the long and mostly sorry record of regional policies, so often voluntaristic, suggests that it is not clear what form such policies should take. And in this respect I find that the new fundamentalism often provides invaluable criticism of unreflecting interventionism.

6.3 Magic, regional development, and population quality

During the Second World War, natives of some Pacific islands saw the arrival of American troops. The Americans cleared and leveled an oblong piece of the jungle, set lights along the edges, and lo! after a while a giant silver bird arrived, bearing all manner of valuable things. This gave rise to a cargo cult among the natives, who, having seen what the Americans had done to attract the silver bird, similarly set about clearing portions of the jungle and then waited by their fires, patiently and reverently, for the arrival of the bird.

In practice, much regional policy resembles these cargo cults. In regions where it wishes to attract economic development, it designates industrial zones, builds some infrastructure, institutes some tax advantages, and then waits for the silver bird of industry. Little is known of where the mysterious bird may come from, but everything must be done to attract it. Sometimes it comes, but more often it does not. This style of planning for regional development, mechanistic in its instruments, thinks magically about outcomes. If the gods are propitiated, they may award gifts which the tribe itself cannot produce.

A quite different type of magical regional development planning has emerged in recent years in nations as different as the United States and China under labels such as "enterprise zones." In designated areas the incubus of governmental overregulation is to be exorcised, and the people there, their minds and energies freed from that demon's oppression, will burst forth entrepreneurially, bringing wealth and riches to themselves and their neighbors. The good "magic of the market," freed from the bad magic of stifling controls, will produce the horn of plenty.

I imagine that the appropriateness and effectiveness of either approach will vary from case to case, and that in many cases neither will be relevant. In portraying them as I have in the last paragraphs, my purpose was not to judge them as policy strategies, but to remind us of how crucial to the concept of regional development is the role which the local population can play in it. The two forms of magic expect very different behavior from the population. In the cargo cult magic the population at large plays a passive role, except for the functionaries who prepare the runway. If economic activity comes, the people will provide the labor, but the organization of economic activity comes from the outside. In the exorcising magic, the role of the population is quite different: they are to provide not only the labor, but the energy and the imagination to organize and indeed conceive economic activity. In the cargo cult the motor of development is exogenous; in the exorcism of the incubus and the magic of the market, it is endogenous.

A key question for either model, of course, is the kind of people involved. What is their culture, what are their institutions, what is their environment? General and economic historians have raised such questions in trying to account for phenomena such as Europe's economic revival in the eleventh century, the rise of the Dutch Republic, the English agricultural and industrial revolutions, and Japan's and now Korea's and Taiwan's rapid industrialization. On the other side of the ledger, Max Weber, for instance tried to explain China's failure to industrialize and develop economically in spite of its intellectual and technological accomplishments by reference to what he called "the Asiatic mode of production."

My reading of this literature is amateurish, of course, but it is my firm impression that, while the best accounts and analyses of each case are richly informative and convincing, they are ad hoc and that no general theory of development is available. Further, these interpretative histories are almost exclusively framed at the level of nations or their contemporary equivalents, and so are of limited help to those concerned with subnational, regional development. Why is it that Catalonia and the Basque country were Spain's leading regions in development? Why is Cartagena renowned for entrepreneurship in Colombia? Why did

Wichita rise in the midst of Kansas's cornfields as a production center for light aviation and sporting goods? Why did the Chinese, who did not achieve economic development in China, become so extraordinarily successful overseas?

Questions in this range seem to me to deal with the *quality* of the population. (Just to be clear, I am not referring to genetic quality, but to the culture and institutions which form individuals and families and within which they operate). Why is it that some people in some locations do generate development, while others elsewhere, often having more generous access to resources, do not?

The brothers Weber, Max and Alfred, who wrote in the early decades of this century, serve to illustrate the basic question. Max Weber, the sociologist, used social concepts, such as Protestantism or the role of bureaucracies, to account for various paths of development. His brother, Alfred Weber the economist, used such concepts as ideal weights and the minimizing of transport costs to account for the location of industry. Max's explanation was endogenous, Alfred's exogenous. Max's explanation relies on the inner fires, Alfred's on comparative advantage. Max dealt with qualitative aspects, Alfred with quantitative. In terms of the two types of magic, Max's thinking relates to exorcising magic, Alfred's to the cargo cult.

The technical literature and technically based policy in regional development traces its principal line of descent to Alfred Weber's branch of social science. It is positivistic and goal oriented, and rejects the qualitative as unmeasurable. It stresses multipliers, marginal and comparative advantages, and the like. This style of analysis has been greatly aided in recent decades by the joining of theory with mathematical formalism, and the availability of quantitative economic data together with extraordinary developments in statistical technique and computational power.

This style of analysis and planning is valuable for questions of location and growth, but it is silent on the question of development in the sense of technical, social and institutional innovation. There are, within what may be called regional science, literatures and theories of innovation diffusion, of cities as seed-beds of innovation, of product cycles, but these are not truly incorporated to the main body of planning practice. This can be seen not only in the absence of any theoretical or empirical bases for the proposed enterprise zones other than faith in a liberated entrepreneurial zeal. It can be seen as well, in North America and in Europe, in the other great fashion of the times in regional development: the pursuit of high tech and the encouragement of innovation. One can be critical of such approaches for their lack of developed theory and empirical support, but one must recognize the importance of developmental processes and how little current regional science has to offer in this respect.

Consider, for instance, the case of Quebec, a province traditionally poorer than Canadian averages. Some years ago its economy suffered some setbacks as French separatism caused the flight of some people and enterprises. But it is a province which is now performing better economically than before, at least in its major urban region. The most interesting aspect of its transformation has been the social one, as evidenced by a stunning decline of its fertility and the career shift of educated French Canadians from the public to the private sector. The social transformation which this evidences, whatever its causes, is certain to have deeper long-term consequences for this province for its development than all of the explicitly regional federal programs.

Regional theory has reached great sophistication in a certain type of analysis, and can assist greatly in certain types of regional policy. But it has chosen to limit itself to Alfred Weber-type problems, and in so doing it has eschewed the social and institutional aspects of development of the Max Weber type, so that it can offer little guidance for policy in this regard.

Would it not be possible to direct more thinking and systematic research in the direction of the social aspects of regional development, at the sources of and obstacles to the endogenous contribution to regional development? Can we go beyond anecdotes to useful generalizations about what I have called the quality of the population? Although I am not certain, I think we can, and that it is important that we try, so that policy can be better informed by both types of knowledge.

7
A review of techniques for regional policy analysis

HARRY RICHARDSON

There have been hundreds of papers written about the tools of regional analysis and policy in the past 20 years.[1] It is impossible to discuss these comprehensively within the space of one relatively brief paper. Accordingly, a few organizing principles may be helpful in selecting the techniques to be discussed and how much attention to give to each. First, the paper looks at existing tools rather than inventing new ones, though some space will be given to relatively recent developments such as qualitative impact analysis and VAR (Vector Auto-Regression) and similar time-series forecasting methods. Second, techniques are primarily analyzed in a policy-related context. However, the relevance of techniques to policy is defined broadly. For example, forecasting techniques are considered relevant because knowing what the future is likely to be helps to determine the need for intervention and its degree. The other, more direct policy issues to be discussed are policy choice (how to select among alternatives) and policy evaluation (the monitoring and assessment of past policies in order to make improvements in the future). Third, the Canadian situation is kept in mind as the appropriate background context. This implies a developed country where regional disparities are sizeable, and where conflicts of interest may arise between national (e.g., federal) and subnational (e.g., provincial) governments and among the subnational governments themselves. Finally, some emphasis is given in the discussion to the problem highlighted in the title of this meeting, that is, whether there is a trade-off or complementarity between regional development and national economic growth.

7.1 Economic base models

In spite of a battery of criticisms over many years, economic base models have nevertheless continued to receive some research attention in recent years, partly because of new studies on the measurement of the base, partly because of their incorporation in regional econometric models (their appeal being a direct link from the national economy to the region within a standard macroeconometric framework). Even so, they have less merit than nonsurvey input–output models which are not much more difficult to construct. The two most common methods of measuring the base are variants of the location quotient method and the minimum requirements method. Less familiar methods are the assignment method (well known but little used); the Mathur–Rosen econometric method (Mathur & Rosen 1974); the industry export share approach, which uses regression methods to determine export shares at the state level as a function of agglomeration economies, relative wages, weight–value ratios and other locational factors (Stevens et al. 1980); and the census survey method (Gibson & Worden 1981). In spite of improvements with the location quotient method, it still flounders on its inability to correct for cross-hauling. Moore's regression approach to minimum requirements (Moore 1975) is simple and fast, but it depends upon the assumption that the export share is an inverse function of population and invariant with economic structure; it fails miserably in regions with highly specialized (i.e. export-oriented) economic structures.

Recent extensions of economic base models move outside the standard Keynesian or input–output framework. One approach is to apply the concept to a central place hierarchy; it can be shown (Thompson 1983) that the economic base multiplier is a special case of the central place multiplier and that multipliers tend to be larger in high-order central places (though this result depends on the sectoral mix). Another is to introduce space explicitly; economic base multiplier impacts decay over distance negative exponentially (Richardson & Gordon 1978).

There is little in the recent research on economic base models to increase confidence in them. A nonsurvey input–output model can be constructed with not much greater effort, and even if its multipliers are not much more accurate, they generate more useful information for regional policy makers and planners, provided it is treated cautiously. The census method of measuring the economic base is promising, but again a "mongrel" input–output table with survey information for key sectors can be developed for a similar cost.

7.2 Input–output models

Of all the tools available to the regional policy maker, regional and interregional input models remain the most widely used. Research over the past 20 years suggests that survey-based models are most acceptable but are too costly, nonsurvey models and other short-cuts are cheap but are inaccurate except as first approximations, and that the future lies with "hybrid" or "mongrel" models which mix survey and nonsurvey techniques and/or which simplify the tables via sectoral aggregation or (within a multiregional context) via spatial aggregation. The summary here draws upon the conclusions reached in Richardson (1985).

This sweeping conclusion needs some modification. Even nonsurvey methods which have been described as "doomed at conception" (Jensen & Macdonald 1982, p. 35) might benefit from simultaneous modification of national to regional input coefficients (i.e. converting a_{ij}^n to a_{ij}^r) and estimation of $t_{ij} a_{ij}^r$, where t_{ij} is the share of requirements of commodity i by sector j supplied locally. Moreover, there are some prospects for estimating the t_{ij}'s using existing (or simulated) interregional commodity flow data; the regional purchase coefficient (RPC) method is promising in this respect (Stevens et al. 1983). Unfortunately, the U.S. Census of Transportation is abandoning the collection of much of its interregional trade flow data.

Although the construction of many survey-based models will be ruled out on cost grounds, the research results on aggregation suggest that the survey approach may be salvaged by aggregation methods, especially by the identification of key sectors and the aggregation of others into broad sectoral groups. In any event, a few more survey models are needed, regardless of their cost. In the United States, the Washington, West Virginia, and Kansas models have had to bear too heavy a burden in being used as the testbed for nonsurvey and mongrel models via comparing the coefficients from these models with the survey coefficients. The survey-based coefficients are not necessarily closer to the "true" coefficients, and in any event the survey tables are too dated. The promising suggestion that "borrowing" a survey-based A-matrix from one region to serve as the initial matrix (prior to adjustment) of another region (Hewings 1977) cannot be implemented until more survey-based models are obtained. Judicious aggregation and efficient sample design may make the cost of new survey-based tables manageable.

Some other issues in regional input–output models have been settled by recent research. For instance, regardless of the many virtues of interregional models, it has been demonstrated that if the analyst is interested solely in the impacts on a single study-region, little is lost by neglecting interregional feedbacks (Miller & Blair 1985). Also, satisfactory techniques are available for measuring the impact of the entry of a new firm into a region without having to make the naive assumption that the new firm will behave like existing firms; the same approach can be used for impact analysis of new industries (Billings & Katz 1982). Other areas of research increase the potential usefulness of input–output models in regional policy analysis, but more work is needed. For instance, in spite of some advances (e.g., Madden & Batey 1983), there is still no systematic integration of regional input–output models and regional labor market analysis. It is possible, though not inevitable, that extensions of demoeconomic models may achieve this. Also, it is unclear whether or not estimating multipliers from the standard Leontief inverse always gives the best results. More experiments on distributed lags, marginal coefficients, and dynamic models may help to resolve this issue. Input–output models are sometimes criticized as a demand-oriented model; the idea that it can be converted to a supply-constrained model (Cronin 1984) is almost too new to be digested, but if workable the approach could be useful in regions suffering from severe resource constraints. There has been substantial research into using regional input–output models for environmental and energy impact analysis (e.g., Johnson & Bennett 1981; Rose et al. 1982), which broadens the scope for regional policy analysis. Other studies on relative price effects have been successful in showing how to measure the intersectoral "ripple" effects of exogenous price shocks, but the substitution effects linking relative price changes to changes in the A-matrix have not been handled as satisfactorily. However, if the policy analyst believes that relative price-substitution effects are very important, perhaps he should choose an alternative technique to the input–output model. One disappointment in the development of subnational input–output models is the failure to build a satisfactory metropolitan model (with intra-metropolitan disaggregation). The structure of such a model would be very different from the standard regional model with a high degree of model closure, sectoral aggregation, disaggregated households, a more detailed government sector, and spatial linkages among subareas.

Regional input–output models are capable of dealing not only with standard economic impact analysis problems, such as changes in final demand associated with the growth and decline of existing industries and the entry of new ones, but also with more direct policy influences such as fiscal incentives to industry (requiring a function relating cost reductions to output expansions) or infrastructrure subsidies (reflected in lower utility and transport input coefficients). The theoretical objections to input–output models remain, but these have been outweighed by the operational usefulness of these techniques. In part because of the massive research devoted to them, regional input–output models have demonstrated again and again their superiority to alternative techniques for measurement of economic impacts and many dimensions of regional policy analysis.

7.3 Shift-share

Shift-share analysis has been widely used as a diagnostic and descriptive device for explaining changes in regional industrial structure, as a forecasting method, and, more rarely, as a guide to policy analysis.[2] For example, Moore and Rhodes (1973) used shift-share to obtain a "no-policy" "backcast" (or *expected* growth in the absence of policy) which could then be compared with *actual* growth to quantify the policy impact. More precisely, Moore and Rhodes estimate the growth path of a region in the absence of policy under the assumption that each industry in the region would have grown at the national growth rate for this industry. This implies that regional policy is completely responsible for the differences between regional and national industry-specific growth rates. This idea is not wholly satisfactory, not only because of the inherent limitations of shift-share but also because a shift-share analysis cannot be purged of all policy influences. Undoubtedly, the widespread appeal of shift-share is based on its simplicity, modest data requirements, and low cost. Stevens and Moore (1980) reviewed 50 studies and suggested that shift-share analysis would still be useful in certain contexts. Their suggestions included:

(a) testing of alternative formulations on a common data set using a common terminology.
(b) abandonment of the alternative assumptions of constant shift and constant share in forecasting applications. For example, a positive shift because of a comparative advantage could be reduced over time as regional growth led to a bidding up of factor prices; or, if it resulted from the generation of agglomeration economies, the shift could increase over time. Similarly, the constant share is implausible because it assumes that regions respond similarly to increases in national demand.
(c) adoption of a refinement developed by Chalmers (1971) to account for changes in regional industrial mix over the period of analysis. This refinement, named the "relative mix modification" (*MM*) is defined as

$$MM = \Sigma_i RS_i \left[(E_i^t/E_i^{t-1}) - (E^t/E^{t-1}) \right]$$

where RS_i = regional shift in industry i, and E = national employment.
(d) making relative shift in each industry a function of changes in production costs in a region relative to national average costs and/or a function of relative profits. This injects some principles of comparative advantage and location theory into shift-share analysis.

(e) the hypothesis that increasing diversification is leading to a common industrial structure across regions. If so, the best predictor of future regional industrial shifts could be the extent to which a region's share of these industries diverged from the national norm.

Whether the adoption of these and other refinements would result in "more promising uses" for shift-share remains open to dispute. In any event, its application in direct regional policy contexts has to be treated with caution.

7.4 Gravity models

The appeal of gravity models to regional scientists is easy to explain. A typical gravity model equation with both mass and distance exponents is a useful short-hand way of summarizing the forces of agglomeration and dispersion that determine the distribution of population and economic activities over space. Moreover, Alonso (1978) showed how a very general formulation, what he called "a theory of movements," can embrace many familiar regional models such as input–output, Markov processes, and economic base models as well as gravity models as special cases. However, an interesting question to discuss is whether gravity models have any application in regional policy analysis. In fact, there have been very few policy applications of the gravity model. Those which readily spring to mind are at the metropolitan level (e.g., the "abstract mode" of transport demand which can be used to explore the impact of untested transport modes without putting them in place) or at the micro level (e.g., selecting sites for shopping malls). Even the forecasting applications of the gravity model (treating forecasting as an adjunct to policy analysis) have been less than satisfactory. A major reason for this is that gravity models are invariably calibrated in cross-sectional context, and there is no reason at all why coefficient values estimated cross-sectionally should remain the same intertemporally. On the contrary, even if we are interested only in the flows between a pair of regions, the criterion of systemic interdependence (i.e., the flow between A and B is affected by all places; Hua & Porell 1979) means that any nonmarginal change anywhere in the system will impact upon the spatial interactions between the two regions under study. Adoption of a systemic model as opposed to a simple pair-wise gravity model can lead to "dramatic parameter shifts and increase in explanatory power" (Porell & Hua 1976).

The implication is that in order to forecast flows between any pair of regions it would be necessary to forecast the future spatial structure of the economic system as a whole. Another difficulty, relevant to the Canadian regional policy context, is whether macroregions such as provinces (as opposed to smaller nodal regions) are appropriate spatial units for the application of gravity models. (Higgins, for example, argues that the macroregions are not the most appropriate spatial unit for regional policymaking and suggests that the focus on interprovincial shifts has hampered the effectiveness of Canadian regional policy.)

7.5 Cost–benefit analysis

Almost all types of policy intervention have to be justified in terms of some kind of cost–benefit analysis, in the sense that no policy actions will be embarked upon if they are not expected to result in a net positive benefit. Higgins (1984) makes three important points about cost–benefit analysis which merit comment: first, benefits may have to be measured at the project, policies, and programs levels; second, a distinction must be made among financial measures (e.g., profitability), economic measures (with price distortions corrected), and social measures (e.g., the extent to which goals, including noneconomic goals, are met); and third, that opportunity costs and benefits at alternative locations have to be taken into account.

Cost–benefit analysis was originally developed as a method of project evaluation, and it becomes more difficult to apply where its context is broadened. For instance, can evaluation of policies and programs ignore the problem of social costs and benefits and the issue of goal achievement (implied by Higgins's second point)? Once the opportunity cost question is raised (the third point), interregional distributional problems cannot be avoided because the costs to one region are often the benefits of others, unless opportunity cost is defined strictly in terms of national economic efficiency criteria. Schofield (1976, 1979), for example, restricted his list of costs and benefits in an evaluation of British regional policy to those affecting economic efficiency (measured via the contribution to national output). The opportunity cost criterion becomes more critical if projects (and economic activities) are footloose and if resources and factors are mobile. Under these conditions Sakashita (1983) has argued that the relative cost-effectiveness of alternative policies in achieving desired ends (e.g., a particular interregional population distribution) is a more appropriate approach than cost–benefit analysis.

The case for cost–benefit analysis as a technique for regional policy analysis is weaker than it was two decades ago because the defects of cost–benefit analysis have not been eliminated, while the criteria for regional policy analysis have broadened. It is increasingly recognized that the social and political consequences of regional policy intervention, ranging from income distribution aspects to the political acceptability of programs to different levels of government and to interest groups, may be as important as the economic effects, yet cost–benefit analysis is weakest when noneconomic costs and benefits are substantial. Moreover, to the extent that government intervention in regional development is based on a broad policy and program mix, cost–benefit analysis becomes less useful because it works better as a technique for evaluating single projects which are less likely to alter relative prices and other background conditions assumed to be exogenous. These considerations imply the superiority of techniques which are interregional, comprehensive, and partially qualitative, such as are examined elsewhere in this paper.

7.6 Structural econometric models

The utility of national structural econometric models (SEMs) as a forecasting tool and as an aid to macroeconomic policy evaluation has led in the past 15 years or so to the widespread application of econometric models to regional analysis. Although there are a few exceptions (see Taylor 1981, for a review), most of the models in the United States have been at the state level. The explanation is obvious. The state may be a very poor functional economic region, as the Four Corners region in the Southwest so clearly illustrates, but it is the only significant subnational planning region. Moreover, the data scarcities which constrain regional econometric research are less serious at the state level than for any alternative way of carving up national geographical space.

Almost all the regional econometric models assume that changes in national demand drive the regional economy. This assumption has several advantages. First, treating national variables as exogenous variables in a regional model enables a direct link to be made between regional and national economic performance, and given the relative abundance of national models this is especially valuable if the analyst is interested in deriving regional forecasts (Courbis 1979). Second, from the point of view of federal policy analysts who are presumably interested in all the subnational units (states, provinces, etc.) the top-down approach implied by the national–regional model permits the most obvious consistency checks that the sum of regional outputs (income, employment, etc.) must add up to a national output (income, employment, etc.). The national–regional approach allows the effects of changes in the interregional allocation of government spending or similar shifts to be measured directly. This suggests a third advantage, namely that this type of model lends itself to direct policy evaluation, especially when the policy variables are national. This explains the superiority of structural econometric models to the time-series models discussed below (pp. 151–2); the latter are much less costly because their data requirements are lighter, but they have negligible policy implications.

The sparser data sets available at the regional relative to the national level account for a major weakness of structural regional econometric models. If information is not available on a key variable (say, regional capital stocks), the operational model is incomplete, in effect misspecified. The result is that models have to be constructed to fit the data even if this involves substantial glossing over the relationships implied by regional economic theory. For example, intraregional relationships are typically given less attention than national–regional interactions. There is very little scope for developing "bottom-up" models, in which national variables can be made endogenous, as alternatives to the standard "top-down" models (Bolton 1979). A similar problem is that the structure of regional models is very similar to that of national models, and they reflect more or less the same theoretical framework. But macroeconomic theory is not necessarily the most appropriate for regional economic analysis, especially in a policy context. Regional policy makers are more concerned with long-term structural change than with short-run demand impacts. This suggests a different type of econometric model, emphasizing perhaps supply factors and stock variables (such as natural resource endowment, infrastructure, and amenities). Although pleas for this type of model have been heard for a long time (e.g., Czamanski 1972), there has been little progress in this area.

The offsetting advantage of regional SEMs is their policy relevance. For example, Milne et al. (1980) explored three types of policy simulations with their multiregional model: the effects of national policies to accelerate economic growth; the regional impact of policy-induced changes in energy prices; and the regional impact of changes in the location of federal government investment (e.g., defense establishments). It should be noticed that the "top-down" structure of the model imposes a severe restriction in that it limits the kind of policy influences that can be analyzed to national policy variables. It would need a different type of model to examine the effects of regional (e.g., state or provincial) or local (e.g., city) policies. Moreover, many of the more obvious applications (e.g., the case for regional stabilization policy made by L'Espérance, 1981) are related to the short-term demand orientation of most of the regional models and do not address the long-term structural issues that are so critical to evaluating the performance of lagging (or prosperous) regions.

There has been some progress in improving the utility of regional econometric models. For example, data constraints resulting from too small a number of regions or from truncated time series can be reduced by using "pooled" time series and cross-sectional data. Model accuracy can be improved by substituting for the familiar recursive models (usually of the export-base type) simultaneous equation models which allow local economic conditions to influence regional income and employment. On the other hand, the standard range of econometric problems (autocorrelation, heteroskedasticity, multicollinearity, errors in variables, small samples, etc.) are often intensified in regional applications. For instance, spatial autocorrelation of variables and residuals may be a major problem with regional models (Cliff & Ord 1981).

7.7 Time-series forecasting models

Time-series models such as Box–Jenkins techniques (Box & Jenkins 1976, Cook & Falchi 1981), autoregressive moving average (ARIMA) models (Eckstein 1981), and vector autoregression (VAR) models (Ratner & Kinal 1985) are alternatives to structural econometric models (SEMs). Their key advantage is that they are much more economical in their data requirements, but they have a serious limitation in that their use is constrained to pure forecasting applications and they are helpless in shedding light on potential policy impacts. This is because, even if they contain government policy variables (this is certainly possible in a VAR model which can forecast the values of a vector of variables), these models do not contain the structural equations which permit measurement of how a particular policy variable impacts upon the other variables to be forecast. Also, a common criticism of these models is their lack of theoretical underpinnings.

It would take up too much space to describe the various time series models. To take the VAR model as a sole illustration, it relates the values of a vector of variables to their past values. Each variable depends not only on its own past values but also on the past values of other variables in the vector. In a modified as opposed to a "pure" VAR model the vector is made up of two subsets, one called the *responding variables* (i.e., the variables to be forecast), the other called the *driving variables*, which are only of interest to the forecaster because they are prime movers of the responding variables. In a regional VAR forecast the driving variables, which are statistically exogenous (being predicted only by their own lagged values), are often national variables (such as GNP, the CPI (consumer price index), or the key interest rate). Because selection of the most relevant driving variables may reflect implicit economic theory, it is too strong to attack the VAR model as being nontheoretical. However, the length of the lags between responding variables and their past values is chosen on statistical not theoretical grounds, and the interdependencies among responding variables are purely empirical.

The chief virtue of this type of model, in addition to its modest data requirements, is that it can generate reasonably accurate forecasts at relatively low cost. One application, forecasting employment, factory output, retail sales and the price level for New York State, showed that a Bayesian version of the VAR model (which restricts the number of parameters by imposing a prior distribution on coefficient values) performed better than other time-series models (Kinal & Ratner 1985), and as well as an available structural economic model (Burtis, n.d.), and justified the conclusion that these models merit more research as a cost-effective approach for regional economic forecasting (Ratner & Kinal 1985; Anderson 1979). However, another application of a family of Box–Jenkins methods to forecast residential household formation in subregions of Idaho, in some versions using employment as a driving variable, was somewhat less successful (Cook & Falchi 1981). Clark (Clark 1982; Clark & Gertler 1983) analyzed gross migration flows at the state level using MA (moving average), AR (autoregressive), and ARIMA techniques, and found that capital flows induced migration except in Texas (where capital and migration were jointly determined) and Florida (where because of the dominance of retirees in migration streams, migration led to a subsequent inflow of capital). Such findings could have direct policy significance. Spatial versions of this type of model have also been developed, either SAR (spatial autoregressive) models (Nipper & Streit 1982) or STARIMA (spatiotemporal ARIMA) models (Bennett 1979), but they have not been applied in a regional economic context.

7.8 Demoeconomic models

The role of population growth, especially migration, in regional development may be critical but complex. Part of the problem is that migrants simultaneously add to labor supply and indirectly, via their demand for goods and services, to labor demand. These impacts may be unequal and are not spread equally over time. Standard population forecasting models are not capable of measuring the economic impacts of population change, but are only useful for providing inputs for an economic model. Yet migration flows are very responsive to changes in a region's economic performance. If population change impacts upon the regional economy, and economic growth impacts upon population, the obvious solution is some kind of simultaneous model. Demoeconomic models represent a desirable type of such a simultaneous model obtained by integrating submodels for the demographic system and the economic system with important interdependencies between them. A more general benefit of the adoption of this kind of model is that it provides a more balanced emphasis on supply and demand factors when compared with the demand-oriented models (e.g., economic base, input–output) which have dominated regional economic analysis.

There are many variants of a demoeconomic model (e.g., Ledent 1978; Ledent & Gordon 1980; Birg 1982), depending on alternative assumptions about determinants of migration, degree of sectoral disaggregation, method of regionalization, and whether the model is single-region or multiregional. However, most of the models share common features. First, there is a focus on the dynamics of labor market behavior because this is the link between net migration and changes in the labor force. Thus, such models typically include the rates of labor force participation, unemployment, and migration as endogenous and simultaneously determined variables. Population (and its natural increase component) and employment are the other key endogenous variables. These variables are obviously related to each other in the following identities:

$$LFPR \equiv \frac{LF}{P} \equiv \frac{E + U}{P_{-1} + NI + NM}$$

where P, P_{-1} = current and lagged population, LF = labor force, $LFPR$ = the labor force participation rate, E = employment, U = unemployment, NI = natural increase, and NM = net migration. Second, employment is usually determined by using a standard type of regional economic model (a version of the economic base model is frequently adopted), with important modifications to reflect the idea that population change stimulates employment growth. Third, the impact of population growth on economic growth is only one of several demoeconomic interactions; in addition, economic changes lead to changes in the number and quality of jobs; the number and quality of jobs induce in-migration and out-migration; and migration is the major determinant of population change, at least in the sense of accounting for rapid change. These four key processes form a simultaneous system in which population and employment (as the index of economic change) continuously interact.

Demoeconomic models are particularly useful for the analysis of regions where rapid economic growth (or decline) stimulates in- (or out-) migration. Measuring the impacts of policy intervention in such regions using models which lack an explicit consideration of the demographic influences on the labor market will probably result in major errors. In spite of the growth of research into demoeconomic models, the use of such models for regional policy analysis remains in its infancy. Moreover, by adopting very simple migration equations, demoeconomic models have not yet caught up with the pace of migration research (Isserman et al. 1985).

7.9 Integrated multiregional models

One of the problems associated with the use of existing tools for regional policy analysis is that each has a limited application. Attempts at comprehensive evaluation may require the adoption of several techniques, each capable of analyzing one particular dimension of the problem. One approach is to select appropriate techniques in ad hoc fashion, varying the choice according to the range of problems to be analyzed. An alternative is to develop an integrated model with the capacity of handling a large number of the interdependent impacts associated with the simultaneous implementation of different regional policies.

One example of such a model that can be used in a multiregional context is the integrated multiregional model developed by Isard and associates (e.g., Isard & Anselin 1982; Lakshmanan 1982; Isard & Smith 1983). This model consists of seven modules:

(a) NATLEC, a national econometric module
(b) CICIOP, an integrated comparative cost, industrial complex input–output and programming module
(c) TRANS, a transportation module
(d) DEMO, a demographic module
(e) REGLEC, a multiregion econometric module
(f) FACTIN, a factor demand – investment supply econometric module
(g) INPOL, a multipolicy formation module

NATLEC generates the components of national final demand which, when they have been disaggregated regionally, help to drive the multiregion input–output model. It also generates price variables (e.g., interest rates and input prices) to drive FACTIN and other national indicators which serve as consistency checks. CICIOP has several functions: to disaggregate national variables by region; to provide information on the basis of industrial location studies, about changing locational patterns which impact on regional final demand; to optimize the regional and sectoral distribution of output, demand for labor, and value added by combining input–output and linear programming; and to generate shadow prices for energy products. The role of TRANS is to generate interregional commodity flows and transport costs by mode and network links, allowing for cross-hauling and input constraints. DEMO is a micromodeling and simulation system, taking account of both natural increase and migration, which generates age- and sex-specific regional populations, labor supply, income distribution and expenditure-savings patterns. REGLEC, on the other hand, is a macro-model which adopts a "bottom-up" approach to determining labor market equilibrium (labor supply, demand, unemployment, and wage rates), and which could be extended to include submodels for regional output, investment, and local government sectors. Given sector outputs and factor prices, FACTIN uses a cost approach to determine the demand for capital, labor, energy, and materials. There are linkages both between and within modules, and several consistency checks to ensure that regional totals sum up to national aggregates (e.g., reconciliation between NATLEC and REGLEC), and that the aggregation of sectors equals national values of output, employment, etc. These reconciliations may have to be achieved iteratively.

All the above modules make use of familiar items in the regional scientist's toolbag, and rely heavily on economics. They cannot easily accommodate the important non-economic aspects of regional policy-making. This is why the seventh module, INPOL, dealing with choosing the most appropriate policy mix, is so important. Because there are different goals and interest groups to be accommodated, the selected policy mix will be a compromise set. Identifying the compromise policy mix requires the use of "conflict management procedures" (Isard & Smith 1983), such as ranking and scaling schemes. Policy choice involves several elements: multiple interest groups influencing government decision-making; the goals of each group; outcomes derived from the other modules of the integrated model; combinations of policy proposals; and policy instruments in a form in which they can be represented in the integrated model. The most important task, in order to keep the policy formation task manageable, is to limit the number of policy mixes to be evaluated because each of these has to be run through the non-policy components of the integrated multiregional model (modules *a–f* above) to determine the outcomes of each policy mix. This pre-selection ("setting the agenda" in the words of Isard & Smith) requires interaction and compromise among the key actors (politicians, officials, interest groups, and behavioral units, e.g., business firms).

To the best of my knowledge, the integrated multiregional model has not been used in a practical context to evaluate the aggregate and interdependent impacts of a set of regional policies and to compare this set with potential alternatives. Clearly, the structure of the model reflects the research interests and expertise of its designers. It is by no means the only form of integrated model which could be developed. For example, with the partial exception of the location factors in CICIOP and transport costs in TRANS, the model is predominantly spaceless. It is more complex than the combination of input–output and econometric models recommended by L'Espérance (1981) or the conjoining of input–output and comparative cost analysis promoted by Stevens et al. (1981), but it follows in the tradition of these approaches. Perhaps the principle of an integrated model is much more important than its specific form. The criteria for a sound integrated model include its ability to consider alternative policy mixes, an attempt to measure impacts comprehensively (linkages among the particular submodels may help to take account of higher-order effects) and incorporation of non-economic impacts.

7.10 Qualitative impact models

It is very obvious that regional policy impacts are not limited to narrowly economic impacts that can be quantified in dollar terms. The restrictions on the application of social cost–benefit analysis in a regional (or interregional) context is a clear illustration of this fact. The problem is twofold. First, there are important economic variables which are qualitative rather than quantitative, or are quantifiable only in physical (not monetary) terms (Stöhr & Tödtling 1984). Examples include the quality of entrepreneurship, the administrative efficiency of regional development agencies, and changes in environmental quality. Second, several of the important consequences of regional policy are not economic but are social and political. For instance, it is unnecessary to stress the criterion of the influence on national cohesion as a measure of effectiveness of regional policy in Canada.

Nijkamp (e.g., Nijkamp 1981, 1983a, 1983b; Nijkamp & van Pelt 1985) is a pioneer of qualitative impact analysis in a regional context. His argument is that impact analysis has to attempt to assess *all relevant foreseeable and expected consequences* of external changes in a system within a given time period. This implies that social, political, spatial, and environmental variables are as relevant components of the system as the standard economic variables. A framework for analyzing these variables is what he calls an impact structure matrix which assesses the effects of i policy measures $(P_1, P_2, P_3 \ldots P_i)$ on j dimensions of regional welfare

($W_1, W_2, W_3 \ldots W_j$), only some of which will be economic. In identifying the cells of this matrix it is necessary to take account of second-order and higher-order impacts of policy measures as well as the first-order (direct) impacts. The tracing of indirect impacts can stop either when the information content is unreliable, or when the number of steps traced has become large. Qualitative impacts are easily included by using ordinal or binary measures, and these can be used for non-economic impacts, for economic impacts for which the data are too scanty to measure precisely, and for the higher-order impacts which are too difficult to quantify. Also, qualitative approaches may be more appropriate when changes are neither marginal nor smooth but dramatic jumps (e.g., catastrophe scenarios). Although the methodology needs further refinement, via its inclusion of non-economic influences and its ability to take account of indirect effects it is a promising approach to a comprehensive assessment of regional policy impacts.

An extension of qualitative impact analysis, again promoted by Nijkamp (Nijkamp & Rietveld 1982, Bloomestein & Nijkamp 1983), is the use of "soft" data (e.g., ordinal measures which are essentially qualitative) for drawing inferences which are ultimately quantitative. There are mathematical and statistical operations available for extracting quantitative (i.e., cardinal) conclusions from qualitative data. For example, multidimensional scaling methods can be used to transform ordinal data (say, an $N \times N$ paired comparison table which describes the dissimilarity between N objects) into cardinal units. The trick of representing these N objects as cardinal coordinates in a Euclidean space is to reduce the number of dimensions, say S dimensions where ($S = 0.5 (N - 1)$): "the transition from higher to lower dimensions implies in general the emergence of degrees of freedom which can be used to extract cardinal information from the underlying ordinal data structure" (Bloomestein & Nijkamp 1983, p. 344). Homogeneous scaling methods are an alternative, though allied, approach based on the idea that different ordinal variables may reflect and measure a common phenomenon. The basic problem is to replace several variables by a single criterion via the principle of maximizing homogeneity. These ideas, originally used in psychology, have had some preliminary applications in regional economics.

7.11 Growth poles

Growth pole analysis is in a different category from the other techniques discussed in this paper because it is less a technique of analysis than a concept (almost a theory of regional development) and a policy instrument. It is included here for two reasons. First, for those who accept its underlying assumptions, it is a tool of analysis because it implies certain types of policy implications (e.g., the priority of economic over social infrastructure, or the agglomeration benefits from investment concentration). Second, the emphasis on growth centers in the economic history of regional policy-making in Canada justifies some attention to the topic.

Cutting through the mound of papers written about growth poles, many of them conflicting from definitions to diagnosis, the following ideas stand out about their implications for *developed* countries such as Canada. In a developing country context the analysis would be different. For example, see Richardson (1978c) and Hilhorst (1979). First, the growth pole approach implies that spatial concentration generates faster and/or more sustained regional development than a more dispersed regional growth pattern, even in conditions where investment resources are reasonably plentiful and human capital is either ubiquitous or highly mobile. Second, the economic stimulus from infrastructure investments will vary according to the infrastructure mix, and emphasis on economic as opposed to social infrastructure is justified in those regions where growth pole strategies are most likely to work (Hansen 1965; Looney & Fredericksen 1980). Third, this implies a continued focus on manufacturing activities, even if the aggregate economy is shifting towards high-order services (but the spatial spillovers from the latter could be greater if the secondary income stimulus to local consumption outweighs backward linkage effects on production). Fourth, regardless of their composition, positive intraregional spillovers may take a much longer time to develop than the planning horizon of electorally responsive policy makers. Fifth, acceptance of growth pole hypotheses implies the relevance of many other analytical techniques from industrial complex analysis to spatial multiplier concepts. Sixth, the piecemeal, ad hoc implementation of growth poles outside the context of a national urban and interregional development strategy will squander resources and dilute impacts. This raises the question of "how many poles?", which implies other issues such as the extent of scale economies, the number of political subdivisions and interest groups, and the volume of interregional mobile economic activities. Seventh, growth pole concepts are inextricably involved with the hypothesis that capital-intensive activities have more dynamic stimulating effects, which suggests the appropriateness of capital-oriented incentives even in subregions with high unemployment rates (Guccione & Gillen, n.d.).

I do not subscribe to all of these ideas. In the context of the subject matter of this paper, the fifth point is worth stressing. The growth pole concept is not technique-neutral. Its acceptance implies that some tools will be useful while others will have little value. For example, its emphasis on dynamics and non-linearities implies that regional input–output models are not very helpful, in spite of their ability to identify backward and forward linkages. Similarly, regional econometric models, at least in their present form, are almost useless because of their lack of spatial differentiation and extrapolations of the past. On the other hand, demoeconomic models might be productive because of their potential for capturing the dynamic effects of migration and one aspect of the qualitative spatial impact models, namely accounting for higher-order interactions among different components of a policy mix, could also be useful, given the multidimensional nature of growth pole strategies.

7.12 Aggregate growth vs. interregional equity

The importance of the efficiency–equity issue in Canadian regional development (Higgins 1984) raises the question of whether or not existing techniques can contribute to an empirical solution. At least one analyst has argued that the trade-off between efficiency and equity "makes no real sense except at the most superficial and naive level" (Clark 1983, p. 41). His argument is based on the difficulty of ranking goals and on the impossibility of purging the concept of efficiency (or national wealth maximization) of distributional and social justice concerns. He concludes: "If regional equity and national efficiency are indeed competing values, there is no common metric to enable any trade-off. If these two concepts are means, then which is more desirable will be decided according to how it advances a third, unstated end, given political preferences for the distribution of costs and benefits. If, on the other hand, one is an end, the other a means (the most likely combination wherein regional equity is the end, national efficiency a means), trade-offs are inconceivable" (ibid, p. 156).

Even if this somewhat philosophical argument is not accepted, there are undoubtedly severe definitional and measurement problems. Measuring interregional equity in spatial equity terms (e.g., measures of dispersion among regions in average regional per capita incomes) tells nothing about what is happening to interpersonal equity. Indeed, because the most direct beneficiaries of regional subsidies are often corporations and landowners, regional development incentives for low-income regions may have perverse distributional effects, especially if financed out of general revenues in a country with a not-too-progressive tax system. Non-monetary dimensions of welfare (e.g., social indicators such as health, education, and amenity indices) are unlikely to be distributed among regions in the same way as income. Average per capita incomes within a geographical area are very sensitive to the size of the spatial unit and its degree of urbanization. The measure adopted by Williamson (1965) in his seminal paper, a weighted (according to regional population shares) coefficient of variation in regional per capita incomes relative to the national average, is very sensitive to how regions are carved up, though this problem is more severe in cross-sectional comparisons across countries than in time-series analysis within one country with an unchanged set of regions.

Efficiency is often regarded as a much simpler concept than equity, but there are some doubts that output maximization subject to stated resource constraints is a sound criterion. For example, relocating polluting industries from a densely populated core to a sparsely populated periphery may lower national output but may not be inefficient if the decline in unpriced negative externalities is greater than the output loss. In such a case, maximizing net social benefits within a cost–benefit framework would be superior to output maximization as an efficiency criterion.

Even when economic efficiency is interpreted very narrowly, there are still practical problems. The allocation of investment among regions should take account of the opportunity cost of capital, but in the absence of data on regional rates of return, there is no direct way of measuring this. One idea might be to use an interregional input–output model and compare the effects on regional gross outputs of regional policy intervention compared with a market-determined investment allocation. But not all policy interventions can be represented in terms of changes in the composition and level of final demand. Some may affect the coefficients in the A-matrix, and such changes may have repercussions on the rest of the interregional model, especially on the interregional trade coefficients. Furthermore, if regional policies primarily impact upon the interregional distribution of investment, a *dynamic* interregional model is required.

The "naive" (Clark's word) way to illustrate the trade-off would be to derive a trade-off function with GNP measured on one axis and a dispersion measure of regional outputs per capita on the other (Richardson 1979). But such a device would have little more than pedagogic value. A programming version of an interregional input–output model could be used to maximize the sum of gross regional products given alternative interregional equity constraints, expressed as limitations on final demands in the more prosperous regions. However, the derived alternative allocations of final demand (and gross output) among regions would reflect what is feasible at one point of time and would be unlikely to hold up over time. Regional development is a dynamic process, and policy-makers trade-off growth and interregional equity over time.

Although the few empirical attempts at measuring the trade-off suggest that the efficiency loss is substantial (Mera 1975 suggested that, to attain interregional income equalization in Japan, GNP would have to fall by 30% in the short run or by 12% in the long run when factors are mobile), it is also possible that in some circumstances efficiency–equity compatibility may exist. Examples include the efficiency gains from reducing inflation by shifting the Phillips curve to the southwest (Higgins 1975); the combination of footloose industries and small interregional differentials in infrastructure and labor quality; and the existence of severe congestion externalities in the core region which are insufficiently reflected in relative prices.

To sum up, the techniques available for understanding the trade-off problem are much more satisfactory than the techniques available for attempting to *measure* the trade-off function itself.

7.13 Concluding observations

This paper has been selective in its discussion of techniques, and each has been treated briefly because of limitations on space. The criterion for inclusion has been policy relevance, but defined loosely to include forecasting and impact analysis as well as policy choice and evaluation. Some general implications may be drawn from the analysis, keeping the Canadian context in mind.

(a) Although the spatial focus could vary according to the policy problem and the jurisdictional home of the policy maker, the most appropriate type of model in the federal–provincial (federal–state) context is an interregional–multiregional model. Even provincial (or state) policy makers should not ignore the effects of their policy intervention on other regions by pursuing beggar-my-neighbor policies. But an interregional focus is critical for federal policy-makers – first, because one federal role is to arbitrate among competing regional interests; and second because an alternative to locational intervention to support lagging regions is to allow the distribution of economic activity to be determined by the market and to tax profits for income transfers to these regions. Furthermore, leakages from investment injections in peripheral regions back to the core may, if demonstrated, win political support in the core region for regional development policies. Moreover, in many circumstances, the impacts of explicit regional policies may be outweighed by the unintended geographical impacts of national macro and sectoral policies (e.g., defense spending), and the latter can be evaluated comprehensively only with an interregional model. Single-region models have only a very limited value, and even national–regional models are incomplete.

(b) There is increasing recognition that techniques which can capture only the economic impacts of regional policies are inadequate. The noneconomic, especially the political, dimensions of regional policy crop up in many countries: those which have historically been vulnerable to independence movements (e.g., Canada, United Kingdom, Ethiopia); those with active or potential insurrectionist groups operating in the periphery (e.g., Philippines, Thailand); those where national political integration is a dominant goal (e.g., Indonesia); those with severe ethnic problems (e.g., Malaysia, South Africa); and those with disputed border regions (e.g., many countries in Latin America and Africa). The social impacts of regional policies are equally important, particularly because of growing dissatisfaction with gross regional product, income per capita, and similar economic measures of welfare. There are three obvious solutions. First, an integrated multiregional model may be developed. The version discussed in this paper is too narrow because the noneconomic module, INPOL, focuses only on policy *formation* with a heavy emphasis on conflict resolution. The second option is to graft on to existing economic submodels which specifically deal with political, social, and other noneconomic aspects. Third, because many noneconomic impacts cannot be quantified cardinally, qualitative assessment methods offer some prospects for estimating them. Measurement is not ruled out via the development of statistical techniques for handling "soft" data. All these areas need much more research than they have received hitherto.

(c) The case for comprehensive models, such as an extension of the integrated multiregional model, is strengthened by the importance of evaluating the overall impact of a package of policies or regional development programs as a whole. It is very difficult to assess the effects of single policy instruments, such as a regional capital subsidy, in isolation from the impacts of other policies – whether explicitly spatial or other economic policies with geographical implications – and from spontaneous economic change. One problem is that there are interactions among policies (secondary, tertiary, and higher-order effects) which can be measured only with an integrated model. Another key issue is that the dominant aim of regional policy makers is to assess the effects of all types of intervention on a region's aggregate economic performance rather than the impact of a single policy. Even if estimates of the effects of individual policies are important for policy evaluation and review, these individual effects are quantifiable only within a framework of a comprehensive model rather than via a partial ad hoc assessment.

(d) Because regional policy makers are primarily concerned with long-run structural change, the most useful techniques are those that can deal with the dynamics of regional development and rapid changes in economic structure. Yet most of the available techniques are static in character and can accommodate structural change, if at all, only via mechanistic coefficient adjustment. The input–output model is a good example, excellent for short-run analysis but increasingly deficient as the time horizon lengthens.

(e) The small sample of techniques reviewed in this paper suggests that even the most trusted and widely used tools have drawbacks. There are some new techniques available (e.g., VAR models, demo-economic models, integrated multiregional policy analysis models, and qualitative impact analysis), but they have not been applied widely enough for their value to be tested. Different techniques may be required for regional forecasting, choosing the policy mix, and policy evaluation. A truly comprehensive model may be able to handle all three tasks, but such models are still in their infancy. Although regional economists and policy makers have some useful tools of analysis which have not proved too difficult to make operational, the search for more effective techniques must continue.

Notes

1 In the context of this paper "tools" are defined as "techniques." An alternative definition might be in terms of "policy instruments." This latter interpretation is avoided in this paper with the exception of the discussion of growth poles, which is a hybrid concept embracing theory, policy instrument, strategy and analytical technique.
2 Policy analysis is generally regarded as an incorrect application of shift-share. I remember attending a conference in Ottawa in 1972 where senior officials of DREE presented a paper which used shift-share analysis to identify priority industries for promotion in the Atlantic provinces. The approach was widely criticized by several of the conference participants.

References

Alonso, W. 1978. A theory of movement. In *Human settlement systems*, N. M. Hansen (ed.), Cambridge, Mass.: Ballinger.

Anderson, P. A. 1979. Help for the regional economic forecaster: vector autoregression. *Federal Reserve Bank of Minneapolis Quarterly Review* 3(3), 2–7.

Armstrong, H. & J. Taylor 1978. *Regional economic policy and its analysis*. Oxford: Philip Allan.

Bartels, C. P. A., W. R. Nicol & J. J. van Duijn 1981. Estimating impacts of regional policies: a review of applied research methods. Laxenburg: International Institute for Applied System Analysis, WP 81–59.

Bennett, R. J. 1979. *Spatial time series*. London: Pion.

Billings, R. B. & J. L. Katz 1982. A technique to obtain accurate impact multipliers for individual firms by means of existing input–output models. *Environment and Planning A* 14, 739–44.

Birg, H. 1982. On the interactions of job creation, migration, and natural population increase within the framework of a dynamic demoeconomic model. *Environment and Planning A* 14, 1141–53.

Bloomestein, H. & P. Nijkamp 1983. Multivariate methods for soft data in development planning: a case study in natural resources. In *Spatial, environmental and resource policy in the developing countries*, M. Chatterji et al. (eds.), 343–60. Aldershot: Gower.

Boadway, R. & F. Flanders 1981. The efficiency basis for regional employment policy. *Canadian Journal of Economics* 14, 58–135.

Boisier, S. 1983. *Economic policy, social organization and regional development*. Santiago: Cuardernos del Instituto Latinamericano de Planificacion Economica y Social, no. 29.

Bolton, R. 1979. Multiregional models in policy analysis. Williamstown: Department of Economics, Williams College. Mimeo.

Box, G. E. P. & G. M. Jenkins 1976. *Time series analysis: forecasting and control*, 2nd edn. San Francisco: Holden-Day.

Burtis, D. [n.d.]. The forecast accuracy of the New York State econometric model. Albany: New York State Division of the Budget. Mimeo.

Cebula, R. J. 1979. A survey of the literature on the migration-impact of state and local government policies. *Public Finance* 34, 69–83.

Chalmers, J. A. 1971. Measuring changes in regional industrial structure: a comment on Stilwell and Ashby. *Urban Studies* 8, 289–92.

Chatterji, M. et al. (eds.) 1983. *Spatial, environmental and resource policy in the developing countries*. Aldershot: Gower.

Clark, G. L. 1982. Dynamics of interstate labor migration. *Annals, Association of American Geographers* 72, 297–313.

Clark, G. L. 1983. *Interregional migration, national policy, and social justice*. Totowa, N.J.: Rowman & Allanheld.

Clark, G. L. & M. Gertler 1983. Migration and capital. *Annals, Association of American Geographers* 73, 18–34.

Cliff, A. D. & J. K. Ord 1981. *Spatial processes, models and applications*. London: Pion.

Cook, T. & P. Falchi 1981. Time-series modelling in a regional economy: an exposition of Box-Jenkins techniques. *Environment and Planning A* 13, 635–44.

Courbis, R. (ed.) 1979. *Modèles régionaux et modèles régionaux–nationaux*. Paris: Editions Cujas.
Cronin, F. J. 1984. Analytical assumptions and causal ordering in interindustry modelling. *Southern Economic Journal* 51, 521–9.
Czamanski, S. 1972. *Regional science techniques in practice*. Lexington, Mass.: Lexington Books.
Eckstein, O. 1981. Econometric models for forecasting and policy analysis: the present state of the art. In *DRI readings in macroeconomics*, A. R. Sanderson (ed.) 2–18. New York: McGraw-Hill.
Engle, R. F. 1975. Policy pills for a metropolitan economy. *Papers of Regional Science Association* 35, 191–205.
Evans, J. P. & R. E. Steuer 1973. A revised simplex method for linear multiple objective programs. *Mathematical Programming* 15, 54–72.
Folmer, H. 1980. Measurement of the effects of regional policy instruments. *Environment and Planning A* 12, 1191–202.
Folmer, H. 1981. Measurement of the effects of regional policy instruments by means of linear structural equation models and panel data. *Environment and Planning A* 13, 1435–47.
Gibson, L. J. & M. A. Worden 1981. Estimating the economic base multiplier: a test of alternative procedures. *Economic Geography* 57, 146–59.
Glickman, N. J. 1977. *Econometric analysis of regional systems*. New York: Academic Press.
Guccione, A. & W. J. Gillen [n.d.]. The optimality of labor subsidies in a regional context: a skeptical note. Windsor: University of Windsor. Mimeo.
Hafkamp, W. & P. Nijkamp 1981. Multiobjective modelling for economic–environmental policies. *Environment and Planning A* 13, 7–18.
Hansen, N. 1965. Unbalanced growth and regional development. *Western Economic Journal* 4, 3–14.
Hansen, N. 1980. Policies for nonmetropolitan areas. *Growth and Change* 11, 7–13.
Hewings, G. J. D. 1977. Evaluating the possibilities for exchanging regional input–output coefficients. *Environment and Planning A* 9, 927–44.
Hewings, G. J. D. 1982. Regional and interregional interdependencies: alternative accounting systems. *Environment and Planning A* 14, 1587–600.
Higgins, B. 1975. Trade-off curves, trends and regional disparities: the case of Quebec. *Économie appliquée* 28, 331–60.
Higgins, B. 1978. Development poles: do they exist? In *Growth pole strategies and regional development policy: Asian experience and alternative approaches*. F.-C. Lo and K. Salih (eds.) Oxford: Pergamon.
Higgins, B. 1981. Regional development planning: the state of the art in North America. Nagoya: United Nations Center for Regional Development. Also in *The Canadian economy: a regional perspective*, D. Savoie (ed.). Toronto: Methuen (1986).
Higgins, B. 1984. Regional and national economic development: trade-off or complementarity. Mimeo.
Higgins, B. 1985. Australian regional development in international perspective. Mimeo.
Hilhorst, J. G. M. 1980. On unresolved issues in regional development thinking. The Hague: Institute of Social Studies. Mimeo.
Hordijk, L. & J. Paelinck 1974. Spatial econometrics: some contributions. Rotterdam: Netherlands Economic Institute. Mimeo.

Hua, C. & F. Porell 1979. A critical review of the development of the gravity model. *International Regional Science Review* **4**, 97–126.

Isard, W. & L. Anselin 1982. Integration of multiregional models for policy analysis. *Environment and Planning A* **14**, 359–76.

Isard, W. & C. Smith 1983. Policy analysis using an integrated multiregional model. In *Spatial, environmental and resource policy in developing countries*, M. Chatterji et al. (eds.), 64–78. Aldershot: Gower.

Isserman, A. M., D. A. Plane, P. A. Rogerson & P. M. Beaumont 1985. Forecasting interstate migration with limited data: a demographic economic approach. *Journal of the American Statistical Association* **80**, 277–85.

Jensen, R. C. & S. Macdonald 1982. Technique and technology in regional input–output. *Annals of Regional Science* **16**, 27–45.

Jensen, R. C., T. D. Mandeville & N. D. Karunaratne 1979. *Regional economic planning: generation of regional input-output analysis*. London: Croom Helm.

Johnson, M. H. & J. T. Bennett 1981. Regional environmental and economic impact evaluation: an input–output approach. *Regional Science and Urban Economics* **11**, 215–30.

Kinal, T. & J. B. Ratner 1985. A VAR forecasting model of a state economy: its construction and comparative accuracy. *International Regional Science Review*.

Klaassen, L. H. 1974. Some further considerations on attraction analysis. Rotterdam: Netherlands Economic Institute. Mimeo.

Klein, L. R. & N. J. Glickman 1977. Econometric model building at the regional level. *Regional Science and Urban Economics* **7**, 3–23.

Lakshmanan, T. R. 1982. Integrated multiregional economic modelling for the USA. In *Multiregional modelling*, B. Issaer et al. (eds.), Amsterdam: North Holland.

Ledent, J. 1978. Regional multiplier analysis: a demometric approach. *Environment and Planning A* **10**, 537–60.

Ledent, J. & P. Gordon 1980. A demometric model of interregional growth rate differences. *Geographical Analysis* **12**, 55–67.

L'Espérance, W. L. 1981. *The structure and control of a state economy*. London: Pion.

Looney, R. & P. Fredericksen 1980. The regional impact of infrastructure investment in Mexico. Monterey: Naval Postgraduate School. Mimeo.

Madden, M. & P. W. J. Batey 1983. Linked population and economic models: some methodological issues in forecasting, analysis and policy optimization. *Journal of Regional Science* **23**, 141–64.

MacKay, R. R. 1979. The death of regional policy – or resurrection squared. *Regional Studies* **13**, 281–95.

MacKay, R. R. & L. Thomson 1979. Important trends in regional policy and regional employment – a modified interpretation. *Scottish Journal of Political Economy* **26**, 223–59.

Mathur, V. K. & H. S. Rosen 1974. Regional employment multipliers: a new approach. *Land Economics* **50**, 93–6.

Mera, K. 1975. *Income distribution and regional development*. Tokyo: University of Tokyo Press.

Miernyk, W. H. 1980. An evaluation: the tools of regional development policy. *Growth and Change* **11**, 2–6.

Miller, R. E. & P. D. Blair 1985. *Input–output analysis: foundations and extensions*. Englewood Cliffs, N.J.: Prentice Hall.

Milne, W. J., N. J. Glickman & F. G. Adams 1980. A framework for analyzing regional growth and decline: a multiregion econometric model of the United States. *Journal of Regional Science* **20**, 173–89.

Moore, B. & J. Rhodes 1973. Evaluating the effect of British regional economic policy. *Economic Journal* **83**, 87–110.

Moore, C. L. 1975. A new look at the minimum requirements approach to regional economic analysis. *Economic Geography* **51**, 350–6.

Nijkamp, P. 1981. Urban impact analysis in a spatial context: methodology and case study. Amsterdam: Department of economics, Free University. Research Memo 1981–5.

Nijkamp, P. 1983a. Qualitative impact assessments of spatial policies in developing countries. *Regional Development Dialogue* **4**(1), 44–62.

Nijkamp, P. 1983b. Qualitative spatial impact analysis. In *Spatial, environmental and resource policy in the developing countries*, M. Chatterji et al. (eds.), Aldershot: Gower.

Nijkamp, P. & M. van Pelt 1985. Spatial impact analysis for developing countries: a framework and a case study. Mimeo.

Nijkamp, P. & P. Rietveld 1982. Soft econometrics as a tool for regional discrepancy analysis. *Papers, Regional Science Association*.

Nipper, J. & U.Streit 1982. A comparative study of some stochastic methods and autoprojective models for spatial processes. *Environment and Planning A* **14**, 1211–31.

Paelinck, J. H. P. & P. Nijkamp 1975. *Operational theory and method in regional economics*. Lexington, Mass.: Lexington Books.

Porell, F. W. & C. Hua 1976. Internal migration policy: Implications from a system model of spatial interaction. Pittsburgh: School of Urban and Public Affairs, Carnegie-Mellon University. Mimeo.

Ratner, J. B. & T. W. Kinal 1985. A comparison of alternative approaches to regional forecasting as applied to New York State. In *Economic Prospects for the Northeast*, H. W. Richardson & J. H. Turek (eds.), 264–83. Philadelphia: Temple University Press.

Richardson, H. W. 1978a. *Regional economics*. Urbana: University of Illinois Press.

Richardson, H. W. 1978b. The state of regional economics: a survey. *International Regional Science Review* **3**, 1–48.

Richardson, H. W. 1978c. Growth centers, rural development and national urban policy: a defense. *International Regional Science Review* **3**, 133–52.

Richardson, H. W. 1979. Aggregate efficiency and interregional equity. In *Spatial inequalities and regional development*, H. Folmer & J. Oosterhaven (eds.), 161–83. Boston: Martinus Nijhoff.

Richardson, H. W. 1981. The relevance and applicability of regional economics to developing countries. In *Training for regional development*, O. P. Mathur (ed.), 39–60. Singapore: Maruzen.

Richardson, H. W. 1985. Input–output and economic base multipliers: looking back and forward. *Journal of Regional Science*.

Richardson, H. W. & P. Gordon 1978. A note on spatial multipliers. *Economic Geography* **54**, 309–13.

Rose, A., B. Nakayama & B. Stevens 1982. Modern energy region development and income distribution: an input–output analysis. *Journal of Environmental Economics and Management* **9**, 149–64.

Sakashita, N. 1983. Evaluation of regional development policy – an alternative approach. *Environment and Planning A* **15**, 1175–84.

Savoie, D. J. 1984a. The toppling of DREE and prospects for regional economic development. *Canadian Public Policy* **10**, 328–37.

Savoie, D. J. 1984b. The continuing struggle for a regional development policy. Mimeo.

Schofield, J. A. 1976. Economic efficiency and regional policy in Britain. *Urban Studies* **13**, 181–91.

Schofield, J. A. 1979. Macro evaluation of the impact of regional policy in Britain: a review of recent change. *Urban Studies* **16**, 251–71.

Stevens, B. H. & C. Moore 1980. A critical review of the literature on shift-share as a forecasting technique. *Journal of Regional Science* **20**, 419–37.

Stevens, B., B. Treyz & D. Ehrlich 1980. On the estimation of regional purchase coefficients, export employment, and elasticities of response for regional economic models. Philadelphia: Regional Science Research Institute, DP 114.

Stevens, B. H., G. I. Treyz & J. K. Kindahl 1981. Conjoining an input–output model and policy analysis model: a case study of the regional economic effects of expanding a port facility. *Environment and Planning A* **13**, 1029–38.

Stevens, B. H., G. I. Treyz, D. J. Ehrlich & J. R. Bower 1983. A new technique for the construction of non-survey regional input–output models and comparisons with two survey-based models. *International Regional Science Review* **8**, 271–86.

Stöhr, W. B. 1982. Alternative strategies for integrated regional development of peripheral areas. In *Regional problems on the periphery of Europe*, D. Seers & K. Ostrom (eds.), London: Macmillan.

Stöhr, W. B. 1983. Changing external conditions and a paradigm shift in regional development strategies. Vienna: Interdisciplinary Institute for Urban and Regional Studies, University of Economics. Mimeo.

Stöhr, W. B. & F. Tödtling 1984. Quantitative, qualitative, and structural variables in the evaluation of regional development policies in Western Europe. In *Regional development problems and policies in Eastern and Western Europe*, G. J. Demko (ed.), 157–73. London: Croom Helm.

Taylor, C. 1981. Econometric modelling of urban and other substate areas: an analysis of alternative methodologies. Mimeo.

Thompson, J. S. 1983. Pattern of employment multipliers in a central place system: an alternative to economic base estimation. *Journal of Regional Science* **23**, 71–81.

Townroe, P. M. 1979a. The design of local economic development policies. *Town Planning Review* **50**, 148–63.

Townroe, P. M. 1979b. Employment decentralization: policy instruments for large cities in LDCs. *Progress in Planning* **10**, 85–154.

Treyz, G. I. et al. 1980. *The Massachusetts economic policy analysis model and its use from 1977 through 1980*. Discussion paper ser. no. 118. Regional Science Research Institute.

Williamson, J. G. 1965. Regional inequalities and the process of national development. *Economic Development and Cultural Change* **13**, 3–45.

Woodward, R. 1974. The capital bias of DREE incentives. *Canadian Journal of Economics* **7**, 161–73.

8
A neoclassical approach to regional economics

THOMAS J. COURCHENE and JAMES R. MELVIN

8.1 Introduction

We are honored to have been asked to present a paper in commemoration of the contributions of Professor François Perroux to the field of regional economics. It was suggested that we undertake a neoclassical analysis of regional economics, and it is with some trepidation that we approach this assignment. As all those familiar with his work are well aware, Professor Perroux has long been a critic of the standard neoclassical approach to economics, and in particular to its application to regional economic questions. In one of his recent books (Perroux 1983), he provides a scathing indictment of the usefulness of neoclassical economics and of its relevance for the analysis of developing economics. He has often argued that while the mathematical tools of classical mechanics (that have served as the analytical basis of the neoclassical paradigm) may have at one time been appropriate for the consideration of economic issues, that time has long since past. He has urged economists to keep abreast of the physical sciences and make use of the more modern and elegant techniques associated with thermodynamics. His strong views are reasonably well captured, we feel, by his statement that "I feel that the *relative* decline of classical mechanics and the advance of thermodynamics cannot be indefinitely ignored by the fanatical partisans of market mechanisms" (1983, p. 61).

A central theme of Professor Perroux's research has been his view that the sterile and simplistic neoclassical general equilibrium approach clouds the underlying issues and, contrary to the generally accepted view, provides neither a lucid presentation of the basic concepts nor a convenient framework against which more complex models can be compared. He endorses Oskar Morganstern's statement that "there is no road leading from L. Walras to reality" (Perroux 1980, p. 154).

We agree with much of Professor Perroux's criticism. Many of the assumptions in neoclassical general equilibrium analysis, purportedly made for the purpose of simplification, abstract from central features of the underlying model and result in conclusions which are at best misleading and at worst incorrect. We have on several occasions, both jointly and singly, undertaken to extend traditional analysis with the hope of contributing to a better understanding of some of these issues (e.g., Courchene & Melvin 1980; Melvin 1985a, 1985b). The purpose of the present paper is to extend some of this earlier work and synthesize some of the implications for regional economics.

At the outset, however, we must make it clear that our approach is *not* the one suggested by Professor Perroux. The mathematics of thermodynamics is well beyond our understanding. Furthermore we are neoclassists through and through and make no apology for this fact. It is our view that the neoclassical apparatus, when properly applied, can provide many more insights into several of the issues raised by Professor Perroux than is generally recognized.

In a recent book, Perroux (1983, p. 64) lists nine basic criticisms of the standard neoclassical general equilibrium model. Of these, two are of particular interest from the point of view of the present discussion:

> the model excludes *structures* and *structural subsets* (industries, regions, social groups).

> It has never succeeded in proposing an identical theory for application to *both* international exchanges *and* domestic exchanges. This is not surprising, since the nation is a structure and an organization and hence beyond the scope of a model which rules out any structure or organization.

We agree that much of standard general equilibrium analysis does suffer from these deficiencies. Furthermore it can be shown that the relaxation of some of these simplifying assumptions requires the development of new theoretical ideas and provides valuable insights into policy analysis.

The literature of regional economics is made up of two distinct strands. The first is the analysis of economic activity in a spatial context, which could be called the economics of a region. The second is the analysis of the economic interaction between regions, which could be called interregional economics. The vast majority of the modern literature concerns the former. The major emphasis in this paper is with the latter, although Section 3 does deal with the economics of a region. Professor Perroux would, we hope, approve of our emphasis, for our approach is very much in the spirit of his two concerns expressed above.

Our major theme is that the identification of regions which differ in some substantial and well-defined way allows an analysis of the interaction among regions and their joint interaction with the rest of the world. In our first example, differentiation between regions is made on the basis of preferences, which implies that the assumption that all individuals in the economy have identical preferences must be relaxed. But before a regional model can be constructed on this basis, it must be shown that an equilibrium exists when consumers have different preferences in the more simple single-region model. This issue is taken up in Section 8.2, and although something of a digression, is essential for the subsequent analysis. It is also of some interest in its own right, for it illustrates that some of the aggregation commonly assumed is not required.

We take up five specific themes. We begin with a disaggregation of the consumption side of the model and ask whether the assumption that all individuals have identical preferences is a harmless one. We find that it is not. We next extend the model to include a notion of distance and thus allow the consideration of regions. We then consider a case where consumers with different preferences work and consume in distinctly different regions. We find that several results from neoclassical analysis must be reformulated. Fourth, we consider an economy consisting of several regions with different endowments, where these regions can trade both with the rest of the world and with each other. We find that this extension has implications both for the standard theory of international trade and for regional economic policy analysis. Finally we draw on our earlier analysis to comment on yet another theme of Professor Perroux's research, namely that one should not expect interregional equality. As he himself has so succinctly put it, "it has become fairly clear that it is the search for a *socially optimal inequality which is really important*" (1980, p. 161).

8.2 The representative consumer

Professor Perroux has a long-standing concern with the aggregation of individual units into "large individuals", and at least since 1950 has been critical of the use of community indifference curves in international trade (Perroux 1950). With this we are in complete agreement. We shall show that assuming all individuals to be identical, while simplifying the analysis, abstracts from domestic transactions among individuals which would normally be expected to take place, and thereby ignores the interaction between international trade and domestic exchange.

The implications of the assumption that all domestic consumers are identical for the basic results of general equilibrium international trade models has received surprisingly little attention. Some early papers by H. G. Johnson (1959) and P. B. Kenen (1957, 1959) considered this issue, but their concerns were with whether or not in such circumstances offer curves could be constructed. In a later paper, V. S. Rao examined the consequences for the Stolper–Samuelson theorem of assuming two distinct groups of consumers in the economy, and found conditions under which the losing factor could be compensated from tariff revenue. None of these papers, however, examined the basic question of whether or not the standard results from international trade theory were sensitive to the simplifications made on the demand side of the model.

The purposes of this section are twofold. First, we shall show that the disaggregation on the demand side to include many consumers, each with different preferences, is not difficult. Second, several examples will be presented to show that the simplification of assuming that all domestic consumers are identical does obscure some important characteristics of the model. We begin with the standard neoclassical trade model but with two consumers (or rather two groups of identical consumers) rather than one. It will then be shown that the generalization to any number of consumers is not difficult.

On the production side our model is the standard one; there are two goods, X and Y, produced with labor (L) and capital (K) under conditions of constant returns to scale. The two factors are in fixed supply for the economy. Thus we have:

$$X = F_x(K_x, L_x) \tag{8.1}$$

$$Y = F_y(K_y, L_y) \tag{8.2}$$

$$K = K_x + K_y \tag{8.3}$$

$$L = L_x + L_y \tag{8.4}$$

These give the standard production possibility curve TT' of Figure 8.1. On the demand side we have two groups of consumers each with identical and homothetic tastes within the group, but with preferences differing between groups. The utility functions are:

$$U_i = U_i(X_i, Y_i) \quad i = 1,2 \tag{8.5}$$

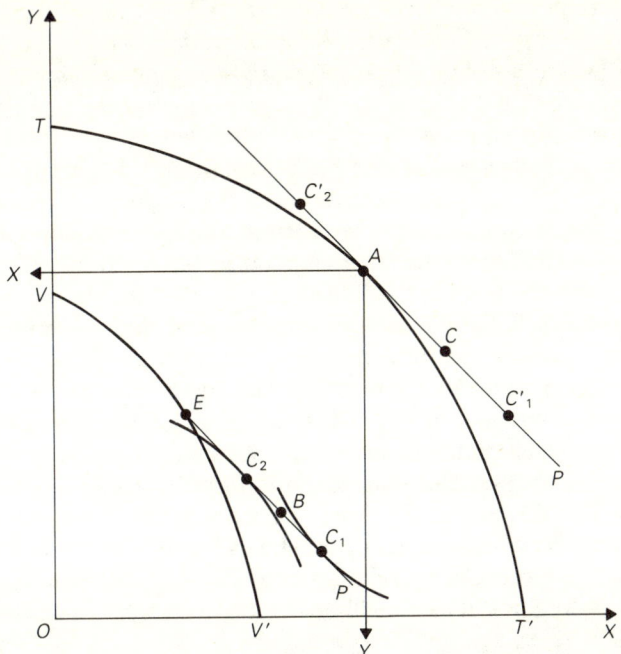

Figure 8.1 General equilibrium for two consumers with different preferences.

Each group has an endowment of capital and labor, L_i and K_i such that $L_i = L$ and $K_i = K$. For any given point such as A on TT' of Figure 8.1, the indifference curves for consumer 1 can be plotted from 0 and for consumer 2 from A giving the contract curve OBA (not shown). In what follows reference to "consumer 1" should be interpreted as meaning the group of consumers whose tastes are represented by consumer 1, and similarly for consumer 2.

One aspect of this model that is seldom taken advantage of in the trade literature is the link between the demand and the supply side formed by the condition that each individual is constrained in his role as consumer by the quantity of the two commodities he receives as factor payments for the provision of capital and labor to the two industries. In a competetive situation he receives his marginal product in quantities of X and Y depending on to which industries he sells his services. The value of the bundles of commodities he receives will be a function only of the commodity price ratio, although the specific endowment point will, in most cases, be indeterminate.

The simplest case occurs when each of the two consuming groups has only labor or capital services to supply. Here laborers will receive a share of the total production of X and Y depending on their marginal products, and similarly for capitalists. This will yield a unique endowment point such as E in Figure 8.1.[1] For A to be an equilibrium production point we must have a price line P tangent to the production possibility curve at A. This same price line through E will allow the determination of excess demands and supplies associated with this price. If the equilibrium consumption points for consumers 1 and 2 are C_1 and C_2, respectively, then C_1C_2 is the vector of net domestic excess demands and supplies. Thus if C_1C_2 (or the identical vector AC) can be obtained through trade, price line P can be a trading equilibrium. Note that the vector AC gives one point on the offer curve for this country, and that the entire offer curve can be constructed by considering all relevant price lines and following the procedure of Figure 8.1. Thus the derivation of an offer curve and the determination of a trading equilibrium is seen not to depend on the existence of community indifference curves.

In Figure 8.1 there will, of course, be a different factor endowment point for each different commodity price ratio, and the locus of these points, VEV', can be constructed and will be called the factor endowment frontier. There is a one-to-one relationship between points on TAT' and points on VEV'. In general there will not be a tangency between the price line and VEV'.[2]

If consumers have endowments of both capital and labor, the story is essentially the same except that now the endowment point E will not be unique but will depend on to which industry the individual consumers sell their factor services. However, given the assumption that factor payments are identical across industries the values of all such endowment bundles (for given commodity prices) will be unique, and thus the net trade vector can be calculated as before. Again these net demand vectors can be used to construct an offer curve for the economy as a whole.

Our analysis has been in terms of two consumers, but it is clear that extending this to three or more consumers is not difficult. With three consumers the total output A must now be divided among three individuals rather than two. Each will face commodity prices P, and given any well-behaved utility function, each consumer will be able to determine his net excess demands and supplies. These excess demands and supplies can be summed to obtain a net excess demand and supply for the economy, this again giving us one point on the economywide offer curve. Of course, we are not restricted to three consumers, and although the diagram becomes difficult, conceptually, any number of individuals can be considered.

To summarize, given the assumptions on the production side of the model, payments to all factors of production are uniquely determined for any commodity price. These payments determine the factor endowment point for each individual, and faced with this endowment and the assumed commodity prices, each consumer can determine his excess demands and supplies for the two commodities. These can be summed to produce one point on the economy's net excess demand and supply function. Thus, the assumption of the existence of community indifference curves is completely unnecessary for the existence of a trading equilibrium.

But does it make a difference in terms of the standard results whether or not community indifference curves are assumed? Clearly if it does not, nothing is gained by the complication of introducing additional consumers, and the traditional aggregation approach is vindicated. An indication that the assumption of community indifference curves does matter can be seen from Figure 8.1. Note that the implicit assumption underlying the traditional trade model is that the domestic economy presents the rest of the world with a unique excess demand and supply vector – a vector in Figure 8.1 equal to AC. This trade vector AC is consistent either with the assumption that all consumers are identical with homothetic preferences or alternatively with the assumption that, while consumers have different preferences, they maximize trade internally before turning to trade with the rest of the world. Note that in Figure 8.1 the traditional trade vector AC can be generated by assuming that the two domestic consumers trade EC_2 with each other, and that consumer 1 then trades the vector C_2C_1 with the rest of the world.

But why would we expect such a trade pattern? In the frictionless world of the traditional analysis, it would be equally appropriate to assume that both consumers trade entirely with foreigners. Thus, consumer 2 would trade the amount EC_2 and consumer 1 would trade the quantity EC_1, where $EC_2 = AC_2'$ and $EC_1 = AC_1'$. Total trade for the economy as a whole is now not the difference between the trade vectors of the two individuals but rather the sum, and is equal to $C_2'C_1'$. Note that we now have a situation where the economy is importing and exporting both commodities. The phenomenon of cross-hauling has often been seen as a puzzle by traditional trade theorists because it is not predicted by the traditional model. We now see that the explicit recognition that consumer preferences may differ within the domestic economy gives this result immediately.

In this frictionless world the total volume of trade, or gross trade, is indeterminate and can be anything between AC and $C_2'C_1'$. However, only the net trade vector AC results in any welfare gains for the economy above what could be achieved in autarky. Thus in some circumstances a significant amount of total trade could be eliminated without any welfare consequences for the economy. This is important because while the vector AC is the vector associated with gains from trade, it is the vector $C_2'C_1'$ which is recorded in international trade statistics. Reductions in this latter quantity need not have welfare consequences.

As an example, consider the effect of a tariff in this model. Because both goods are imported, a tariff on either (or both) commodities is possible. A tariff on X will have quite different welfare consequences than a tariff on Y, however. First suppose a tariff is imposed on the imports of commodity Y, the net export good. In this frictionless world, this will result in a shift of domestic consumers from foreign suppliers to domestic suppliers. The trade volume will immediately shrink from $C_2'C_1'$ to AC but no loss of welfare for any consumer will have been generated. A tariff on commodity X, on the other hand, will initially have the effect of reducing the volume of trade to AC and will subsequently have the traditional effect of the tariff found in the standard trade literature. Thus in this model the welfare consequences of tariffs depend upon on which commodity the tariff is levied. A similar argument applies to the imposition of quotas (see Melvin 1985a).

8.3 Different consumers within a region

The frictionless world of the previous section is completely unrealistic and not at all helpful in analyzing regional questions. It is easily shown, however, that the results do not depend on this very special assumption. Suppose, rather than a frictionless world, that transportation costs between any two economic units are some positive function of distance. Assume two countries such as Canada and the United States with a common border, each with producers and consumers of both commodities, and for the moment ignore the international boundary. If all economic units are allowed to trade freely with whomever they choose, an equilibrium will be reached in which total transportation costs are minimized.

Now suppose that into this geographic space we introduce the international border. The volume of international trade is, of course, just the measure of trade flows that cross this line. This flow tells us nothing about the importance of international trade for the welfare of the citizens of these two countries, however. As before we would also expect cross-hauling, for consumers of X in Windsor would buy from producers in Detroit rather than producers in Toronto, and consumers of X in Buffalo would prefer to buy from suppliers in Toronto rather than suppliers in Detroit. The indeterminancy of the trade volume found in the frictionless model will be reduced, but presumably not eliminated. There will be domestic and international sources of supply equidistant from some domestic consumers; the choice of a supplier will be arbitrary.

As before, tariffs on X and Y will have quite different effects. A tariff on Y will switch domestic consumers from foreign to domestic suppliers, and this will reduce the welfare of the domestic consumers if domestic suppliers are farther away. But this welfare reduction is of a completely different kind than that associated with traditional tariff analysis, for it is associated with higher transportation costs rather than with changes in the relative prices faced by domestic consumers. Furthermore, it will be borne entirely by the individual who is required to pay the higher transportation cost.

A tariff on X will have two effects. It will internalize trade, which will reduce welfare by the same argument as used for a tariff on Y. It will also increase the domestic price of X to all domestic producers and consumers and thus will produce the traditional welfare costs associated with a tariff.

8.4 Preference differences in the traditional model

But all countries do not have a long common border such as exists between Canada and the United States. Do the traditional trade results hold in models where it is assumed that all foreign markets are farther distant than domestic markets? To illustrate that they do not, consider the effect of an improvement in the terms of trade on the welfare of our two groups of consumers. We know from the Stolper–Samuelson theorem that any change in the terms of trade will be beneficial to one factor and harmful to another. To neutralize this effect we make the simplifying assumption that all consumers have identical allocations of capital and labor. This implies that from the point of view of factor rewards, they will always be treated identically by any change in the terms of trade. This assumption has the added attraction of allowing us to construct the commodity endowment frontier for our two consumers in a very simple way. Since the two consumers have identical endowments of capital and labor, their endowments must be exactly proportional to the endowments of the economy, and the commodity endowment locus of both will be the line WAW' of Figure 8.2. With initial prices P the factor payments give an endowment of A for both

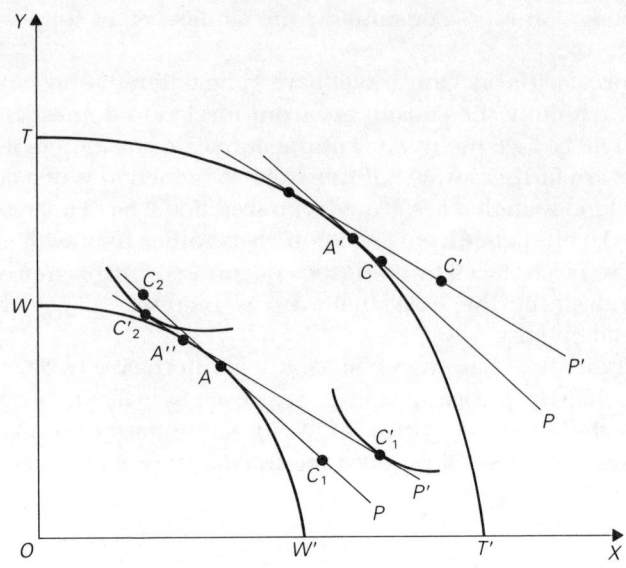

Figure 8.2 Terms of trade changes with differences in preferences.

consumers, and a total output for the economy of A', where A is on the straight line OA'. With consumer 1 assumed to have a preference biased towards commodity X, we have the two consumption points C_1 and C_2. The difference between the trade vectors AC_1 and AC_2 gives the net trade vector $A'C$.

Now, consider an improvement in the terms of trade to relative price P' (This is considered to be an improvement in the terms of trade, since it is an increase in price of Y, the net export good.) This improvement has increased the utility of consumer 1 but reduced utility for consumer 2. Thus an improvement in the terms of trade makes some consumers better off but others worse off. Furthermore, this effect is quite separate and distinct from that associated with the Stolper–Samuelson theorem. It is also of interest that the effects of an improvement in the terms of trade on consumers are not monotonic. This is illustrated in Figure 8.3 where a larger terms-of-trade change is considered. We find that with a large relative increase in the price of Y both consumers become importers of commodity X. In moving from the initial price line P the welfare of consumer 2 initially falls and, as autarky for this individual is reached, subsequently rises. In fact, the final equilibrium at C_2' in Figure 8.3 shows a situation where the total effect on consumer 2 has been an increase in welfare from C_2 to C_2'. This provides a further illustration

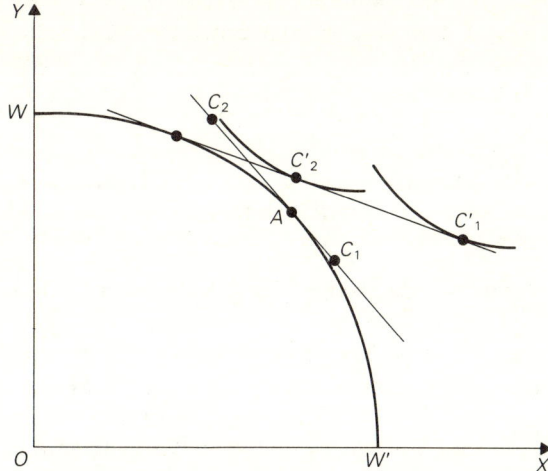

Figure 8.3 Welfare changes with changes in the terms of trade.

that this result is not related to the Stolper–Samuelson theorem. Indeed, we can think of this as the demand side counterpart to the Stolper–Samuelson theorem – a result which has heretofore been ignored because of the concentration on single consumer models.

A similar result can be shown for the effects of tariffs: any tariff will make one consumer better off and the other worse off (Melvin 1985a). It can also be shown that with different consumers the proposition that any tariff can be duplicated by a system of domestic taxes and/or subsidies no longer holds. Without going into detail, the reason is that while a tariff reduces the welfare of the individual importing the commodity and increases the welfare of the other, a tax reduces the welfare of anyone who consumes the product. A tax collected by the domestic government creates a distortion between all domestic consumers and foreigners. A tariff, on the other hand, creates a distortion between domestic *importers* and foreigners, but allows some domestic consumers, namely those with an excess supply of the tariff-ridden commodity, to benefit from the price increase as they essentially collect the tariff. The significance for the present discussion is that this important distinction between the effects of domestic taxes and tariffs has also been obscured by the concentration on the single-consumer model.

These examples serve to illustrate the point made earlier, namely that the assumption that all consumers are identical with homothetic preferences does obscure important aspects of the general equilibrium model. The use of community indifference curves has resulted in a general acceptance of results which are not correct when less restrictive demand conditions are considered. Professor Perroux was quite correct in his criticism of the use of community indifference curves in international trade theory.

8.5 An interregional model with differences in preference

The model of consumer differences can be given a regional interpretation by assuming that our two groups of consumers live in different regions, where transportation costs between these two regions are high relative to transportation costs to neighboring foreign markets. Such a model has an obvious application for countries like Canada where distances between Toronto and Buffalo or between Vancouver and Seattle are small relative to the distances between Toronto and Vancouver. To simplify further we will assume that international transportation costs are zero and that both regions face the same world prices.

Figure 8.4 illustrates an initial equilibrium with production in both regions at A, and consumption in regions 1 and 2 at C_1 and C_2, respectively. Several results are immediate. Because of our transportation costs assumption, both regions trade with the rest of the world and we have cross-hauling of identical commodities for the economy as a whole. It is also clear that any change in the terms of trade will increase welfare in one region and reduce it in the other, thus creating regional disparities. Note that because a change in the terms of trade leaves commodity and factor prices the same between regions, the regional disparity is entirely due to the differences in preferences. Per capita incomes will remain the same between regions.

Now consider the imposition of a tariff on commodity X. This tariff only affects consumers in region 1, for region 2 does not import X and therefore cannot be affected by a tariff. In region 1, the price of X will increase for both consumers and producers, and the standard tariff result is obtained. Production will move to B_1, consumption to D_1, and the volume of trade will be reduced from AC_1 to B_1D_1. We thus see immediately that tariffs have distinctly regional effects. In particular a tariff only affects the region which imports that commodity.

Figure 8.4 also illustrates the fact that the tariff has changed the pattern of trade – a result which is not possible in the traditional international trade model. In the initial equilibrium, net trade was equal to $AC_1 - AC_2 = AC$ so that the economy as a whole is a net importer of commodity X. With the tariff on commodity X, imports change from AC_1 to B_1D_1, and clearly the economy is now a net exporter of commodity Y.

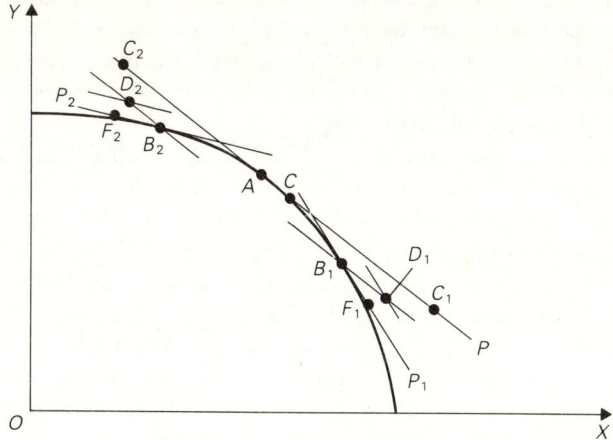

Figure 8.4 Regional consequences of differences in preferences.

Those who are still concerned with explanations of the so-called Leontief Paradox can add tariffs in a regional economy to their list.

A tariff on commodity Y produces a symmetrical result for consumers in region 2. Production will move to B_2 and consumption to D_2, resulting in a welfare loss for consumers in this region. The volume of trade will be reduced from AC_2 to B_2D_2. Consumers in region 1 will be unaffected by this tariff, of course.

The implicit assumption made to this point has been that the tariff has been smaller than the transportation cost between the two regions. Now suppose that the tariff rate and the transportation costs have become identical, and for simplicity, suppose that this occurs for the tariff illustrated in Figure 8.4. Now with any small increase in the tariff on X, consumers in region 2 will find it profitable to import X from region 1 rather than from the rest of the world. But note that this will result in a further reduction in welfare for consumers in region 1, for they now lose the gains from the trade they formerly enjoyed. With production at B_1, consumption would be at F_1 if consumers were forced to trade at prices P_1. With the possibility of foreign trade at prices P consumers can move to D_1, and thus the distance F_1D_1 represents the gains from international trade. With the switch from international to interregional trade these gains are lost, and residents of region 1 will consume at F_1. Thus the switch from international to interregional trade results in a discrete welfare loss from D_1 to F_1.

This welfare loss occurs because the switch from international to interregional trade has been accomplished by transforming the tariff revenue into a transportation cost. The tariff revenue, of course, was a gain to society but the additional transportation cost is a loss to society since the added transportation uses up scarce resources whereas the tariffs did not. It is therefore clear that tariffs which generate interregional trade impose a cost on society well beyond the cost calculated in traditional tariff analysis.

Does this model have implications for factor mobility? At first glance it may appear not to be the case, even though tariffs result in different factor prices between the two regions. Since all individuals have the same relative endowments of capital and labor, it is not clear how they would be affected by, say, an increase in the wage rate combined with a reduction in the return to capital. The differences in preferences also complicate the issue, since residents of one region have a different evaluation of any relative price change than do residents of the other region. A closer examination shows, however, that tariffs will result in factor mobility. Consider the situation shown in Figure 8.4 where a tariff on commodity X results in a reduction in the welfare of all consumers in region 1. Assume no tariff on commodity Y, so that residents of region 2 will be unaffected and continue to consume at point C_2. An individual consumer in region 1 will observe that by migrating to region 2 he can reestablish his consumption at C_1, for in region 2, there are no imports of commodity X and therefore the tariff cannot be effective. Similarly, a tariff on commodity Y will encourage all consumers in region 2 to move to region 1. Thus, a substantial amount of factor mobility has been generated by the tariff but not, as we have already noted, because of the changes in factor prices.

8.6 An interregional model with endowment differences

An alternative method of regionalizing the economy is to follow the Heckschler–Ohlin approach and assume that the two regions differ, not in terms of preferences, but in terms of their endowments of factors of production (Melvin 1985b). This model is again in the neoclassical tradition and assumes the production structure given in Equations 8.1–8.4 of Section 8.2. In order to focus on the effects of differences in endowments, we assume that all individuals in both regions of the economy have identical preferences, and that the regions differ in terms of their endowments of capital and labor. Specifically, it is assumed that region E is relatively well endowed with factor K and that region W is relatively well endowed with factor L. Each region has access to the same technology for the production of X and Y, both of which are assumed to be produced under conditions of constant returns to scale. It is again assumed that significant transportation costs exist between the two regions and that there are zero transportation costs internationally. Both regions are assumed to face the same set of given world prices, and in the initial equilibrium it is assumed that both regions produce both goods.

The production possibility curves for the economy and for the two regions are shown in Figure 8.5, where TAT' represents the production possibility curve for the economy as a whole. Subscripts E and W refer to the production sets for the two regions. With P the world price vector, region E produces at A_E and region W at A_W, and the addition of these points gives point A, the production point for the economy. With identical homogeneous tastes in both regions, the consumption points for the two regions and for the economy as a whole will lie along some straight line through the origin such as OC.

This model has some obvious similarities to the one described in Section 4. For example, in the equilibrium illustrated in Figure 8.5, region E exports Y while region W exports X; the economy as a whole is exporting and importing both commodities, and we again have cross-

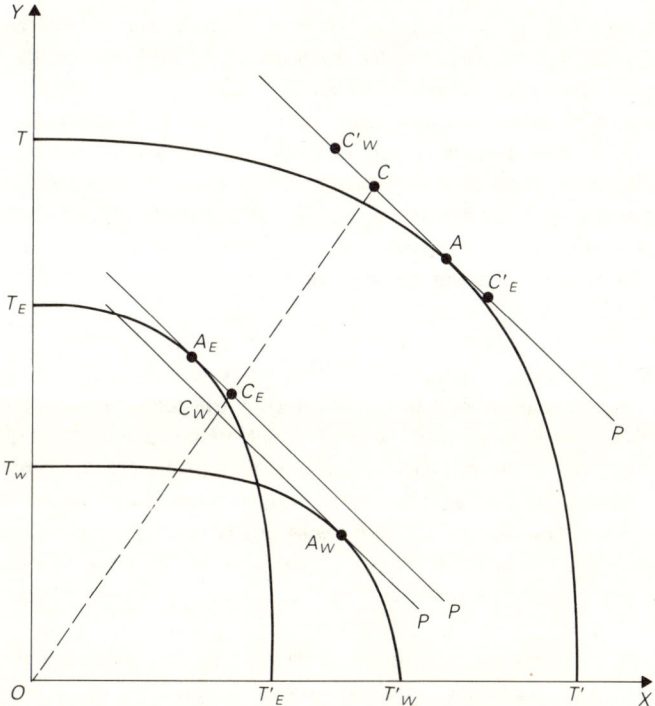

Figure 8.5 Cross-hauling in a regional trade model.

hauling. The difference between the trade vectors of the two regions gives the net trade vector AC, while the total trade vector for the economy is $C_W'C_E'$.

Now consider an exogenous increase in the relative price of commodity X. While this would be considered as an improvement in the terms of trade for the economy as a whole, since X is the net export commodity, it is clear that such a relative price change does *not* increase welfare in both regions. In particular, per capita income in region W will rise and per capita income in region E will fall. Thus a change in the terms of trade will have differential welfare consequences for the two regions as long as the trade patterns of the two regions differ.

Such changes in the relative per capita incomes of the two regions might be seen as a regional disparity and could prompt the federal government to "correct" this disparity through an interregional transfer from W to E. But, while per capita incomes have changed in the two regions, the terms of trade change *has not resulted in differences in factor payments between regions*. Given the assumptions of our model, the equalization of commodity prices between regions and the fact that both regions produce both goods implies that factor prices will be equalized between regions. This statement is true both before and after any terms-of-trade change, and thus it is clear that no factor in E has been disadvantaged relative to the corresponding factor in W by the increase in the price of commodity X.

Any interregional transfer to consumers in region E would be financed, we assume, through taxation of all consumers in region W. This will result in all factors being made better off in region E than their counterparts in region W, even though the terms-of-trade change increased per capita income in W (both relatively and absolutely). Thus while the terms-of-trade change does not create a real disparity, the attempt to correct it does.

This somewhat paradoxical result can be explained by noting that, while factors have not been disadvantaged according to their location, relative factor prices have been affected by the terms-of-trade change. In particular, since commodity X is labor intensive, an increase in the price of X will, by the Stolper–Samuelson theorem, increase the real reward to labor and reduce the real reward to capital. This, however, will be true in both regions. The observed changes in per capita income result from the fact that region W has relatively more of the factor labor whose price has risen while region E is relatively well endowed with capital whose return has fallen. Thus the observed differences in per capita income in the two regions is simply a consequence of the fact that factors exist in different proportions in these two regions. Such "disparities" are not something that should be corrected, at least not through interregional transfers.

Figure 8.6 illustrates the imposition of a tariff on commodity Y, the

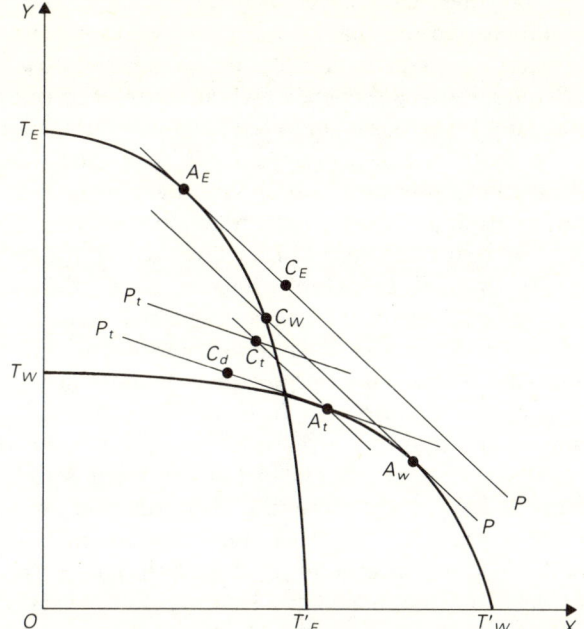

Figure 8.6 Tariffs in a regional trade model.

import of region W. Production moves to point A_t and consumption to C_t, and thus the welfare of the region W has been reduced. Region E, which imports commodity X will not be directly affected by such a tariff. The analysis of Figure 8.6 will, however, generally underestimate the cost of such a tariff to region W. The gains from trade for region W, associated with the fact that it can still trade at prices P, are equal to the distance C_dC_t, this being the amount of tariff collected and redistributed to consumers in region W. But a tariff collected by the federal government will generally not be returned entirely to the region from which it was collected. Under the more normal assumption that the tariff revenue is allocated to all consumers in the economy, we would find that consumers in E would benefit from this tariff, and consumers in region W would suffer a further welfare loss. Thus, even for a small open economy, a region may have an incentive to encourage the federal government to impose tariffs on the imports of the other region.

The costs associated with the generation of interregional trade in this model are similar to those described in Section 8.4. A tariff high enough to overcome the transportation cost barrier will immediately result in consumers in region W moving from point C_t to C_d. What was formerly collected as tariff revenue is now used up in the unnecessary transportation of goods from one region to another. Note that under such circumstances, an optimal strategy for region W, and indeed for the economy as a whole, would be to introduce a restriction on interregional trade, thereby forcing a switch from interregional back to international trade. There has been much discussion in Canada in recent years about the costs of interprovincial trade restrictions. Our analysis suggests that in the face of tariffs, such regionally imposed restrictions may in fact increase both regional and national welfare.

This model has quite different implications for factor mobility than does the earlier model in which regions were differentiated by preferences. The tariff illustrated in Figure 8.6 will reduce the real and relative wage rate and increase the real and relative return to capital in region W, but will have no effect on factor payments in region E. Thus tariffs can clearly be a source of interregional differences in factor prices. If factors are free to move, as we would assume them to be within a country we would expect labor to move from W to E and capital to move from E to W. But note that on the margin such factor movements will not result in any reduction in factor-price differentials. As long as both regions continue to produce both goods, and as long as commodity prices are unchanged, the Rybczynski theorem tells us that real factor rewards will not be affected by factor movements. Of course, if factor movements are large enough to change trade patterns which in turn will result in commodity price changes, factor price differentials will narrow and eventually be eliminated. But this will occur only when the relative endowments of the two regions have also become equal. The point is that, in this model, factor mobility cannot be seen as a cure for interregional differences in factor prices.

A variety of other results can be derived from this model (see Melvin 1985b) but these brief comments will suffice for present purposes, namely to demonstrate that the failure to consider the underlying regional structure of an economy will result in a failure to appreciate the fundamental interactions between regions, and between regions and the rest of the world. This failure to recognize the regional nature of an economy may result in an incomplete and misleading picture of both domestic and international policy issues.

8.7 The natural rate of interregional disparities

Professor Perroux has long understood that differences in the economic activities of regions would be expected to produce interregional disparities (see for example, Perroux, 1955, p.101). The quote presented at the end of Section 8.1 also makes it clear that he feels that such disparities should be expected to persist in any optimum. This view, which we support, is quite sharply at variance with much of the popular regional policy analysis, at least as practiced in Canada. Disparities are almost seen as undesirable and as things which must and can be corrected if only the appropriate policy instrument can be brought to bear on them. Vast amounts of resources have been allocated to the task of correcting Canadian interregional disparities, and in many cases the policy actions have almost certainly been the cause rather than the cure of observed interregional differences.

But of course the problem of identifying the causes of regional disparities is not a simple one. While many observed differences are undoubtedly the consequences of natural equilibrating processes, others are not. For example, disparities which are caused by either federal or regional policies are not "natural" and should probably be eliminated. There are also perceived disparities which are not real disparities at all, but which nevertheless sometimes receive a considerable amount of attention. We feel that the principal policy task of regional economics is, first, to decide when disparities exist; and second, to decide whether or not these disparities are in need of correction. Some of these distinctions can be illustrated with reference to the earlier analysis.

In the model with regional endowment differences, it was shown that an exogenous terms-of-trade change would increase per capita income in one region and reduce it in the other. Such apparent disparities, however, were seen to be entirely a function of the distribution of factors between the two regions, and it was found that individual factor owners were not disadvantaged relative to factors in the other region by such a terms-of-trade change. This is an example of a situation where there is no real disparity at all, unless, of course, one regards the change in relative factor prices as a distortion. But in such a case the losing factor should be subsidized *regardless* of location. Otherwise the observed change in per capita income does not require policy action, for the disparity is completely illusory.

Now consider the effect of a change in the terms of trade in the model with regional taste differences. Here there can be no illusion about the disparity, for all individuals in the economy are exactly identical with respect to their ownership of factors. A terms-of-trade change makes some of them better off and others worse off. But while this is an obvious disparity, it is entirely due to the difference in consumers' preferences and is not something with which the government should be concerned. Relative price changes always affect individuals differently, depending on their tastes for the products in question, but this should not be seen as a matter for government concern.

For the case of a tariff in the model with regional differences in endowments, the observed disparity is real and should be eliminated. It is obviously the consequence of government policy and not associated with the natural equilibrating mechanisms of the economy. But even here care must be taken, for many policies introduced to solve the problem will be ineffective, or indeed may make things worse. The optimal solution is clear – the tariff should be eliminated.

Many causes of regional disparities not discussed in this paper could be enumerated, and some would be found deserving of policy action and others not. To provide just a few examples, if natural resources are unequally distributed among regions, there is every reason to expect that factor payments will also differ. Whether or not these differences should be corrected depends on whether one views natural resources as belonging to regions or to all citizens of the country. The existence of increasing returns to scale in industries which are important for certain regions will almost certainly generate factor price differentials. Such differentials would generally not be seen as candidates for policy action. Differences in the level of regional minimum wages or the strength of unions can result both in differential unemployment rates and differences in factor prices across regions. Most would agree that these differences, because they are artificially produced, are inappropriate and should be subject to policy action.

A taxonomic approach to regional disparities hardly seems necessary to illustrate our principal point, namely, that sensible regional policy cannot be formulated without a clear understanding of the source of the difficulty, if indeed any difficulty exists. While it may well be true that more powerful models could usefully be brought to bear on these questions, our view is that much can be learned from the appropriate use of the simple general equilibrium models at our disposal.

8.8 Conclusions

Professor Perroux has long been a critic of neoclassical general equilibrium models and has argued that many of the simplifying assumptions are at such odds with reality as to make the conclusions of the model at best worthless and at worst harmful. The main purpose of our paper has been to lend some support to this claim by demonstrating that many of the simplifying assumptions mask a whole range of interesting issues, and that until these issues are understood, little progress can be made towards the formulation of sensible regional economic policy.

Professor Perroux goes further and argues for the abandonment of the neoclassical methodology in favour of a more sophisticated approach based on the modern theory of thermodynamics. We do not find ourselves completely convinced by this argument. One reason for our doubt may well be the fact that we are completely incapable of coming to grips with this new methodology. An equally important reason, however, is our view that much of the problem lies not with the methodology but with its application. As we hope to have demonstrated, some progress can be made by a more careful application of the general equilibrium tools that are already well understood. Finally, we feel that the neoclassical general equilibrium model, imperfect as it is, does provide, at least in many cases, clear policy direction. At least at the present this is not the case for the new methodology proposed by Professor Perroux.

Notes

1 As an example consider the two Cobb–Douglas production functions $X = K^a L^{1-a}$ and $Y = K^b L^{1-b}$. The marginal product of K in X is aX/K and the marginal product of K in Y is bY/K. Thus capital shares of X and Y are aX and bY respectively. Similarly labor shares in the two industries are $(1-a)X$ and $(1-b)Y$, and thus the shares of labor and capital define a unique point in output space – a point such as E in Fig. 8.1.
2 If the two groups of consumers have identical endowments of both factors then the price line P will be tangent to VEV'. This case is assumed in Melvin (1985a).

References

Courchene, T. J. & J. R. Melvin 1980. Energy revenues: consequences for the rest of Canada. *Canadian Public Policy* **6**, 192–204.
Johnson, H. B. 1959. International trade, income distribution and the offer curve. *Manchester School* **27**, 241–60.
Kenen, P. B. 1957. On the geometry of welfare economics. *Quarterly Journal of Economics* **71**, 426–47.
Kenen, P. B. 1959. Distribution, demand, and equilibrium in international trade: a diagrammatic analysis. *Kyklos* 629–38.
Melvin, J. R. 1985a. Domestic taste differences, transportation costs and international trade. *Journal of International Economics* **18**, 65–82.
Melvin, J. R. 1985b. The regional economic consequences of tariffs and domestic transportation costs. *Canadian Journal of Economics* **18**, 237–57.
Perroux, F. 1950. Economic space: theory and applications. *Quarterly Journal of Economics* **64**, 89–104.
Perroux, F. 1955. Note sur la notion de pôle de croissance. *Économie appliquée*. D. L. McKee et al. (ed.) (1970) *Regional economics: theory and practice*. New York: The Free Press.
Perroux, F. 1980. Peregrinations of an economist and the choice of his route. *Banca Nazionale de Lavoro Quarterly Review* **133**, 147–62.
Perroux, F. 1983. *A new concept of development*. London: Croom Helm (for UNESCO).

PART III
Canadian experiences

9
Regional development and efficiency of the national economy

BENJAMIN HIGGINS

This essay resembles those by François Perroux in Part I above in four respects: (a) It is based upon a conviction, reached after many years of observation and study, that regional economics should not be thought of as a "branch" of general economic theory, standing a bit apart from the main body of doctrine, but as an essential part of any complete and realistic general economic theory. No national or international economy can be thoroughly understood without analyzing its regional structure, the nature and functioning of the various regional economies comprising it, their interactions among themselves, and their relationships to the national and world economies. (b) The essay brings together components of a more general theory that has been evolving for two decades or more, but is still incomplete. (c) This system is designed to offer an alternative to both the neoclassical and the neo-Marxist systems, which will provide a better basis for prescribing policy and formulating plans for development. (d) The central argument of the essay is that one cannot really speak of "regional development" and "increasing the efficiency of the national economy" as though these were two quite distinct things, between which any society with limited resources must make marginal choices. Rather, regional development is a key component of any policy or program for raising the efficiency of the national economy.

The entire general theory cannot be presented in any essay shorter than a book; and such a book is now nearing completion. As it stands, however this essay provides a bridge between Parts II and III of the present volume. It is concerned with scope and method, and with the design of new approaches to economic analysis. To that extent its arguments are applicable to any country. On the other hand, its illustrations are derived mainly from Canada, and its policy applications are made mainly to Canada. Some of the general ideas are derived from Canadian experiences.

The neoclassical paradigm

There are two possible ways of persuading adherents to the prevailing neoclassical paradigm that some new system is worth consideration. One is to attack the neoclassical system in its own backyard, accepting its definition of scope and method, and demonstrate the weaknesses of the system within its own framework. The other is to show that there are types of behavior and kinds of interaction which are important for the operation and development of national economies, but which are not part of the neoclassical system. The first kind of attack takes a lot of time and space; many people are engaged in it, and I have already devoted two articles to the subject (Higgins 1977, 1978a). In this paper I shall therefore concentrate on the second approach within the specific context of regional and national development, and show that there are kinds of feedback relationships between the two that do not normally enter into the neoclassical analysis.

9.1 The concept of "efficiency"

When we ask whether programmes to develop particular regions are in conflict with economic efficiency at the national level, the term "efficient" can only mean that resources are allocated in a way that enhances welfare of the entire national society. If all the technical and philosophical assumptions of neoclassical welfare economics are granted, so that prices are indeed a measure of welfare gained, and costs are a measure of welfare sacrificed; and if the ethics of income distribution under pure competition are ignored; it is then possible to identify "efficiency" in the national economy with level and growth of gross national product. The question becomes, "Would GNP be higher and grow faster with or without the regional development programs?"

These are of course very big "ifs," and any debate concerning national efficiency versus regional development plunges us deep into the hornet's nest of the current controversy over the validity of neoclassical welfare economics. My own conclusion (or value judgement) is that not much remains of pure neoclassical welfare economics; a different approach is needed to estimating the impact on "national efficiency" of any economic or social policy, regional development policy included. A goodly proportion of the participants in the workshop seem to have reached the same conclusion. But even for those who have not yet reached it, there are considerations that any objective scholar must take into account when discussing the topic of this paper. These considerations may be grouped under five major headings: market failure; the mechanism of the market, including both behavioral assumptions and the way the "machine" operates as a result; elements of welfare that the market mechanism leaves out; philosophical underpinnings; and specific interactions between regional disparities and the operation of the national economy.

9.2 Market failure

The elements involved in market failure are well known to any trained economist and I shall not give them a long recital here. The debate is not about what the elements are, but about how important they are in the real world. Robert Solow's pronouncement on the subject is so apt and so elegant that I cannot resist quoting him once again:

> Some of us see the Smithian virtues as needles in a haystack, as an island of measure zero in a sea of imperfections. Others see the imperfections as so many ticks on the thick hide of an ox, requiring only an occasional flick of its tail to be brushed away. (Solow 1980, p. 2)

This debate can be resolved only by empirical study. The answer will vary from country to country, from region to region, from sector to sector, and from industry to industry. With regard to the industrialized market economies (IMEs) as a whole, I belong to the "sea of imperfections" school. I might add that, despite the supposed injurious role of the multinationals, I believe that the market economies of many developing countries operate in a manner closer to the neoclassical ideal than do those of most of the IMEs. Nothing could approximate pure competition, perfect knowledge, and equal access to information better than village markets in developing countries. I also believe that in the IMEs imperfect knowledge, imperfect foresight, externalities, indivisibilities, and slow and unequal diffusion of information do more damage to "efficiency" than exercise of monopoly power as such. So far as I can see, those with a lot of monopoly power seldom use it to limit production so as to maximize profits, but rather try to maximize growth of the firm within restraints, as Robin Marris would have it (Marris 1967). The few entrepreneurs who try to maximize profits are those who, like the Indian shopkeeper in Fiji, working 14 hours a day, seven days a week, to send his children to school, have no choice but to maximize profits because otherwise they will go under. Their counterparts may be found in the Atlantic Provinces and Quebec.

I am not asking anyone to accept my judgement on such factual matters at face value. I am insisting only on the need for study of market structures and decision-making by managers, workers, and consumers, at the regional level, before judgement is exercised on the positive or negative effects of regional policies on national efficiency.

9.3 The mechanism of the market

Here there are two separate but overlapping issues. The first is a very big issue indeed, and relates to the whole methodology of economics. I am one of the growing body of economists, which includes Herbert Simon, François Perroux, Janos Kornai and many others, who believe that we should sever the fetters that bind us to the methodology of physics, and especially of mechanics, leaving us free to model our analyses on the methodology of biology instead. For me this means, among other things, abandoning the attempt to build general theories on simple assumptions about supposedly universal characteristics of individual human behavior, like maximization of utility or profits, in favor of semi-anthropological studies of social groups, on the spot and at the community level, to find out who the real actors are whose decisions and actions determine the course of development, what motivates them, and how they respond to various situations.

Such an approach makes a lot of difference. Models constructed to fit the behavior of peasants in Haiti or the African Sahel, for example, who minimize risk measured in terms of possible starvation, give very different results, and have very different policy implications, than models based on an assumption of profit-maximizing by commercial farmers. So do models based on the behavior of leisure-loving and business-hating French Canadian entrepreneurs, a type that dominated francophone enterprises in Quebec until the last decade or so, but who are now being replaced by hard-driving, ambitious, francophone growth-maximizers. Here again, of course, we are confronted with questions of fact that cannot be answered without study of actual behavior. (I may as well record here my disagreement with Milton Friedman, on the methodological issue as to whether the validity of behavioral assumptions can be tested by looking at the macroeconomic *results* of such behavior. I don't think they can.)

The other issue is rather different, and relates to the question as to whether the operation of "the market," left to itself, tends to bring convergence of regional employment and income, or whether it tends to bring cumulative movements away from equilibrium and ever increasing regional disparities. Simplistic application of pure neoclassical models leads to the conclusion that the operation of a free market leads sooner or later to the elimination of regional gaps. On the neoclassical theory as such, there are by now a good many books presenting critical attacks on it, including its application to urban growth and regional development (for example, Kornai 1971; Hollis & Nell 1977; Bensusan-Butt 1978; Perroux 1983, 1984; Lekachman 1976; Lutz & Lux 1979). A book is what it takes to do a proper job, but I may be forgiven one observation. Italy, West Germany, and France all have market economies that have performed reasonably well since World War II; but the gap between per capita output in the richest and the poorest regions of each country ranges between 210 and 260%. The United States is often regarded as an example of a successful free market economy. Yet it took that country 120 years to reduce the gap in per capita income between the richest and the poorest region from over 400%, as it was in 1860, to about 30% today, which might be regarded as tolerable. I doubt that the inhabitants of the poorer regions in Canada are in a mood to wait that long for their positions to be improved.

Moreover, in the United States, as Harry W. Richardson has pointed out, there is at least a possibility of the gaps being reversed and becoming cumulatively worse again:

> In the relatively near future, an opportunitity will develop to test the appropriateness of the neoclassical compared with the cumulative causation model. The key question is whether regional per capita income will stabilize close to equality (i.e., an approximation to neoclassical equilibrium) or whether they will cross over, with the four lower income regions (South Atlantic, East South Central, West South Central and Mountain) then becoming progressively richer than the four regions of the Northeast and Midwest. The latter development would be more consistent with the cumulative causation model. The competing hypotheses of interregional income equilibrium and the "cross over" is the most intriguing question in contemporary regional economics. (Richardson 1984, pp. 22–3.)

Translating Richardson's question into the Canadian context is not altogether simple because current trends are not clear. Quebec has made remarkable gains in the past two decades, and the gains seem to be accelerating. Alberta and British Columbia have also made rapid progress in the past ten years, surpassing Ontario in per capita income, but are now slowing down, if not stagnating or worse. The Atlantic Provinces show little sign of catching up with the other provinces. Is Quebec on its way to becoming Canada's richest province? With the new dynamism displayed by the French Canadian population of that province, it is not beyond the realm of possibility.

But whatever one thinks of the logical consistency, validity of behavioral assumptions, and empirical relevance of the neoclassical model, we must at least take into account the fact that it is not unrivaled. There are, as offshoots of the neoclassical theory itself, the rival doctrines of cumulative causation and polarization. From the radical political economists and other Marxists come theories of dependency and uneven development. The concept of cumulative causation was applied by Roy Harrod and Evsey Domar to market economies as a whole, leading to the vision of such economies as being poised on a "knife-edge," with steady growth about as likely as a camel getting through the eye of a needle, and hyperinflation or deep and chronic unemployment the probable result of falling off the knife edge. Gunnar Myrdal applied similar reasoning to regional disparities (Myrdal 1957). Regions with an initial advantage will tend to attract both labor and capital. Investment in the advantaged region will tend to raise both wages and profits there, leading to further inflows and further expansion. The accelerated population growth in more prosperous regions will itself encourage investment there. Because of linkages between advantaged and disadvantaged regions, expansion of the more prosperous regions will generate both "spread effects" (favorable impacts) and "backwash effects" (unfavorable impacts) on the less prosperous ones, but the backwash effects will prevail. For example, emigration from the lagging region will discourage investment there. So the rich regions get richer and the poor regions get poorer, and regional disparities get worse and worse.

François Perroux elaborated his well known doctrine of polarization (not to be confused with the later application – or misapplication – of growth pole strategies by some of his disciples, and by others who did not really understand Perroux at all), which also argued that rather than a market economy bringing "balanced" development in space it brings instead a concentration of development in particular centers (see Higgins 1981a, 1983). The Perroux and Myrdal theories are obviously interrelated.

I have always found it impossible to deal with neo-Marxist theory in short compass, and here I shall not try. But the school has too many adherents to ignore, and they are in any case not wholly wrong. A recent and typical example of the application of neomarxist doctrine to development within space is Neil Smith's book *Uneven development*, where he writes:

> capital is like a plague of locusts. It settles in one place, devours it, moves on to plague another place. Better, in the process of restoring itself after one plague the region makes itself ripe for another. At the very least, uneven development is the geographical expression of the contradictions of capital. (Smith 1984, p. 52.)

The process of capitalistic accumulation leads to concentration of wealth, not only in the hands of a particular social class, but in particular places as well, leading to polarization of development. Underdevelopment in some regions and cities is the opposite side of the coin of development in others.

Elsewhere I have criticized the Radical Political Economists for their failure to provide empirical evidence regarding the manner in which decisions are made and the way in which power is exercized; as a rule, they merely report *results* of the operation of the system, and the results can be explained in alternative ways (Higgins & Dung 1981). But one need not be a neo-Marxist to recognize the importance of power, other than monopoly power exercised in the market, for the outcome of the operation of any economic system. As John Kenneth Galbraith says in a recent book:

> The young are taught that in a democracy all power resides in the people. And that in a free enterprise system all authority rests with the sovereign consumer operating through the impersonal mechanism of the market. Thus is hidden the public power of organization – the Pentagon, the weapons firms, and other corporations and lobbyists. Similarly concealed by the mystique of the market is the power of corporations to set or influence prices and costs, to suborn or subdue politicians, and to manipulate consumer response ... Yet power, per se is not a proper subject for indignation. The exercise of power, the submission of some to the will of others, is inevitable in modern society; nothing whatever can be accomplished without it. (Galbraith 1983, pp. 12–13.)

The point about the exercise of power is not that it leads inevitably to an allocation of resources inferior to, or less "efficient" than, a market ruled by atomistic competition, but that once power enters the stage, the market no longer gives direct evidence of the efficiency or inefficiency of resource allocation. Even monopoly power hides from direct view marginal costs of any enterprise, and without knowing marginal costs as well as prices one cannot judge the "efficiency" of resource allocation, even within the neoclassical framework. But with the introduction of the sort of power that intrigues Galbraith, all links between the market and measurement of efficiency and inefficiency are broken. It is not that markets where such power is exercised are impossible to analyze. I have constructed several models to do just that, one concerned with nationwide wage determination which is presented as a game played by trade union leaders, top managers, and top government policy makers (Higgins 1981c).

The intervention of government in wage determination may be as direct and pervasive as the Australian Arbitration Commission, which sets the basic wage on which all wages are determined, or as direct as a central bank threat to impose a restrictive monetary policy with high interest rates if the wage settlement is too generous to labor. Each player in the game has "rational expectations" about the strategy that will be pursued by the other players. If bargaining power is evenly distributed, if a sense of fair play prevails, if government policy is foresighted and astute, such a game may produce a wage settlement as good or better for the welfare of the society as a whole as a free competitive market where wages are determined by individual employers and employees. But with such a model it is impossible to predict the outcome, or evaluate the "efficiency" of the market after the event, from the wage settlement alone. The outcome is indeterminate. One may know that Dr. Sinkorswim will probably open the chess match with the Jugoslav variant of the king's Indian defense, but that is not enough to predict the outcome. And to evaluate the outcome it must be studied in detail and in all its aspects, to determine its impact on the economy and on the society. It cannot be said that the wage settlement is "good" just because the "market" produced it.

Whether industrialized market economies are characterized by movements back toward equilibrium in the wake of any disturbance or, in the absence of favorable shocks or effective government intervention, by cumulative movements away from equilibrium, is again a question of fact that cannot be settled by any exercise in pure theory alone. The answer is probably "sometimes the one, sometimes the other." Theories of economic fluctuations, or business cycles, of different durations depend upon alternations of movements towards with movements away from equilibrium. These can be applied to regional disparities as well as to national economies as whole. I have combined some of these theories in a special way to explain why depressions have been longer and deeper in Quebec than in the more prosperous provinces in the past. I shall return to the question of regional business cycles below, but it should be already clear that we cannot take for granted a tendency for uninhibited market forces to bring rapid and substantial reductions in regional disparities.

9.4 Things the market leaves out

Then there are the things that the market leaves out. First among these, perhaps, is the enormous and increasing range of public goods – health, education, transport, energy, the environment, nutrition, defense, internal security, etc. These nonmarket decisions are more important for welfare in the industrialized market economies than the sum total of market decisions. Moreover, the collective decisions become more and more "lumpy" as megaprojects become more important. How does a society decide whether or not to go through with the $150 billion project to separate James Bay from Hudson Bay, turning James Bay into a freshwater lake, turn its gigantic inflow of water – twice that of the Great Lakes system – around into the Great Lakes and then to the Mississippi, selling Canada's vast water surplus to the Americans at a good price?

But there are less dramatic things, which must be taken into the calculus of costs and benefits of regional projects, and which are not priced in any market. Among these are:

(a) the contribution to the welfare of people in disadvantaged areas of being able to earn a satisfactory living where they are, rather than emigrating;
(b) the contribution to the welfare of other Canadians of having people in the disadvantaged regions stay where they are, rather than emigrating and competing in other areas for jobs, housing, public transport, public utilities, and so on;
(c) the addition to the welfare of Canadians in prosperous areas through knowing that gaps between them and people in the poorer areas have been narrowed ("altruism");
(d) the satisfaction of people in the poorer areas in knowing that gaps between them and other Canadians have been narrowed;
(e) the gain to other Canadians when people in high unemployment areas get jobs and stop living on unemployment insurance or social welfare;
(f) the value to the unemployed of not working (leisure);
(g) the increased satisfaction of people in high unemployment areas through having a job rather than living on unemployment insurance or social security;

(h) the increase in incomes (and welfare) through migration from poorer to more prosperous areas (if any);
(i) the increase in incomes of people in prosperous areas through migration of people from poorer areas (if any);
(j) the loss of infrastructure in the form of housing, public utilities, transport, schools, and hospitals in regions where net emigration takes place, including the impact of the tendency of such emigration to become cumulative once started;
(k) the cost of providing such infrastructure in the areas of net immigration, once again considering the tendency for such movements to become cumulative.
(l) the cost to those who remain in disadvantaged regions of emigration of young, well-trained, ambitious, high-need-achievement people of their community, leaving behind a distorted age and social structure, and broken families.

While the market provides no direct estimate of these costs and benefits, they can be estimated as part of a regional planning exercise.

9.5 Philosophical underpinnings

I have dealt with the underlying philosophical assumptions of neoclassical welfare economics in two earlier papers (Higgins 1977, 1978), and can do little more than record my major conclusions here. These are:

(a) Maximizing "welfare, in the sense in which the term is used in "welfare economics," which requires equalizing marginal satisfaction of all individuals in society, makes no philosophical sense. It requires redistributing income in favor of the "super enjoyers" and away from those with less capacity for enjoyment.
(b) The Pareto optimum makes no sense either. It tells nothing about the true level of social welfare in any society. One cannot possibly say that a society which is in a state of Pareto optimum is better off than a society that is not, or even than the same society when it is not in Pareto optimum. The only thing the Pareto optimum does is to permit the retention of the facade of *Wertfreiheit*, which is not a good thing to do anyhow. A good society should, and most societies do, go well beyond the Pareto optimum, to make common sense and generally accepted value judgements about weights to be attached to incomes of different social groups – the poor, the unemployed, the very young, and the very old, and so on.

(c) Freedom to choose has value in itself, but that does not mean that the choices actually made are good for society. In fact, all societies inhibit individual members' freedom to choose in the interest of society as a whole: thus access to drugs, firearms, pornography, and the like may be restricted. Once started on this road, it is hard to know where to stop. In developing countries, or even very poor regions of IMEs, malnutrition may be a more serious threat to welfare than alcohol or drugs, and perhaps freedom to decide what kinds of foods to produce, sell, buy, and consume should be restricted too.

(d) It is impossible to prove that market choices are rational, or even consistent. One cannot present choices in different sequences simultaneously. Thus one cannot distinguish inconsistency from changes in taste.

(e) One must make allowances for altruism and for what Amartya Sen calls "commitment" (sense of moral obligation to a social group or to a cause). Doing so breaks the link between prices, costs, and "efficiency" in the neoclassical sense. If some people pay unnecessarily high prices or wages out of sympathy, others may have to meet those prices and wages who do not feel the same sympathy (Sen 1979).

(f) Consistency of choice does not make the choices "good." It merely permits the welfare economist to construct his model. The model states only that the choices were made. To arrive at the conclusion that the choices contribute to the welfare of the individual, one must make the value judgement that whatever choice an individual makes is good for him, just because he makes it. The alternative judgement is to have a point of reference outside the range of individual choices which reflects collective choice, a social contract, a "constitution." I prefer the second value judgement. So does François Perroux (Perroux 1984).

(g) In almost all societies, true social welfare can be improved more, and more quickly, by measures to redistribute income than by measures to improve resource allocation. Value judgements about income distribution among social groups and among communities, and thus among areas in space, are an essential aspect of economic and social policy.

(h) Even if the price structure provides information about relative marginal utility, it tells nothing about average or total utility. Some people will consume more of a particular commodity than others in the course of bringing relative marginal utility to the same level, and so derive more total satisfaction than others. The equality of average or total satisfaction among members of a society is a

philosophically more acceptable goal than equality of marginal satisfactions.
(i) The price structure as such tells nothing about relative costs, and therefore nothing about degrees of monopoly power.

Most of the *individual* choices made repeatedly and frequently are of little importance for *social* welfare anyhow. Whether individuals of any society eat more beef or more lamb, drink more wine or more beer, more tea or coffee, wear white dinner jackets or black, is not in itself important for welfare of the society as a whole. There may be health implications in some of these choices, but if people cannot be taught or persuaded to make the right choices, the problems must be dealt with by *intervention* in the market, not by free choice. On the other hand, freedom to choose has a value in itself; and since the choices that must be made collectively with an admixture of expert advice, if even a second- or third-best approximation to the optimal level of social welfare is to be attained, are so many and so complicated, we may as well leave these unimportant choices to the market.

What the market cannot do is to assure good choices in areas where the choices must be collective (health, nutrition, education, security, transport, energy, the environment), or assure full employment without inflation, or most important of all, turn a poor and stagnant society into a growing and eventually a prosperous one, or a rich and declining society into a reinvigorated one. In most societies, it is not that the market system is terribly bad; it just isn't very good. We are not speaking here of distributive justice or "fairness"; no *system* can guarantee those. Only "sympathy" and moral behavior can guarantee those.

9.6 Interactions of regional and national development

Let us turn now to various types of interaction between regional and national development which must be taken into account when formulating regional policy.

Regional disparities and national development

Some decades ago, when he was still Executive Secretary of the Economic Commission for Europe, Gunnar Myrdal showed that regional disparities in the less developed European countries tended to be large and increasing, whereas in the more advanced economies they were small and diminishing. In a cross-section analysis made some years later, Jeffrey Williamson (1965) showed that regional gaps tend to increase in the earlier stages of development and to diminish in the later stages. (These particular results should be taken generally and applied to particular countries only with supreme caution).[1] But it is apparent that Myrdal's findings can be applied in a general way throughout the world.

From the observations alone, one might conclude that any nation wishing to reduce regional disparities should adopt policies designed to accelerate growth of the national economy; or one might conclude that in order to accelerate growth of the national economy, one should adopt policies designed to reduce regional gaps. It is not easy to demonstrate the validity of one of these conclusions and the invalidity of the other. Indeed, both may be true; diminishing regional gaps and higher rates of growth may reinforce each other. My own historical studies of interactions between regional and national development, however, lead me to believe that the more unshakeable truth lies in the second proposition. For example, the dramatic story of regional convergence and achievement of one of the world's highest standards of living in the United States is, I am convinced, the result of a special kind of "ratchet effect" in regional development. As a consequence of the wide dispersal of good land and other natural resources, the ever-moving frontier, the extraordinary mobility of the American people, the "frontier spirit" and "rugged individualism," no large regions in the United States ever slipped from stagnation into decay. Time and time again a lagging region was converted into a leading region. Growth of each region reinforced the growth of others in the long run. Industrialization and urbanization were spread with a remarkable degree of uniformity throughout the whole country. New England lost her textile and pulp and paper industries to the South and her boot and shoe industry to the Midwest, but attained even higher levels of productivity and incomes on the basis of higher-technology activities. Now hi-tech industries are moving to the South too, but New England is not suffering. The Great Lakes region is presently in some difficulty, but I have no doubt that a basis will be found for a resurgence even there. This unique performance of the American economy was more owing to government policy than is usually acknowledged, but it was largely the result of market forces. The almost child-like American faith in the market as a source of regional and national development is founded on a certain reality. But the structure of the American economy, the nature of its natural and human resources, are also unique, and cannot be replicated elsewhere (Higgins 1981b).

The interactions of regional and national development are extraordinarily complex, and differ from country to country. To arrive at recommendations for regional policy in any particular country on the basis of *any* general theory is a dangerous game to play. Each case must be carefully studied on its own, just as each medical patient must be examined individually before a prognosis is made and a prescription given. The available evidence suggests that opportunities for mutual reinforcement are greater where all regions are strong, and that a national economy is healthier where all regions are healthy than if some are in splendid health but others are sick. A prescription to make the healthy ones still stronger and to ignore the maladies of the sick ones may result in spreading the disease to the healthy ones and killing off the sick ones.

Regional disparities and trade-off curves

In my contribution to the volume of essays in honour of Paul Rosenstein-Rodan, I demonstrated that the height of national trade-off curves varies directly with the index of regional dispersion of per capita income. For Canada, I was able to show that the height of regional trade-off curves varies directly with the dispersion index for subregions

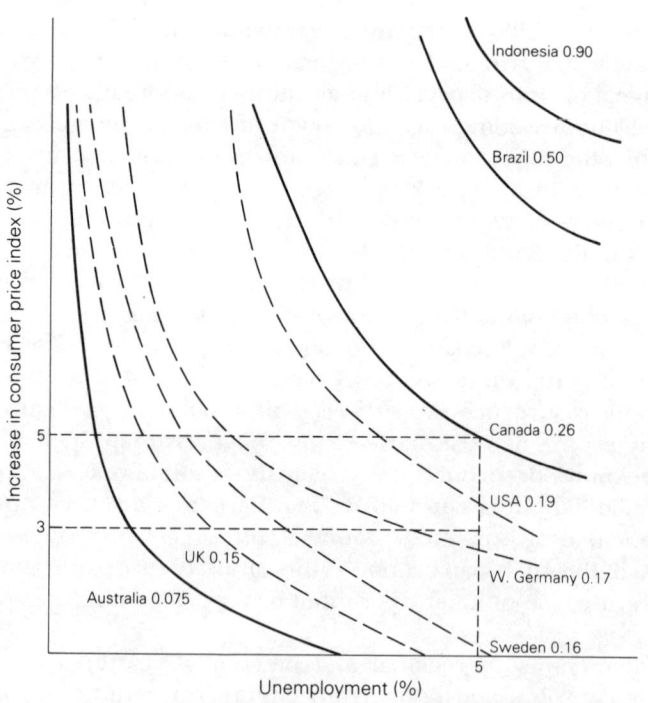

Figure 9.1 Trade-off curves for selected countries, 1960–65.
Sources: Bodkin et al. (1965), Williamson (1965), and Chernick (1966).

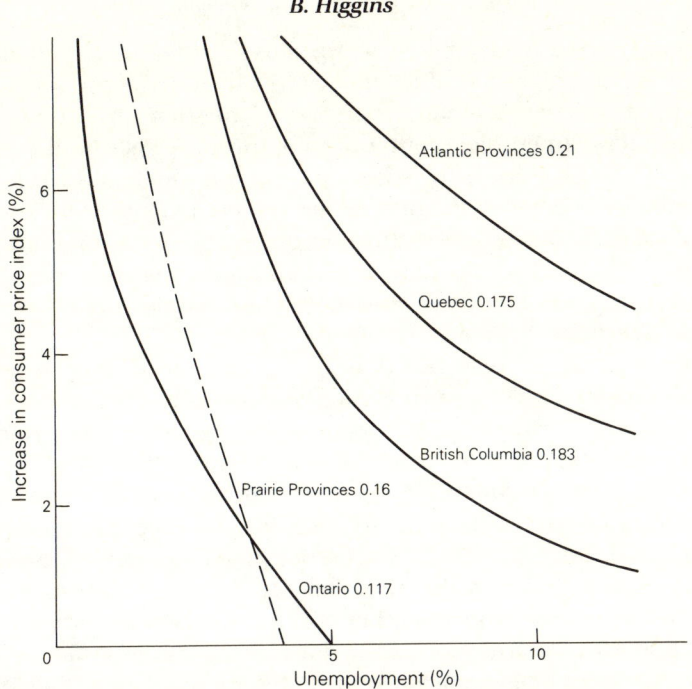

Figure 9.2 Trade-off curves for Canadian regions, 1963–67.
Sources: Chernick (1966), and Bodkin et al. (1965).

(Higgins 1972). These results are reproduced here as Figures 9.1 and 9.2. Finding ready-made trade-off curves *and* dispersion indices for the same countries or regions is not easy, and I have been unable to bring this study up to date. However, I have little doubt that more recent data would confirm the observation.

There is no reason to be surprised by these conclusions. We don't have much by way of a theory of trade-off curves, but what we have suggests that the greater the degree of fragmentation or disintegration within the economy, the more frictional and structural unemployment there can be, and the longer can be the lags in adjustment of prices. Fragmentation in space, as evidenced by large regional gaps, can be especially pernicious in permitting the continued existence of unfavorable trade-off curves.

Price spreads for transportable goods and services cannot for long exceed costs of transportation in any one country. Even prices of nontransportable goods (such as houses) tend to follow after a lag of some duration. Unemployment, however, need not be rapidly diffused. If the lagging regions are to a significant degree economically, culturally, or politically separate from the leading ones – as they are in Canada – the amount of net emigration of labor towards the more active areas of the country may well be less than the growth of the labor force. Under these circumstances, unemployment may continue to rise in the lagging regions. There are powerful socio-cultural and political forces which limit mobility of labor in the Atlantic Provinces, and still more powerful ones in Quebec. Moreover, with unemployment above 8% even in the most prosperous regions, there is no assurance that migration to the leading regions will guarantee employment, unless one has special skills that are clearly in short supply.

Conversely, capital may not flow from richer to poorer, from low-unemployment to high-unemployment regions as it is supposed to do in the neoclassical textbooks. With nationwide bargaining and minimim wage laws, wages may vary less than productivity from one region to another, and the high-unemployment regions may actually be high-cost rather than low-cost regions. In any case, regions where unemployment is high and incomes relatively low do not provide attractive markets. If costs are really lower in the retarded region it may pay to establish enterprises there for export to other countries or regions, but only if the production cost advantage exceeds the transport cost disadvantage of locating far from where the most favorable markets exist. Increasingly important too is the desire of entrepreneurs, managers, scientists, and technicians to be "where the action is." They don't want to resettle in a backwater.

In short, and in more technical terms, the position of a country's trade-off curve is related to the amount of frictional and structural unemployment that exists (or would exist) when prices are stable. In Lipsey's terms (Lipsey 1960), it is a matter of the level of unemployment when excess demand for labor is zero, or $(d-s)/s=0$ where $d=$ the demand for labor and $s=$ the supply. In Milton Friedman's terms (Friedman 1968, 1977), it is a matter of how high is the "natural" rate of unemployment; that is, the amount of unemployment that is consistent with stable prices. Intuitively one can see that these levels of unemployment are likely to be higher when the so-called "national economy" is a loosely knit bundle of distinct regional economies than when the national economy is the tightly knit, closely integrated unity that it is assumed to be in textbooks on macroeconomics. There is, in any case, a good deal of evidence that large regional disparities and particularly unfavorable trade-off curves tend to go together, as we have seen.

From this analysis emerges a very important conclusion: in an economy like Canada's, the way to tackle unemployment and inflation simultaneously and push the trade-off curve back towards the origin is to attack regional disparities head on.

Regional trends and regional fluctuations

Elsewhere I have presented a model analyzing the relationship of interactions between cycles and trends to regional disparities (Higgins 1975). The model is essentially an elaboration of John R. Hicks's model of the "trade cycle" (Hicks 1950, Higgins 1955). In the model there are two kinds of investment: "induced," stimulated by past increases in sales, and "developmental," brought on by population growth, technological progress, and resource discovery. An essential feature of the model is that induced investment depends not only on changes in consumer spending and sales in the recent past, but partly also on changes that occurred in the more remote past. Once a boom starts (as the result, let us say, of a technological innovation, or a resource discovery), it becomes cumulative until it hits a ceiling imposed by the maximum rate at which output can increase when all known resources are fully utilized, through growth of the labor force, technological progress, and resource discovery alone. Once the ceiling is hit, growth inevitably slows down. As time passes, and the economy "creeps along the ceiling," periods of high growth in the more distant past become ineffective in decision-making, and recent periods of slow growth dominate investment decisions. Eventually the whole impact of past changes in consumer spending becomes negative, investment falls, and a cumulative downswing ensues. It continues until the "floor" is hit, determined by the rate of growth of national income that results from whatever developmental investment remains, less the reduction in the stock of capital through failure to replace it as it wears out. If the floor is upward sloping, periods of falling sales in the more distant past are gradually replaced by more effective recent periods of increasing sales, induced investment increases again, and a new cumulative upswing begins.

With this model, it is easy to see that the underlying long run growth brought about by increasing population, technological progress, and resource discovery is a crucial factor in the timing and amplitude of economic fluctuations. If long run growth is rapid, hitting the ceiling does not make much difference and the regional economy can "creep along the ceiling" for a long time before investment actually falls. Even when it does, the regional economy will soon hit a steeply rising "floor," and it will not be long until investment increases again and recovery ensues. Booms will be prolonged, depressions will be short and shallow. But if the ceiling is flat, the net impact of changes in consumer spending on induced investment soon becomes negative, the boom is quickly over, and a steep downswing sets in. Moreover, the floor is flat too; hitting it doesn't do much good, and the depression can last a long time. Indeed, if the floor is completely flat, the depression will go on forever, in the absence of favorable shocks or astute government policy.

During the decades between 1950 and 1980, the long-run growth of the Quebec economy was comparatively slow. Population growth was at a low ebb; the province lagged in terms of technological progress; and resource discovery, while it took place, was not measurably in advance of that in Alberta, British Columbia, and Ontario. Floor and ceiling were relatively flat. Therefore Quebec had short booms, entered the downswing comparatively early, and suffered deep and prolonged depressions. This unfavorable configuration of the regional business cycle contributed to the prolongation of disparities between Quebec and more prosperous provinces.

The recent tendency towards convergence of the Quebec and Ontario economies has lasted too short a time to permit us to say for sure whether or not a new trend has set in. But there is reason to think that it has, based mainly upon a new wave of technological advance, upgrading of skills, and improvements in product mix and occupational structure, as evidenced by the rapid rise in productivity. If all that is true, we can expect an improvement in the pattern of Quebec business cycles too, and the whole catching-up process could become cumulative. Once again, will Quebec be Canada's richest province at the end of the century?

There are also questions as to the degree to which the recent improvements in Quebec's relative position on the Canadian totem pole are the result of policy – federal and provincial – and to what extent they are the result of developments in the market economy, including the relative decline in the Ontario economy, and the new values and attitudes of Quebec's younger generation, who show none of the reluctance to train themselves for managerial and entrepreneurial positions, in Quebec's still anglophone-dominated economy, displayed by their older brothers and sisters. I have discussed these questions elsewhere, and shall not attempt to answer them here (Higgins 1986). But in the interactions of cycles and trends we see another kind of cumulative causation, and one that regional policy must take into account, however complicated a task that may turn out to be.

Regional disparities and shifting trade-off curves

Another analysis explains why economic fluctuations since 1950 have taken the form of shifting trade-off curves, unemployment, and inflation increasing together in recessions and decreasing together in recoveries (Higgins 1981c). The model is partly macroeconomic and partly microeconomic, and regional fragmentation is only one element, so I shall not try to summarize it here. The basic conclusions, however, are needed for the argument of the rest of this section, so I shall merely state them. The model has three parts, which I label The Machine, The Structure, and The Game. The Machine presents the theory of interacting long waves and shorter cycles presented above, and shows that a long wave downturn, or even flattening of longer-run trends, can bring the appearance of an outward shift of the trade-off curve (TOC), but does not explain simultaneous movements of unemployment and inflation. The Structure has itself three components. The first is regional fragmentation, which permits inflationary pressure to be generated mainly in one or two regions while unemployment is concentrated in one or two others. The second is the distortion of the global economy by a century of colonialism and protectionism, so that the international division of labor is almost the exact opposite of the one that comparative advantage would dictate. Countries like Canada and Australia whose comparative advantage is obviously in agriculture have tiny fractions of their labor force in that sector, and too many workers in traditional manufacturing (textiles, boots and shoes, metal work) where these countries have an obvious comparative disadvantage. Some developing countries with an obvious comparative advantage in manufacturing have most of their labor force in agriculture. This situation contributes both to unemployment and to high costs and prices, and to protectionist measures in recession which tend to keep prices up without providing more jobs.

The third is a tendency for the period of investment (capital:output ratio) to lengthen (increase) in recession – the converse of the von Hayek theory. In recession, private enterprises tend to continue their long-gestation, capital-intensive projects (pipelines, mines, tankers, new plant), to cut orders for equipment, and to let inventories run down. Governments switch to investments with infinite capital:output ratios (no product is sold), like unemployment insurance and public works. Thus a given investment produces less output for sale on the market, aggravating inflation, and provides fewer jobs, deepening unemployment.

The Game is the same one that has been outlined above. It is played in such a way that it tends to increase both unemployment and inflation for most of the time. One constant in The Game is that the unions tend always to bargain for some increase in wage rates, no matter what, although how much increase they bargain for and will accept depends somewhat on levels of unemployment and on expected price increases, and on what they think government and employers will do about it. Since many of the unemployed these days are not union members, the trade union leadership is quite prepared to bargain for steep wage increases even when unemployment is increasing. (This behavior appears quite clearly in the case of the Canadian and Australian construction industries.) Foreigners enter The Game mainly by raising export prices, which raises costs in importing countries and has an impact similar to that of a wage increase. While the outcome of The Game is indeterminate, it tends to be highly inflationary in its impact.

Employers more often than not accept higher wages or higher import prices in the expectation that they can raise their administered prices, and that government will bail them out through monetary expansion on a sufficient scale to make the new and higher wage–price level stick. To simplify the discussion, the not unrealistic assumption is made that major wage settlements are made once a year and that other wage settlements follow. The government then sets its monetary and fiscal policy in response to the expected impact of the settlements on unemployment and price increases. Out of all these decisions comes some level of unemployment and inflation; we have one point on a trade-off curve. Expectations are revised accordingly, the process is repeated, and another trade-off point emerges, which may or may not be on the same curve as the first one.

Let us now proceed to look at the behavior of national and regional trade-off curves in Canada. The curves are presented in Figures 9.3 to 9.12. They are not quite what is usually presented as TOCs; they are not constructed on the assumption that unemployment is a function of price increases, or vice versa; consequently, they are not derived from any equation relating unemployment to inflation. The underlying theory is rather that both unemployment and inflation are the outcome of all the forces operating in the economy during any one period, including forces emanating from abroad. The operation of The Machine, The Structure, and The Game generates every year (or quarter, or month) some movement of prices and some level of unemployment. These constitute one point on a TOC. To say that several points lie on the same TOC means, in my conception of TOCs, that during the whole period covered by the curve, the government could have achieved any of the points on it by money management (orthodox macroeconomic monetary and fiscal policy) alone. Deciding what points lie on the same curve is a somewhat rough and ready but very laborious process; first, the points must look as though they lie on the same curve; and study of the whole economic situation must lead to the conclusion that all the combinations of unemployment and inflation which are attributed to the same curve were in fact options open to the government throughout the entire period covered by the curve. (Higgins (1982) presents such a study for Australia, using quarterly data covering the period 1950–80.) Similarly, attributing a shift to a TOC must be based on some event or events (such as a major wage settlement, or a steep increase in prices of a major import like oil, or a clear-cut downturn or upturn in the economy, a major resource discovery or innovation, etc.).

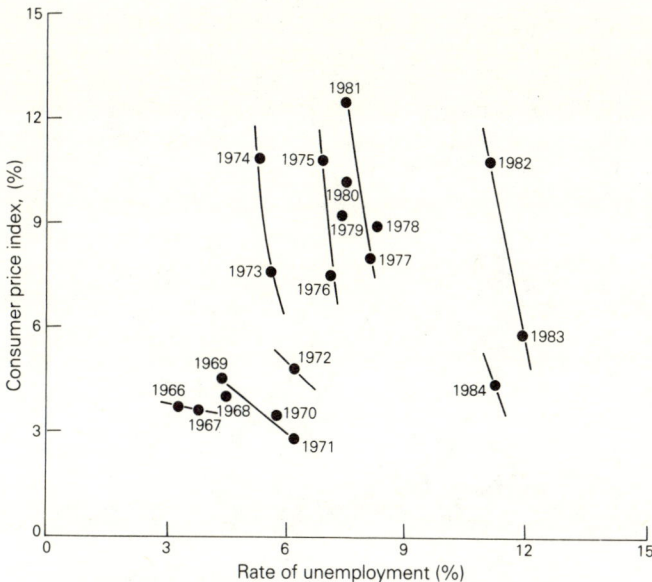

Figure 9.3 Trade-off curves for Canada, 1966–84.
Source: Statistics Canada.

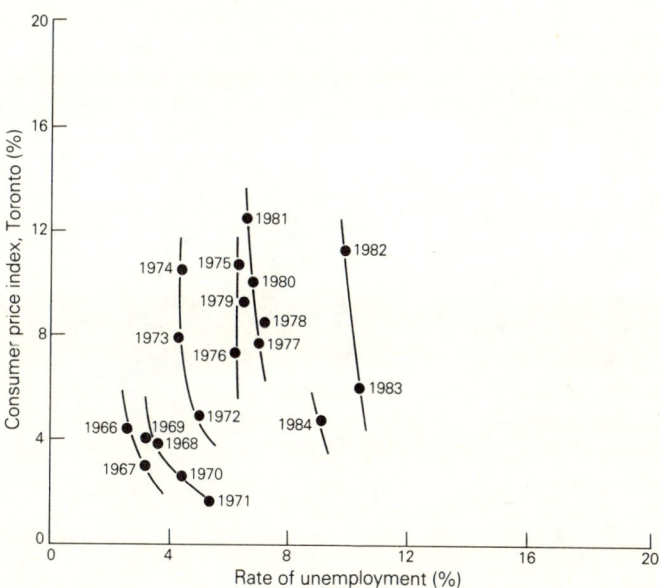

Figure 9.4 Trade-off curves for Ontario, 1966–84.

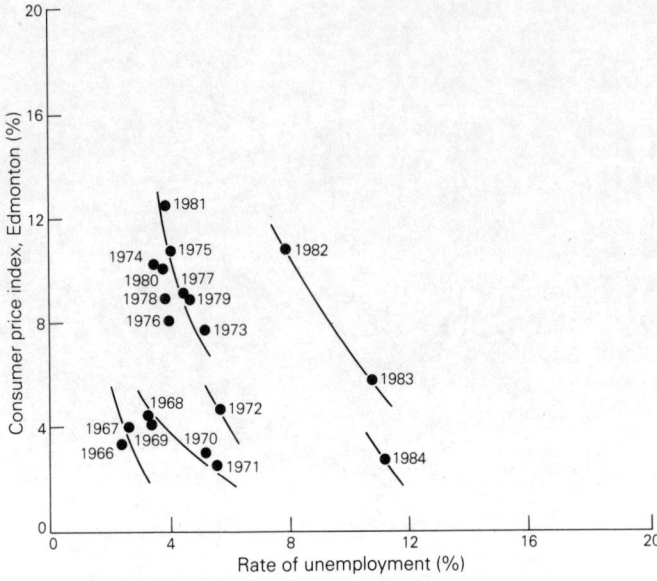

Figure 9.5 Trade-off curves for Alberta, 1966–84.

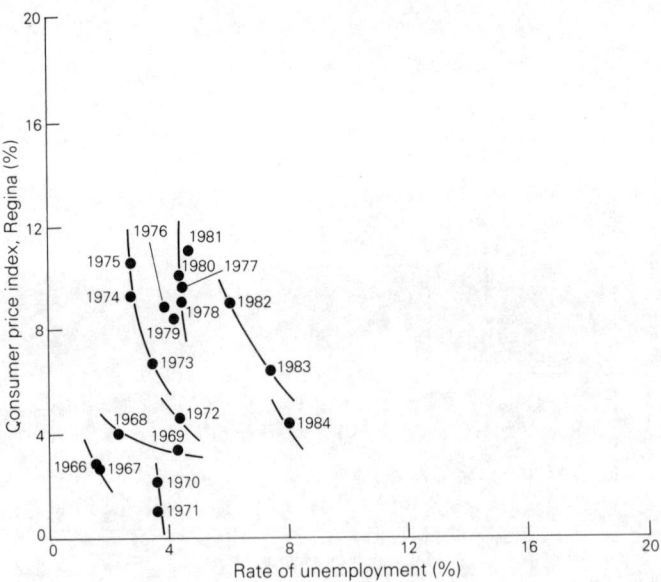

Figure 9.6 Trade-off curves for Saskatchewan, 1966–84.

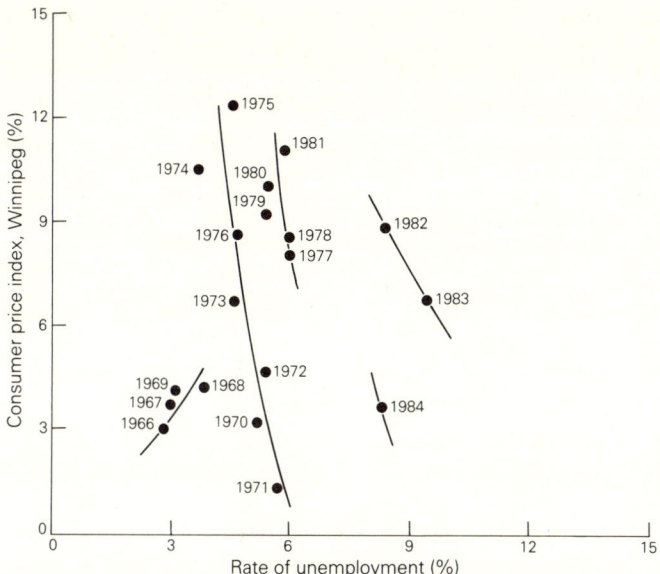

Figure 9.7 Trade-off curves for Manitoba, 1966–84.

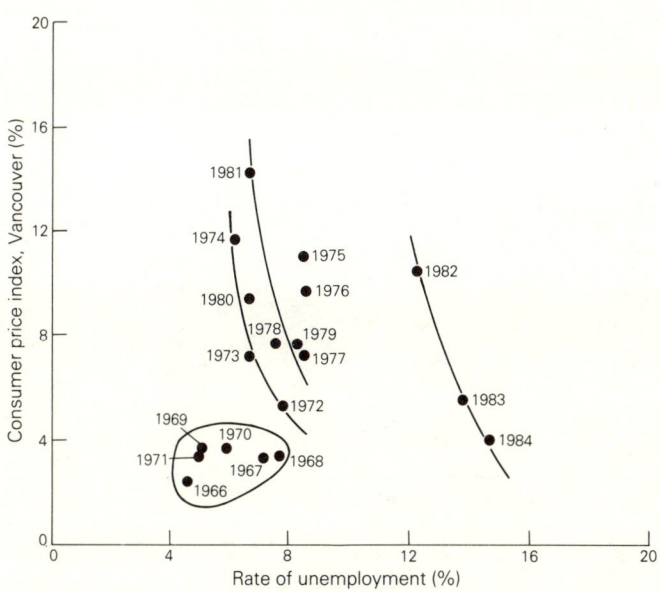

Figure 9.8 Trade-off curves for British Columbia, 1966–84.

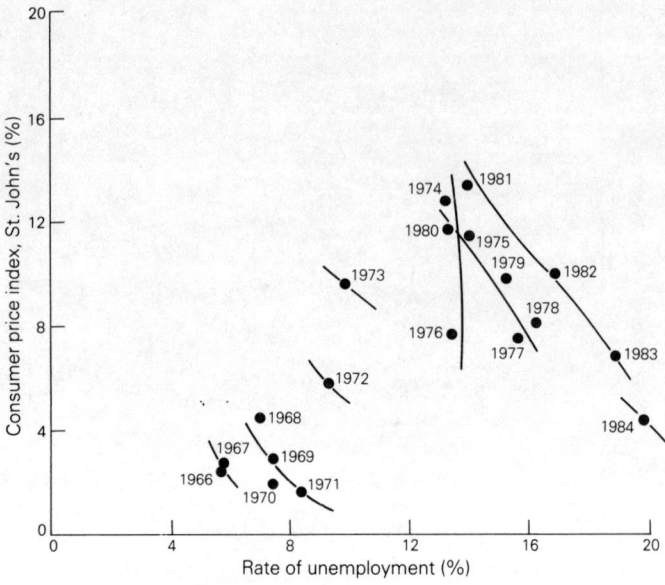

Figure 9.9 Trade-off curves for Newfoundland, 1966–84.

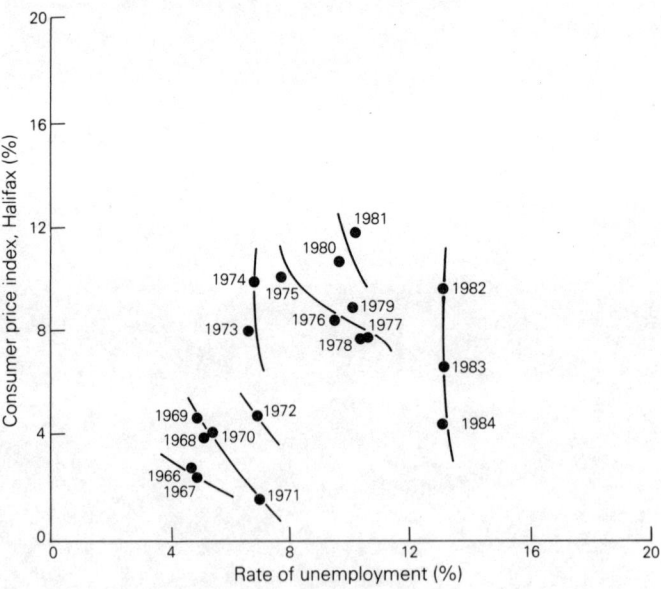

Figure 9.10 Trade-off curves for Nova Scotia, 1966–84.

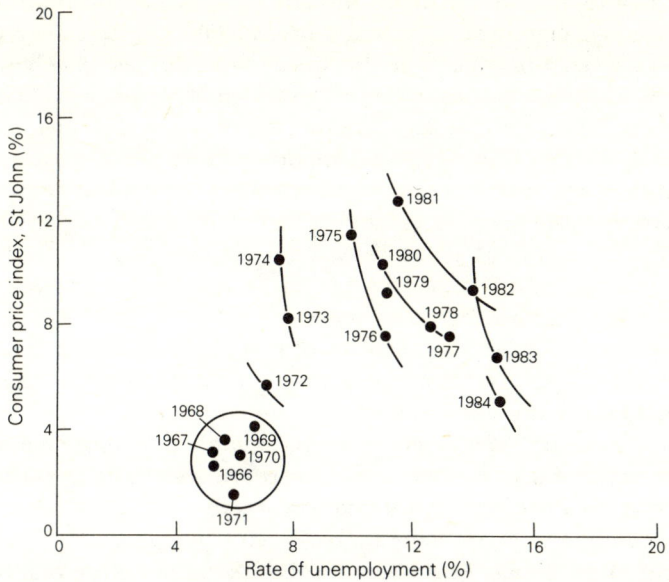

Figure 9.11 Trade-off curves for New Brunswick, 1966–84.

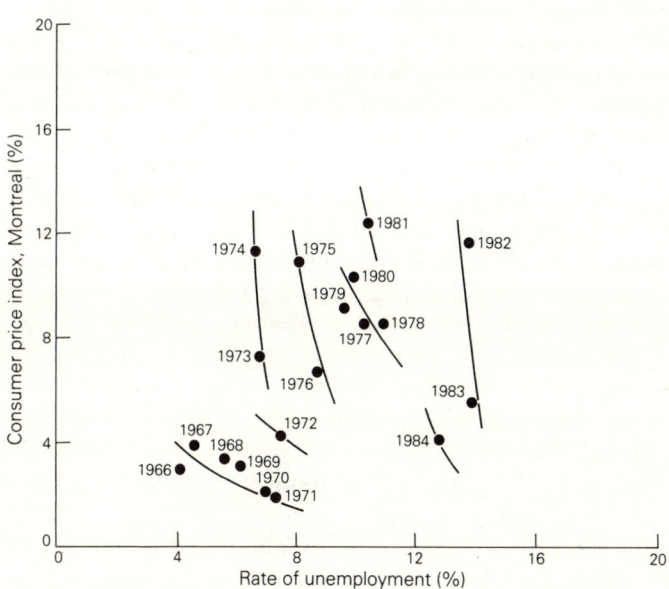

Figure 9.12 Trade-off curves for Quebec, 1966–84.

For Canada as a whole, with TOCs defined as above, the curve began to shift outwards in 1967, from an already unfavorable position (Higgins 1978b). It also became steeper and more unstable. By the early 1980s, it had become so unstable that the question arises as to whether the course of events might not be better described in terms of cyclical loops, of which more below. It looks as though the outward shift has continued up to 1983 or 1984; I have been unable to conduct a sufficiently detailed study of the Canadian economy in recent years to decide whether or not the 1983 and 1984 observations should be regarded as being on the same curve. I suspect not. These years saw a mild recovery in the Canadian economy, and according to my model, the curve should have shifted towards the origin during those years.

More interesting for the purposes of this paper, I also found that the chronic regional disparities in Canada are reflected in marked differences in the configuration and behavior of regional trade-off curves. Inflation in Canada had until then been generated mainly in Ontario and Alberta. The TOCs for those regions were steep and near the vertical (price increase) axis. Moreover, in the national recession they tended to shift more up than out. Unemployment had been concentrated in the Atlantic Provinces and Quebec. The TOCs of those provinces were relatively flat and well out to the right on the unemployment axis. As they shifted in recession, they shifted more out than up – that is, inflation was aggravated most where it was already severe, and unemployment was aggravated where it was already concentrated.

In those circumstances, another kind of trade-off appeared. The Canadian government could buy a substantial reduction in inflationary pressure in the national economy, at very low cost in terms of increased unemployment, by postponing relatively low-priority spending in Ontario and the Prairies. It could buy a significant reduction in unemployment by bringing forward ("telescoping") badly needed projects in the Atlantic Provinces and Quebec, at very low cost in increased inflationary pressure. Thus without changing either its total spending or its budget deficit, it could reduce unemployment and inflation together by planning carefully the *place* as well as the *timing* of its expenditures. Such a policy also conformed to the high-priority objective of reducing regional gaps.

In the 1980s, the pattern has changed again, marked especially by the appearance of high levels of unemployment, even in Ontario, and by sharp reductions in rates of inflation throughout the country. In Ontario, the TOC continued to shift outwards until 1983, when there was an abrupt decline in the rate of inflation and a slight increase in unemployment. Points Q and R *might* be on the same curve. In 1984, there is clearly a shift toward the origin. In Alberta there appears to have been a shift in 1972 and a second shift in 1982, with no clear evidence of a shift toward the origin in 1984. It depends upon whether point S is on the same curve as Q and R or not. We shall need more observations, and a detailed study of events in the Alberta economy, to be sure. Saskatchewan displays a pattern somewhat similar to Alberta's. Manitoba hardly shows any pattern at all, but if there is a TOC for Manitoba it shifted toward the origin in 1984, as the Canadian TOC did.

The patterns for the Atlantic Provinces and British Columbia differ from those of the other provinces, in that up to 1984 unemployment was still increasing, and reached very high levels in that year. There is some suggestion that the TOC has become steeper both in British Columbia and in the Atlantic Provinces; that is, reducing unemployment by standard Keynesian policies risks greater aggravation of inflationary pressures than it would have done in the 1970s. However, I do not have sufficiently detailed knowledge of the functioning of these provincial economies from 1981 to 1984 to express an opinion as to whether or not the observations Q, R, and S were on the same curve or not. The criterion is, let us reiterate, whether these points were really options, attainable through orthodox money management alone, throughout these three years. Over the entire period covered, the Ontario and British Columbia economies show the most marked deterioration. The Newfoundland economy is in the worst condition, but the situation in that province has been very unsatisfactory since 1972. Quebec shows clear-cut improvement in the 1980s, but still has a very high level of unemployment, from which not even Montreal is spared.

For the Canadian economy as a whole – loose and fragmented aggregation of regional economies that it is – there is strong evidence that the TOC is becoming steeper. The reduction of the rate of inflation is of course to be welcomed. But the indications are that a sincere attempt to bring down levels of unemployment to, say, 4% in all provinces, by Keynesian or monetarist policies alone, could bring sharp increases in inflation, probably to a level above 10%.

The picture is not more pleasing if we interpret Canadian experience with unemployment and inflation as cyclical loops rather than shifting trade-off curves. Fig. 9.13 presents such loops for the period 1955–84. Gaston Luthi prepared such a diagram for the period up to 1978, and I have added the later years. It appears that the amplitude of the fluctuations is increasing. If the loop which started about 1978 is completed, as the earlier ones were, Canada could have both unemployment and inflation above 20%. Economic fluctuations in the industrialized market economies since 1950 are not well understood, and there is no single and generally accepted theory to explain behavior like that shown in Figure 9.13. Luthi has at least an interesting idea:

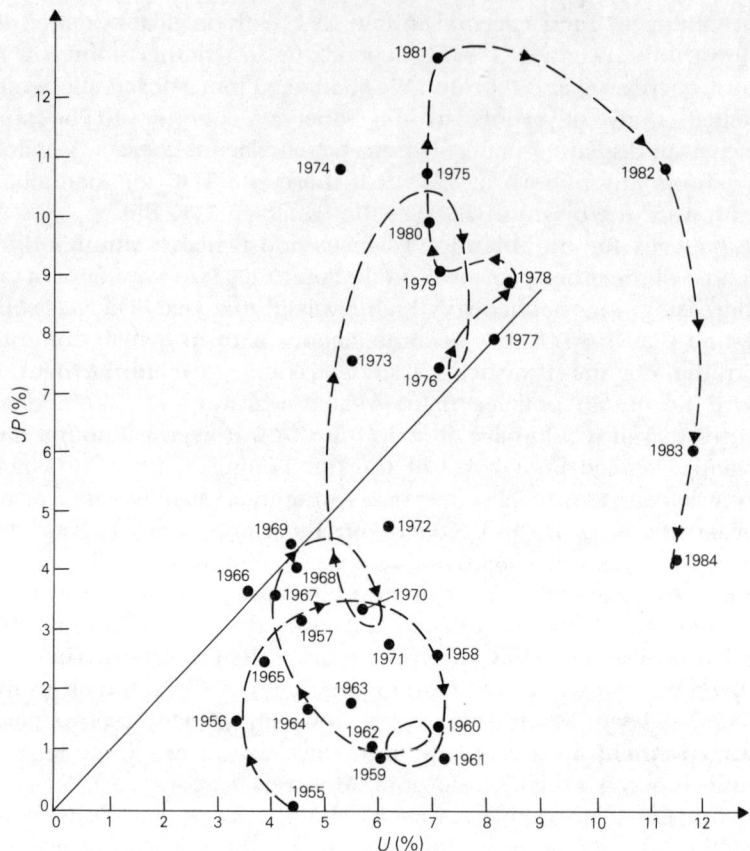

Figure 9.13 Inflation and unemployment in Canada, 1955–84.

We observe in this figure three distinct general loops starting in 1955 and spanning over a period of approximately 20 years. The average duration of each of these general loops is 7 years. Looking closer and accounting for the effect of small loops built into the general loops we note a quite consistent sequence of 4 and 3 years. Subsequently, could it not be that these loops are in effect representations of Juglar cycles for the general configuration and Kitchin cycles when decomposed? In any case, the evidence correlating the cyclical pattern of the economy to the loops of the inflation and unemployment spiral is quite suggestive.[2]

It is worth stressing the fact, obvious though it may be, that when movements of unemployment and inflation are interpreted as loops the two variables are always moving together in one direction or another. A true trade-off exists only in periods when the inflation rate is falling and unemployment increasing or vice versa. Luthi finds for the annual Canadian data that the majority of the observations suggest a trade-off; but with 1979 to 1984 added, it can also be said that a significant proportion of the observations do not suggest trade-off, since both unemployment and inflation are either rising or falling together, indicating shifts in TOCs rather than movements along them.

It is these *differences* in the position configuration and shifts of provincial TOCs that provide the opportunity, through a finely tuned fiscal policy that determines both the *timing* and the *placing* of federal government expenditures according to the situation in each province, to reduce unemployment and inflation simultaneously in Canada. It can no longer be implemented at the provincial level. Each province should be broken down into three types of subregion: those that are doing well; those that have unutilized potential (resource frontier regions); and those with severe problems in the form of unemployment and underemployment, low incomes, and inadequate infrastructure and public services. The third group should be treated as "less-developed regions" in much the same way that "less-developed countries" are treated internationally. They should be carefully studied to uncover hidden potential, plans for their development should be made accordingly, and funds provided for the execution of the plans. In this way it would still be possible to plan the timing and placing of expenditures, at all three levels of government, including appropriate subsidies to private enterprise, so as to reduce unemployment, inflation, and regional disparities all at once.

The regional structure, regional planning, and regional development in Canada are not something on the periphery of the national economy, or of national economic policy, or of national economic development and the "efficiency" of operation of the national economy. (One can scarcely speak of "national economic planning" because no such thing exists.) The national economy is an aggregation of regional economies, some of which may have closer ties to the world outside of Canada than to some of the other regions within it. In a country like Canada, the performance of the national economy would be more "efficient" with a collection of well-founded regional economic policies and no national policy, than with a national economic policy, no matter how well founded, and no regional policies. "Efficient" national policy in Canada must consist largely of an aggregation of efficient and effective regional policies.

9.7 Conclusion

If the various arguments in this paper are added together, they lead to the conclusion that well-construed regional development policy, far from redistributing income in favour of retarded regions at the expense of reduced efficiency of the national economy, can increase the efficiency of both the regional and the national economies. To begin with, today's free market is a "sea of imperfections," and cannot cope with the really important choices, which are almost wholly collective rather than individual choices. The alternative, however, is not centralized planning and mastodonian bureaucracies. The achievement of an efficient allocation of resources requires intervention in the market process, but not necessarily the intervention we have. A "free" market in an industrialized society will certainly function imperfectly, and perhaps badly; but misguided intervention or cumbersome centralized planning can make it even worse.

But why take either risk? We can make happen what we want to happen, through a system of multilevel planning, with major emphasis on regional, local, and community planning in close collaboration with target populations.

Notes

1 Williamson (1965). Since Williamson's study was based on a cross-section econometric analysis of a large number of countries, it was limited to the statistics that were available, and to the definition of 'region' adopted for collecting and publishing statistics in each country. Thus 'regions' might mean the ten provinces of Canada; the six Australian, nineteen Brazilian, or fifty American states; or the 149 *municipios* in tiny Puerto Rico. Obviously these are conceptually very different organisms, and there is no reason to expect them to behave identically. Second, when individual cases are examined historically, the similarities tend to disappear. Thus, the United States went through several cycles of alternating convergence and divergence over the one and a quarter centuries of narrowing regional disparities, and the initial appearance of large regional gaps was linked to patterns of settlement rather than to different trends in per capita income for people already settled. Australia does not follow the pattern at all, either in terms of initial divergence or of subsequent convergence. Canada showed no clear signs of convergence for two centuries after *La Conquête*. In general different countries show markedly different patterns with respect to *timing* of divergence and convergence. In a goodly number of countries where some convergence has been achieved in recent decades – Brazil, Greece, Italy, Yugoslavia, Malaysia, Thailand and many more – it has been the result of massive government intervention, not of "free market forces" alone. The same is true of Canada and of Quebec.

If indeed Canada is now launched on a process of regional convergence, which shows more distinctly for Quebec than for the Atlantic provinces, it is in large measure the result of deliberate regional development policies of the Federal and Quebec governments. As for Montreal, it is inevitably involved in this process through a two-way feedback system.

2 Figure 9.13 is taken from the Ph.D. dissertation of Gaston Luthi, *Business cycle theory and stabilisation policies in a world of shifting trade-off curves*, University of Ottawa, 1979, which was started under the present writer's direction and completed under the direction of Professors R. Bodkin and O. Mehmet. The quote is from p. 155.

References

Bensusan-Butt, D. 1978. *On economic man*. Canberra: Australian National University Press.
Bodkin, R. G., E. P. Bond, G. L. Reuber & T. R. Robinson 1965. *Price stability and high unemployment*. Ottawa: Economic Council of Canada.
Chemick, S. E. 1966. *Inter-regional disparities in income*. Ottawa: Economic Council of Canada.
Friedman, M. 1968. The role of monetary policy. *American Economic Review* 18(1), 1–17.
Friedman, M. 1977. Nobel lecture: inflation and unemployment. *Journal of Political Economy* 85(3), 451–72.
Galbraith, J. K. 1983. *The anatomy of power*. Boston, Mass.: Houghton Mifflin.
Hicks, J. R. 1950. *A contribution to the theory of the trade cycle*. Oxford: Oxford University Press.
Higgins, B. 1955. Interactions of cycles and trends. *The Economic Journal* 65, 594–614.
Higgins, B. 1972. Trade-off curves and regional gaps. In *Economic development and planning: essays in honour of Paul Rosenstein-Rodan*, J. N. Bhagwati & R. S. Eckhaus (eds). London: Allen & Unwin.
Higgins, B. 1975. Trade-off curves, trends and regional disparities: the case of Quebec. *Economie Appliquée* 28(2–3), 331–60.
Higgins, B. 1977. Welfare economics and the unified approach to development planning. In *Social issues in regional policy and regional planning*, A. Kuklinski (ed.), 91–114. The Hague: Mouton.
Higgins, B. 1978a. Economics and ethics in the new approach to development. *Philosophy in Context* 7, 7–29.
Higgins, B. 1978b. *Growth and stability in construction*, Ottawa Public Works Canada.
Higgins, B. 1981a. Growth poles: do they exist? In *Polarized development and regional policies*, A. Kuklinski (ed.), 19–36. The Hague and New York: Mouton.
Higgins, B. 1981b. Economic development and regional disparities: a comparative study of four federations. In *Regional disparities and economic development*, R. Mathews (ed.), 21–80. Canberra: Australian National University Press.
Higgins, B. 1981c. Stagnation with shifting trade-off curves. Homage to Alvin Hansen. *Croissance et stagnation dans les pays capitalistes 1973–1980 Économies et sociétés* 28. Paris: ISMEA.

Higgins, B. 1982. The postwar trade cycle as shifting trade-off curves: the case of Australia. Occasional Paper No 28. Canberra: Centre for Research on Federal Financial Relations, Australia National University.

Higgins, B. 1982. *The rise – and fall? – of Montreal*. Moncton, N.B.: Institut canadien de recherche sur le développement régional.

Higgins, B. [n.d.] Trade-off curves, trends and regional disparities: the case of Quebec. *Economie appliquée,* 28(2–3), 331–60.

Higgins, B. & N. T. Dung 1981. Dualism and dependancy in continuing underdevelopment. In *Changing perceptions of development problems,* R. P. Misra and M. Honjo (eds). Nagoya, Japan: UNCRD.

Hollis, M. & E. Nell 1977. *Rational economic man: a philosophical critique of neo-classical economics*. Cambridge: Cambridge University Press.

Kornai, J. 1971. *Anti equilibrium: on economic systems theory and the tasks of research*. London and Amsterdam: North Holland.

Lekachman, R. 1976. *Economists at bay: why the experts will never solve your problems*. New York: McGraw-Hill.

Lipsey, R. 1960. The relationship between unemployment and the rate of change of money wage rates in the United Kingdom. 1862–1957: a further analysis. *Economica* (new series) Vol. 27 February, 1–21.

Lutz, M. & K. Lux 1979. *The challenge of humanistic economics*. Menlo Park, Cal.: Benjamin-Cummings.

Marris, R. 1967. *The economic theory of managerial capitalism*. London: Macmillan.

Myrdal, G. 1957. *Economic theory and underdeveloped regions*. London: Duckworth.

Perroux, F. 1983. *A new concept of development*. Paris: Croom Helm for UNESCO.

Perroux, F. 1984. Au-delà du Welfare State: une société pleinement économique. *Économie appliquée* 37(1), 99–121.

Richardson, H. W. 1984. Approaches to regional development theory in Western-market economies. In *Regional development: problems and policies in Eastern and Western Europe,* G. Demko (ed.), 22–3. London: Croom Helm.

Sen, A. 1979. Rational fools. In *Philosophy and economic theory,* F. Hahn & M. Hollis (eds), 87–109. Oxford: Oxford University Press.

Smith, N. 1984. *Uneven development*. New York: Basil Blackwell.

Solow, R. 1980. On theories of unemployment. *American Economic Review* 70(1), 2.

Williamson, J. 1965. Regional inequality and the process of national development: a description of patterns. *Economic Development and Cultural Change* 13(4).

10

Regional development in a federal state

ANDRÉ RAYNAULD[1]

This conference in honor of Professor François Perroux brings me a good thirty years back when I had to pass an oral exam before him. His first and only question was about the definition of monopoly power. I began my answer by saying that a monopoly was a market structure. Professor Perroux stopped me right there and said: "Malheureux! monopoly power is not one but a whole set of market structures each of them having its own characteristics and functional properties." I must have said something additional, since in the end Professor Perroux gave me a very generous mark.

The purpose of this paper is to examine the rationale and impact of government policy in regional development. The setting being Canadian, I hope to show that the analysis requires specific and formal recognition of the federal form of government that we have in Canada as a major determining factor in the rise and fall of regions.

10.1 The political process in a federal state

Heterogeneous preferences

One of the key features of a federal as opposed to a unitary form of government is heterogeneous preferences among the consumer-citizens and the geographic concentration of groups with similar preferences forming local communities, provinces or states. Those preferences, on a strict basis of welfare or efficiency, will call for diversity in the supply of public services and hence for decentralization of powers and resources. Different preferences will also lead to different mixes of private goods and different end results in most indicators of welfare.

Breton and Scott (1980) identified the main sources of welfare gains from decentralization of government: it is less costly for individuals to reveal their preferences; it is easier and less costly for governments to identify those preferences and adjust their policies to meet them. More efficient policies, in turn, reduce the need for and cost of migrations as well as those of shifting business activity.

It is generally assumed that preferences and demand differences are particularly acute in Canada because of distances, the diversity and location of its resources and economic activity, and above all, its linguistic and cultural stratification. In view of what will be said below on the influence of pressure groups on shaping policy, it can be added that the whole institutional framework is likely to produce a different structure of public services. Examples of diverging preferences include local control of industry such as in Quebec, progessivity of the taxation system, the emphasis on income as opposed to employment, language requirements, the role of government relative to the private sector, and so on.

It is obvious that with all preferences having their price, significant disparities can develop between regions or provinces. To the extent that these disparities reflect deliberate choice, however, they are desirable and contribute to welfare. As Professor Perroux puts it, there is such a thing as a socially optimal inequality. One might say today that there is a natural rate of inequality. The remarkable paper by Courchene and Melvin for this conference presents elegant proofs of such a proposition.

Production and trade

If matters rested there, a case could be made to elevate the smallest homogeneous community to the rank of an independent country. However, production technologies and requirements are such that differences may be counterbalanced by communality of interests. In other words, to insist on full satisfaction of particular preferences may turn out to be very costly compared with benefits lost from integration.

A rational consumer is expected to weight the cost and benefit of standing alone or living with others. Now, it appears that there are substantial economies of scale in the provision of public goods such as defense, internal security, general administration, national institutions, research, the arts, and communications. In some other cases, spillovers and externalities will indicate that it is more efficient to produce goods and services at a higher level of government than at a lower one. Finally, and most importantly, there are considerable gains from trade in private goods that will make it in the interest of all regions to secure and maintain full access to the national market.

The policy implications, this time, and again for reasons of efficiency alone, will lead towards more centralization and harmonization; free movement of goods and services, of people, capital, and enterprise; and recognizing the advantage of uniformity in regulation as opposed to stressing the merit of originality. The existence of federal countries such as Canada is a recognition through provincial entities that people do value their differences but also acknowledge that what they have or get in common is more important than what separates them.

The public interest

It is not possible to understand regional policy without first understanding the nature of the government decision-making process. In the last 20 years, this field of enquiry has been revolutionized with the landmark contributions of Tullock, Olson, Stigler, Breton and Scott, and several others. Citizens engage in political activity to reduce the costs to them of the public goods supplied by governments and to secure transfers or rents at the expense of others. They will find it useful to form distributional coalitions to secure those advantages when the transaction costs of doing so are less than the expected benefits. The more concentrated the benefit and the smaller the number of participants, the more chance there is that a coalition will be formed; hence the name given to the approach, "the special interest group" theory of government. If this assumption is accepted, then the coalitions become the prime instrument for the delivery of votes.

Politicians in turn will appeal to these groups to get elected and will develop a set of discriminatory policies designed to win a majority. Different combinations of grass-roots coalitions will identify the various political parties. The result of this process is that the so-called public interest sought, or the social utility function adopted by governments, is no more than a weighted and moving average of the special interests of the grand coalition. Let me add that shifting majorities and election results are evidence of strong competition among pressure groups, so that a privilege extended to one is often nullified by a benefit given to another.

Intergovernmental trading

This analysis of the political process must be extended to take federal forms of government into consideration. While governments apply coercion in their jurisdictions, they cannot do so, at least in principle, when they deal with another government. Conflict resolution is thus made substantially more difficult and costly. The only alternative to coercion among civilized partners is trading. Indeed, intergovernmental relations in Canada can be seen as an exchange where rights and resources are traded, without interruption, by direct negotiations at all levels, and by public appeals and polls. I would venture to say that there is not a single federal decision today, in any field, that is not the subject of provincial scrutiny, support, or opposition. Similarly most provincial decisions are scrutinized by the federal government.

Several observations can be derived from this model of government decision-making. First, regional interests and policy are much more prominent in a federal political system because of the support of provincial governments whose raison d'être it is to serve their own electorate. One would thus naturally expect more decentralization and more resources devoted to achieve regional balance, however defined and preferably left undefined.

Second, federalism implies a certain form of competition among provincial governments and between the provinces and the federal government. In the latter case, it is competition for legitimacy, for expenditure priorities, for sources of taxation, for jurisdiction. However, this intergovernmental rivalry has none of the virtues of genuine competition. It does increase output, but more government output means higher rather than lower prices and leads to less efficiency rather than more, for the simple reason that exchanges are not voluntary but imposed on the consumer-citizen. I would prefer to visualize this pseudo-competition as that of an oligopoly with more or less arbitrary access to resources. But as far as I know, no determinate equilibrium solution has yet been found in such a market, in spite of the originality and efforts of recent researchers (Boyer & Moreaux 1983).

These views are not inconsistent with Albert Breton's (1985) model of competititve federalism. Taken as a broad concept, competition is an inescapable fact in a federal system, as our notion of intergovernmental trading implies. Indeed, competition is the rule internationally among all governments, whatever their nature. I am not prepared to assume, however, that intergovernmental competition has or can have the virtues of private competition. It will be sufficient to say in this regard that such a theory has no predictive power, while genuine competition theory leads to neat and clear conclusions. Citizens are not "free to choose" (Milton & Rose Friedman) but consumers are, in a competitive market.

Third, the goals of governments in trading with one another are not necessarily and always short-term benefit from a narrow viewpoint. Equity and redistribution considerations enter into the equations. The evidence in the second part of this paper indicates clearly, I hope, that huge transfers take place in favor of the poorer provinces in Canada. There are three possible reasons for this phenomenon. One is that the principle of equity receives more or less unanimous support in Canadian society. This assumption would account for the fact, for example, that fiscal equalization and equality of opportunities are now part of the Canadian constitution. A second reason would be the threat of conflict and ultimately of separation. Finally, there is the cold calculation of my colleague Doug Hartle (1984), who says that it is often much less costly to give than to fight.

Fourth, government trading may involve cooperation rather than conflict and trade-off, in those instances where there is complementarity between regional and national development. It is easy to imagine cases where resource development – mining, forestry, energy or agriculture – will be beneficial to both the region involved and the country as a whole through final or intermediate demand linkages. The same may be said of situations where large disparities exist in unemployment, provided that appropriate reference prices are used for evaluation purposes, as my colleague Fernand Martin indicates in the next chapter. Several authors have shown that national efficiency may be compatible with regional development in certain circumstances, among them Benjamin Higgins (1973) and Raymond Courbis (1981).

10.2 Regional transfers of resources in Canada

Governments nowadays have the power and resources to build or destroy regions. In Canada, the federal government redistributes huge amounts of money among the provinces through fiscal policy and regulation. Since this paper will concentrate on fiscal transfers, let it be qualified at the outset by the fact that the regional impact of federal regulation is probably more important than visible flows. In this respect, one can think of transportation, farm, or energy policy as illustrations. Energy policy alone, according to the Economic Council of Canada, shifted $14 billion to the Canadian East in 1980, which is close to total intergovernmental transfers in that year.

Before proceeding with the federal government transfers, it will be useful to draw a brief picture of regional disparities in Canada.

Unemployment

The first and most significant indicator of disparity is the rate of unemployment. Regional differences are at least twice as large in unemployment as in income; they are fairly constant through time and the business cycle (Table 10.1). In the second half of the 1970s, the extreme situations were those of the Prairie provinces with about 4% unemployed and the Atlantic provinces with 12%, giving a ratio of one to three. There is a surprisingly large consensus to the effect that no more than a third of this unemployment is related to aggregate demand deficiency. The evidence is presented in Fernand Martin's paper to which I contributed. Among those who support this view I would add the Economic Council of Canada (1982) and Thirsk (1973) to Siedule and Newton (1979) and Miller (1985). Martin goes on to a further decomposition of contributing factors, specifying, for example, unemployment insurance which is one among many federal transfers with differentiated regional impact, minimum wage regulations in the provinces, seasonality, and so on.

Table 10.1 Regional unemployment rates.

	1966–9		1970–6		1977–81		1982–4	
	%	Index	%	Index	%	Index	%	Index
Atlantic Provinces	5.6	140.0	8.8	144.3	11.9	152.6	14.8	129.8
Quebec	5.1	127.5	7.4	121.3	10.2	130.8	13.5	118.4
Ontario	3.2	80.0	5.1	83.6	6.8	87.2	9.8	86.0
Prairies Provinces	2.8	70.0	4.4	72.1	4.4	56.4	8.6	75.4
British Colombia	5.2	139.0	7.5	123.0	7.6	97.4	13.5	118.4
Canada	4.0	100.0	6.1	100.0	7.8	100.0	11.4	100.0

Source: Statistics Canada, Historical Labor Force Statistics, cat. 71–201.

Taking a more analytical view of unemployment disparities, one would develop a model with the following features: (a) there is less than perfect adaptation of production functions to resource endowments, with persisting differences in productivity; and (b) unit labor costs are higher in depressed regions because of pressures for wage parity. These pressures originate in nationwide bargaining, federal government wage policy, minimum wage legislations, and large public sectors in the depressed regions (Table 10.2). This latter factor is particularly important as a larger segment of the labor market is less exposed to competition. Public expenditure as a proportion of gross domestic product was 41% in Canada in 1981, 27% in Alberta, and 37% in Ontario, but 49% in Quebec and 78.6% in the Atlantic Provinces.

Such a model obviously implies that labor mobility is insufficient to restore full employment; to stimulate aggregate demand would not succeed either, even if the stimulus could be restricted to target areas (which is unlikely). Policy should rather be directed toward improving the efficiency of labor markets, notably by enhancing the flexibility of

Table 10.2 Public expenditures (all government levels) as a percentage of GDP, 1961–81.

	Atlantic	Quebec	Ontario	Alberta	Canada
1961	47.9	26.7	27.5	29.6	30.4
1970	53.1	35.5	33.6	31.9	35.7
1975	72.6	44.8	37.4	26.7	40.3
1979	66.8	45.8	35.5	25.9	39.4
1980	81.6	47.9	36.2	25.5	40.4
1981	78.6	49.3	36.8	26.7	41.4

Source: Statistics Canada, Provincial Economic Accounts, cat. 13–213, 1984 edn.

wage rates. Alternatively, efforts should be made to increase labor productivity up to the national wage level, although this latter prescription is easier said than done.

Incomes

The most widespread indicator of regional disparities is income per capita. It also contributes least to understanding the situation because income per capita is an aggregate number of several components that need to be identified.

One can write:
$$\frac{Y}{P} = \frac{Y_t + Y_I + Y_e}{P} \qquad (10.1)$$

where Y = personal income, P = population, Y_t = transfer income, Y_I = investment income, and Y_e = earned income. In other words, personal income can be decomposed into the three major categories of earned income, investment income, and transfer income. Income earned from work and from investment is market income.

In turn, earned income per capita can be disaggregated further as follows:

$$\frac{Y_e}{P} = \frac{Y_e}{E} \cdot \frac{E}{P} \qquad (10.2)$$

where E is the number of persons employed. Now E/P is a critical ratio incorporating several hidden dimensions. It is obvious, for example, that if P_x is population of working age and L the labor force, then:

$$\frac{E}{P} = \frac{P_x}{P} \cdot \frac{L}{P_x} \cdot \frac{E}{L} \qquad (10.3)$$

Since L/P_x is the participation rate p and E/L is $1 - U$ where U is the rate of unemployment, equations 10.2 and 10.3 can be rewritten in a more elegant way:

$$\frac{Y_e}{P} = \frac{Y_e}{E} \cdot \frac{P_x}{P} \cdot P \cdot (1-U) \qquad (10.4)$$

Finally, one can take all factors into account with respect to personal income per capita by writing:

$$\frac{Y}{P} = \frac{Y}{Y_I + Y_e} \cdot \frac{Y_I + Y_e}{Y_e} \cdot \frac{Y_e}{E} \cdot \frac{P_x}{P} \cdot P \cdot (1 - U) \qquad (10.5)$$

This component analysis indicates that disparities in personal income per head may be increased or reduced by a number of factors, some of which are policy-induced such as transfers; others are purely demographic or exogenous such as population of working age; while others still are endogenous and reflect economic conditions, namely earnings per worker, participation rates, and unemployment.

The first question to be addressed is the size and time trend of income disparities in Canada. Compared with the United States, regional disparities in personal income per capita are slightly higher in Canada.

Table 10.3 Personal income per capita selected years (Canada = 100).

	1926	1949	1959	1970	1980	1983
Newfoundland	—	50.92	54.02	63.37	65.27	67.78
Prince Edward Island	56.23	55.53	59.12	66.54	70.61	74.27
Nova Scotia	67.85	74.53	75.61	77.45	78.91	80.42
New Brunswick	64.71	69.36	66.90	71.98	72.87	74.14
Quebec	84.66	85.12	86.73	88.67	94.18	92.54
Ontario	114.34	119.20	118.86	118.41	107.61	109.18
Manitoba	108.28	103.43	99.06	92.89	88.75	93.07
Saskatchewan	101.86	96.76	82.29	72.45	91.09	93.69
Alberta	113.80	105.37	101.62	99.25	109.13	108.20
British Columbia	124.55	121.21	117.02	108.82	111.49	105.89
Yukon and N.W. Terr.	—	—	111.59	94.61	101.48	105.47
Canada	100.00	100.00	100.00	100.00	100.00	100.00
Mean deviation						
Unweighted	21.04	21.70	20.49	18.18	15.27	13.89
Weighted	19.36	18.67	16.38	14.94	9.68	9.49

Note: Number of regions: 1926–9, 1949–10, since 1959–11.
Source: Statistics Canada, National Accounts, cat. 13–502, 13–201.

Based on the same number of regions in both countries and an unweighted standard deviation measure, disparities were 37% higher in Canada in 1981 according to Mansell and Copithorne (1984). The general view is that over time, income disparities in Canada have been reduced very slowly or not at all. Table 10.3 indicates indeed that personal income per capita did not show much convergence between 1926 and 1959.[2] During the last two decades, however, the situation has changed substantially. Taking the simplest measure of dispersion, that is, the mean relative deviation such as:

$$\frac{(Y_i/Y) - 100}{N} \qquad (10.6)$$

where Y_i is any measure of regional income per capita, Y, the national average, and N, the number of regions, disparities in personal income per capita have been narrowed by 32%, – that is, from a mean deviation of 20.49% in 1959 to 13.89% in 1983. An interesting modality of the deviation index is to weigh the disparities by population in each region (see Appendix Eqn. A6). On this more significant basis, disparities stood at less than 10% in 1983, a reduction of 42% from 1959. The difference between the weighted and the unweighted deviation shows that disparities involve less people now than was the case in 1959.

Table 10.4 Earned income per capita selected years (Canada = 100).

	1926	1949	1959	1970	1980	1983
Newfoundland	—	50.29	51.28	57.97	57.60	59.82
Prince Edward Island	—	52.91	55.24	61.18	63.86	67.91
Nova Scotia	69.17	73.00	73.88	76.01	77.48	79.91
New Brunswick	66.97	67.17	63.66	69.33	69.27	70.49
Quebec	84.10	84.23	86.51	88.33	92.56	90.32
Ontario	111.18	120.45	120.08	119.96	110.08	112.86
Manitoba	108.64	105.88	99.94	92.47	87.12	91.44
Saskatchewan	108.94	98.15	80.87	68.78	85.40	87.18
Alberta	118.88	108.74	102.83	100.56	111.09	108.62
British Columbia	126.14	116.49	114.79	107.46	111.32	104.41
Yukon and N.W. Terr.	—	—	124.72	108.00	117.04	122.04
Canada	100.00	100.00	100.00	100.00	100.00	100.00
Mean deviation						
Unweighted	19.19	22.58	22.82	20.17	19.66	18.26
Weighted	21.23	19.47	17.08	15.91	11.85	11.97

Note: Number of regions: 1926–9, 1949–10, since 1959–11.
Source: Statistics Canada, National Accounts, cat. 13–502, 13–201.

The major component of personal income is earnings. The deviations from the national average in earned income per capita are given in Table 10.4. The disparities weighted by population were reduced in this case by 30% between 1959 and 1983. This is an encouraging trend for those concerned with income disparities. Contrary to what one might have expected, the reduction in disparities over time is not mainly due to government transfer payments; in fact, close to three-quarters of the overall reduction, 30% out of 42%, can be attributed to changes in earnings per capita.

This finding is compatible with an important role for transfers in explaining the level of disparities in any one year, such as 1983, as opposed to explaining variations in disparities over time. In 1983, the deviation index reached 11.96% for earned income and 9.49% for personal income, the difference being imputable to transfer payments.[3]

Depending on the number of regions and provinces used in the calculations, the weighting procedure accounting for population may or may not produce large differences in the results. In the present case, using 11 provinces and territories of very unequal size, the weighting is necessary and significant. As Tables 10.3 and 10.4 indicate, income disparities diverge considerably when an unweighted index is chosen; when the size of population is taken into account in 1983, for example, average disparities are reduced by about one-third for both personal and earned income.

Table 10.5 Contribution of factors to the weighted mean deviation in earned income per capita (%).

	1966	1983	1966–83
earned income per employee (w_i)	58.7	46.20	51.40
participation rate (p_i)	28.9	42.40	35.80
population of working age (a_i)	10.8	4.10	6.90
rate of employment (u_i)	3.6	9.20	7.90
interaction effects (m_i)	−2.0	−1.80	−2.00
Total	100.0	100.00	100.00
mean deviation[a]	14.2	11.97	13.09

Note: For notation, see Appendix.
[a]: Based on ten provinces, the Yukon and N.W. Territories having been removed from the calculations.

The next question is more analytical. Referring back to Equations 10.4 and 10.5, it is possible to determine the contributions of the factors associated with income disparities either at a point in time such as 1983 or the average for a period, such as 1966–83, or again by looking at changes over time. The statistical procedures involved are described in the Appendix. Table 10.5 provides some results. It indicates that of the disparities in earned income per capita over the period 1966–83 more than 50% can be imputed to earned income per employee, and 36% to the participation rate; while differences in both population of working age and the rate of employment (the reciprocal of the rate of unemployment) account for about 15%. Interaction effects between the variables are small if not negligible, but tended to increase disparities during the period.

There is no reason to believe that the role of each factor in increasing or reducing income disparities is the same across provinces. One province can be poor because wages are lower, another because there are fewer people working, and so on. Table 10.6 throws light on this complex question. Earned income per capita is substantially lower than the national average in the four Atlantic provinces. The main reason is, in all cases, that wages are lower. Lower participation rates are the second most important reason. Prince Edward Island shows the lowest wages, compensated to a certain extent by a relatively favorable participation rate. Quebec and Ontario are close to the national results given in Table 10.5. Wages contribute to 50% of the overall disparity in both provinces, but in Quebec they are lower than the national average, while in Ontario they are higher than the national average, as is earned income per capita. In Alberta, the situation is very different. Income in total is above average, mainly because participation rates are exceedingly high by national standards and so is the rate of employment. Because wages and population of working age are relatively less favorable, Alberta's overall edge is lower than it would otherwise be.

Table 10.6 Contribution of factors to the relative position of each province in earned income per capita 1966–83 (%).

	w_i	p_i	a_i	u_i	m_i	Total	D_i
Newfoundland	−36.5	−48.1	−21.9	−12.8	+19.2	100	−41.9
Prince Edward Island	−75.3	−19.3	−10.3	−6.9	+11.8	100	−39.0
Nova Scotia	−47.4	−41.8	−12.6	−6.8	+8.6	100	−23.6
New Brunswick	−48.2	−41.7	−13.4	−8.8	+12.0	100	−30.6
Quebec	−51.8	−42.3	+9.8	−18.2	+2.5	100	−9.9
Ontario	+47.6	+31.4	+9.3	+7.4	+4.4	100	+14.7
Manitoba	−112.2	+13.4	−24.4	+24.5	−1.4	100	−6.6
Saskatchewan	−78.7	−23.1	−32.5	+24.8	+1.8	100	−12.4
Alberta	73.6	+199.4	−65.5	+46.9	−8.2	100	+4.7
British Columbia	+90.3	+1.3	+19.3	−11.3	+0.6	100	+8.5

Note: When the sign is the same as for the disparity D_i in the last column, the factors are contributing to the disparity; when the sign is different, the factors involved reduce the disparity.

The changes that have taken place during the period 1966 to 1983 are also revealing. Disparities in earned income per capita have been reduced by two percentage points (weighted). This reduction is associated with a substantial narrowing in earnings per worker across the provinces, and to a lesser extent in population of working age. However, widening differentials occurred at the same time in both participation rates and the rates of employment, maintaining wider disparities in earned income per capita than would otherwise have been the case.[4]

Summarizing the findings so far, one can think of transfer payments to persons as reducing market income disparities by some 24%. Disparities in earned income per capita, in turn, can be imputed, to the extent of about 50%, to earnings per employee (or the level of wages); and to regional differences in participation rates for about an additional third. Differentials in the rate of unemployment among provinces account for less than 10%, a finding which is a bit surprising.

Earnings per employee being the dominant factor in income disparities, this factor is worth further consideration. Indeed, this subject has been thoroughly investigated by the Economic Council of Canada (1977), which found that such disparities have been associated with differences in capital per employee, following the standard neoclassical approach. An additional 20% was related to an index of labor quality involving age, sex, and education, with the emphasis on the latter.

Net fiscal benefits

The purpose of the above analysis was not so much to measure disparities as to provide the background to the role of the federal government in reallocating resources among the provinces, to which I now turn.

The transfers to persons included in the previous income per capita series give a very partial view of the government's impact on the regional situations. For one thing, transfers to persons exclude interest paid on the public debt and obviously exclude also transfers or subsidies to the business sector. In addition, transfers to persons are only one category of public expenditure. The other categories involve as much if not considerably more shifting of real resources across the provinces. Expenditure on goods and services, for example, are anything but neutral in terms of regional development. For several authors, some subcategories of those expenditures are indeed the only expenditures that count, namely public investment projects designed specifically to stimulate regional development. Then there are the intergovernmental transfers which are typical of the Canadian federal system. These include fiscal transfers such as equalization and established programs in

Table 10.7 Provincial distribution of federal expenditures and taxes in dollars per capita (Canada 1983 = 100).

	Goods and services[a]	Transfers to persons[b]	Intergovernmental transfers[c]	Total expenditures	Total taxes receivable[d]	Net fiscal benefits[e] ($ million)	($/capita)	(% of GDP)
Atlantic	174.0	116.0	177.0	141.0	58.5	6,911.00	3,050.00	29.5
Quebec	71.5	90.2	150.0	98.3	82.6	4,129.00	634.00	4.6
Ontario	113.0	106.0	54.8	97.1	112.6	−5,249.00	−595.00	−3.5
Manitoba	115.0	92.5	123.0	103.4	54.9	1,126.00	1,077.00	7.5
Saskatchewan	78.6	94.3	78.1	87.7	82.0	200.00	202.00	1.2
Alberta	71.8	100.0	68.9	87.9	164.9	−6,827.00	−2,900.00	−12.1
British Columbia	84.8	89.0	67.9	83.9	95.5	−1,270.00	−449.00	−2.7
Canada[f]	100.0	100.0	100.0	100.0	100.0	—	—	—
(in dollars per capita)	782.45	2,195.21	751.43	3,729.08	3,729.08	—	—	—

[a]: Current expenditure plus investment less capital allowances.
[b]: Including subsidies to business and debt service.
[c]: Including value of special abatement to Quebec on personal income tax (16.5 points = $1,339.00 millions).
[d]: Taxes collected adjusted for the federal deficit and distributed as taxes collected.
[e]: Federal expenditures less taxes payable.
[f]: Yukon and N.W. Territories and non-residents have been included in calculations but not reported here.

the field of health and postsecondary education as well as a host of smaller departmental transfers. For consistency purposes, the value of the special tax abatement for Quebec has been included in government-to-government transfers. Table 10.7 presents the per capita regional distribution of the three categories of federal expenditures mentioned, as well as the total. Of the three categories of expenditures only the transfers to governments are specifically designed to equalize fiscal capacity and income among the provinces, but the end result is given by total expenditures rather than any one component. In spite of the very wide dispersion of particular federal expenditures per capita, total expenditures obviously contributed to reduce regional disparities with the possible exception of Saskatchewan, where personal income per capita is about the same as in Manitoba (see Table 10.3).

But this is only the first part of the story. The second is taxes paid to the federal government to finance the expenditures. Given our uniform and progressive federal tax structure, poorer provinces will pay less tax per capita than richer provinces. The case of the Atlantic provinces is striking in this respect. Federal expenditures per capita in the Atlantic provinces exceed the national average by 41%, but federal taxes paid by the residents in those provinces are also 41% less than the Canadian average. They gain from both sides of the ledger. To measure this overall gain, the notion of net fiscal benefit is introduced – that is, federal expenditure less federal taxes paid per capita. Table 10.7 gives the total amounts of net fiscal benefits by province or region. This calculation could be described as the extent of the net redistribution of federal funds that took place in 1983. The Atlantic provinces received close to $7 billion net, Quebec $4.1 billion and Manitoba $1 billion. Almost $7 billion of these funds were contributed by Alberta, $5.2 billion by Ontario, and $1.3 billion by British Columbia. Total funds transferred on a net basis reached $12.4 billion, or 13% of total federal expenditure.

As the first part of this paper has shown, the theoretical issue raised by the regional distribution of federal net fiscal benefits is whether this distribution can be rationalized by efficiency, equity, or political market considerations.

Efficiency would call for enough distribution of fiscal benefits per worker to prevent unproductive migrations. For example, if labor productivity is 20% below the Canadian average in a given province, one would not want to encourage migration away from the more productive provinces by closing the gap, so to speak, in terms of total income per worker, through fiscal benefits. If productivity is approximated by earned income per worker, efficiency can only be achieved if fiscal benefits are distributed across the provinces in the same way as earned income per worker. Earned income per worker was $21,952 in Quebec in 1983 and $23,941 in Ontario. Efficiency considerations would have called for higher net fiscal benefits per worker in Ontario than in Quebec. From Table 10.7, it is possible to recalculate net fiscal benefits on a per worker basis. In 1983, net fiscal benefits per worker reached +$1,563 in Quebec and −$1,282 in Ontario, an absolute difference of $2,845 in favor of Quebec workers. Efficiency clearly cannot be used as the rationale for the federal government redistribution that takes place.

Table 10.8 Impact of total federal transfers to the provinces on fiscal capacity, 1980–1981.

	Own revenue[a]	Own revenue plus transfers	Variation in fiscal capacity (%)
Newfoundland	53	87	64
Prince Edward Island	51	92	80
Nova Scotia	66	86	30
New Brunswick	62	88	42
Quebec	79	90	14
Ontario	99	88	−11
Manitoba	77	88	14
Saskatchewan	99	99	0
Alberta	206	193	−6
British Columbia	111	104	−6

[a]: "Own revenue" equals own revenue proper plus federal taxes paid to finance the transfers. It is calculated as provincial tax bases at national rates per capita and includes all revenue sources plus local property taxes. Figures in the first two columns are expressed as provincial revenues per head with Canada = 100.
Source: Economic Council of Canada (1982, Table 2–3).

Equity is an awfully elusive concept, as we all know. I will not try to outclass anybody by judging whether present fiscal benefits are equitable or not. However, one aspect of equity can be made meaningful because it is defined in the Canadian constitution. It has to do with "providing essential public services ... at reasonably comparable levels of taxation" (article 36). The question is whether or not intergovernmental transfers contribute, and to what extent, to the achievement of this obligation. Table 10.8 summarizes the results of an analysis done by the Economic Council of Canada. The key concept is fiscal capacity – that is, the revenue that provinces can raise at national taxation rates before and after federal transfers. The table indicates that federal transfers contribute to a considerable reduction in disparities. Alberta aside, the extreme deviations from the national average go from 51 to 111 before federal transfers, and to 86 and 104 after transfers. The disparities are reduced on average by 46%, and seven provinces find themselves with essentially the same fiscal capacity. The exception is Alberta, which remains at twice the average. It can be concluded that federal transfers achieve their stated purpose in giving the provinces the ability to provide equivalent public services.

Beyond the provision of public services, equity should probably mean that federal net fiscal benefits should be distributed equally on a per capita basis. In fact, net fiscal benefits are distributed anything but equally, as is shown in Table 10.7. In the Atlantic provinces, they reach $3,050 and in Alberta −$2,900 per capita. Ontario loses $595 and Quebec gains $634. These amounts represent some 30% of GDP in the Atlantic provinces but substantially less in other regions.

If net fiscal benefits do not reflect efficiency or equity considerations, one is left with intergovernmental trading as the major source of explanation or rationalization. This result is disappointing insofar as this theory leads to indeterminate conclusions and therefore has no predictive power.

Appendix: factors contributing to income disparities – standardization procedure

Equation 10.4 in the text is written:

$$\frac{Y_e}{P} = \frac{Y_e}{E} \cdot \frac{P_x}{P} \cdot P \cdot (1 - U) \tag{A.1}$$

To facilitate derivations, the notation is changed as follows:

Let

$\frac{Y_e}{P} = Y_e$, earned income per capita

$\frac{Y_e}{E} = W$, wage rate

$\frac{P_x}{P} = A$, population of working age in total population.

Then

$$Y_e = W \cdot A \cdot P \cdot (1 - U) \tag{A.2}$$

To determine the contribution of each component to the mean deviation of Y_e, one can take each factor's own deviation in region i from the national average.

The deviations can be written as follows:

$$\frac{Y_e}{\bar{Y}_e} = (1 + e_i), \quad \frac{W_i}{\bar{W}} = (1 + w_i), \quad \frac{A_i}{\bar{A}} = (1 + a_i), \quad \frac{P_i}{\bar{P}} = (1 + q_i)$$

$$\frac{(1 - U)_i}{(1 - \bar{U})} = (1 + u_i) \quad (1 - \bar{U})$$

where $\bar{X}$ = the relevant national average.

Equation A.2 can then be expressed in terms of deviations from the national averages:

$$\bar{Y}_e (1 + e_i) = \bar{W}(1 + w_i) \cdot \bar{A}(1 + a_i) \cdot \bar{P}(1 + q_i) \cdot \overline{(1 - U)}(1 + u_i)$$

$$\bar{Y}_e (1 + e_i) = \bar{Y}_e (1 + w_i)(1 + a_i)(1 + q_i)(1 + u_i) \tag{A.3}$$

$$(1 + e_i) = (1 + w + a + q + u + m)_i \tag{A.4}$$

where $m_i = [w(a+q+u) + a(q+u) + qu + w(aq+au+qu) + aqu + waqu]_i$, which are the interaction effects between the variables.

Equation A.4 can be multiplied by 100 to translate the deviations in percentages, that is:

$$100\, e_i = 100\, (w + a + q + u + m)_i \quad (A.5)$$

Now, if the deviations in each series or province are $D_i = |\bar{X}_i - 1|$ as defined above, then mean deviation indices can be obtained by summing the D_i's

$$V = \sum_i \left| \frac{X_i}{\bar{X}} - 1 \right| N_i \times 100$$

where $N_i = 1/N$ the number of regions or provinces included in the income series. N_i can also be equal to N_i/N if the deviations are to be weighted by population.

Finally, one gets

$$V = \sum_i N_i \; |w_i + a_i + q_i + U_i + m_i| \times 100 \quad (A.6)$$

which is the contribution of each province i through its own characteristics to the mean deviation for the country as a whole.

Since a D_i below the average tends to reduce disparities and a D_i above the average increases disparities, it is necessary to introduce a term A_i in Equation A.6 which will be equal to 1 if $D_i \geq 0$ and equal to -1 if $D_i \leq 0$. Then,

$$V = \sum_i 100\, N_i w_i A_i + \sum_i 100\, N_i a_i A_i$$
$$+ \sum_i 100\, N_i U_i A_i + \sum_i 100\, N_i u_i A_i + \sum_i 100 N_i m_i A_i \quad (A.7)$$

in which each element, $\sum_i 100\, N_i X_i A_i$, measures the contribution of factor X_i for all provinces to the mean deviation for Canada as a whole.

Earned income per capita, y_e, has an unweighted mean deviation, V, of 18.26% and a weighted mean deviation of 11.96% in 1983. These are the V's to be explained by each of the components included in Equations A6 and A7. The contributions of the components are expressed in percentage points. In the text, as in Table 10.5, they have been divided by V to get percentages.

Notes

1 I wish to thank Robert Gagné and Jean-Pierre Vidal for their expert assistance in preparing this paper.
2 The coefficient of variation V is very sensitive to the number of regions N in Equation (10.6), and the time series available since 1926 is not uniform in this respect, as Table 10.3 indicates. Another series based on seven regions (not shown here) reveals a reduction of 10% in disparities between 1926 and 1959.
3 The equalizing virtue of government transfers is underestimated somewhat when the comparison is made between earned income and personal income. Market income, that is, earned income plus investment income, is a better reference point. The fact is that investment income, and therefore market

income, increases disparities. The weighted deviation index for market income in 1983 was 12.48%, compared with the 9.49% for personal income. Transfers would thus have reduced market income disparities by 24%.

4 These observations are based on direct examination of the data but can also be derived from a comparative reading of the first two columns in Table 10.5.

References

Broadway, R. W. 1980. *Intergovernmental transfers in Canada*, Toronto: Canadian Tax Foundation.

Broadway, R. W. & F. Flatters 1982. Efficiency and equalization payments in a federal system of government: a synthesis and extension of recent results. *The Canadian Journal of Economics*, 15, 613–33.

Boyer, M. & M. Moreaux 1983. Conjectures, rationality and duopoly theory. *International Journal of Industrial Organization* 1, 25–41.

Breton, A. 1985. Commentary on the report of the Royal Commission on economic union and development prospects for Canada, vol. III, 554–600 in the French version.

Breton, A. & A. Scott 1980. The design of federations. Montreal: The Institute for Research on Public Policy.

Courbis, R. 1981. The national and multinational impact of regional policy. Regional Science Association Meetings, Montreal.

Courchene, T. J. 1970. Interprovincial migration and economic adjustment. *The Canadian Journal of Economics* 3, 550–76.

Courchene, T. J., 1978. Economics and federalism. *Transactions of the Royal Society of Canada* series 4, 16, 71–87.

Courchene, T. J. 1980. Towards a protected society: the politization of economic life. *The Canadian Journal of Economics* 13, 556–77.

Courchene, T. J. 1983. Canada's new equalization program: description and evaluation. *Canadian Public Policy* 16, 458–76.

Economic Council of Canada 1977. Living together, a study of regional disparities. Ottawa.

Economic Council of Canada 1982. *Pénurie et carences*. Ottawa. Table 2–1.

Government of Canada 1979–80. Tax expenditure account. Ottawa: Department of Finance.

Hartle, D. 1983. The theory of "rent seeking: some reflections". *The Canadian Journal of Economics* 16, 539–54.

Hettich, W. & S. Winer 1983. Vertical imbalance in the fiscal systems of federal states. Paper presented at the meeting of the Canadian Economics Association, Vancouver.

Higgins, B. 1973. Trade-off curves and regional gaps. In *Development and planning: essays in honour of Paul Rosenstein-Rodan*, J. Bhagwati & R. S. Eckaus (eds.), 152–77, London: Allen & Unwin.

Lithwick, H. 1984. Federal government regional economic development policies: an evaluative survey. Preliminary paper prepared for the Royal Commission on the Economic Union and Development Prospects for Canada.

Mansell, R. L. & L. Copithorne 1984. Canadian regional disparities: a survey. Preliminary paper prepared for the Royal Commission on the Economic Union and Development Prospects for Canada.

Miller, F.-C. 1985. The unemployment effects of regionally discriminating fiscal policies. The Canadian Regional Science Association. Mimeo.

Olson, M. 1965. *The logic of collective action.* Cambridge, Mass.: Harvard University Press.
Olson, M. 1982. *The rise and decline of nations.* New Haven, Conn.: Yale University Press.
Siedule, T. & K. Newton 1969. The unemployment gap in Canada, 1961–1978. Discussion paper no. 145, Economic Council of Canada, Ottawa.
Stigler, G. 1971. The theory of economic regulation. *Bell Journal of Economics and Management Science* **2**, 3–21.
Thirsk, W. 1973. Regional dimensions of inflation and unemployment. Prices and Income Commission, Ottawa.
Tollison, R. D. 1982. Rent-seeking: a survey. *Kyklos* **35**, 575–602.
Tullock, G. 1967. The welfare costs of the tariffs monopolies and theft. *Western Economic Journal* **5**, 224–32.
Winer, S. L. 1983. Some evidence on the effect of the separation of spending and taxing decisions. *Journal of Political Economy* **91**, 126–41.

11

The influence of unemployment insurance benefits upon the social cost of labor in lagging regions

FERNAND MARTIN

11.1 The problem

Many social studies evaluate projects with the purpose of justifying subsidies, tax expenditures, or other forms of encouragement to locate manufacturing activities in lagging regions. Following the suggestion of the Treasury Board (Treasury Board of Canada 1976), these studies shadow the price of various inputs and outputs of projects, notably of labor. Indeed, by resorting to the shadow price of labor, the calculated cost of a project is reduced, since the social cost of labor is usually smaller than its nominal cost in the case of unemployment. This approach, however, understates the cost of labor and thus the social cost of projects because, as we will show below, the shadow price of labor depends (among other things) upon the length of the unemployment spells of the temporarily unemployed workers, which in turn is a function of the availability of unemployment insurance and other social security payments. The upshot is that the social cost of labor is understated because, in the absence of these social measures, it would be higher. The implication, then, is that if the welfare function is national, the calculation method of the government departments that rely on the Treasury Board manual to do their cost–benefit studies, understates the social cost of labor, especially in lagging regions where unemployment insurance benefits (UIB) have, relatively speaking, the greatest impact. (The differential regional impact of UIB has been suggested by Mati (1975).) This has the effect of giving the false impression that industrial projects cost much less if located in lagging regions. Or, if the subsidy given to business firms corresponds to the difference between the nominal wage bill and the social cost of this wage bill, it is greater than it should be. In both cases there is a misallocation of resources; that is, too many economic activities are sent to the lagging regions.

11.2 The definition of the social cost of labor

The task of this essay is to establish the relationships hypothesized above between unemployment insurance, length of the unemployment period of temporary workers, and the social cost of labor (SCL). To that effect, we must first of all define the social cost of labor. In the case of a real economy such as in Canada, characterized by imperfect markets, externalities, and public goods, it is necessary to enable the government, through shadow pricing the inputs, to take optimum (second-best) decisions regarding the subsidization of projects in lagging regions. Over the years the federal government has, to that effect, codified its practice of cost–benefit analysis (see Treasury Board of Canada 1976). In the field of labor shadow pricing, special efforts have been made by Jenkins and Kuo (1978)[1] and a few others. DREE immediately adopted the Jenkins–Kuo method which is still in use.[2] The social cost of labor of a temporary worker in the most simple case is computed as follows:

$$SCL = W_t (52 - D) + DV$$

where: SCL = social annual cost of labor of a temporary worker;
      52 = is the 52 weeks in a year;
      D = probability of not working during a year, which is some kind of function of the unemployment rate[3] expressed in weeks of non-work;
      W_t = weekly social income of the temporary worker when he works. It is equal to the gross weekly wage of the worker, plus the social security paid by the employer and the fringe benefits; and
      V = weekly value of nonwork activities, i.e., the minimum weekly wage sufficient to induce the temporary worker to reduce his unemployment by one week.[4]

V is measured at the margin of working and not working. It is determined as follows:

The welfare of a particular temporary worker is measured by:

$$I = W_1 (52 - D) + D [fU (1 - t) + V]$$

where: f = the proportion of unemployed time during which the worker collects UIB,
t = marginal tax rate,
U = weekly benefits received from unemployment insurance, and
W_1 = the weekly wage plus fringe benefits, but without wage bill taxes paid by employers to the government.

An unemployed worker will then accept a job only if

$$W_1 (1 - t) \geq fU (1 - t) + V$$

Note that the right member in this expression is a way to express the reservation wage.

Then

$$V = (W_1 - fU)(1 - t)$$

$$V \leq W_1$$

The above equations illustrate the problem referred to above. Indeed, if f, U, or t are increased, V will decrease. Ceteris paribus this will reduce SCL. Since we show below, in Section 11.4, that an increase in UIB also increases D (Feldstein & Poterba 1984), we can say that any increase in UIB in whatever form (i.e., f or U) will have the effect of reducing SCL. The same reasoning can be extended to other types of social security payments which diminish the hardship (opportunity cost) of nonwork periods.

The same approach can take into consideration other aspects of imperfect markets, such as the monopolistic component of labor markets (hereafter represented by $B = 4/3$ (MacDonald & Evans 1981),[5] and other social welfare payments (represented by A). The equilibrium equation becomes then:

$$\frac{W_1 (1 - t)}{B} = fU (1 - t) + gA (1 - t) + V$$

where:

$$V = \frac{W_1 (1 - t) - B (fU + gA)(1 - t)}{B},$$

g = proportion of the unemployed period over which social security payments are received, and A = weekly payments of social security.

11.3 Types of unemployment

The shadow price of labor is not easily established because labor supply and demand functions are difficult to establish, both in specific cases and in the aggregate. The reasons are numerous.

First, there are many labor markets, differentiated by industries, professions, occupations, and space. There may not even be communication among some of these markets, so that the analyst may have to deal with non-competing groups. Second, demand for a particular labor may shift because of changes in aggregate demand or because of modifications of the industrial structure due to technological changes, international trade, or geographical shifts of the industry. Third, the supply of labor is also variable because of changing participation rates, notably of women who go in and out of the labor force for all sorts of reasons. Fourth, it is even more difficult to extrapolate the future demands and supplies of labor because the previously mentioned difficulties are compounded by anticipations. Fifth, these difficulties are also reflected in the measurement of the unemployment rate; this notion is ambiguous because its definition is based on at least two different paradigms (neoclassical and Keynesian), and also because some of the virtually unemployed are not visibly so. This is a reference to disguised unemployment (not usually included in the published unemployment rate) which consists in workers discouraged, unemployed and hoarded (by big firms).

The paradigms show that unemployment cannot be defined simply by examining the demand and supply of labor; the impact of the state of labor markets (in equilibrium or in disequilibrium) upon the state of commodities markets must also be considered. This is how shifts in demand and supply of labor, which are baffling in elementary analysis, are mastered.

The neoclassical paradigm consists mainly of frictional and structural unemployment where the "cause" largely consists of transaction and mobility costs. The Keynesian paradigm consists in cyclical unemployment. It is tempting to use the distinction between the two to generalize as follows: cyclical (Keynesian) unemployment is involuntary, non-cyclical (neoclassical) unemployment is voluntary. But, here also, things are not that simple.

In the Keynesian paradigm there is an ambiguity because, there, the unemployment is taken as voluntary only if "in case of a small increase in prices, both the aggregate supply of labor at the current wage and the demand for labor at this wage are established above the existing level of employment," (Hung & Lefebvre 1981). Also, it is not clear what is meant by "current wages": is it the last wage received, or the full employment wage, or the next "expected" wage,[6] or even the socially optimal reservation wage (Feldstein & Poterba 1984)? Depending upon the answer, the Keynesian paradigm leads to many different measures of involuntary unemployment, so that some portion of total unemployment becomes voluntary.

On the other hand, the neoclassical unemployment cannot be completely voluntary because the workings of the labor markets imply some inevitable transaction costs – i.e., at the going wage, labor markets do not clear. Note that nonclearing markets are also present in Keynesian unemployment. Similarly, when workers are dismissed because their former employer has disappeared or because technological changes have rendered their skills obsolete, their unemployment is initially involuntary. However, voluntary unemployment arises when the non-work period is prolonged beyond what it would have been otherwise because of UIB and other social security payments. These policy measures affect the willingness of the participants in the labor force to work.[7]

The distinction between voluntary and involuntary unemployment seemed, up to 1975, to be essential for inferring some welfare proposition concerning unemployment; for instance, part of the "voluntary" unemployment (if such a thing exists) might be assimilated to consumption, while another portion could consist in search activities considered necessary to ensure a better allocation of workers among jobs. However, today (as we shall see below) studies are based on the reservation wage, so that the distinction between voluntary and involuntary unemployment does not necessarily enter into the formulation of welfare implications.

11.4 The effects of unemployment insurance benefits upon the unemployment rate: the theory

The effect of the availability of UIB upon the observed unemployment rate can be assessed through two theoretical approaches: (a) the moral hazard approach; and (b) the reservation wage approach. Both approaches conclude that the availability of UIB induces unemployed workers to extend the length of the non-work period whatever the surrounding conditions (macro and micro). Furthermore, both approaches lend themselves to econometric explorations.

In the moral hazard approach, the non-work period is extended because, for an individual, the opportunity cost of remaining unemployed one more week is not the wage foregone by not working, but that wage minus the UIB benefits (all this net of taxes). The control of the Unemployment Insurance Commission over such decisions is imperfect.

In the reservation wage approach, UIB is shown to raise the reservation wage; this in turn extends the length of the non-work period.

Both approaches are quite convincing in their attempt, at the theoretical level, at demonstrating the proposition that UIB causes some net unemployment, even taking into account the positive effects of this built-in macroeconomic stabilizer. What has been (and is still) under dispute (among economists)[8] is the magnitude of the effect.[9]

11.4.1 The moral hazard approach

The effect of unemployment insurance benefit (UIB) upon the observed unemployment rate u is hypothesized to be positive – i.e., an increase in UIB induces some members of the labor force to quit their jobs and/or, if laid off, to extend somewhat the non-work period. This proposition is based upon a rational choice model (having its origins in Grubel & Maki (1978), p. 365ff.) which has the following features:

(a) Nonwork is not a Giffen good, so that if its price (the opportunity cost of not working) is reduced, more is consumed.
(b) For many members of the labor force, there is a trade-off between income from work and utility from non-work (in whatever form: search activities, leisure, goods produced by do-it-yourself work, income from underground activities, the value of a homemaker's work, etc.).
(c) The UIB shifts the budgetary constraint of the temporary unemployed worker to the right, thus reducing the opportunity cost of non-work periods.[10]
(d) There is an absence of a fully experience-rated unemployment insurance tax system where firms also compete for workers; so that moral hazard and adverse selection proliferate (see Section 11.5 below).
(e) The hypothesis that UIB increases the length of the non-work period does not require that each and every member of the labor force has this preference function, nor that all of the unemployment be voluntary throughout the whole period; what is voluntary is some extension of the non-work period.[11]

A common-sense model (based on Grubel et al. 1975) (in the moral hazard approach) for expressing the relationship between UIB and the unemployment rate takes the following form:

$$u = f(SU, TU, CU, UI),$$
where: u = unemployment rate,
SU = structural changes in the economy,
TU = seasonal effects in the economy,
CU = cyclical effects, and
UI = unemployment insurance effects.

Other factors such as the minimum wage and other general welfare programs are disregarded because of lack of suitable data. But, since the effect of these variables are likely to be of the same type as UIB, the worst that can happen is that the measured UIB effects might include some of the effects of these variables. We will deal with this point in Section 11.6.2.

Grubel et al.'s (1975) econometric model corresponding to that approach, GMS, assesses the effect of UIB upon the Canadian unemployment rate during the period 1953–72 in the form of an elasticity measurement.

The formula is:
$$e_{u,\,UIB} = \frac{\Delta (U/E)/U/E}{\Delta(UIB/AWW)/UIB/AWW}$$

where:

$e_{u,\,UIB}$ = elasticity relating the unemployment rates of UIB;
U = number of people unemployed:
E = labor force;
UIB = unemployment Insurance Benefits; and
AWW = average weekly wage.

The model holds TU and SU constant but incorporates the cyclical effects in the form of variations in GNP, the effect of UIB in the form of variations in the replacement rate (UIB/AWW), the variations in the labor force participation rates of males and females, and finally the variations in the enforcement of unemployment benefit eligibility rules (Grubel et al. 1975, p. 183). Their results show that for 1972, 22% of the unemployment rate was accounted for by UIB (p. 187). Green & Cousineau (1976) and Ren (1977), using somewhat similar models, attributed 17% and 25%, respectively, of the unemployment rate in 1972 to UIB. Maki (1975), also using a similar model, computed the effect of UIB upon the regional unemployment rates in Canada for 1972; for instance, he found that in the Atlantic region, UIB accounts for 41% of the local unemployment rate. In the same test, UIB accounted for only 6% of the unemployment rate of Ontario, also for 1972.

The GMS model (and those akin to it, e.g., models using time-series data, replacement ratio, etc.) have been criticized as follows:

(a) It does not incorporate seasonal and structural changes.
(b) Since it uses time series, it confuses the effect of the trend in the data with the specific effect of UIB.
(c) The model does not use the real benefits and wages effectively received by the temporary unemployed worker.
(d) The relationship between UIB and u is nonlinear.
(e) The elasticity computed for one particular year cannot be extrapolated to other years or cover extreme changes in the coefficients.

The first three criticisms can be answered satisfactorily (see Raynauld & Martin forthcoming). We deal with the latter two as follows. The fourth main criticism blames the GMS method for producing coefficients that are acceptable only for a certain range of values – that is, the relationship between UIB and u for 1972 cannot be simply extrapolated to other unemployment rates. For instance, Hamermesh (1978), by stipulating a linear relationship between UIB and u, has shown that such extrapolations may lead to ludicrous results. This suggests that the relationship is probably nonlinear for a certain range of values. Actually, here is how this criticism is attenuated: taking the lead from GMS (Grubel et al. 1975, pp. 187–8) and from Feldstein and Poterba, I hypothesize (Section 11.6.1) that there are low levels of UIB/AWW where UIB does not shift the labor supply curve – that is, does not cause any unemployment.[12] However, we also suppose that once a threshold (in the ratio) is attained, further increases in UIB/AWW shift the labor supply curve to the left. According to the experts, the years 1955–56 represent this threshold (i.e., at that time, UIB had no influence upon u) (GMS 1975, p. 187, Economic Council of Canada). It turns out that the UIB/AWW ratio was 0.30 in that period (GMS 1975, p. 182). We then suppose that any increase in the ratio will, in some proportion, increase the unemployment rate;[13] this proportion is mathematically expressed by the elasticity e_u, UIB (see formula above).[14]

The final criticism holds that the results of time series apply only for a given year or period (in the case of GMS, for 1972). Consequently, since the ratio of UIB/AWW has since changed, the results might not be applicable to more recent periods (such as the period 1972–82 used in Section 11.6.1). The answer to the criticism is as follows. First, we do not need all the results of the GMS study in order to proceed; only the elasticity measure is actually used. Second, the use of the original measure of elasticity of GMS is legitimized by the fact that an elasticity describes a behavior, not specific events.[15] Consequently, except if the workings of the Canadian labor market of the period 1972–82 have been influenced by different variables (different from the period 1953–73), the original elasticity measure should be usable.[16] However, the specificity of the period 1972–82 (e.g., the changes in the ratio UIB/AWW), is accounted for by combining the measures of elasticity with known recent changes in UIB/AWW (see Section 11.6).

Finally, absolute agreement in econometric estimations is never attained. For instance, Rea (1977) notes that "in terms of the aggregate unemployment rate, UI increases the extent of voluntary unemployment but not necessarily the measured unemployment rate" (p. 263). Note that this author got this result not through empirical work but through simulations. Similarly, Hung and Lefebvre (1981) have shown that unemployment benefits stimulate aggregate consumption through multiplier effects and thus employment. On the other hand, if UIB is financed by taxes, these taxes have a negative multiplier effect and thus reduce employment. It is then difficult, a priori, to determine the net effect. To assess that, Hung and Lefebvre (p. 550) propose the use of a disequilibrium econometric model. But, already Boadway and Flatters (1981) have shown through a theoretical model (involving a poor and a rich region) that if UIB are financed by a tax per employed worker in both regions, "... the opportunity cost of creating a job always exceeds the market wage and no case can be made for subsidizing jobs" (p. 73). In the light of the above remarks, the elasticities we used must consequently be interpreted because of their empirical basis as measuring *net effects* after and including the workings of keynesian multipliers.

11.4.2 The reservation wage approach

The theoretical and econometric difficulties of the moral hazard approach (either in time series or cross-section analyses) are diminished by a complementary approach, the reservation wage approach, which does not apply directly to the notion of "voluntary" unemployment (Feldstein & Poterba 1984, p. 142), a notion linked to the "moral hazard," which is itself derived from a peculiar psychological attitude. The first part of the reservation wage model is purely econometric: it establishes a relationship between the replacement ratio and the reservation wage. Then, through a probabilistic model, the reservation wage is related to the duration of unemployment. Since the replacement ratio is a function of UIB, through a transitive reasoning, the level of unemployment can also be related to the level of UIB.

The reservation approach is based upon a simple unemployment model, as illustrated by Figure 11.1. The model is simple in that it has only two labor markets – unionized and non-unionized – and it is very general, simultaneously incorporating three main reasons for persistent

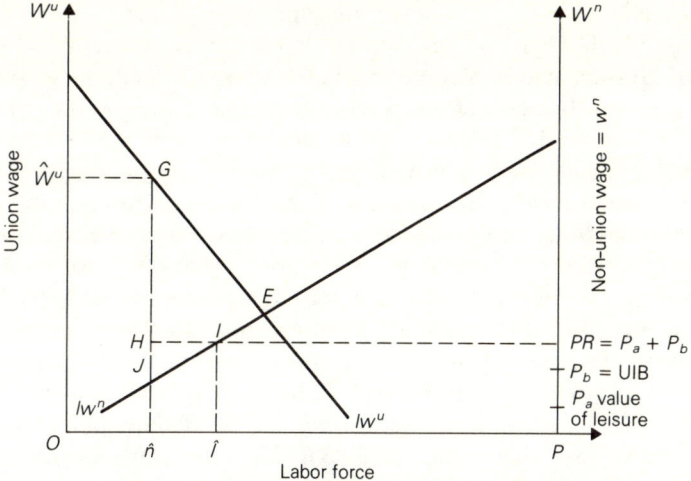

Figure 11.1 Unemployment equilibrium model.
Source: adapted from Greenhalgh et al. (1983), p. 2.

unemployment: the trade union effect, the UIB effect, and the taxation effect.

In Figure 11.1, OP is the total labor force, W^u is the union wage, W^n is the non-union wage, lw^u is the demand for the union labor (read from left to right), and lw^n is the demand for non-union labor (read from right to left). If the union can enforce G (this point corresponding to preferences) as the level of its wages, only $O\hat{n}$ employees are hired in the union sector. The remaining labor force $\hat{n} P$ can be absorbed at the competitive wage $\hat{n} J$ (in the non-union sector). The first conclusion of the model is that provided that the competitive wage does not drop below P_a (the value of non-work activities, or the value of leisure plus other non-work activities) and that there are no taxes or UIB available, and that labor is homogeneous, labor unions do not cause unemployment. However, with P_b representing UIB available (but no taxes), the conclusion is different. In that case, the reservation wage becomes $P_a + P_b = PR$. At that level of wages (unemployed people do not accept wages below PR), only $P\hat{I}$ workers are hired, leaving $\hat{I}\hat{n}$ (or HI) unemployed. Consequently, the simultaneous presence of labor unions and UIB "cause" some unemployment. The introduction of taxes (not shown in the diagram but incorporated by shifting the lw^u to the left and the lw^n to the right) would further increase unemployment, provided that the unions keep their original target wage (now after taxes) and unemployment benefits are not taxed at a higher rate than is income.[17] To add some realism to the model, transaction costs could be incorporated that would increase further unemployment. Not all the components of the model lend themselves easily to econometric measurements – e.g., demand curves are unavailable. But, as shown by Feldstein & Poterba (1984) the reservation wage can be known through a survey.[18] Their survey showed that in general the reservation wage ratio equals 1.07, and that this ratio diminishes with the length of the unemployment spell. Through a multiple regression analysis which included as independent variables the replacement rate, the age and color of the respondent, marital status, the presence of supplementary benefits, etc., and as a dependent variable, the reservation ratio, Feldstein and Poterba then found that the variables had a negligible effect except the replacement rate, itself a function of UIB (ibid., p. 159). Furthermore, the effect of UIB on reservation wage, and thus on the reservation ratio, is non-linear (ibid., p. 160). (For instance, completely eliminating the unemployment insurance does not reduce to zero the mean probability of a reservation wage ratio greater than unity.) This convinces the authors that "higher unemployment benefits ... increase the reservation wage" (ibid., p. 151). Finally, through a probabilistic model simulating a certain frequency of job offers, the authors establish the proposition that the higher the reservation ratio the lower the probability of facing suitable job offers, and consequently the longer the duration of unemployment spells (ibid., pp. 160 ff.). Not only does the model solidly connect UIB and the duration of the period of unemployment, but with the aid of plausible standard deviations the authors quantify this relationship to the extent that they conclude "that reducing unemployment insurance benefits (especially at high levels of the replacement ratio) could significantly lower the average duration of unemployment and the relative number of long duration spells" (ibid., p. 165). Consequently, studies that negate the effect of UIB on u are suspect.

11.5 Welfare implications of UIB

The surprising result of introducing welfare theory in the analysis is to end up saying that even if it can be demonstrated that UIB causes some unemployment (as we have done in Section 11.4), that alone does not necessarily mean this induced unemployment is wasteful. Indeed, it can be demonstrated that some UIB-induced unemployment of the so-called neoclassical type can be compatible with a second-best Pareto optimum – that is, there may be no better way to ameliorate the aggregate level of output, given search costs and/or the value of non-work activities; indeed, it can be shown that a second-best pareto optimum is a legitimate goal of social policy.[19] The conditions for reaching that optimum, for which mathematical proofs can be found in Mortensen &

Rosen (1983, pp. 13 ff.), are as follows:

(a) The unemployment insurance scheme should be experience-rated – i.e., there should be no cross-subsidization among industries and firms (Mortensen 1983, p. 68).
(b) The insurance scheme should not be government subsidized.
(c) UIB should be fully taxed (Mortensen 1983).

Optimality is attained by diversifying away all risks (except the macroeconomic risks), so that the unemployment insurance premiums are optimal (Rosen 1983, p. 7). Furthermore, it is assumed that

(d) Workers are risk averse and income constrained (while they are unemployed), and that
(e) The unemployed search optimally for employment, and workers enter into implicit contracts with their employers.

That means that if people refer to the optimum social reservation wage[20] they may remain unemployed without jeopardizing the social optimum. The income constraint prevents moral hazard from leading to non-optimal situations, and competition among firms (which are paying premiums according to their unemployment experience) prevents adverse selection (Rosen 1983, p. 35).

Conversely, to include, in the presence of UIB-induced unemployment, at social non-optimality (and thus at the necessity of shadowing the prices of inputs and outputs in cost–benefit analyses), some of the above conditions must be violated. In that case, there will be misallocation of resources. See Rosen, pp. 36–7. For instance, a non-experience rated scheme "promotes excessive unemployment instability in the economy and may add a percentage point or two to the natural rate" (Rosen, p. 41).

This translates into unwarranted extensions of the non-work period, that is, individuals are subsidized by UIB for producing non-work goods; consequently, too many non-work goods are produced (Rosen 1983, p. 40).

In Canada many of the conditions of social optimality in the presence of UIB are violated since (a) the system has not been set at its optimal level;[21] (b) it is not experience rated; and (c) it is highly subsidized out of government general funds. Economic distortions consequently exist among industries and regions (to the extent that regions do not pay their share according to the experience of their unemployment). The results are that:

(a) Interregional migrations are reduced.
(b) Seasonal and unstable employment are encouraged.
(c) The participation rate in the labor force is increased.
(d) The duration of employment spells is increased.

The above effects are stronger in high unemployment regions since the UIB system is more nonoptimal in these regions.

On the other hand, some people note that the analysis does not credit the UIB system enough for its useful macroeconomic function as an automatic stabilizer, as depicted by its multiplier effect in small lagging regions afflicted by high unemployment. There is no doubt that there is some substantial beneficial local distribution effect in the Canadian scheme (Osberg 1979). But at the aggregate Canadian level the net macroeconomic impact is negative. First, on the demand side, there is an increase in labor requirements due to the increase of net transfers, but on the supply side, the availability of UI benefits induces an expansion of the labor force.[22] Second, at the aggregate level, UI benefits have annoying side-effects. For instance, they impede the efficiency of regional employment policy.[23] Similarly, the redistribution portion of the scheme, like all measures designed to bring about interregional equity, "appears to involve a substantial reduction in the income of richer regions without producing corresponding increases in the incomes of the poorer regions (Aziz et al. 1983). The intuitive reason is that the UIB income transfers are financed by taxes in the more efficient regions, thus reducing the number of projects undertaken there, while the lagging regions lack good projects, or at least their projects are inferior to those of the rich regions, so that the productivity of the funds made available to the lagging regions is lower.

Finally, comparative advantage is not operational between regions in interregional traded goods; only absolute advantage counts. Not all regions, then, are assured of viability without transfer payments.

11.6 Empirical measurement of the impact of UIB upon the unemployment rate in Canada

In Canada, the main contribution to the empirical measurement of the effect of UIB upon the unemployment rate has been provided by GMS (Grubel et al. 1975) and by Green and Cousineau (1976). Both these groups of authors worked through the moral hazard approach using time series. Other Canadian authors have also contributed (see the citations in Section 11.4.1 and the table of the Appendix) on particular aspects of the unemployment problem, some of them using cross-section analysis. The contributions have been of two types: (a) the direct method, where authors relate UIB directly to the unemployment rate through multiple regression analysis; and (b) the distribution method, which allocates the total aggregate unemployment rate among various paradigms (cyclical and non-cyclical unemployment), and other identifiable causes of unemployment besides UIB. The function of the presentation of these data is to make sure that there exists an unallowed residue (in the aggregate rate) large enough to accommodate the UIB contribution to u.

11.6.1 Empirical results of the direct method

Table 11.1 presents results of the computations of the share of the observed unemployment rate in Canada in 1972, and from 1980 to 1982. Our method of computation is based upon the principles established in Section 11.4.1, and proceeds as follows: Given that UIB/AWW = 0.30 is the threshold of impact of UIB, a ratio of 0.41 (the one of 1972) will account for

$$(0.41 - \overline{0.30}) \times 0.69 = 25.3\%$$

of the unemployment in the year 1972, provided that the elasticity is 0.69. From that, the impact of the enforcement of unemployment benefits eligibility rules (INEL) is subtracted. That reduces the contribution of UIB to the unemployment rate to 22%. Since the unemployment rate in 1972 was 6.3%, 1.4% was due to UIB and to the level of INEL

Table 11.1 Proportion of unemployment accounted for by UIB for 1972, 1980–82, for Canada, Quebec, and Nova Scotia (e_u, UIB = 0.69).

	Observed rate of unemployment (%)	UIB/* AWW	e_u, UIB	Rate of unemployment accounted for by UIB (%)	Proportion of unemployment accounted for by UIB (%)
1972					
Canada	6.39	0.41	0.69	1.59	25.3
Quebec	7.50	0.43	0.76	2.47	32.9
Nova Scotia	7.0	0.43	1.22	3.70	52.9
1980					
Canada	7.50	0.38	0.69	1.38	18.4
Quebec	9.8	0.38	0.76	1.99	20.3
Nova Scotia	9.7	0.42	1.22	4.73	48.8
1981					
Canada	7.5	0.37	0.69	1.21	16.1
Quebec	10.3	0.37	0.76	1.83	17.7
Nova Scotia	10.2	0.41	1.22	4.56	44.7
1982					
Canada	11.0	0.37	0.69	1.77	16.1
Quebec	13.8	0.37	0.76	2.45	17.7
Nova Scotia	13.2	0.40	1.22	5.37	40.7

* Source of basic data: Statistics Canada, cat. 72002, 73001, 71201.
Source: For 1972: GMS (1975) for Canada, and Maki (1975) for Quebec and Nova Scotia; for the other years, author's calculations.

Table 11.2 Proportion of unemployment accounted for by UIB for 1972, 1980–82, for Canada, Quebec, and Nova Scotia (e_u, UIB = 0.56).

	Observed rate of unemployment (%)	UIB/AWW[a]	e_u, UIB[b]	Rate of unemployment accounted for by UIB (%)	Proportion of unemployment rate accounted for by UIB (%)
1972	6.39	0.41	0.56	1.3	20.6
1980	7.50	0.38	0.56	1.1	14.5
1981	7.50	0.37	0.56	1.0	13.1
1982	11.0	0.37	0.56	1.4	13.1

[a] *Source*: Statistics Canada.
[b]: *Source*: Green & Cousineau (1976) for 1972; for the other years, author's calculations.

in that year. The same reasoning can be used to compute the impact of UIB in various regions relying upon the regional elasticities computed by Maki (1975). The results of my own computations for 1980–2 are available in Table 11.1. The results of the same computations made for Canada using the elasticity of 0.56 (suggested by Green and Cousineau 1976) are given in Table 11.2. They are compatible with those of Table 11.1, showing that a somewhat different method, and period studied, produces similar results. Furthermore, for Canada, the contribution of UIB to *u* is then of the order of 15% for 1982, while it was around 35% in 1972. It seems to have been diminishing ever since 1977.

This compares favorably with opinions of other US experts. For Hamermesh (1978) "if UI would be abolished slightly less than one third of the insured unemployed would be at work." For Feldstein (1978) "one third of temporary layoffs are by an increase in the UIB replacement ratio." Canadian authors who have studied the recent period also corroborate these results.[24]

11.6.2 The distribution method

Ideally, we should be able to break down the total unemployment rate into its cyclical and non-cyclical components; and then further identify the non-cyclical components more specifically as structural, frictional, seasonal, minimum wage, UIB, etc.[25]

Unfortunately, besides the distribution between cyclical and non-cyclical, not many studies have successfully allocated the rest. The Appendix table resumes what is available for Canada. The results here are tentative (as other econometric results), yet they show that since 1970, the imperfection of the labor markets is becoming relatively more and more important (although this is not to say that cyclical unemployment could not have become more important in the years 1980–2). It also shows that there is a possible role for the impact of UIB upon the aggregate unemployment rate. In other words, the cyclical, frictional, and minimum wage "causes" of unemployment do not account for the whole of the aggregate rate of unemployment.

11.7 The extent of the underevaluation of the SCL in Canadian cost–benefit studies

Building upon the proposition demonstrated above that UIB contributes to D, we can now illustrate the extent of the consequential underevaluation of SCL by the following simulation. Without UIB, D periods would be roughly 15% shorter (see Table 11.2),[26] and $(1-D)$ periods would be longer; consequently, the elimination of UIB will produce an increase in SCL depending upon the relative sizes of W_t and U. To appreciate the importance of the effect of eliminating UIB, upon SCL, suppose the following case which is based on a real life example: $W_t = \$409$, $W_1 = \$391$, $f = 72\%$, $g = 8\%$, $U = \$189$, $A = \$140$, $t = 25\%$, $B = 4/3$, $D = 30.7$ weeks.
In that case:

$$V = \frac{391\,(1 - 0.25) - 4/3\,[0.72\,(189)\,(1 - 0.25) + 0.08\,(140)\,(1 - 25)]}{4/3}$$

$$V = \$109.48$$

This figure may look high compared to those of Gera (1985, p. 22) but Gera's values concern only unskilled would-be workers, while our sample is more general.
The social cost of such a temporary worker is then:

$$SCL_1 = 21.3\,(409) + 30.7\,(109.48) = 12{,}073$$

Without unemployment insurance, D would be 26.09 weeks,[27] and V would be:

$$V = \frac{W_1\,(1 - t) - B\,(gA)\,(1 - t)}{B} = 211.54^{28}$$

$$SCL_2 = 25.91\,(409)^{29} + 26.09\,(211.54) = 16{,}116.27$$

The new SCL_2 is 33% bigger than the former SCL_1.

The values obtained above represent a minimum because the alternatives envisaged were limited to the region. If migration is envisaged,[30] especially from lagging regions to regions with high job prospects, the opportunity cost of labor in the lagging region must be increased (Jenkins & Kuo 1978).

Appendix: partial distribution of components of total unemployment rate, various periods, Canada and some provinces

Source	Region	Period	Percentage points	Share in total unemployment(%)
Cyclical unemployment				
Siedule & Newton (1978)	Canada	1961–69	2.7 (av.)	44.8
	Canada	1970–79	2.8 (av.)	35.7
Duncan & Wilson (1982)	Canada	1954–69	1.0 (av.)	20
	Canada	1970–78	1.0 (av.)	15
Miller (1985	Canada	1961–74	2.9 (av.)	56
	Canada	1975–83	2.7 (av.)	32
	Atlantic	1961–74	2.6 (av.)	33
	Atlantic	1975–83	2.8 (av.)	23
	Quebec	1961–74	1.5 (av.)	22
	Quebec	1975–83	2.5 (av.)	24
	Ontario	1961–74	2.9 (av.)	83
	Ontario	1975–83	3.1 (av.)	42
	Prairies	1961–74	1.9 (av.)	56
	Prairies	1975–83	1.6 (av.)	30
	British Columbia	1961–74	3.2 (av.)	52
	British Columbia	1975–83	2.9 (av.)	32

Frictional unemployment

Author's computations	Nova Scotia	1961–69	0.52	9
	Nova Scotia	1970–82	0.51	6
	Quebec	1961–69	0.51	9
	Quebec	1970–82	0.49	6

Minimum wage

Maki (1978)	10 provinces	1970–78	0.7	9
Swidinsky (1978)	Canada	1950–75	1.0	10
Fortin (1978 & 1983)	Quebec	1966–82	1.0–1.5	5–10

Seasonal

Beaudry (1978)	Canada	1955	1.7	38.6
	Canada	1961	2.3	32.4
	Canada	1969	1.3	27.7
	Canada	1972	1.3	20.6
	Canada	1975	1.3	18.3
	Atlantic	1955	3.2	49.2
	Atlantic	1961	4.8	42.9
	Atlantic	1969	2.6	34.7
	Atlantic	1972	2.7	30.0
	Atlantic	1975	3.3	28.4
	Quebec	1955	2.8	45.2
	Quebec	1961	3.1	33.7
	Quebec	1969	1.7	24.6
	Quebec	1972	1.7	20.5
	Quebec	1975	1.8	20.5

11.8 Conclusion

Our point, throughout this essay, has not been that the shadow pricing of labor is a non-optimal method. Quite the contrary, government departments should be commended for that. But, our demonstration points at a case of perverse interpretation between measures favoring equity and measures to bring about social efficiency. That means that, in the search for equity, more neutral methods should be devised to help the unemployed.

Notes

1 Their formulation is at first partial equilibrium but this approach tends toward general equilibrium by incorporating multiplier effects and interregional migrations. Yet it always remains a potential Pareto optimum in spirit.
2 That does not mean that social cost–benefit analysis is the only basis for government decision. Local political considerations also intervene. Only the case of the temporary worker is interesting because the permanently employed worker has an SCL equal to his earnings and the out of the labor force will not by definition be used in a project. Temporary workers register the functioning of the local labor market, i.e., the place of a temporary worker who takes up a permanent job is taken by another temporary worker or by somebody formerly outside the labor force, and so on.
3 D is determined empirically in the place and time of the project. In their work on the Cape Breton case (1972–4) Jenkins and Kuo (1978) examined the records of a 10% sample of temporary unemployed workers and concluded that $D = 39.4$ weeks, on the average (ibid., p. 233). The source of the unemployment is not made explicit, but its location surely takes into consideration seasonal effects, other miscellaneous effects, and the cyclical effects (ibid., p. 221).
4 As economists we must consequently fall back upon observed values, i.e., observe how people trade off work for non-work periods without fully comprehending the mechanisms that are at work in microdecisions. We are, however, aware that non-work periods do not necessarily mean only leisure, but also household work, do-it-yourself work, underground economy activities (including crime, investment of own time in culture, education and health activities), and finally search activities. All these things represent private values that are taken into consideration in work/non-work decisions. Furthermore, these non-work values are not negligible: Lamonde (1985) has recently reported that underground activities in Quebec are as important as the whole budget of the government of the province – $14 billion involving 200,000 persons. In Italy, one-third of the labor activities are underground (Burton 1984, p. 113).
5 In 1976 MacDonald and Evans had suggested 4/3, which they reduced to 6/5 in 1981, and kept with some variations in 1983 (see MacDonald 1983).

Recently Simpson (1985) came out with a slightly smaller ratio. However, these figures are not regionalized. In Quebec, because of the relative importance of the public sector, the ratio of 4/3 seems appropriate.

6. Since today the studies are based upon the replacement rate, it is important to have a sure basis to establish the denominator (and also the numerator) of that ratio (the replacement rate). (We shall see later that the numerator is also difficult to determine). See Dilnot and Morris (1983, p. 325), Feldstein and Poterba (1984, pp. 142–4), Nicksell (1979, pp. 37–8), Osberg (1979, p. 230).

7. Note that this approach does not require that an employed worker who 'voluntarily' extends his unemployment spell by one week considers himself better off than working one more week at his former job. Actually, most unemployed people consider their welfare position inferior to the one they enjoyed before being laid off. However, they may extend their unemployed period because the present job opportunities are inferior to the level of their welfare, given the fact that they have access to UIB, social security payments, help from relatives and friends, income from underground economy sources, etc.

8. Yet not all economists agree (see Osberg 1979).

9. That's why a low estimate of the impact of UIB upon the unemployment rate is used in Section 11.7

10. Before the availability of UIB, the opportunity cost of a week of non-work equals the weekly wage. If UIB equals 2/3 of the weekly wage, this reduces the opportunity cost of a week of non-work to 1/3 of the weekly wage. For simplicity we ignore taxes, qualifying period, maximum UIB, and other administrative constraints. One could, however, criticize the above reasoning on the grounds that it is only valid when envisaging an individual beneficiary of UIB. The criticism holds that if the permanent workers, who are taxed to finance UIB paid to others, are included, these people will see their budgetary constraints shifted to the left, thus inducing them to increase the number of weeks worked during the year, so that, in macro reasoning, the aggregate number of weeks worked by the total labor force in the economy will not change (because the loss, in weeks suffered by temporary workers is compensated by an increase, in weeks, produced by permanent workers). This reasoning is flawed for at least two reasons: (a) the elasticity of the response to taxes to finance UIB differ between permanent and temporary workers: it is almost nil for the first because they already work all the available time and empirical data show that high income wage earners are not responsive to taxes except at extremely high levels; (b) the number of weeks worked in the economy in the aggregate is not pertinent because the unemployment rate is computed as the ratio of unemployed persons (not weeks) over the total labor force. There is of course a social efficiency aspect to this problem, which will be dealt with in Section 11.5.

11. Obviously, it is unlikely that a woman who maintains a family in which nobody else is employed will voluntarily increase her unemployment spells. But as mentioned before (see Shaw 1985, p. 155), not all cases of unemployment correspond to that situation.

12. In this respect Feldstein and Poterba (1984, p. 160) have proven "the nonlinear character of the effect of unemployment insurance on reservation ratios" and later "the nonlinear response of the unemployment duration of the reservation wage" (p. 165). Consequently, unemployment and unemployment insurance benefits are likely to be nonlinearly related.

13 The nonlinearity could be accentuated by using an exponential function to relate UIB and u.
14 Two authors have computed such an elasticity: GMS (1975, p. 187) suggest 0.69; and, from the computations in terms of numbers of unemployed of Gree and Cousineau (1976, Table 5.5, p. 95), an elasticity of 0.56 is deduced.
15 Note the behavior of the unemployed worker facing UIB has been ascertained under all sorts of circumstances: business cycles, drastic changes in the level of UIB/AWW, etc. Note also that in this respect, time-series results are much more extrapolable than cross-section results, which by definition have not been influenced by different market conditions.
16 I do not see any, i.e., if the regression were redone for 1972–82 we would still use GNP, and UIB/AWW, etc. I do not see any institutional changes in 1972–82 that would modify this judgement. For instance, Beach and Kaliski (1983, p. 171) while studying the period 1976–80, still talk about induced unemployment through UIB. (This reinforces my use of the elasticity established for 1972.) They show that a reduction of the UIB/AWW ratio increased the probability of finding a job (if unemployed before), and diminishes the probability of remaining unemployed if already unemployed. They show that the reduction in "induced" unemployment took the form of a shorter duration of unemployment spells rather than a reduced frequency.
17 In England, this type of model enables Minford (as reported by Nicksell 1984, p. 952) to impute 65% of the unemployment to union activities, 17% to UIB and the rest to payroll taxes upon employers and income taxes upon employees. Because the unionized sector is much smaller in Canada, the proportions imputed to the different causes of unemployment would likely differ.
18 Feldstein and Poterba (1984) used the US Current Population Survey of May 1976. This questionnaire reveals not only the reservation wage for each individual in the survey, but its reservation wage ratio. The reservation wage ratio is the ratio of the reservation wage (as declared by the respondents in the questionnaire) to the last wage earned, i.e., $R_w/W_t - 1$. In general R_x/W_{t-1} = 1.07 1.0.
19 The conclusions that follow in the demonstration below apply to both a search model (people quit their job) or to a layoff model (see Mortensen 1983, pp. 69 ff).
20 Defined as the one that "reflects a balancing of the gains of additional job search (measured by the increase in the individual's marginal product in a better job) against the cost of search (measured by the value of the foregone production net of the value of leisure during the period of additional search)" (Feldstein & Poterba 1984, p. 143). See also the equation of Dilnot and Morris (1983, p. 324) and Mortensen (1983, p. 79).
21 In Canada because of the presence of many distortions in the economy and the desire of the government to force some redistribution of income, the setting up of an optimal level of UIB would require that the "degree of experience rating be adjusted away from one to offset the distorting effects of taxation and unemployment benefits. It is in a sense an application of the Second Best Theorem ..." (Boadway & Oswald 1982, p. 20). In other words, not only should the unemployment insurance scheme be government-operated, but the setting up of its optimal level should be influenced by second-best considerations. This is not done at the moment. Furthermore, it has not been set at the optimum level for the following reasons. First of all,

the occurrence of the event (becoming unemployed) is in some cases completely under the control of the "insured." This is the classic case of moral hazard. This happens either when a person now employed voluntarily quits his job or when he is laid off. In both cases, he controls the amount of the compensation since he can extend the length of the unemployment period. These two possibilities differentiate unemployment insurance from other types of insurance, such as fire insurance, since the first case corresponds to the situation where the insured could voluntarily burn the insured property and nevertheless be compensated, while in the second case, the insured could, once the fire has occurred, determine the amount of the compensation. Since none of this is experience rated (contrary to many insurance shemes) in the Canadian unemployment insurance scheme, the insurance content is not optimal. Secondly, given the above reasoning, if the "insurance" aspect of UIB is low, that means that the scheme is largely a welfare system since its deficits are financed by the general fund of the federal government. On an interregional perspective this is very strong in Canada. For instance, in 1977 "UI benefits paid in the three Maritime provinces totalled $455.8 millions against premium collections of $145.7 million" (Osberg 1979, p. 224). The transfer payment function is then quantitatively twice the size of the "insurance" function.

22 For 1972 (after the liberalization of the UI scheme in Canada in 1971), Bodkin and Cournoyer (1978, p. 83) estimate that the impact on the supply side was greater than on the demand side so that the net macro effect was to increase total measured unemployment by 74,000 persons, or a 3/4 percentage point.

23 In that case, "the opportunity cost of creating a job always exceeds the market wage" so that "no case can be made for subsidizing jobs." (Boadway & Flatters 1981, p. 71). In a two-region model, these authors show that "the desirability of creating jobs in the low income region depends upon the parameters and technology of the economy. We may even wish to subsidize employment to a greater extent in the full-employment region" (ibid., p. 75).

24 See, for instance, Beach and Kaliski (1983) and Osberg (1979, p. 223) who argued "that under 1978 conditions, the work discentive impact of UI Benefits on aggregate unemployment is quite small". Since he does not say how small, it would seem reasonable to keep the estimation of 15%.

25 Section 11.4.1 shows that these categories are not completely mutually exclusive with UIB. There is also another way to reclassify the causes of unemployment by including labor unions and tax effects; see the general model of Section 11.4.2.

26 Since UIB "causes" roughly 15% of the unemployment (in Canada), we apply this percentage to D since that variable represents the period of non-work activities in a year for an average temporary worker. D is then a linear function of the unemployment rate. For our purpose it is immaterial whether the unemployment rate varies because of more or less frequency or because of more or less duration (D_u), because the total number of weeks a temporary unemployed person will be unemployed (d) is the product of the duration of each unemployment spell multiplied by the number of times that person becomes unemployed during the year. Furthermore, Hasan and de Broucker (1985, p. 41) show that these components have been moving in the same direction, with duration (D_u) being relatively more important since 1976.

27 By reducing D proportionately by 15% we do not distinguish between

unemployment caused by short spells and by long spells. There is, however, an implicit assumption that some long spells are partly financed by UIB because Feldstein and Poterba (1984) have shown precisely that UIB, by raising the reservation wage, extends the duration.

28 The example may be a bit artificial since in that case social assistance might increase. But even at the former level of $V=109.48$, the conclusion arrived at below would still hold.

29 It might be more realistic to suppose that faced with the elimination of UIB, the temporary unemployed might not only increase the length of his working period, but more importantly accept a job below the old level of remuneration. The reason is that the sudden increase in the labor supply might drive down the wage level. Indeed, it would pay the temporary unemployed to accept any job (for the additional weeks of work) that would pay more than 211.54 (net of taxes).

30 The problem is worth studying because UIB are reputed to retard migrations or even introduce reverse flows of migrations into lagging regions. See Cousineau (1979).

References

Atkinson, A. B., J. Gomulka, J. Micklewright & N. Raw 1984. Unemployment benefit, duration and incentives in Britain: how robust is the evidence? *Journal of Public Economics* **23**, 3–26.

Aziz, R., D. Butterfield, & A. Kubursi 1983. Regional equity and efficiency: some experiments for Canada. *Journal of Regional Science* **23**(3), 397–413.

Beach, C. & S. F. Kaliski 1983. The impact of the 1979 unemployment insurance amendments. *Canadian Public Policy* **9**(2), 164–73.

Beaudry, R. 1978. L'Importance du chômage saisonnier dans les disparités de chômage au Canada. *La Revue canadienne d'economique* **11**(2), 333–45.

Boadway, R. & F. Flatters 1981. The efficiency basis for regional employment policy. *The Canadian Journal of Economics* **14**(1), 58–77.

Boadway, R. & R. J. Oswald 1982. Unemployment insurance and redistributive taxation. Discussion Paper no. 466, Kingston, Ontario: Queen's University.

Bodkin, R. G. & A. Cournoyer 1978. Legislation and the labour market: a selective review of Canadian studies. In Grubel & Walker (1978).

Bruner, K. & A. H. Meltzer (eds.) 1983. *Variability in employment, prices and money*. Carnegie-Rochester conference series on public policy, vol. 19. Amsterdam: North-Holland.

Burton, J. 1984. The instability of the "middle way". In *Hayek's serfdom revisited*, Barry et al. (eds.) London: The Institute of Economic Affairs, Hobart Paperback 18.

Conseil économique du Canada 1982. *Pénuries et carences, travailleurs qualifiés et emplois durant les années 80*. Ottawa: Approvisionnement et Services Canada.

Cousineau, J. M. 1979. La mobilité interprovinciale au Canada: le cas de l'Ontario, du Nouveau-Brunswick et de la Nouvelle-Ecosse. *L'Actualité économique* **55**(4), 501–15.

Dilnot, A. W. & C. N. Morris 1983. Private costs and benefits of unemployment: measuring replacement rates. In Greenhalgh, Layard & Oswald (1983).

Duncan, D. P. & T. A. Wilson 1982. Potential GNP: performance and prospects. Report series no. 10, Institute for Policy Analysis, University of Toronto.

Feldstein, M. 1978. The effect of unemployment insurance on temporary layoff unemployment. *American Economic Review* **68**(5), 834–46.

Feldstein, M. & J. Poterba 1984. Unemployment insurance and reservation wages. *Journal of Public Economics* **23**, 141–67.

Fortin, P. 1978. Une évaluation de l'effet de la politique québécoise du salaire minimum sur la production, l'emploi, les prix et la répartition des revenus. Ministère du Travail et de la Main-d'oeuvre. Québec.

Fortin, P. 1983. L'Effet des variations du salaire minimum sur l'emploi et les heures hebdomadaires de travail dans sept secteurs industriels du Québec, 1966–82. Cahier 8321, Département d'Économique, Université Laval.

Gera, S. 1985. The employment tax credit: an evaluation of the 1978–81 Canadian wage subsidy program. Paper presented to CEA Meetings, University of Montreal.

Green, C. & J. M. Cousineau 1975. *Chômage et programme d'assurance-chômage*, Conseil économique du Canada. Ottawa: Approvisionnement et Services Canada.

Greenhalgh, C. A., P. R. G. Layard & A. J. Oswald 1983. *The causes of unemployment*. Oxford: Clarendon Press.

Grubel, H. & D. Maki 1978. The effects of unemployment benefits on U.S. unemployment rates. In Grubel & Walker (1978).

Grubel, H., D. Maki & S. Sax 1975. Real and insurance-induced unemployment in Canada. *The Canadian Journal of Economics* **8**(2), 174–91.

Grubel, H. & M. Walker 1978. *Unemployment insurance*. Vancouver: Fraser Institute.

Hamermesh, D. 1978. Unemployment insurance and unemployment in the United States. In Grubel & Walker (1978).

Hasan, A. & P. de Broucker 1985. *Chômage et dynamique du travail au Canada*. Ottawa: Conseil économique du Canada.

Hung, N. M., & P. Lefebvre 1981. Sur l'impact de l'assurance-chômage dans une économie keynésienne. *Actualité économique* **4**, 525–53.

Jenkins, G. & C. Y. Kuo 1978. On measuring the social opportunity cost of permanent and temporary employment. *The Canadian Journal of Economics*, **9**(2), 220–39.

Lamonde, P. 1985. Televised interview at CBFT, Montreal (March 16).

MacDonald, G. M. 1983. The size and structure of union–non-union wage differentials in Canadian industry: corroboration, refinement and extension. *The Canadian Journal of Economics* **16**(3).

MacDonald, G. M. & J. C. Evans 1981. The size and structure of union–non-union wage differentials in Canada. *The Canadian Journal of Economics* **14**, 216–31.

Maki, D. 1975. Regional differences in insurance-induced unemployment in Canada. *Economic Inquiry* **13**, 389–400.

Maki, D. 1978. The effects of changes in minimum wage rates on provincial unemployment rates. Discussion paper 78-3-2, Burnaby, British Columbia: Simon Fraser University.

Miller, F. C. 1985. The unemployment effects of regionally discriminating fiscal policies (mimeo). Paper presented at the meeting of the Canadian Regional Science Association (May 30).

Minford, P. 1984. Response to Nicksell. In *The Economic Journal* **94**, 954–9.

Minford, P. with D. Davies, M. Peel & A. Sprague 1983. *Unemployment, cause and cure*. Oxford: Martin Robertson.

Mortensen, D. T. & S. Rosen 1983. A welfare analysis of unemployment insurance on second-best themes. In Brunner & Meltzer (1983), 67–102.

Nickell, S. J. 1984. Review of: *Unemployment: cause and cure* by Patrick Minford, with David Davies, Michael Peel & Alison Sprague. *The Economic Journal* **94**, 946–53.

Osberg, L. 1979. Unemployment insurance in Canada: a review of the recent amendments. *Canadian Public Policy* **5**(2), 223–35.

Raynauld, A. & F. Martin (forthcoming) *Le Coût économique du travail et le développement régional*. Moncton: Institut canadien de recherche sur le développement régional, Université de Moncton.

Rea, S. 1977. Unemployment insurance and labor supply: a simulation of the 1971 unemployment insurance act. *The Canadian Journal of Economics* **10**, 263–78.

Rosen, S. 1983. Unemployment and insurance. In Brunner & Meltzer (1983), 6–49.

Shaw, R. P. 1985. Unemployment in Canada. *Canadian Public Policy* **11**, 143–60.

Siedule, T. & K. Newton 1979. The unemployment gap in Canada, 1961–78. Discussion paper no. 145, Conseil économique du Canada, Ottawa.

Simpson, W. 1985. The impact of unions on the structure of Canadian wages: an empirical analysis with microdata. *The Canadian Journal of Economics* **18**(1), 164–81.

Swidinsky, R. 1978. Minimum wages and teenage unemployment in Canada. Discussion paper, 1978–4, University of Guelph, Department of Economics.

Treasury Board of Canada 1976. *Benefit cost analysis guide*. Ottawa: Treasury Board Secretariat, Planning Branch.

12

Regional disparities: a model with some econometric results for Canada[1]

JOHN VANDERKAMP

12.1 Introduction

Regional disparities in economic fortunes present a vexing problem in regional analysis. Disparities in wages, incomes, and unemployment between Canada's provinces and regions have a long history. Over the last half century, earned income per capita has been below the Canadian average in the five Eastern provinces and in Manitoba and Saskatchewan. Moreover, during the last four decades unemployment rates have been above the Canadian figures for the five Eastern provinces as well. Such disparities create social and political stress, particularly in the context of Canada's confederate system of government (see also André Raynauld, Ch. 10 in this volume).

The analytical question is, Can we explain the existence and persistence of regional disparities? The attempt to answer this question represents the primary aim of this paper. The policy question is whether we can devise policies and programs which will help to reduce or eradicate disparities. While the paper contains some discussion of policy issues and the impact of certain programs, it is not intended as a policy review; the reader is referred to the review paper (Vanderkamp 1986) for this purpose.

The persistence of regional disparities presents a number of analytical challenges. In connection with this it is useful to consider briefly a number of theoretical issues which will help in the development of a model in the next section.

The traditional view of economics is that the migration of labor constitutes an "automatic" equilibrating mechanism in a country's regional system. Labor has a tendency to flow from regions with low wages and high unemployment to regions with high wages and low unemployment. The result is that migration will contribute to the system's adjustment towards equilibrium, which is presumably characterized by equality in regional wages and employment opportunities. A common empirical approach is to examine regional income disparities to see whether they have a tendency to disappear. As a methodological approach this is rather weak. The very existence of disparities suggests that there are also disequilibrating forces – i.e., shocks which disturb the regional system. To look for equalizing tendencies in regional incomes or wages over time is therefore to accept as an implicit item of faith that such shocks are absent or of minor importance in the period under study. As a corollary, the persistence of regional disparities does not provide proof that the equilibrating tendencies are absent.

To be sure, not all economic theory comes to the conclusion that regional disparities will disappear or will even be absent in long-run equilibrium. Two strands of thought may be mentioned in this context. First, there are models, particularly in international trade theory, which show that under certain circumstances migration may result in widening wage differentials. Such models typically use a number of industrial sectors which have different technologies and may employ different types of labor and other factors (see, e.g., Gerking & Mutti 1983). Such models are difficult to implement empirically because of data requirements. Moreover, it is useful to explore the empirical validity of the simple model of the link between disparities and migration before proceeding to more complex versions.

The other strand of thought is that if wage or income disparities have been quite stable for a long time they must be equilibrium disparities. Because of the availability of non-private goods such as climate, scenery, amenities, and public goods and services, it is often possible to argue that almost any pattern of regional incomes is compatible with regional equilibrium. For example, if enough people prefer living near to the ocean, then the existence of this amenity in Atlantic Canada will be compatible with a low income level there. From a methodological point of view this strand of thought has little to recommend it since an "anything can happen" prediction is not helpful. Moreover, the empirical fact of fairly persistent migration flows is surely inconsistent with the label equilibrium in the long run.

Nonetheless, it is important to consider the influence of amenities and public goods on migration behavior. The empirical literature in the United States has quite a few recent examples of empirical work on migration which includes variables associated with climate and other amenities. A number of recent Canadian migration studies consider the importance of various fiscal variables such as tax levels, provincial government expenditures, and also personal transfer schemes such as unemployment insurance. While the results of these Canadian studies are mixed, they show the potential impact of government policy on migration and regional adjustment (see Grant & Vanderkamp 1983 for a review).

It is sometimes argued that migration is too slow a process, and the persistence of regional disparities is part of the evidence. One allegedly important reason for the slowness and inadequacy of the migration process is the existence of a range of federal government programs associated with transfers to individuals and to provincial governments. These programs may be initiated for equity reasons but they have serious consequences for the allocation process. Thus federal–provincial transfers and unemployment insurance retard out-migration from labor-surplus regions. The clear message is that regional problems are exacerbated by redistributive policies (see Vanderkamp 1986).

The name of Myrdal is associated with a view that migration may be ineffective because it works in part in the opposite direction: there is no question about migration flows being inadequate, in fact they may well be too large. It is argued that migration is a highly selective process in terms of age, human capital, drive, ambition, and entrepreneurial ability. Thus, out-migration regions lose their best people, and in-migration regions are invigorated further by the new migrants. This tendency may be reinforced in the short run by a multiplier–accelerator process. The result is that the migration process may in principle become destabilizing, which in our context means that it may widen regional disparities. The empirical question becomes how large this destabilizing aspect of migration is in comparison with the usual equilibrating tendency.

The final challenge to be discussed concerns the relationship between different types of regional disparities, and in particular between wage and unemployment differentials. There is a common notion that wage and unemployment disparities are simply two different sides of the same coin. This suggests a strong, negative correlation between regional wages and unemployment. Such a correlation does indeed exist in terms of Canadian interprovincial comparisons, but the correlation is quite weak; for example, British Columbia is typically high in terms of wage rates but also above average in unemployment; Manitoba has one of the lowest unemployment rates but it is also below average in wage rates. The common notion is presumably based on the argument that certain shocks which affect the regional system have opposite impacts on wages and unemployment. For example, a decline in comparative advantage for a region's major industry is likely to raise its unemployment rate and depress its average wage.

But there are other theoretical links between wages and unemployment. First, there is the conventional excess demand hypothesis which forms the basis of the Phillips curve relation. In line with this hypothesis a region's wage rate will rise in relative terms when unemployment is low (and job vacancies high). Second, a high regional wage will ceteris paribus tend to create a high unemployment rate. The upshot is that the relation between wage and unemployment disparities is likely to be quite complex.

The model to be developed in the next section will attempt to deal with the various challenges posed above by incorporating the different approaches into a consistent framework. In principle the questions raised here become answerable and the various impacts can be measured empirically. Because of the empirical interest, the model is structured to fit in with available data. There is no doubt that the model should be made more complex (e.g., by including industrial and occupational dimensions of labor markets), but such a model would be difficult to estimate with available Canadian data.

12.2 The model

The model consists of three principal components: supply, demand, and wage adjustments. While these are the traditional components in economics modeling, the emphasis here is on change or adjustment. As a consequence the model is set up to explain changes in regional labor supply, changes in regional employment, and changes in relative regional wages. Because of partial wage adjustment, the regional labor markets will in general not be in balance, which means that the model also explains the regional excess supply or demand situations. There are three structural relationships and an identity plus a pseudo-identity, which can also be estimated.

The first concern is with the supply side, with is formulated in terms of changes in potential labor supply – that is, changes in the population 15 years and over, the population of working age. The reason for concentrating on potential labor supply instead of actual labor force is largely a matter of necessity. To obtain a good view of evolving regional disparities (and to increase the number of statistical observations), the data period extends back to the 1930s (and for lagged variables back to the 1920s). Prior to 1945 there are no consistent labor force series. Moreover, it is not possible to obtain data on labor force migration, as one source of supply adjustment. In short, there are good data on population of working age and the model is therefore constructed in terms of this as potential regional labor supply.

Potential labor supply changes (PC) can be broken down into two components: net out-migration from a region (NOM), and natural increase (NI). The NI component is treated as exogenous in the model as it is related to prior birth rates and to mortality during the period under consideration.

For the reasons given in the previous paragraph, it is not possible to obtain consistent unemployment data back to the prewar period. I therefore use a variable X which is intended to be a proxy for excess labor demand in the region and therefore negatively related to unemployment. The X variable is defined as the ratio of employment to potential labor supply, a variable which fits quite naturally into this model. It is of course negatively related to the unemployment rate, but it is also positively related to the participation rate. There is an important advantage in this combination since low participation rates are also an indicator of a weak labor market. We can think of X as representing regional labor market pressure in terms of employment opportunities. The limited evidence available suggests that X is also positively related to regional job vacancies.

The major analytical component of potential labor supply change is net migration. The first structural relation therefore relates to migration.

$$\text{NOM} = a_0 + a_1 W + a_2 X + a_3 \text{NFB} + a_4 \text{PT} + \qquad (12.1)$$

$$+ a_5 \text{AGR} + a_6 \text{URB} + a_7 \text{SAS} + a_8 \text{AGE}$$

in which NOM is net out-migration as a proportion of regional population 15 years and over. The signs of all the coefficients are indicated in brackets after the definitions of the other variables, which are:

W = wage rate in the region (−ve); X = employment ratio of the population aged 15 years and over (−ve); NFB = net fiscal benefits (provincial expenditure − residence-based taxes) as proportion of earned income (−ve); PT = personal transfers as a proportion of earned income (−ve); AGR = proportion of employment in agriculture (+ve); URB = proportion of population in a region resident in urban areas (+ve); SAS = dummy for Saskatchewan in the 1930s (−ve); and AGE = proportion of labor force population in 15–35 age group (+ve)

This relation is derived from traditional human capital considerations in which the migration investment is compensated by higher earnings (W), higher employment prospects (X) and greater provision of public good (NFB). Equation (12.1) may be derived from individual choice behavior, with the probabilities translating into migration flows, and the flows netted into a single net out-migration variable. Thus as W increases, the probability of in-migration increases, with the converse for out-migration. This means that both W and X are expected to have negative parameters.

Wages and employment opportunities can be considered as private pay-offs to migration, with the net fiscal benefits variable representing a kind of public pay-off. A province with a high level of public goods provision and a low level of taxes is an attractive location for potential migrants; the parameter of NFB is therefore anticipated to be negative. The size of NFB is largely determined by intergovernmental transfers which a province receives from Ottawa and by the level of natural resource revenues.

The federal government is also heavily involved in various personal transfer programs, from family allowances to unemployment insurance. It has been argued that such personal transfers tend to retard out-migration; PT is then expected to have a negative coefficient (for a review of the literature, see Vanderkamp 1986). There are two problems with this argument. First, most of the personal transfer programs are available regardless of location and should therefore have little impact on migration decisions. This is clearly true for family allowance but probably less so for unemployment insurance, particularly since regional differentiation came into effect in 1971. But this leads into the second problem with PT: this variable is bound to have higher values in those provinces which have high unemployment and low wages. PT may therefore act as a proxy for less favorable regional fortunes, and it may therefore have a positive impact on the level of net out-migration. In short, the expectation regarding the sign of the PT coefficient is not very firmly held.

The AGR and URB variables are included to represent autonomous aspects of migration. It is assumed that people in agriculture and people in large urban areas have higher propensities to migrate, given any set of opportunity variables. The coefficients of these two variables are therefore expected to be positive. The SAS dummy is set at unity for the 1930s for Saskatchewan to reflect the unusually low level of farm income in this province due to exceptionally poor weather conditions. The AGE variable is intended to capture the effect that young people are more mobile.

The second equation reflects the supply identity.

$$PC = NI - NOM \qquad (12.2)$$

PC is the proportional change in potential labor supply consisting of natural increase (NI), also expressed as a proportional rate of change, and the previously defined NOM. The NI variable is assumed to be exogenous in the context of this model.

Moving over to the demand side, the third equation is designed to explain the proportional change in employment in a region (EC).

$$EC = b_0 + b_1 W + b_2 \text{ NOM} + b_3 \text{ BASIC} + b_4 X^0 \qquad (12.3)$$

The W and X^0 variables are designed to represent a simple traditional demand-for-labor function which, because of slow adjustment, has a lagged dependent variable; X^0 is the lagged employment–potential supply ratio which is used as a convenient substitute for the lagged employment variable. I see the employment decision as embodying the capital investment decision, and the adjustment speed will therefore reflect both adjustments on the capital investment and employment change side. The parameter of W thus combines the static demand elasticity and the costs of adjustment. The coefficients W and X^0 are both expected to be negative, and if the speed of adjustment is very slow, then both coefficients will be small in absolute size.

BASIC measures the proportional rate of change in employment in basic industries to represent the shifts in a region's demand-for-labor function. This variable is related to the export base notion common in the regional literature, and it can be thought of as representing changes in a region's comparative advantage or terms of trade or resource endowment; BASIC's impact is expected to be positive.[2]

The NOM-variable in Equation 12.3 is a simple way of representing the Myrdal effect already referred to. The coefficient is expected to be negative since a greater level of out-migration will have a (negative) multiplier effect and will reduce the pool of entrepreneurial and risk-taking talent in the region's work force, thus producing a lower rate of employment growth. The empirical question is whether NOM is significant in determining employment changes. Since we are considering a simultaneous system, there is also an indirect relation whereby employment change, through its impact on W and X, has a negative effect on NOM. By recognizing this simultaneity in the estimating method, it will hopefully be possible to disentangle both of these channels of causation.

The fourth equation is a pseudo-identity designed to relate the changes in our X variable to current and lagged changes on the potential supply and employment side.

$$X = k_1 X^0 + k_2 (\text{EC} - \text{PC}) + k_3 (\text{EC}^0 - \text{PC}^0) \qquad (12.4)$$

The X^0 variable refers to the employment–potential supply ratio prevailing in the previous period, and EC^0 and PC^0 are the previous period's proportional rates of change in employment and potential supply, respectively. Since X and X^0 relate to the average levels of employment and potential supply, it is clear that the change in this variable $(X - X^0)$ is a nonlinear function of present and past changes in employment and potential supply. While the k_1 parameter will be estimated, it is fully expected to be unity, and the k_2 and k_3 coefficients are anticipated to be positive.

The final structural equation attempts to determine the way in which the regional relative wage is adjusted and it basically relies on the excess demand hypothesis mentioned above. Two versions are used in the estimating process, the second one allowing a role for the level of personal transfers (PT) and the average Canadian level of transfers (CPT) to capture the notion of induced wage rigidity.

$$W = c_0 + c_1 W^0 + c_2 X + c_3 X^0 \tag{12.5a}$$

$$W = c_0 + c_1 W^0 + c_2 X/PT + c_3 X^0/PT + c_4 CPT \tag{12.5b}$$

The pure excess demand aspect is represented by the X and X^0 variables to permit a current and lagged effect; c_2 and c_3 are expected to be positive. As this formulation represents a wage change equation, the c_1-parameter should be unity, although it will be freely estimated. Equation 12.5a represents the simple specification of the excess demand hypothesis.

In Equation 12.5b PT variables are introduced to allow for possible wage rigidities caused by personal transfer programs. The basic argument is that a higher level of support provided by these transfer programs, particularly unemployment insurance, will make wage adjustment more rigid, especially in the downward direction. In Equation 12.5b, the PT variables are included in inverse form in the complex variables, which allows for the possibility that the response of wage change to excess demand may be lower when the level of personal transfers is relatively high. The CPT variable in Equation 12.5b permits an upward shift in the wage-adjustment relation over time as the average level of personal transfers has risen over the recent half-century.

This closes the model. The five equations jointly determine the five endogenous variables: NOM, EC, PC, X, and W. All the other variables are exogenous or predetermined. To shed particular light on regional disparities variables (W and X), the system can be represented in the following two reduced-form equations.

$$X = f_0 + f_1 X^0 + f_2 W^0 + f_3 (EC^0 - PC^0)$$
$$+ f_4 [AE + (1 + b_2)(AM_1 + AM_2) - NI]. \quad (12.6)$$

$$f_2 < f_3, f_4 > 0$$

$$W = g_0 + g_1 X^0 + g_2 W^0 + g_3 (EC^0 - PC^0)$$
$$+ g_4 [AE + (1 + b_2)(AM_1 + AM_2) - NI]. \quad (12.7)$$

$$g_3, g_4 > 0$$

Each of the f and g coefficients is, of course, a complex of parameters derived from Equations 12.1 through 12.5, and the expected signs of the coefficients in Equations 12.6 and 12.7 are based on the anticipated signs of all the structural parameters indicated above. For convenience, the various autonomous shock variables have been separately identified in Equations 12.6 and 12.7, as follows:

$AE = \quad b_3$ BASIC — autonomous employment change

$AM_1 = \quad a_3$ NFB $+ a_4$ PT — autonomous out-migration associated with policy variables

$AM_2 = \quad a_5$ AGR $+ a_6$ URB $+ a_7$ SAS $+ a_8$ AGE — other autonomous compotents of migration

$NI = \quad$ natural increase

These autonomous shock elements have an impact on wage and excess demand disparities, both working in the same direction. Thus, a region with a low rate of natural increase in potential labor supply, a high level of autonomous out-migration (because, e.g., NFB or AGR is low) and a high rate of increase in autonomous employment (perhaps because of favorable changes in the terms of trade) will have a high W and X. It will be noted that I am assuming that the Myrdal effect is not so large that the system becomes unstable (i.e., $1 + b_2$ is assumed to remain a positive fraction). The effects of autonomous shocks on X and W imply that the two disparities should be positively correlated or that regional wage and unemployment rates should be negatively correlated. This tendency is however muted by the effects of past wage and excess demand variables, which provide the system with a memory. For example, if for some reason a region's wage level became too high in the past (W_0), then this will lead to lower excess demand (see Equation 12.6 with $f_2 < 0$) or higher unemployment.

The quantitative effects of autonomous shocks on W and X depend on many of the structural parameters. Two points are worth making. If the migration responses to wage and excess demand disparities are strong (and if employment change is responsive to regional wages), then the effects of shocks on both W and X will be muted. We can think of the extreme case of perfect mobility as a very high migration response which will not lead to any regional disparities at all in the face of favorable or unfavorable shocks. Second, the effects of a shock on X versus W will depend on the wage adjustment parameters (Equation 12.5). If regional wages respond little to excess demand, then the main impact of a shock will be in terms of X disparities, with little impact on W disparities. In the extreme case of no wage adjustment, all the impact of shocks will be on excess demand and unemployment. In the specification of Equation 12.5 it was argued that the degree of wage responsiveness was partly determined by the level of personal transfers. If as a result of policy changes PT levels are raised, then this will lead to lower wage responsiveness. One possible consequence of increased social benefit measures over the last 50 years or so is that a large part of the shocks affecting the regional system are taking the form of excess demand or unemployment disparities.

12.3 Data

The transition to an empirical model requires two important specification decisions. First, in order to eliminate short-term fluctuations it was decided to use decades as the time periods. Because of the timing of the Canadian census these are intercensal decades, with some variables (such as W and X) becoming average values for the decade, and others (such as EC and PC) being defined as rates of change over the decade. Second, the model is not designed to explain the Canadian pattern of the endogenous variables from one decade to another. For this reason most of the variables are expressed in terms of the Canadian average figures for the respective decades. For example, W is calculated as the regional wage level (earned income per employed person) expressed as a proportion of the Canadian average wage level during the decade. Similarly, EC is the proportional rate of change in regional employment minus the Canadian rate of change over the decade.

Table 12.1 provides some basic details about the variables employed in

Table 12.1 Variable definitions and means.

Symbol	Brief definitions		Means ($N = 48$)
*NOM	net out-migration of labor force population (population aged 15+)	as proportion of labour force population at the start of the decade	0.0054
*NI	natural increase in labor force population		0.1064
*PC	potential change in labor supply (change in labor force population)		−0.0390
*W	earned income per person employed (decade average)	current decade	0.9009
*W⁰		previous decade	0.8835
*X	ratio of employment to labor force population (decade average)	current decade	0.9629
*X⁰		previous decade	0.9702
NFB	provincial government expenditure minus residence-based taxes as proportion of earned income (decade average)		0.0859
PT	personal transfers as proportion of earned income, decade average (CPT is Canadian average for this variable)		0.1384
AGR	proportion of employment in agriculture at start of decade		0.1862
URB	proportion of total population in large urban areas at start of decade		0.3186
AGE	proportion of population (15+) in 15–35 age group		0.4531
*EC	employment change over decade as proportion of employment at start		−0.0451
*BASIC	change in employment in primary industries and manufacturing as proportion of total employment at start of decade		−0.0159
*EC⁰	proportional employment change over previous decade		−0.0563
*PC⁰	proportional change in labor force population in previous decade		−0.0470

Note: For more detailed definitions and statistical sources, see Appendix. Variables marked * are expressed in relation to the Canadian average figures for respective decades.

the empirical work. There are 48 observations, a combination of cross-section and time series with 9 provinces over 5 decades (1930s–1970s) plus Newfoundland for 3 decades (from 1950s on). The variables marked with an asterisk are all expressed in relation to the Canadian figures for the relevant decade. The appropriately weighted averages for these variables are therefore 0 (as in the case of PC and EC) or unity (in case of W and X). The unweighted averages reported in Table 12.1 reflect the fact that all provinces have equal weights in these calculations; thus W is about 0.9 since a number of smaller provinces are below average in wage levels, while some large provinces are above the Canadian average. This also explains the negative means reported for PC and EC.

The main sources are the national accounts (for earned income and

PT), the various censuses 1921 through 1981 (for population, EC, BASIC, AGR, URB, and AGE), vital statistics (for mortality figures to compute NI) and provincial finance accounts (for NFB). NOM is calculated as the residual between PC and NI which is derived by a simple survival method. The Appendix provides further definitions and sources.

12.4 Empirical results

There are two versions of the model, based on the two versions of the wage adjustment relation in Equation 12.5. The estimating methods are two-stage least squares (2-SLS) and three-stage least squares (3-SLS), both of which are designed to deal with the obvious simultaneity of the basic model. The difference between the two estimating methods is that 3-SLS allows for interrelationships among the stochastic error structures of the different equations. Table 12.2 presents two estimated models: Model I uses Equation 12.5b and is estimated by 2-SLS, while Model II employs 12.5a and 3-SLS as the estimating method. While the choice of wage adjustment specification makes some differences to the rest of the system, most of the differences between the two estimated models in Table 12.2 arise from the different estimating method.

Most of the coefficients in the NOM-equation are significant and carry the expected signs. The negative parameters of W and X in (I-1) are roughly the same size, which suggests that a change in average earned income per member of the working age population has the same effect on migration regardless of whether it comes out about as a change in the wage level or an equivalent change in X. In (II-1) the W and X coefficients are more significant and larger (in absolute value) and the X parameter is roughly twice as large as the W coefficient. This suggests that X disparities (employment opportunities) are a more potent motivation for migration than wage differentials. The migration response to W and X is not large: an increase of 10% in a region's wage level (e.g., from 90% to 100% of the Canadian average) will cause an increase in its potential labor supply of about 6–7% over a ten-year period, and the same change in X produces a 6–15% change in potential labor supply over a decade.

The NFB coefficient is negative and surprisingly large in absolute value. And the results are quite different in the two models in Table 12.2. For example, a massive increase in average earned income from 70% to 100% of Canadian average in a particular province which at the same time experiences a reduction in federal transfers so that NFB goes from 30% to 10% (a scenario quite in line with the recent cross-section pattern) would produce an *increase* in the rate of net out-migration of about 5% per decade in terms of its working age population according to

Table 12.2 Estimated models.

Model I (2-stage least squares)

(1) NOM = 0.83 − 0.60 W − 0.63 X − 1.12 NFB + 1.26 PT
       (2.1)   (3.9)   (1.6)   (2.6)   (2.8)
  + 0.48 AGR + 0.36 URB − 0.28 SAS + 0.22 AGE
    (2.6)   (2.2)   (2.4)   (0.6)
  $R^2 = 0.597$

(3) EC = 0.06 − 0.04 W − 0.54 NOM + 0.76 BASIC − 0.02 X^0
      (0.4)   (0.4)   (3.8)   (3.0)   (0.1)
  $R^2 = 0.774$

(4) X = 0.999 X^0 + 0.48 (EC − PC) + 0.38 (EC^0 − PC^0)
       (581.7)   (7.7)   (8.8)
  $R^2 = 0.9999$

(5) W = 0.14 + 0.77 W^0 − 0.003 X/PT + 0.008 X^0/PT + 0.39 CPT
       (2.0)   (16.0)   (0.7)   (1.9)   (1.0)
  $R^2 = 0.855$

Model II (3-stage least squares)

(1) NOM = 1.90 − 0.71 W − 1.46 X − 0.82 NFB + 0.56 PT
       (2.9)   (4.5)   (2.6)   (1.9)   (1.1)
  + 0.63 AGR + 0.60 URB − 0.15 SAS − 0.26 AGE
    (3.0)   (2.9)   (1.2)   (0.6)
  $R^2 = 0.473$

(3) EC = −0.009 − 0.05 W − 0.40 NOM + 0.98 BASIC − 0.06 X^0
       (0.1)   (0.6)   (2.9)   (4.2)   (0.4)
  $R^2 = 0.737$

(4) X = 0.999 X^0 + 0.52 (EC − PC) + 0.36 (EC^0 − PC^0)
       (612.3)   (9.3)   (9.5)
  $R^2 = 0.972$

(5) W = 0.01 + 0.75 W^0 − 0.34 X + 0.57 X^0
       (0.1)   (14.2)   (0.7)   (1.1)
  $R^2 = 0.846$

Note: Figures in brackets are absolute values of *t* statistics.

Model I, but it would engender a decrease of about 5% in potential supply according to Model II. If a dollar of public expenditure were equivalent to a dollar of private expenditure in terms of utility, this combination of events would increase average welfare in the province by about 20% in relative terms, and it is difficult to believe that this would be accompanied by increased net out-migration. This suggests that Model II is more believable than Model I in this regard.

Contrary to results in other studies, the PT coefficient is positive. This result is not entirely unexpected (as was indicated in a preceding section), but it implies that we have to be careful in our interpretation. The earlier argument suggests that a positive impact of PT on NOM may be related to excess supply (labor market hardship) aspects which are not adequately or fully captured by the X variable. For example, the X measure is reduced by an increase in a region's unemployment rate and by a reduction in its average participation, and it is entirely possible that the former may have a bigger impact on out-migration than the latter. The PT measure is likely to be more strongly affected by an increase in unemployment. It is interesting to note that in Model II the PT coefficient is much smaller, and insignificant by conventional standards. In fact a comparison of (I–1) and (II–1) reveals that the reduction in the PT coefficient is accompanied by an increase (in absolute value) of the X parameter. This result lends some weight to the interpretation of the role of the PT variable in the migration equation.

The other variables in Equation 1 perform as expected, except that the AGE variable is not significant. The net result of AGR and URB is to reduce the rate of net out-migration from the four Atlantic provinces. The negative coefficient on the SAS dummy confirms that the earned income level in Saskatchewan during the 1930s was unusually low. The proportion of population speaking French was also tested as an autonomous migration variable but it was not statistically significant.

Equation 3 in Table 12.2 contains two surprises. First, while the W and X^0 variables attain the expected signs (except for X^0 in II–3), the coefficients are completely insignificant. This suggests that the regional demand for labor is insensitive with regard to wage rates. While such a conclusion may be quite acceptable to a regional specialist, it is difficult to accept for an economist. The second surprise is the relatively strong performance of the NOM variable, which has the expected negative coefficient and is statistically significant although it is clearly a fraction – in line with the stability assumption discussed earlier. Assuming that the estimating method has coped with the obvious simultaneity between EC and NOM, this result suggests that the Myrdal effect may be of considerable importance. The coefficient implies than a higher level of in-migration adding an extra 10% to a region's labor force population over a decade will boost its employment growth over that decade by about 4–5%. The coefficient of BASIC approaches unity, particularly in (II–3), which suggests that the conventional employment multiplier is roughly equal to unity, which is low by comparison with other regional studies.[3]

Equation 4 is intended to be a linear approximation of an identity and its estimated coefficients are in line with that. The X^0 parameter is virtually unity.

Finally, Equation 5 presents a number of puzzles; the empirical results are hard to accept. Judging from quite a few tests it is difficult to discover a role for the excess demand variables in regional wage adjustment. Most often, as in Table 12.2, both X variables have parameters which are not significant and display a typical "minus (X) − plus (X^0)" sign pattern. It should be noted that the X parameter in Equation 5 is crucial in terms of the relationship between W and X disparities; if the X parameter's is negative, then the real regional shocks will initially have opposite effects on X and W disparities. Now it is true that a higher positive coefficient of X^0 will compensate for this twist in the next ten years, but the net impact is small. In (II–5) a permanent increase of 10% in the X variable (e.g., from 0.9 to 1.0) would produce a long-run increase of 2% in the regional wage level, if we accept the insignificant coefficients as estimated. The difficult conclusion is that regional wage rate differences appear to be unrelated to excess demand conditions in the labor market.

Equation 5 in Model 1 allows for personal transfers, including particularly unemployment insurance, to have an impact on wage sensitivity. With PT in the denominator, a positive coefficient of the X/PT variable would imply that the response of relative regional wages to excess demand goes down when the level of personal transfer payments is increased. But as Equation (I–5) shows, the results are mixed with a minus–plus pattern of coefficients, and only the X^0/PT being close to significant; X and X^0 do not appear in Equation 5 because given the presence of the more complex variables they were totally insignificant. The net effect of the X/PT and X^0/PT variables on W is very small: with PT = 0.2, a permanent 10% increase in X would increase the region's wage by only about 0.3% in relative terms. The CPT variable has a positive coefficient but it is not significant.

The final puzzle in the wage equations in Table 12.2 is the coefficient of W^0, which in all tests turns out to be significantly less than unity. This implies that a simple change formulation in the tradition of the excess demand hypothesis is inappropriate. It is not clear how to interpret this result. It literally means that the wage change is smaller, for any given set of excess demand conditions, the higher the wage level in the previous decade. This may have something to do with downward wage rigidity, but further work on this subject is clearly required.

12.5 Implications and simulations

While the model and its specifications are perhaps best termed tentative, it is interesting to raise a series of questions at this point. The first question relates to the predictive power of model. How well does it "predict" the endogenous variables for the most recent decade? Table 12.3 answers this question. The predicted values are fairly

Table 12.3 Actual and predicted values for the 1970s.

	Actual	Model I	Model II		Actual	Model I	Model II
W				**X**			
Nfld.	0.84	0.83	0.79		0.79	0.79	0.80
PEI	0.69	0.67	0.67		0.91	0.94	0.91
NS	0.85	0.82	0.79		0.88	0.88	0.89
NB	0.84	0.81	0.79		0.86	0.87	0.88
Que.	0.96	0.96	0.95		0.93	0.97	0.98
Ont.	1.06	1.08	1.08		1.07	1.06	1.05
Man.	0.93	0.93	0.93		1.01	1.01	1.01
Sas.	0.93	0.90	0.90		0.98	0.95	0.96
Alb.	0.97	0.96	0.97		1.10	1.07	1.06
BC	1.08	1.06	1.03		1.00	1.02	1.02
MAPE		0.017	0.029			0.017	0.019
NOM				**PC**			
Nfld.	0.14	0.20	0.15		−0.02	−0.08	−0.04
PEI	0.04	0.07	0.00		−0.03	−0.07	0.01
NS	0.05	0.03	0.06		−0.06	−0.04	−0.06
NB	0.06	0.12	0.12		−0.03	−0.10	−0.10
Que.	0.07	0.12	0.11		−0.05	−0.11	−0.09
Ont.	−0.00	−0.04	−0.07		−0.02	0.03	0.05
Man.	0.10	0.05	0.06		−0.12	−0.07	−0.08
Sas.	0.13	0.11	0.12		−0.11	−0.09	−0.11
Alb.	−0.25	−0.11	−0.13		0.28	0.14	0.16
BC	−0.16	−0.04	−0.04		0.13	0.00	0.01
MAPE		0.059	0.052			0.064	0.052
EC							
Nfld.	0.04	−0.02	0.03				
PEI	−0.08	−0.05	−0.02				
NS	−0.06	−0.01	−0.03				
NB	−0.02	−0.06	−0.05				
Que.	−0.11	−0.07	−0.05				
Ont.	−0.01	0.03	0.03				
Man.	−0.13	−0.06	−0.07				
Sas.	−0.08	−0.11	−0.12				
Alb.	0.35	0.12	0.13				
BC	0.15	0.04	0.04				
MAPE		0.070	0.066				

Note: Predicted values of variables for 1970s are obtained from Model I and Model II estimated equations in Table 12.2 using actual values of exogenous and predetermined variables applicable to the 1970s. MAPE is the mean absolute prediction error.

reasonable, but there are some major discrepancies, particularly in the cases of NOM and EC. Table 12.3 shows the mean absolute prediction error (MAPE) at the foot of the columns of predicted values; the differences between prediction errors of NOM and PC are due to rounding. The rate of net out-migration is overpredicted in the cases of Newfoundland, New Brunswick, and Quebec, and underpredicted for Manitoba, while the rate of net in-migration is grossly underpredicted for Alberta and British Columbia, and over-predicted for Ontario. The rate of employment growth (EC) is overpredicted for Prince Edward Island, Nova Scotia, Quebec, Ontario, and Manitoba, and underpredicted for the other five provinces, particularly for Alberta and British Columbia. The predictions regarding W and X are on the whole much closer, but this is partly the result of the very persistence of these disparities. Equations 4 and 5 contain the lagged dependent variables on the right-hand side and this feature obviously increases predictive power under these circumstances.

The second question relates to the internal dynamics of the estimated model. What would happen to the system if the situation of the 1970s continued for a few more decades? Or, put more technically, would provincial disparities tend to disappear if the exogenous variables all maintained their 1970s values for two more decades? I define the absence of disparities as a hypothetical situation in which potential supply and demand growth are identical for all regions, and wage and excess demand levels are the same as well. Table 12.4 provides the evidence for both models. Generally speaking there is indeed a tendency for regional disparities to diminish. This is most clearly true for the relative wage variable (W), and the tendency is least strong in the case of the excess demand variable (X); for example, in both Models I and II, X moves the "wrong" way in Prince Edward Island, Saskatchewan, and British Columbia. Still the X variable is by no means "out of control," partly because of the feedback loops whereby X affects labor supply growth (Equation 1) and wage levels (Equation 5) which in turn have an impact on potential supply (and demand). The X variable to a large extent takes on the role of shock-absorber in the short run.

The third question is what happens to the regional system if we make some of the exogenous shocks more equal. Will disparities have a tendency to disappear if all provinces are exposed to some of the external shocks in the same way? To avoid completely unrealistic simulations (e.g., based on the AGR or URB variables, which are unlikely to ever have the same values for all provinces) the following three scenarios are chosen:

(a) The rate of natural increase in working age population takes on the same value (average for the 1970s) for all provinces; this is fairly

Table 12.4 Simulated values of endogenous variables for 1970s and 1990s.

	Model I		Model II			Model I		Model II	
	1970s	1990s	1970s	1990s		1970s	1990s	1970s	1990s
W					**X**				
Nfld.	0.83	0.86	0.79	0.78		0.79	0.86	0.80	0.86
PEI	0.67	0.77	0.67	0.78		0.94	0.92	0.91	0.85
NS	0.82	0.87	0.79	0.83		0.88	0.91	0.89	0.92
NB	0.81	0.86	0.79	0.82		0.87	0.91	0.88	0.91
Que.	0.96	0.96	0.95	0.94		0.97	1.02	0.98	1.01
Ont.	1.08	1.06	1.08	1.06		1.06	1.06	1.05	1.04
Man.	0.93	0.96	0.93	0.96		1.01	0.99	1.01	0.99
Sas.	0.90	0.93	0.90	0.92		0.95	0.93	0.96	0.95
Alb.	0.96	0.99	0.97	1.00		1.07	1.03	1.06	1.03
BC	1.06	1.03	1.03	1.01		1.02	1.08	1.02	1.06
NOM					**PC**				
Nfld.	0.20	0.14	0.15	0.07		−0.08	−0.02	−0.04	0.05
PEI	0.07	−0.01	0.00	−0.00		−0.07	0.01	0.01	0.01
NS	0.03	−0.01	0.06	−0.00		−0.04	0.01	−0.06	−0.00
NB	0.12	0.07	0.12	0.05		−0.10	−0.05	−0.10	−0.03
Que.	0.12	0.09	0.11	0.06		−0.11	−0.08	−0.09	−0.04
Ont.	−0.04	−0.03	−0.07	−0.03		0.03	0.02	0.05	0.02
Man.	0.05	0.00	0.06	0.02		−0.07	−0.03	−0.08	−0.04
Sas.	0.11	0.11	0.12	0.13		−0.09	−0.09	−0.11	−0.12
Alb.	−0.11	−0.10	−0.13	−0.10		0.14	0.13	0.16	0.13
BC	−0.04	−0.06	−0.04	−0.08		0.00	0.02	0.01	0.05
EC									
Nfld.	−0.02	0.01	0.03	0.07					
PEI	−0.05	−0.01	−0.02	−0.03					
NS	−0.01	0.01	−0.03	−0.00					
NB	−0.06	−0.03	−0.05	−0.02					
Que.	−0.07	−0.06	−0.05	−0.03					
Ont.	0.03	0.02	0.03	0.02					
Man.	−0.06	−0.04	−0.07	−0.05					
Sas.	−0.11	−0.11	−0.12	−0.12					
Alb.	0.12	0.11	0.13	0.12					
BC	0.04	0.05	0.04	0.06					

Note: Simulated values for 1970s are from Table 12.3 (predicted). For the 1990s, exogenous variables maintain actual values applicable to 1970s but predetermined variables take on values simulated for preceding decade.

realistic since provincial birth rates have become quite similar recently (labeled as simulation 2 in Tables 12.5 and 12.6).
(b) The NFB variable (net fiscal benefits as proportion of earned income) takes on the same value (average for the 1970s) for all provinces; this is a possible policy option which the federal government could entertain although it is not likely (labeled as simulation 3 in Tables 12.5 and 12.6).
(c) The BASIC variable (the rate of change in the regional employment base) takes on the same value (average for 1970s) for all provinces; although not likely, this scenario might arise from fortuitous circumstances or from a very interventionist government policy (labeled simulation 4 in Tables 12.5 and 12.6).

The simulation results for models I and II are presented in Tables 12.5 and 12.6 respectively. All exogenous variables other than those specifically mentioned above maintain the values actually prevailing in the 1970s; the predetermined variables (W^0 and X^0) take on the simulated values for the preceding decade. All the simulated values for the wage level (W), the excess demand variable (X), and for net out-migration (NOM) reported in Tables 12.5 and 12.6 relate to the 1980s to permit an evaluation of the impact of the simulated shocks beyond the immediate period. Simulation 1 in Tables 12.5 and 12.6 represents the "status quo," included for comparison purposes. Simulation 5 combines the three impacts of 2, 3, and 4, with NI, NFB, and BASIC all taking on their same respective values for each province.

There is little tendency towards convergence in the case of the provincial wage levels. In fact W values change little; in the case of model I (Table 12.5) the W variable does not change at all because excess demand has virtually no impact here. The X and NOM variables show some tendency towards reduced disparities comparing simulations 1 and 5, but there are quite a few exceptions. These exceptions arise from the fact that for some provinces equalizing a shock variable increases the disequilibrium. For example, equalizing BASIC implies a reduced growth of the employment base for Newfoundland which increases excess supply, and the equalization of NI reduces the rate of increase in Alberta's working-age population, thereby increasing the need for in-migration.

Simulation 2 shows that the equalization of NI has a particularly strong impact in the case of Newfoundland, and also in British Columbia and Manitoba. Simulation 3 indicates that the equalization of net fiscal benefits (NFB) increases out-migration from the Atlantic provinces, reduces out-migration from Quebec and Saskatchewan, and increases the rate of in-migration to Ontario and British Columbia. The equalization

Table 12.5 Simulations for the 1980s using Model I.

	(1)	(2)	(3)	(4)	(5)
W					
Nfld.	0.85	0.85	0.85	0.85	0.85
PEI	0.73	0.73	0.73	0.73	0.73
NS	0.85	0.85	0.85	0.85	0.85
NB	0.84	0.84	0.84	0.84	0.84
Que.	0.96	0.96	0.96	0.96	0.96
Ont.	1.07	1.07	1.07	1.07	1.07
Man.	0.94	0.94	0.94	0.94	0.94
Sas.	0.92	0.92	0.92	0.92	0.92
Alb.	0.98	0.98	0.98	0.98	0.98
BC	1.04	1.04	1.04	1.04	1.04
X					
Nfld.	0.83	0.95	0.90	0.76	0.94
PEI	0.94	0.93	1.02	0.97	1.04
NS	0.90	0.88	0.94	0.91	0.92
NB	0.90	0.91	0.92	0.90	0.94
Que.	1.00	1.00	0.96	1.01	0.97
Ont.	1.06	1.03	1.00	1.05	0.96
Man.	1.01	0.97	0.98	1.05	0.98
Sas.	0.94	0.94	0.91	1.00	0.97
Alb.	1.05	1.07	1.06	0.99	1.02
BC	1.05	1.00	1.01	1.03	0.93
NOM					
Nfld.	0.17	0.09	0.26	0.21	0.24
PEI	0.01	0.02	0.14	−0.01	0.12
NS	0.01	0.02	0.06	0.00	0.07
NB	0.09	0.08	0.12	0.09	0.11
Que.	0.11	0.11	0.05	0.10	0.04
Ont.	−0.04	−0.02	−0.12	−0.03	−0.10
Man.	0.00	0.03	−0.04	−0.02	−0.04
Sas.	0.10	0.10	0.06	0.07	0.02
Alb.	−0.11	−0.12	−0.09	−0.07	−0.07
BC	−0.05	−0.01	−0.11	−0.03	−0.07

Assumptions for simulations:

(1) As in Table 12.4, all exogenous variables maintain actual values for 1970s through 1980s.

(2) As (1), but natural increase in population held at same value for all provinces through 1980s (value of NI is actual average for 1970s).

(3) As (1), but NFB (net fiscal benefits) held at same value (average for 1970s) for all provinces through 1980s.

(4) As (1), but BASIC (change in employment base) held at the same value (average for 1970s) for all provinces through 1980s.

(5) Combines assumptions of (2), (3), and (4), so NI, NFB, and BASIC all are held at same respective values for all provinces through 1980s.

Table 12.6 Various simulations for the 1980s using Model II.

	(1)	(2)	(3)	(4)	(5)
W					
Nfld.	0.78	0.76	0.77	0.79	0.76
PEI	0.74	0.74	0.73	0.73	0.72
NS	0.81	0.81	0.80	0.81	0.80
NB	0.80	0.80	0.80	0.80	0.79
Que.	0.94	0.94	0.95	0.94	0.94
Ont.	1.07	1.08	1.08	1.07	1.08
Man.	0.95	0.95	0.95	0.94	0.94
Sas.	0.91	0.91	0.92	0.90	0.91
Alb.	0.99	0.99	0.99	1.01	1.00
BC	1.01	1.02	1.02	1.02	1.03
X					
Nfld.	0.84	0.93	0.89	0.77	0.90
PEI	0.88	0.88	0.94	0.91	0.96
NS	0.91	0.90	0.94	0.92	0.93
NB	0.90	0.91	0.92	0.91	0.94
Que.	1.00	1.00	0.97	1.01	0.98
Ont.	1.04	1.02	1.00	1.04	0.97
Man.	1.00	0.97	0.98	1.04	1.00
Sas.	0.95	0.95	0.93	1.01	0.99
Alb.	1.04	1.06	1.05	0.98	1.00
BC	1.04	1.00	1.01	1.02	0.95
NOM					
Nfld.	0.10	−0.01	0.14	0.20	0.12
PEI	−0.02	−0.01	0.03	−0.06	0.00
NS	0.02	0.04	0.04	0.01	0.05
NB	0.08	0.07	0.09	0.07	0.07
Que.	0.08	0.08	0.06	0.06	0.04
Ont.	−0.04	−0.01	−0.07	−0.04	−0.04
Man.	0.00	0.04	−0.01	−0.05	−0.03
Sas.	0.13	0.13	0.11	0.05	0.03
Alb.	−0.11	−0.13	−0.11	−0.03	−0.05
BC	−0.07	−0.01	−0.09	−0.04	−0.01

Notes: For assumptions, see notes to Table 12.5.

of BASIC (simulation 4) has a particularly strong impact in the Atlantic and Prairie provinces, but the direction of impact is different for Newfoundland and Alberta compared with other provinces.

In short, the simulations suggest that wage disparities are unlikely to disappear or even change much over a decade or two, even in the face of major changes in exogenous variables or policy measures. On the other hand, the shock-absorber role played by the X variable implies that this variable responds much more strongly to changes in the pattern of shocks or policies. The net result of the three scenarios in Tables 12.5 and 12.6 is a reduced dispersion of excess demand (and unemployment) across the provinces, but this does not imply that migration is eliminated or even reduced. In fact, the combination of the various events increases out-migration from the Atlantic provinces. In principle it would be possible to provide further simulations into the future to trace the evolution of the endogenous variables, and in particular to see whether regional wage disparities will eventually narrow in response to the equalization of these shocks and policy measures. But the dynamics of the model are not sufficiently well specified in the context of decennial patterns, and such an exercise would take us too far out on a limb.

12.6 Concluding comments

The paper is only modestly successful in explaining Canada's regional disparities. It appears that migration is only moderately responsive to differentials in economic fortunes, which implies that because of external and internal shocks substantial disparities are bound to arise and persist. In recent times, relative wages appear to be quite unresponsive to differential excess demand pressures. This in turn means that most shocks to the regional system will have a primary impact on unemployment (and participation rates), and little effect on wage disparities. This also implies that it will be very difficult to reduce or eliminate existing wage disparities. All this leaves a puzzle why the disparities in wages would ever have arisen in the past, unless that past was characterized by considerably more wage flexibility, with wages indirectly responding to exogenous shocks which have tended to persist into more recent periods. The observed Myrdal effect has contributed to this persistence syndrome.

There is long-standing debate in the migration literature about the relative importance of wage differentials and differences in employment opportunities in motivating interregional migration behavior. The results of this paper suggest that both are important, but at least one set of empirical estimates (Model II) implies that job opportunity differences (as represented by the X variable) are more powerful. This is particularly significant in a world in which, according to the evidence presented here, regional wage levels are quite rigid. In essence the adjustment path through relative wages becomes inoperative, with the consequence that the adjustment path through job opportunities (X variable) becomes more important. It is an interesting question whether policy measures to promote greater wage flexibility would be welfare-improving under these circumstances. For example, a regional shock (a change in comparative advantage) might require out-migration, which could be accomplished by a 10% reduction in the relative wage or by a 6% decline in our excess demand measure. Would wage flexibility then be preferable, as is often argued by economists, particularly if an increase in flexibility is itself costly? (For some more discussion of this topic see Vanderkamp 1986).

Although migration is not perfect or even very responsive, the general conclusion which emerges from this paper is that migration constitutes a crucial part of the inter-regional adjustment process. Regional employment change does not appear to respond to wage differentials or excess demand, which means that migration is primarily responsible for holding regional disparities in check. If migration could be more responsive to disparities, then disparities would be less of a problem (particularly with some wage flexibility); but it should be recalled that migration is an expensive process. The adjustment role of migration is, of course, reduced by the Myrdal effect. If the Myrdal effect as estimated here is indeed caused by the selectivity of migration, then the resulting complication for the adjustment process is probably an inevitable result of accepting individual freedom of choice.

What role can policy variables play in reducing regional disparities? With regard to wage disparities the tentative answer which emerges from the results is "very little." Since the role of our personal transfer variable is not very clear, it appears that a change in federal policies (e.g., related to unemployment insurance), may not have a decisive impact on disparities. On the other hand, a more equal distribution of federal transfers to the provinces is likely to result in some reduced dispersion of job opportunities (X). This effect is largely the result of increased out-migration from the Atlantic region and increased in-migration to Ontario and British Columbia. As already indicated, increasing migration is not a costless exercise, and such a policy shift would also run counter to the equity principles recently enshrined in the Canadian constitution.

It is sometimes argued that Canada has too little migration. One interpretation of this opinion is that we have a number of policies, such as federal–provincial transfers and agricultural support programs, which tend to keep people in the low-income and rural regions. In contrast, it is often stated that many underdeveloped countries suffer from excessive rural–urban migration with consequent overpopulation of major urban areas. In line with the above interpretation this argument may also be related to policies pursued by the national governments in those developing countries. The hypothesis might be that rural–urban migration is partly induced by policies which favor urban areas. It is alleged that in many developing economies the provision of social services and the investment in social capital is heavily slanted toward urban areas. The control of agricultural prices in many countries may also contribute to the economic disadvantages of rural regions. An examination of this hypothesis would constitute a fascinating component of a study of regional disparities in developing economies.

Appendix: definition of variables

Earned income

Earned income is the sum of the following four items: (a) wages, salaries and supplementary income; (b) military pay and allowances; (c) net income of farm operators from farm production; and (d) net income of nonfarm unincorporated business

These four components are summed for each year. The average annual level of earned income for the decade is computed by dividing the sum of the ten relevant years by ten for each decade 1931–40 through to 1971–80. This decade average of earned income is expressed on a per worker basis (i.e., the decade average of earned income is divided by average employment of the decade for each province). These provincial figures are then expressed as a proportion of the Canadian value of the same variable.
Assigned names: W, W^0.
Source: National accounts.

Employment

This variable reflects the average demand for labor for each decade for each province. Computation proceeded in the following manner. The average level of employment for the decade was calculated by summing the levels of employment at the beginning of the decade and the end of the decade and subsequently halving this sum. This figure was then expressed as a proportion of the average labor force population 15 years of age and over which was computed in a similar manner. These provincial figures were then expressed as a proportion of the Canadian value of this variable for each decade and each province.
Assigned names: X, X^0.
Source: Census

Employment change

This variable captures employment growth over each decade for each province. To compute this variable, the difference in employment between the beginning and the end of each decade for each province is expressed as a proportion of employment at the start of the decade. These provincial figures are then differenced from the Canadian value of employment change for each decade. For example, the value of employment change for the 1950s would be calculated as follows: the employment level in 1951 (start of decade) is subtracted from the

employment level in 1961 (end of decade). This difference is then expressed as a proportion of employment in 1951. This proportion is then expressed as a difference from the Canadian figure, which is calculated using Canadian levels of employment for the same time period.
Assigned name: EC.
Source: Census

Personal transfers

This variable refers to personal transfers from all levels of government to individuals. To compute the decade average of personal transfers, the annual levels are summed over the decade and divided by ten. This decade average of personal transfers is expressed on a per capita basis (i.e., the decade average of personal transfers is divided by the decade average of the labor force population 15 years of age and over for each province). These provincial figures are then expressed as a proportion of the average of earned income of the province. The Canadian value of this variable was derived in the same manner using Canadian decade averages for personal transfers and population.
Assigned names: PT, CPT.
Source: National accounts.

Net fiscal benefits

Net fiscal benefits is defined as the magnitude of the difference in the total gross provincial government expenditure less interest payments on the public debt, and total gross revenue less revenue from corporate taxes, natural resources, and intergovernmental transfers. The sum of this difference is computed annually and then the average of the decade is taken. However, it should be noted that the decade average for the period 1931–40 is the average of eight years since data was not available for the years 1937 and 1938. This decade average of net fiscal benefit is expressed on a per capita basis (i.e., the decade average of net fiscal benefit is divided by the decade average of the labor force population 15 years of age and over for each province). These provincial figures are then expressed as a proportion of the average earned income of the province.
Assigned name: NFB.
Source: Provincial finance accounts.

Population change

Labor force population refers to the total of individuals aged 15 years and over. To compute the average rate of change over the decade, the difference between the two census years is taken and expressed as a proportion of the labor force population at the start of the decade for each province. For example, for the period 1931–40, the difference in the labor force population in 1931 and 1941 is taken and expressed as a proportion of the labor force population in 1931 for each province. These provincial figures are then differenced from the Canadian value of this variable.
Assigned name: PC.
Source: Census.

Natural increase

Natural increase refers to the average increase in the "domestic" labor force population. Natural increase was derived in the following way. Using the 1960s as an example, the population 5 years of age and over in 1961 less the population 15 years of age and over in 1961 was computed and subsequently purged of those individuals 5 years of age and over in 1961 who died in the period 1961–70. This figure was then divided by the population 15 years of age and over in 1961. This was done for each province. Once the provincial figures were derived, they were then differentiated from the Canadian value of the variable.
Assigned name: NI.
Source: Census.

Net out-migration

Net out-migration refers to the difference between the rate of natural increase in the labor force population and the rate of the actual change in the labor force population. If positive, this variable reflects provincial out-migration, and if negative, it reflects provincial in-migration. The provincial figures are differenced from the Canadian figure (see *PC* and *NI*), with the result that Canadian net immigration is excluded.
Assigned name: NOM.
Source: Census.

Basic industry employment growth

Basic industries, for our purposes, are agriculture, forestry, fishing, hunting, trapping, mining, quarrying, and manufacturing. To compute the average rate of change in employment in these industries over the decade, the difference between the two census years is taken and expressed as a proportion of total employment at the start of the decade. For example, for the period 1971–80, the difference in employment in basic industries in 1971 and 1981 is taken and then expressed as a proportion of total employment in 1971 for each province. These provincial figures are then differenced from the Canadian value of this variable for the relevant decade.
Assigned name: BASIC.
Source: Census.

Agricultural employment

This variable reflects the role that agriculture plays in a province's total employment opportunities. To compute this variable, the decade average of employment in agriculture is expressed as a proportion of average total employment for the same decade for each province.
Assigned name: AGR.
Source: Census.

Urban population

This variable captures the degree to which a region's population is urbanized. The urbanized population, for our purposes, refers to that population living in urban centers of 30,000 or more. To compute this variable, the decade average of a region's urbanized population is expressed as a proportion of the decade average of that region's total population.
Assigned name: URB.
Source: Census.

Age composition of population

This variable expresses the population 15 to 35 years of age as a proportion of the population 15 years of age and over for each province. This variable is included in the analysis to isolate differences in provincial migration flows with respect to the proportion of its population in the young age group.
Assigned name: AGE.
Source: Census.

Saskatchewan dummy

This variable was designed to capture the severe influence of the drought of the 1930s on the economy of Saskatchewan. Since this variable is a dummy, it takes on a value of unity for the 1930s in Saskatchewan and zero elsewhere.
Assigned name: SAS.

Notes

1. The theoretical model used in this paper provides the analytical underpinning for part of my recently completed review paper "The efficiency of the interregional adjustment process" prepared for the Macdonald Commission (Vanderkamp 1986). This forms part of a project funded by the Social Science and Humanities Research Council of Canada, and the support is gratefully acknowledged. I am grateful to the conference participants for a number of suggestions and comments which are reflected in the revision.
2. The level of government employment may also be looked at in the same light, i.e. as largely exogenous. It has been suggested in particular that changes in the provincial distribution of federal government employees might appear in Equation 12.3 as a shift variable analogous to the BASIC variable (see also Raynauld, this volume). Unfortunately, data on such a variable prior to the 1950s are not available.
3. It has been suggested that the impact of changes in the regional employment base (and the Myrdal effect) should be allowed to vary with the size of the region. To capture this idea, both BASIC and NOM variables were also included interactively with the provincial population aged 15+, but the interaction variables were both completely insignificant.

References

Economic Council of Canada 1982. *Financing confederation, today and tomorrow*. Ottawa.

Economic Council of Canada 1977. *Living together*. Ottawa.

Gerking, S. D. & J. R. Mutti 1983. Factor rewards and the international migration of unskilled labour: a model with capital mobility. *Journal of International Economics* 14(4), 367–80.

Grant, E. & J. Vanderkamp 1983. Regional demand and supply projections and migration. In *Canadian Labour Markets in the 1980's*. Kingston, Ontario: Industrial Relations Centre, Queen's University.

Hanushek, E. A. 1981. Alternative models of earnings determination and labor market structures. *Journal of Human Resources* 16(2), 238–59.

Johnson, G. E. 1983. Intermetropolitan wage differentials in the United States. In *The measurement of labour costs*, NBER Studies in Income and Wealth, vol. 48, Jack E. Triplett (ed.), 309–30. Chicago: University of Chicago Press.

Mueller, C. F. 1982. *The economics of labor migration: a behavioral analysis*. New York: Academic Press.

Polèse, M. 1981. Regional disparity, migration and economic adjustment: a reappraisal. *Canadian Public Policy – Analyse de Politiques* 7(4), 519–25.

Pissarides, C. A. 1978. The role of relative wages and excess demand in the sectoral flow of labour. *Review of Economic Studies* 45(3), 453–67.

Pissarides, C. A. & I. McMaster 1984. Regional migration, wages and unemployment: empirical evidence and implications for policy. Centre for Labour Economics, London School of Economics, Discussion Paper no. 204.

Raynauld, A. Regional development in a federal state, Ch. 10, this volume.

Swan, N. M. & P. J. E. Kovacs 1981. *Empirical testing on Newfoundland data of a theory of regional disparities*. Ottawa: Economic Council of Canada, Ministry of Supply and Services.

Vanderkamp, J. 1986. The efficiency of the interregional adjustment process. In *Disparities and interregional adjustment*, Kenneth Norrie (ed.), 53–108. Volume 64 of Research Studies of the Royal Commission on the Economic Union and Development Prospects for Canada, University of Toronto Press, Toronto, 1986.

Winer, S. L. & D. Gauthier 1982. *Internal migration and fiscal structure: an econometric study of the determinants of inter-provincial migration in Canada*, Economic Council of Canada, Ottawa, 1982. See also their working paper, Supplement with Interprovincial Migration Data.

Wrage, P. 1981. The effects of internal migration on regional wage and unemployment disparities in Canada. *Journal of Regional Science* 21, 51–63.

Yap, L. 1976. Internal migration and economic development in Brazil. *Quarterly Journal of Economics* 90(1), 119–37.

PART IV
Experience in other countries

13

Some lessons and implications of the World Bank's experience in urban development

LLOYD RODWIN[1]

Even after a decade of activity (1972–82), formal urban lending of the World Bank barely exceeded 4% of total Bank loans (World Bank 1983, p. 2).[2] So in scale at any rate, these efforts do not amount to much in terms of Bank loans. This does not come as a surprise. What does, however, is that the Bank is operating in this field at all. When it was created in 1946, the Bank's immediate job was to finance the rebuilding of the war-ravaged economies of the more developed countries (MDCs). Still later – from the mid-1950s through the 1960s – its emphasis shifted to the promotion of growth and development, in particular the financing of the economic infrastructure of the Third World countries (TWCs) (Malson & Asher 1973, chs. 1 & 2). Only after 1972, when the worldwide issue of poverty and inequality aroused widespread concern, did the Bank begin to explore urban development as one of several ways to come to grips with these problems.

Understandably, after a decade of these efforts, the Bank has paused and reviewed what it has done. It has examined how and why these activities were initiated, the successes and failures to date, and its plans for the future (World Bank 1983). This self-assessment stands almost alone, for there have been almost no other studies of the Bank's urban development programs. The neglect is odd considering the influence of the Bank's activities on urban development policy in TWCs and the ways in which they mirror the concerns and trends, the concepts and methods – and, no doubt, some of the hopes and illusions – of our time.

My paper is a response to this neglect.² It explores the World Bank's urban program as a subsystem of one of the current international systems of aid, and, in particular, the Bank's evolving experiments in program planning, institutional learning, and the training of national bureaucracies. Then it reviews briefly what the Bank has done with regard to urban development, and to a lesser extent, regional development, and what the Bank thinks might be learned from these efforts. The final section looks at what the cities think, as well as some of the problems that loom ahead in trying to carry out the programs on a significant scale.

13.1 The system of international aid

In the existing international aid systems, most developing countries can get assistance for urban and regional development in two ways. They can negotiate bilateral agreements with the assistance agencies of the more affluent nations, or they can negotiate the terms of assistance with the World Bank or other multilateral agencies. Multilateral agencies function like a flexible federation. Goals are set; and various kinds of assistance, mainly loans, grants, and technical aid, are provided for members, subject to various conditions. Although the MDCs control the organization, the international agencies provide for TWC participation in their management; and their staff is drawn from TWCs as well as MDCs.

Under this system, nations – like local authorities in the United States – can opt not to participate. Officials of the international agencies are subject to many other pressures as well, including the need to show that significant service is being rendered or sought. In the functioning of this system, there is little reason to expect that the allocation of this aid would not often be influenced by political factors. To be sure, the reasons vary. In some cases, there may be concern about turbulence and instability; in others an effort to help "friends"; and in still others, to secure sources of supply, to reinforce defense arrangements, or to encourage cooperation for other purposes. But, more often than not, such political considerations tend to be more influential in bilateral rather than multilateral programs; and they are apt to involve agriculture, port and industrial development, the building of dams, or commodity and exchange agreements rather than assistance with urban and regional problems.³

Even if we make allowance for these factors, the urban and regional programs of the World Bank appear less subject to political manipulation for two reasons: first, unlike bilateral agencies, their policies and programs are not directly linked to the interests of particular donor countries; and, second, they are not subject to pressure for "tied aid" – for the purchase or use of the goods and services of the assisting country (Malson & Asher 1973, p. 19).

Another special circumstance is that until the early 1960s, the World Bank had no field offices; and although the number is now increasing, it is still small. The Bank's relatively centralized operations in Washington D.C. insulated it from certain client-oriented political pressures. This distance from the activities and programs being financed also limited the Bank's responsiveness, not to mention knowledge about conditions in the field. In part, this may explain why UN and AID favored urban and regional policies and programs for housing a decade or more before the World Bank.

Despite these differences, however, the views of UN, AID, and the Bank on urban matters in many ways converged. They veered in the same direction because these agencies found their staffs had to cope with the same problems and pressures for action. The World Bank and the other assistance agencies were unable, or perhaps were just unwilling, to continue sidestepping the persistent issues faced by high level officials in TWCs. These were, as we have noted, the problems of what to do about big cities, urban public services, urban finance, regional pressures, priorities for the location of infrastructure, national urban policy, urban management, or the best ways of training staffs, of creating new institutions, or of improving or redesigning them so that more of the things done to promote growth and development were likely to work and to be implementable on a national scale.

13.2 International learning and the training of national bureaucracies

In effect, the Bank is now functioning under the auspices of the more developed countries as one of several international planning and educational agencies for the bureaucracies of the poorer nations of the world. It has been called the "world's largest antipoverty agency" (Ayres 1983, p. 1).

One of the functions of this international bureaucracy is to advise how the bureaucracies of the participating TWCs might manage the development and, more recently, some of the economic welfare components of a modern state (Deutsch, n.d.); still another is to assess their performance. Many of the bureaucracies of the TWCs value or depend upon the technical assistance and review, and do not particularly resent it. Others will only accept tutelage grudgingly; some not at all.

The World Bank programs have evolved in several phases. First, they moved from the finance of economic infrastructure to social infrastructure. Then, as a result of a variety of studies and the monitoring of experience, institutional innovations were proposed, including new organizations and policies to implement programs. For example, the senior staff has serious reservations about public housing. They support instead public land programming or development, geared, if possible, to facilitate the incremental self-help efforts of low income households. They are also very cautious, if not dubious, about spatial strategies, but they strongly back measures to reform land tenure, to promote urban land management, to revise price policy for public services, and to handle urban finance, urban management, and even national urban policy. Currently, the Bank is also shifting emphasis from so called "retail" to "wholesale" functions – that is, from funding of individual projects to the promotion of national programs. The extensions reflect the World Bank's activist efforts to make their assistance less experimental and more significant.

The Bank's influence rests in large part, on the effectiveness of its 'if–then' incentives in providing capital. That is to say, as in federal systems, where the subnational units of government agree to certain conditions if national funds and/or assistance is provided to achieve certain outcomes, so, too, national and subnational agencies are accepting certain conditions of the Bank in order to obtain financial and technical assistance. However, the requests are not coming only from the national units; more often than one might suppose, they are being encouraged or induced by the Bank.

Of course, there are pressures for the Bank to produce successful outcomes and to ensure that there are reasonable returns on such investments. For the client states too, there are pressures to augment existing resources and assistance, preferably with the maximum permissible autonomy. The interests of the Bank and the client overlap, but they also differ; and the differences lead to sensitive negotiations on policies and standards. Examples are the emphasis to be placed on the public or private sectors, the channeling of funds to particular ministries or agencies, or the matching commitments in terms of local resources, financial and human.

Still other examples are the decisions whether to provide or to accept assistance and its scale. There is often an element of cajolery and bluff in the negotiations. The Bank can hold out the promise of more generous assistance, or threaten to withhold approval of the request for assistance; and the applicants may sometimes be reluctant to accept assistance on the stipulated terms, or may opt for the role of attractive "partners" if the terms are "right."

In the domain of urban lending, there are already strong efforts to produce changes in the system. Pressures are growing to raise the Bank's resource allocations for urban activities. The first studies have already been published documenting the relatively limited investments in shelter and urban services compared to the projected increases in the magnitude of the problems.[4]

There is also a strong inclination, internally and externally, to reduce or at least to transform the tutelage of the Bank as such. For example, the Economic Development Institute, the formal educational arm of the Bank, which used to bring technical staff from the TWCs for short-term training programs, is now arranging seminars and conferences between high-level staffs from countries with common problems so that they – and the Bank – might profit from each other's experience. To improve managerial performance, innovative studies are also being initiated of how the World Bank staff function when they are in the field, in order to understand better the customary procedures, behavior, assumptions, and values. Increasingly, also, the Bank – as well as other external assistance agencies – is persuaded that in the process of expanding and improving programs, more effort is necessary in each of the countries to develop techniques of analyzing manpower and training requirements and the design of indigenous or world regional training programs which over time might reduce as well as transform the character of outside assistance.

13.3 The nature of the urban and regional programs

As noted, in its initial urban and regional programs, neither the Bank (nor for that matter other multilateral or bilateral assistance programs) hoped to do more than spur significant demonstrations. Ideal investments, senior staff felt, should be high yield, low cost, and affordable by poor or moderate income families. They should tap private savings, involve a large amount of self-help and be self-sustaining. Even if the standards were initially low, they should be improvable, linkable with programs in other sectors, and ultimately carried out on a regional and national scale.

In the first decade, the emphasis was on sectoral programs – in the main shelter and transportation. These activities involved 66% of the total loans and 62% of the total urban project costs (World Bank 1983, p. 3 and ch. 4). Integrated urban development – linked citywide investment programs or multisectoral projects, and regional projects extending beyond individual cities – accounted for the rest.

Most of the programs were initiated in the poorest countries: in Africa (Senegal, Tunisia, Botswana, Kenya, Tanzania, and Zambia); in South and Southeast Asia (India and Indonesia) and in Latin America and the Caribbean (El Salvador, Nicaragua, and Jamaica) (World Bank 1983, pp. 14–18 and 508).

Two-thirds of the 38 projects approved in the first period (1972–6) were for programs providing, initially, "sites and services" in lieu of shelter, and later, the upgrading of the physical conditions of the shantytown settlements of the poor – the improvement of water supply, drainage, electricity, sanitation, footpaths, streets, and so on. These were the new approaches vying to replace the expensive subsidized public housing projects serving the less critical needs of higher-income families.

The other programs involved transport and integrated urban and regional development. The transport projects were quite limited: in fact, reduced to two or three a year, mainly in Brazil. They had several aims: to provide bus service and road access to zones where the poor lived; to improve traffic management in congested commercial areas; and to increase the ability of local officials to "appraise and execute project investments" (World Bank 1983, pp. 18–19).

The integrated urban and regional programs were more ambitious. Initiated in Calcutta, India, in Seoul, and the Kwangju region in Korea, they were intended to show effective ways of linking different programs: sites and services, water supply, transportation, employment, and the like.

Because of limited experience, approaches were supposed to be flexible. In principle, there was a willingness to adapt these programs to different traditions, administrative abilities, resource endowments, and other circumstances. Far from deterring Bank officials, the differences spurred them to monitor and evaluate projects and to finance studies of the experience of different types of countries with relevant housing, land, municipal finance, and national spatial and urban policies.

After a decade or more of activity, the Bank now has had a hand in the financing of more than 100 projects in different stages of operations. On the basis of this experience, the urban staff has persuaded the senior Bank management – and the officials of many TWCs – that there are feasible, more technologically appropriate alternatives to existing expensive public housing, transportation, and other infrastructure investments: alternatives that are affordable, improve the environment, and can serve the poor. For the most part, it appears that such programs can be self-financing, produce savings in foreign exchange, and avoid taking resources from the rural sector or from other institutions.

The Bank reports success stories, albeit not always unequivocal, in Brazil, Colombia, Ecuador, India, Indonesia, Jordan, Kenya, Korea, Mali, Mexico, Morocco, the Philippines, Tanzania, Thailand, Tunisia, and elsewhere. The economic returns are reported to be substantial, ranging from 14% to 38%. Urban transport projects had the best payoffs. But sites and services and area improvement programs are also highly regarded: the projects accommodate a substantial number of households (an average of 40,000); security of tenure is often achieved; a significant share of the funds reach persons directly below the poverty level; and the costs often are recovered either by direct charges or tax revenues (World Bank 1983, p. 40, ch. 5, and Tables 10–13).[5]

For the World Bank, these projects were innovative. But in 1972, when it first began to finance urban and regional projects, a decade or more had elapsed since other organizations such as AID and UN had developed somewhat comparable policies and programs. The actual ideas and experiments, especially the provision of sites and services, or the upgrading of existing housing settlements of the poor, had been explored earlier in a number of places – India, Puerto Rico, Peru, Venezuela, and elsewhere; and several of these experiences had been taken into account when the World Bank decided to move into the urban field.

With World Bank support, however, the main ideas are becoming – or indeed have become – the "new orthodoxy" for this component of urban development strategy in Third World countries. The Bank itself has increased by 1½ times the projects planned for the 1982–6 period compared with those financed in the previous decade – half with repeater projects expanding existing programs (World Bank 1983, pp. 49–50). The lending is also being extended to another 25 countries. The Bank's experience has enabled it to develop a long view of these processes, since it is now aware that the first projects do not function easily and that the problems – after the first year when enthusiasm and backing is at the peak – often get worse, until about the fourth year, after which there appears to be some improvement.[6]

As we shall soon note, there are many differences in views on the value of these activities; but before examining them, a final observation is in order about the ways they may grow. The odds are that, sooner or later, these financing opportunities might be extended by the Bank, or by Bank influenced organizations in the TWCs, to other activities, or additional ones beyond those already undertaken. Possible examples are resource-conserving efforts involving energy, water, land, and human resources. A program for potable water supply and sanitation might develop parallel to it prototypes in local water reuse, recycling, and pricing. Or a transport development program might be matched by programs evolving and expediting low-powered and human-powered vehicles. The same holds for either management training, or a variety of other training or idea-exchange programs, linked to existing agencies or educational institutions providing extension services.

13.4 Why the Bank changed its views in urban policies and programs

The Bank's explanation for the shifts of policies and programs was that the financing of economic infrastructure and directly productive activities were not benefitting the poor – or at any rate, not significantly and not quickly enough. Robert MacNamara, in 1973, shortly after he became President of the Bank, proposed to help the poor more directly as well as provide increased assurance that subsidized urban programs would be less apt to drain resources from rural areas (MacNamara 1973). As the implications of his ideas were explored, new departments or emphases emerged in the Bank to promote a broader concept of urban projects (1972), of agricultural and rural development (1973), and of projects dealing with population, health, and nutrition (1979).

Soon thereafter, Bank studies began to attach more importance to the fact that the processes and indeed the successes of economic development were generating an increasingly stressful urban expansion (World Bank 1972): a projected growth of more than 150% of the world's urban population by the year 2000; a tripling or quadrupling of the urban dwellers in the poorer regions of the world; and demanding and often turbulent pressures for infrastructure – not just roads, water, sewage facilities, and electricity, but housing, schools, and health services. A large proportion of the public capital available for investment, and quite substantial subsidies, were being channeled into these investments (World Bank 1983, pp. 1, 3). That fact troubled many top officials; there were increasing misgivings about where and when these infrastructure investments should be made and the groups that should be served by them. There was also the suspicion that much of the actual needs – given realistic standards – might be funded by the urban sector on an affordable basis.

The World Bank's inattention to these matters before the 1970s gave it little leverage for spurring change. Almost the contrary, in fact: for its help to TWCs for directly productive investments made it all the more feasible for TWC officials to use their own funds to meet some of the infrastructure investment pressures which, unlike the Bank, they felt less able to ignore.[7]

In other words, the choice over time turned out to be less between "social" investments and "productive" investments – for the former were complementary to the latter – and more the question of whether – and if so how – the World Bank could influence the social investments. The staff concluded that they could do so. This would be by promoting projects to demonstrate ways of financing urban infrastructure and services largely with private savings. The necessary conditions were that the investments would be properly planned and managed, with favorable rates of return, and based on realistic standards so that they might be put into effect on a national scale. Still other positive effects were anticipated – to the extent that decision-making processes and institutional capabilities for dealing with these and related problems could be improved. That at any rate was the justification advanced on behalf of the switch in emphasis.

These altered views reflected a worldwide change in the climate of opinion. Behind it lay many concerns. One, of course, involved the conditions of health and the prospect of breakdowns in the provision of essential public services in the big cities, especially the capital cities. There was, also, the more specific repugnance of the well-to-do and the governing groups in the client countries with the depressing physical conditions – attitudes shared by the visiting international bureaucrats and technical advisers. Still other factors reinforced these attitudes: for example, the earlier efforts along these lines by the bilateral assistance programs; in addition, the urban improvement programs designed to remedy much better urban conditions in the more developed countries; the continuing requests by the client countries for help in coping with these problems; and the fact that some 50% or more of GNP originated in cities – in large measure because cities provided the indispensable infrastructure required by the economic activities located there.

13.5 Learning by doing?

Shelter policies and national spatial strategies in relation to urbanization patterns and trends provide two examples of how these issues were reinterpreted. With regard to shelter, there was agreement on two items: the utter inadequacy of the public investments for traditional public housing, which as a rule did not serve the poor; and the need to adjust future housing standards to affordability. The harsh facts were that most of the households were already obliged to fend for themselves and that substantial improvements were possible by having public policy not impede these efforts but encourage and extend them.

As for spatial strategies, the great concern was how to redress the balance between rural poverty, lagging or undeveloped regions, unequal distribution of income, and the inordinate expansion of the mega cities. Admittedly congested, costly and hard to manage, the mega cities both evidenced and contributed to the imbalance of income, public services, and patterns of regional growth. But explicit spatial strategies favoring rural development and/or intermediate-size cities as ways of coping with these problems turned out to have serious limitations (Richardson 1977, Renaud 1979). Aside from the inability to identify optimum urban sizes or patterns and the well-known ineffectiveness of controls, there were the hazards of formulating general rules for developing countries without taking adequate account of their levels of income or of their institutional and administrative constraints. In addition, there were the political pressures to disperse infrastructure and other investments regardless of growth potential; the difficulties of ensuring firm commitments to the policies for a long enough period to make them effective; the sheer administrative complexities inherent in multisectoral programs; and the countervailing, indirect, hard-to-influence spatial effects of other sectoral and macroeconomic policies.

Given these complications as well as the long-term and the uncertain outcomes of explicit spatial strategies, only a small number of regional projects were approved (two in Korea and one in Mexico by 1982, and another in Turkey in 1985); and, in the main, the emphasis in these projects by the World Bank was not on efforts to achieve a theoretical or even a pragmatic balance of income or level of development between regions. Instead the main focus was on the region's comparative advantage and development potential. The Bank's advisers also favored programs providing assistance for small and intermediate-size cities serving as processing centers or handling procurement, marketing, and servicing functions for the surrounding rural hinterland.

Loathe to back regional projects unless the prospects of success were substantial, the Bank staff reemphasized the advantages of the mega cities and ways of making them more manageable as well as more efficient. They also jousted against the indirect, often unintended, policy bias in TWCs which, it was believed, increased significantly and unjustifiably the advantages of the large cities.[8] Thus they pressed for the elimination or reduction of urban price controls on food and energy; for the reduction, if not the elimination, of subsidies for urban infrastructure; and for reduction of the concentration of administrative power and decision-making in the capital cities. But, unfortunately, these preferred policy options were also extraordinarily difficult to implement.

Most of these ideas and the pressures to support them came initially from outside the World Bank. The Bank thought its contribution was to explore, to adapt, and to try them out. By financing such programs, particularly those designed to serve the poor, and by monitoring the impact on the poor of these and other Bank activities affecting urban areas, the officials hoped to demonstrate the opportunities as well as risks of these programs and the diverse ways of promoting them.

Interpreted in retrospect in relation to the learning process, in the first phase key Bank officials concluded that financing shelter and urban settlement programs did not immediately or necessarily benefit the poorer segments of the population; and, in the second phase, these officials perceived that many of the client government's policies in the realms of shelter and settlement policy were questionable, inadequate, nonreplicable, and grossly inconsistent with the aims of the Bank. Coupling these insights made it easier for Bank officials to experience a *Gestalt* shift in perspective, and to see that the migrant shantytowns and the mega cities which appeared to be the problem, might also be, with some reasonable guidance, if not *the* solution, then a part, perhaps even a significant part, of the solution.

From this point of view, it may be somewhat misleading to stress, as the Bank's staff does, that its urban program involved in the main deliberate "learning by doing" (World Bank 1983, chs. 3 & 5). This rhetoric omits the factors that influenced the things to do. There was really a more complex sequence: first, learning by failing, learning by misunderstanding, and "cognitive dissonance"; then a second phase of reformulating the problem, of altering goals and criteria and, hopefully, making them more specific and relevant; next, a search for solutions (some not new but developed by others); and then a process of testing and adapting these solutions to serve the reformulated aims.

13.6 Ideological and pragmatic critiques

So much for how the Bank's urban programs are seen from the Bank's official perspective. But, as might be expected, there are many persons who scorn these efforts. The critiques have come in the main from two sources. There was the ideological opposition – the right wing hostile to the very existence of the Bank, the left wing skeptical of the Bank's constraints and motivations. There were also the pragmatic reformers – both right and left – anxious to make the programs more effective.

The ideological critics on the right (Bauer 1981, chs. 4 & 5) argued that the investments would prove questionable since capital for productive enterprises could be gotten from existing financial institutions. They predicted high opportunity costs, with the transfer of resources from more efficient to less efficient activities; and the formation of coalitions of TWCs to articulate and intensify the pressures for still more assistance. There was concern, also, that the efforts would often support wasteful and even tyrannical governments. Not least was the warning that the bulk of the assistance would probably not reach the poor in these countries; and that, in the end, the programs would not assuage the "false" assumption of guilt stemming from unease with a heritage of imperialism or exploitation.

On the left, the ideological critics split into two main groups. There were those who were suspicious of power, of large organizations, of the state, and of the forces favoring large programs, legality, and similar measures that would decrease flexibility and increase costs.

There were also the views of the more traditional leftists, who looked at the Bank as the chosen instrument of the more developed countries to help the international economic system function and to serve the needs of the groups in power in the TWCs as well as the MDCs. After all, the Bank's goals and rules were under the control of a governing board representing the different participating countries, roughly in proportion to their capital contributions and their political clout in world affairs. Even in circumstances when the bulk of the World Bank loans and assistance went to the poorest countries, as was the case with projects in the urban field, on the basis of dollar volume the middle income TWCs were the main beneficiaries. What is more, the proportion, some 4%, was paltry. This outcome, of course, is not unexpected from the point of view of these critics.

The reformer's concern was to make the policies and programs more "realistic" or more "effective." For example, the right-wing pragmatists wanted to get rid of expensive public housing and of ambitious and costly spatial development strategies. Site and service programs, upgrading, making the mega cities manageable, served these aims and promoted the private sector.

Left-of-center pragmatists, on the other hand, wanted the programs to go beyond rhetoric. They scoffed at several things: the amount of capital resources allocated or available for demonstrations of how to organize and manage urban programs; the snail-like pace and the uncertainty of even minor institutional reforms, such as the introduction of cost-recovery pricing policies; the delays in establishing cadastral systems, and in improving the production of local building materials and industries.[9] They underlined, too, the reluctance to modernize land and improvement taxes, and to adopt measures sharing the increases of value produced in large measure by the public infrastructure investments. One of their deepest concerns was the fear that the successes achieved to date would prove trivial if the policies and programs were not carried out on a significant scale without external assistance. That won't come easily, say Bank officials, because the main snags in expansion are the institutional hurdles: reforming land tenure; recasting standards of housing and services; obstacles in ensuring cost recovery; dilemmas of community participation and politics; and the sheer lack of trained staff and of efficient management. Add to all of this the lack of funds, staff and power of most local authorities, and the pressures as well as the traditions of centralization and national sovereignty.

13.7 Organizational behavior and implementation

In addition, other necessary and well-intentioned features of the Bank's operations have created special difficulties. Take, for example, the terms for obtaining assistance and the monitoring of how the funds are used. These conditions, reasonable as they may seem, are not easily satisfied by the TWCs. Delays ensue and strains develop. The problems are aggravated in circumstances where the funds have to be put to work promptly and where the international bureaucracy has limited confidence in the ability of the client states, or of their national or subnational agencies, to do what needs to be done: that is, to formulate implementable proposals and the necessary justifications; and to assure fairly responsible and noncorrupt administration. These concerns led to the creation or extension of the supervisory and tutelage functions. These functions are deemed necessary even before the proposals are submitted as well as after they are approved. For example, the Bank understandably insists on pre-investment and feasibility studies prior to the formal submission of project proposals.

Before final decisions are made, there must also be acceptable cost analyses and justifications on the basis of diverse technical criteria. These involve affordability, poverty impact, training and employment effects, institutional strengthening or innovation, and the relative merits of projects, as indicated, for example, by rates of return, and evaluations of project feasibility and prospects of implementation. The weight to be assigned to these criteria, and therefore the importance of different programs, have often led to strong divisions within the Bank's staff.

In addition, the Bank's representatives favored decentralized administration, efficient agencies and administrators, and specific types of organizations noted for their relative insulation from politics: autonomous agencies, action agencies controlling capital budgets or public works, and "mixed" enterprises. There was a preference, too, for highly visible, if not always large, projects; and, sooner or later, there was a disposition to explore how the emphasis might be shifted from individual projects to program loans to accommodate clusters of related activities. This depended on whether there was satisfactory performance, reliable monitoring by local institutions, and, when appropriate, a sequence of more or less successfully completed scheduled programs.

Some critics dub these conditions "dependency", whereas the international bureaucracies say they will minimize political meddling, facilitate training and learning, and ensure the soundness of the enterprise. Both views may be correct. But some people, Judith Tendler for example, take comfort in the fact that it is more a technical effort, perhaps correctable – not an imperialistic imperative: the aims being to achieve the kind of information, power or minimum control most organizations desire in order to cope more effectively with an uncertain and in many ways a precarious "task environment" (Tendler 1975, chs. 4 & 8).

Lisa Peattie has sensitized us to still other unanticipated and not altogether desirable consequences of efforts by the Bank to make these programs work (Peattie 1982). In contrast to the autonomous building of shantytowns by the poor, the administration of sites and service programs, even by sympathetic authorities, raises problems and costs. So do rules about initial down payments, even of very modest sums. The requirement of regular payments eliminates the families with casual employment and unsteady income. In addition, large-scale projects shift the developments to outer areas; and rationalization of building processes tend to favor large, single contractors and the use of more expensive and perhaps even less appropriate materials. Also, standardization of lot sizes, rules about resale, and inflexibility in the timing and character of public services (water, sanitation, electricity, paving, and the like) limit the variety of solutions appropriate for diverse households with vastly different needs. All these changes tend to eliminate households from the program, foster more homogeneous development, and add to the problems of the unserved poorer families dependent for their income and other forms of help on providing services for the more successful families. Actually much progress has occurred on these matters – for example, in the greater use of small subcontractors, in diversifying lot size, and increasing the flexibility of rules of resale. But the trade-offs in costs and relative inflexibility in return for institutional support are still significant and hard to eliminate.

Still other difficulties grew out of the effort to ensure the maximum effect for a given investment of resources. This drive led to a search for critical linkages, complementarities, and leverage points for interrelated or more comprehensive policies and programs rather than self-contained projects; and these efforts, in turn, spurred intersectoral and multilevel integration and sometimes centralization. For example, the senior Bank management concluded that strengthening of the economy and employment creation strategies were more effectively dealt with at national and regional levels, but not at the local level (World Bank 1983, ch. 2, p. 23). Similarly, a water project in Lahore, Pakistan, produced pressures for an urban investment plan providing information about the future population rate of growth and spatial development in the city. On the national level, programming of water projects in Indonesia led to pressure on the Ministry of Public Works to produce or promote a national urban policy (Rodwin 1980). The World Bank – the financer of action projects around the world – for its own protection became also the financer of comprehensive studies and plans that might lead to more reliable decisions.

Unfortunately, most of the experience with planning in the MDCs over the past two decades has reinforced the shift of a significant segment of professional opinion away from comprehensive land use planning to ad hoc incremental planning. It has proved difficult, and in most situations impossible, to make comprehensive land use planning work in the MDCs. Administrative capability and power were too limited and there were many quasi-independent powerful organizations and groups with their own goals and priorities (Rodwin 1981). The experience in the TWCs was no different on this score; and the limitations applied all the more to the "sophisticated" analytical models which might support these efforts (Mohan 1979).

However, ad hoc incremental programs based on appraisal and justification of individual projects often produced absurd outcomes: mind-boggling traffic congestion; ports, bridges, and industrial areas without complementary infrastructure, or shelter without water or other public services and too far away from sources of employment. The failings were frustrating and costly: they hobbled development, even though on occasion they proved self-correcting.

So there was a search for something short of comprehensive land use planning and beyond ad hoc sectoral planning. The need was for some way of pragmatically reconciling the two. This was a widespread problem in many countries, and the Bank's staff rediscovered it anew. Their compromise was to distinguish integrated from comprehensive planning. Although the integration was intended to improve linkages between the more important elements of multisectoral programs, the major emphasis was only on one or two of these sectors (World Bank 1983, pp. 19–20). When successful, especially in improving the capacity of the development authority to dovetail economic, financial, and physical planning, or to manage several interrelated programs, as appears to have been the case in Calcutta, the payoff is attractive. But the management of such enterprises is complicated, time consuming, and hazardous. It is anything but easy to reconcile the needs and pressures of diverse, articulate, and often powerful agencies and interest groups with the intricate requirements of "integrated" plan-making processes. The degree of cooperation and consensus necessary make success feasible only in particular environments and historical settings: in short, more likely in atypical circumstances rather than the less felicitous settings characteristic of most TWCs.

13.8 Concluding observations on growth theory and World Bank practice

In support of their urban policies, the World Bank staff could argue that no one knows when the big city is too big or simply badly organized and managed; and they were loathe either to see the big cities subsidized or to help opponents conduct skirmishes against them. In any case, if their programs were to succeed, they had to yield reasonable returns. What is more, since the Bank's perspectives were relatively short term, their programs also had to be swift paced: this despite limited theory and experience, not to mention the need to observe collaborative proprieties.

The Bank's activities presupposed that the lessons of this assistance would over time help to create self-sustaining development. But this development was not likely as long as the ventures – ranging from shelter and infrastructure to land management, public services, and integrated programs were ad hoc and more in the nature of experiments and "pilot" efforts. At some profit, however, a decision had to be made on whether what had been done and learned could be turned into durable, national programs.

Ultimate success required more than a resolve of national decision makers to expand these programs. Recognizing this fact, Bank officials concluded that the critical problems of the future were management and institutional change. These notions, however, tend to oversimplify. The changes necessary involve more than simple techniques which can be taught, or the implementation of not-so-simple adaptations of institutions, or institutional innovations. Something else is needed – something which we do not quite understand and which requires much more insight than is provided by our present theories and analytical techniques.

Two of the papers presented here – those of Hansen (1978) and Alonso (1987), authors with different analytical orientations and policy inclinations – point to this serious limitation.

Niles Hansen, presenting a shrewd assessment once again of the prospects of small and intermediate-size cities, observes that the large metropolitan areas with external economies of agglomeration, "the places where development-inducing innovations [were] most likely to be adopted, are in fact ... [now] losing population and economic activity as a result of many market forces, particularly the cumulative effects of technological change"; but he suggests that small and medium-size cities while no longer condemned to mere "lower order" central places ... require *"sufficient indigenous adaptability* [my emphasis] ... to take advantage of these opportunities as well as *internal dynamism* [my emphasis] based on regional social, technical, organizational, and industrial structures and their adaptation to a changing national and international division of labor" (Hansen 1985).

But what is meant by "indigenous adaptability" and "internal dynamism"? How can these traits be generated and sustained? And will the improvements now favored by the World Bank in management training and institutional adaptation or innovation make this happen? We really do not know.

Entirely independently – that is, with no special focus on Hansen's ambiguities – Professor Alonso suggests that the big uncertainties surrounding urban and regional development will not be resolved by our positivistic, Alfred Weber-type ways of coming to grips with problems. Those methods, he suggests, may tell us a good deal about questions of location and growth, but they are silent on how to unleash the energies of cities and regions and thereby promote and sustain durable social and technical innovations and development (Alonso 1985). Some additional approach, he suggests, more qualitative perhaps, albeit empirically rigorous, may be needed to disclose what we need to know. What this might be, however, he is unable to say.

That is all the more the pity because the Bank finds itself now at the threshold of this most perplexing issue. It has shown in a reasonably orthodox fashion that we can deal institutionally with small, manageable problems. This is no small accomplishment; but neither is it a great one. The critical test lies ahead: it is whether training in management, changes in administrative processes, and the creation of new institutions can ensure (not simply reflect) long-term and self-sustaining programs on a national scale.

This is the same question that faces the Canadian Atlantic towns. That some of these small and medium–size cities may be potential centers for some of the relocated economic activities of the more footloose, decentralized economy which appears to be evolving in the future is one thing; but the probability that they would be is another. In between (for the policy- and decision-maker) is the gap of what needs to be known and done to invigorate energies and create innovators and entrepreneurs.

Whether scholars can produce these insights is anyone's guess. Meanwhile, candor obliges us to confess our present inability, as yet, to spell out many of the necessary, let alone the sufficient conditions to produce the desired transformation.

Notes

1 This paper is more accurate and in some respects different because of suggestions made by Michael Cohen. He is not responsible, of course, for any remaining errors or inadequacies.
2 The World Bank provided approximately two-thirds of the non-concessional aid of the multilateral agencies (OECD 1983, pp. 95–100 and Table C-1, p. 214). According to the only study currently available (Donelson et al., n.d.), the loan commitment for urbanization (sites and services, slum upgrading, housing, urban development, and urban transport) of multilateral agencies averages about 2.2% of total loans.
3 Aside from these influences, it is possible that the MDCs which contribute most to the multilateral organizations obtain the bulk of the contracts of the multilateral agencies.
4 See for example Donelson et al. (n.d.), and other studies on this subject by the International Institute for Environment and Development.
5 See also Keare and Parris (1982), and Churchill (1979). Cost recovery is still one of the more difficult problems to solve.
6 In the fourth year, the Bank reports that 32% of the projects (22 out of 62) had no problems, 55% (down from 73% in the third year) had moderate problems, and 13% (up from 10% in the third year) had major problems. World Bank (1983, p. 29, Table 6).
7 "The availability of foreign assistance, in sum, has caused the borrower country to quite rationally switch around its priorities and increase the foreign exchange component of its public sector investments in order to get more investment out of the same amount of domestic revenue" (Tendler 1975, p. 83).
8 Professor Remy Prud'homme (University of Paris, Cretail) has told me that recent studies he and his colleagues made in Casablanca and elsewhere indicate that large cities contribute disproportionately to the cost of infrastructure and other investments in small and intermediate-size cities and rural areas, and that he now believes the bias may not be in favor of the smaller communities and rural areas.
9 This problem is often made worse by the financing of the foreign exchange components of projects creating excess reliance on foreign materials. This is "because it is politically cheaper to repay or reschedule payments on loans than make the necessary changes in the tax and land holding structure which would obviate or reduce the need for foreign assistance" (Donelson et al., n.d., p. 72). For a more extended discussion of the problem, see Tendler (1975, ch. 21).

References

Alonso, W. 1987. Population and regional development. In *Regional economic development*, B. Higgins & D. J. Savoie (eds.), 131–41. London: Allen & Unwin.
Ayres, R. L. 1983. *Banking on the poor*. Cambridge and London: MIT Press.
Bauer, P. A. 1981. *Equality, the Third World and economic delusion*. Cambridge, Mass.: Harvard University Press.
Churchill, A. A. 1979. Basic needs in shelter. Washington, D.C.: World Bank. Mimeo.

Deutsch, K. [n.d.]. From the national welfare state to the international welfare state. Berlin: International Institute for Comparative Social Research.

Donelson, S., J. E. Hardoy & S. Schkolnik [n.d.]. Aid for human settlements in the Third World: a summary of the activities of multilateral agencies. London: International Institute for Environment and Development.

Hansen, N. 1987. Small and medium-size cities in development. In *Regional economic development*, B. Higgins & D. J. Savoie (eds.), 318–29. London: Allen & Unwin.

Keare, D. H. & S. Parris 1982. *Evaluation of shelter programs for the urban poor: principal findings*. World Bank, Urban and Regional Report no. 81–25.

MacNamara, R. 1973. Address to the Board of Governors. (24 September, Nairobi, Kenya).

Malson, E. S. & R. E. Asher 1973. *The World Bank since Bretton Woods*. Washington, D.C.: The Brookings Institution.

Mohan, R. 1979. *Urban economic and planning models: assessing the potential for cities in developing countries*. Baltimore, M.D.: The Johns Hopkins University Press.

Organization for Economic Cooperation and Development (OECD) 1983. *Development cooperation – 1983 review*. Paris: OECD.

OECD 1984. *Development cooperation – 1984 review*. Paris: OECD.

Peattie, L. 1982. Some second thoughts on sites and services. *Habitat* 6(1–2), 131–9.

Renaud, B. 1979. *National urbanization policies in developing countries*. World Bank Staff Working Paper no. 347. Washington, D.C.: The International Bank for Reconstruction and Development.

Richardson, H. W. 1977. *City size and national spatial strategies in developing countries*. World Bank Staff Working Paper no. 252. Washington, D.C.: The International Bank for Reconstruction and Development.

Rodwin, L. 1980. Urban development policy. United Nations Development Programme, Project Document, INS/78/059/A/01. Jakarta, Indonesia: United Nations.

Rodwin, L. 1981. *Cities and city planning*. New York: Plenum Publishing.

Tendler, J. 1975. *Inside foreign aid*. Baltimore, M.D.: The Johns Hopkins University Press.

World Bank 1972. Urbanization sector working paper (June). Washington, D.C.: The International Bank for Reconstruction and Development.

World Bank 1983. *Learning by doing: World Bank lending for urban development 1972–1982*. Washington, D.C.: The International Bank for Reconstruction and Development.

14

Small and medium-size cities in development

NILES HANSEN

The roles that small and medium-size cities may play in regional development processes and strategies depend on the context in which they are being considered. As pointed out in the section that follows, city size does not necessarily provide a good indication of the functions a city performs. The latter depend in great part on the geographic setting of cities in relation to the larger urban system of which they are a part. However, mere descriptions of the functions cities perform do not necessarily shed much light on larger issues concerning development processes. During the 1960s and early 1970s, it was common to analyze spatial development processes in terms of a hierarchical spatial diffusion of innovations. In this paper, a brief presentation of the policy implications of this orientation is followed by evidence suggesting that this hierarchical diffusion paradigm has lost much of its validity, at least with respect to more economically developed countries. The final section discusses some implications of the newly emerging spatial division of labor, with particular emphasis on consequences for small and medium-size cities.

14.1 City size and city functions: the static setting

A small city in a megalopolitan setting may be primarily a residential area with relatively few economic functions, though its inhabitants may have easy access to a wide range of employment and shopping opportunities in a large nearby city. In contrast, a small city in a sparsely settled area may have few such opportunities. Nevertheless, some small cities in non-metropolitan areas – for example, tourism and recreation centers – may possess a wide range of high-quality goods and services. In yet other instances, small cities may be major regional service and employment centers. For example, in the mid-1970s, the US Department of Commerce divided the United States into 183 relatively small-contained functional economic areas, each having an urban core and an associated hinterland. In principle, the urban cores were metropolitan areas – that is, urban concentrations with respective central cities of at least 50,000 population. However, because much of the Great Plains lacks metropolitan areas, it was necessary to choose smaller core cities for functional economic areas. These included such cities as Salina, Kansas (1975 population: 38,960); Grand Island, Nebraska (33,304); Rapid City, South Dakota (48,156); Bismark, North Dakota (38,378); and Minot, North Dakota (32,790). Despite their small populations, these cities performed central functions for functional economic areas that were larger in size (in some cases, equivalent to half a state) than the national average. Finally, as will be discussed, relatively recent decentralization tendencies have been expanding the functions performed by many small and medium-size cities that were once primarily dependent on a rural-agricultural economic base.

14.2 City size and city functions: the hierarchical diffusion paradigm

During the 1960s and early 1970s, many countries adopted policy measures designed to achieve more "balanced growth," a somewhat vague objective which nonetheless implied a more geographically equitable allocation of resources. Typically this involved subsidies to promote the decentralization of population and economic activities from large metropolitan areas in favor of regions, often relatively rural in character, that were lagging economically. Strategies in this regard gave a prominent role to small and medium-size cities in the context, sometimes explicit and sometimes implicit, of the hierarchical spatial diffusion paradigm. The latter essentially takes the classical central place network of Christaller (1933) as a kind of locational matrix or landscape within which development-inducing innovations diffuse through time and over space from higher-order centers (large metropolitan areas) to lower-order places. The induced development of small and medium-size cities could thus be viewed as a "filling-in" of the urban hierarchy so that diffusion could take place more rapidly and over larger geographic areas. More specifically, within this framework, small and medium-size cities could perform three functions. First, their own development would in itself represent decentralization. Second, their development would result in spread, or trickle-down, effects that would benefit their respective hinterlands. Finally, their increased ability to retain population and attract migrants would make them counter-magnets to the further expansion of large metropolitan areas.

As will be discussed in more detail, the decentralization objectives just outlined here have tended to be realized in many developed countries. However, the reasons have had more to do with spontaneous factors than with government decentralization policies, which typically were tentative in terms of the resources made available as well as commitments to specific strategies. In addition, the hierarchical diffusion model, as it applies to developed countries, has been shown to rest on weak theoretical and empirical foundations. Von Boventer (1973), for example, has convincingly argued on theoretical grounds that particular rank-size distribution parameters with respect to urban hierarchies are no help in national planning decision processes, and that satisfactory economic growth and the personal well-being of a country's citizens are compatible with a wide range of differences in the degree of spatial concentration of population and economic activity. Pred's (1977) studies of the diffusion of growth-inducing innovations that affect city system development indicate that the intricate web of economic interdependence contradicts central place hierarchy depictions of city systems. Growth-inducing linkages run not only from large cities to smaller cities, but also from large cities to even larger cities, from smaller to larger cities, and between cities of comparable size. And the most important non-local linkages are not those between a city and its hinterland, but rather those between cities.

In a related vein, a key tenet of the hierarchical diffusion model is that large metropolitan areas are the places where development-inducing innovations are most likely to be adopted. Moreover, in the 1960s and early 1970s there was a clear consensus among urban economists that the external economies of agglomeration generated by large metropolitan areas made them the most efficient locations for a wide range of manufacturing and service activities. Although such areas might also generate external diseconomies, the net social product associated with further population growth was likely to be greater than it would be in alternative locations. Thus, policies designed to curb the growth of large cities would be inconsistent with efficient spatial resource allocation. The favorable view of large cities was buttressed by the results of empirical research suggesting that productivity increases with urban size. For example, Sveikauskas (1975) found that wages in manufacturing increased by about 5% with each doubling of metropolitan population, and that productivity in manufacturing was 6% greater in a metropolitan area of 2 million population than in one of 1 million population. Segal (1976) similarly found that metropolitan areas of 2 million population and larger had a return to factors that was 8% higher than in other metropolitan areas, a result he attributed to agglomeration economies that more than offset congestion costs.

Yet even while the advantages of large urban size were being "confirmed" by expert theory and research, many large US metropolitan areas were in fact losing population and economic activity as a result of market forces. Employment declines were especially evident in the manufacturing sectors of major northern industrial centers. The data in Table 14.1 indicate that between 1970 and 1980, northern metropolitan areas with over 2.5 million population, as a group, experienced absolute population decline. Northern metropolitan areas in the 1–2.5 million population-size class had a growth rate less than one-third the national average during this period. For the United States as a whole, the overall average annual metropolitan growth rate was 1.00% between 1970 and 1980, well below the corresponding non-metropolitan rate of 1.34%. Nor was this a peculiarly American phenomenon. Evidence indicated that similar tendencies were being experienced in many European countries (Berg et al. 1982; Hall & Hay 1980; Vining & Pallone 1982).

As evidence became increasingly available that all was not well with many large metropolitan areas, a major shift of emphasis occurred in the relevant scholarly literature. For example, Moomaw (1981) reinterpreted the empirical studies by Sveikauskas and by Segal to show that both had exaggerated the productivity advantages of large cities. Hoch (1976) argued that the benefits of large city size seemed to be outweighed by the costs. The higher per capita incomes observed in large cities represent a wage premium that must be paid to compensate workers for higher living costs and net disamenities in large cities. In more broadly regional terms, by the late 1970s there was a large and growing literature contrasting an inevitably rising sunbelt and a declining frostbelt, which had previously been regarded as the industrial heartland of the United States. Although many studies in this regard exaggerated sunbelt-frostbelt differences or overlooked the considerable heterogeneity within these broad regions, it was nonetheless evident that a great deal of fundamental regional restructuring was taking place.

Various explanations have been given for the relatively recent changes in the spatial division of labor. In the US context they have included improved transportation and communications accessibility, changing life styles, weather differences, air-conditioning, a growing number of footloose retirees, changing energy relationships, differing "business climates," and regional differences in federal taxation and spending

Table 14.1 Population change by region and by size of metropolitan area.

	United States				North				South and West			
	Population (thousands)		Annual average % change		Population (thousands)		Annual average % change		Population (thousands)		Annual average % change	
	Total 1982	Change 1980–82	1980–82	1970–80	Total 1982	Change 1980–82	1980–82	1970–80	Total 1982	Change 1980–82	1980–82	1970–80
Total	231,663	5,117	0.99	1.08	108,266	265	0.11	0.22	123,396	4,851	1.78	1.94
Metropolitan	176,207	4,089	1.04	1.00	85,287	177	0.09	0.08	90,920	3,912	1.95	2.00
over 5 million	47,772	683	0.64	0.33	29,863	98	0.15	−0.20	17,909	585	1.48	1.32
2.5–5 million	23,838	661	1.25	1.01	11,107	−143	−0.57	−0.22	12,731	804	2.90	2.33
1–2.5 million	36,182	955	1.19	1.15	16,129	89	0.25	0.07	20,053	866	1.96	2.15
500,000–1 million	26,609	642	1.08	1.20	11,535	49	0.19	0.26	15,074	593	1.78	2.02
250,000–500,000	20,684	544	1.18	1.50	8,577	50	0.26	0.69	12,107	494	1.85	2.13
100,000–250,000	18,875	517	1.23	1.63	7,109	23	0.14	0.65	11,766	495	1.91	2.31
less than 100,000	2,247	87	1.75	1.43	967	10	0.48	0.92	1,281	76	2.74	1.86
nonmetropolitan	55,456	1,027	0.83	1.34	22,979	88	0.17	0.77	32,477	939	1.30	1.79
counties with more than 15% commuting to metropolitan cores (261 counties)	5,577	118	0.95	1.72	2,530	10	0.18	1.21	3,048	108	1.61	2.18

Source: US Department of Commerce (1984).

policies. Evaluation of the relative importance of these factors is beyond our scope here, but it does seem clear that the hierarchical diffusion paradigm, whatever its validity in the past, does not provide an adequate frame of reference for analyzing current changes in the distribution of population and economic activities. Before giving further attention to the significance of recent spatial–temporal development processes, it is necessary to examine the evolution of small and medium-size cities more closely.

14.3 Patterns of urban change

The absolute population declines experienced by numerous large US metropolitan areas in the 1970s suggested to some observers that "counterurbanization has replaced urbanization as the dominant force shaping the nation's settlement patterns" (Berry 1978, p. 42). The data in Table 14.1 do not support this contention. It is true that all population-size classes or northern metropolitan areas either declined in population or grew less rapidly than the national rate of population increase. However, northern non-metropolitan areas also grew less rapidly than did the national population. In contrast, in the South and West all size classes of metropolitan areas grew more rapidly than did the national population; and metropolitan areas as a whole grew more rapidly than non-metropolitan areas. The highest rate of population increase in the South and West was in fact registered in large metropolitan areas in the 2.5–5 million class.

Considering the United States as a whole, the most rapid rates of population growth between 1970 and 1980 were in small and medium-size metropolitan areas (those in the three metropolitan classes below the 500,000 population level), and in non-metropolitan areas with relatively high commuting rates to metropolitan cores.

Data for the 1980–2 period indicate that nationally metropolitan areas were again growing more rapidly than non-metropolitan areas, but this was largely attributable to rapid metropolitan growth in the South and West, which accounted for 96% of US metropolitan growth. In the South and West, the average annual growth rate in each of the three metropolitan size-classes below 500,000 population exceeded the overall growth rate of 1.78%. However, it would be imprudent to draw firm conclusions from so short a period, especially since the fact that it was a time of marked economic recession could make it untypical.

A study of 35 comparable metropolitan regions in 12 European countries and Japan found that there was an inverse relationship between the rate of population growth and urban size (Korcelli 1982). In the mid-1970s, 13 of these regions were experiencing absolute population decline; the number was projected to increase to 21 by the year 2020. During the 1970s, traditional rural-to-urban migration streams became largely reoriented toward smaller cities and peripheral regions. The higher growth rates observed in the smaller metropolitan areas resulted from migration from still smaller urban and rural communities, rather than from moves away from the larger metropolitan regions.

The case of France is particularly interesting because of the remarkable reversal of regional development patterns in recent years (Aydalot 1984). The higher-ranking regions in terms of total employment change between 1968 and 1975 were the lower-ranking regions in terms of total employment change between 1975 and 1981. For 15 out of 21 regions, the change in rank was at least eight ranks. The eight regions where the rate of employment growth increased between the two periods were precisely those that had been regarded as the least well off economically: Brittany, Lower Normandy, and six regions in the Southwest. With certain exceptions in the Paris suburbs, newer high technology activities have been locating in the South, in small and medium-size cities (such as Aix, Toulouse, Grenoble, Montpellier, La Gaude, Antibes), that previously had little industry.

14.4 Technology and decentralization

What accounts for the decentralization tendencies that are occurring in so many industrialized nations? A number of possible factors have already been mentioned in the context of the US sunbelt. However, the sine qua non is technological change.

It is instructive to consider the relationship among technology, efficiency, degree of industrial concentration, and degree of spatial centralization in historical perspective (Blair 1972, pp. 87–151). From the late eighteenth century until well into the twentieth century, technological developments provided a strong impetus toward greater concentration and centralization of economic activity. The substitution of the steam engine for water power was particularly instrumental in fostering the growth of large industrial plants. Steam power and the substitution of steel for wood made possible the development of continuous mass production techniques using highly specialized machines and processes. A host of mechanical improvements raised the number of stages of production that could be carried out in a single plant involving large-scale operations and large capital outlays. Meanwhile, a revolution in transportation was also promoting concentrated, centralized industrial structures. Railroads brought materials from a few major deposit sources to a relatively few terminal centers that became increasingly congested with population and manufacturing enterprises. The advent of the steamship greatly increased the quantities of raw materials that could be brought economically to major manufacturing centers, and made possible world distribution of finished goods. Although concentration of ownership was often well beyond that required by technology, the fact that control over the market was moving in the same direction as the consequences of technological change gave the trend toward greater concentration and centralization an aura of inevitability.

The impact of these phenomena created a conceptual dilemma for classical economists who observed a correlation between size and efficiency but also believed in the virtues of competition. No such dilemma troubled Marx, who regarded competition as a passing phase in the evolution of capitalism. Marx not only observed that the new technologies brought with them a larger scale of operations, but went further and elevated a transient phase into an inevitable "law of concentration" that would steadily diminish the number of capitalists and prepare the way for a social revolution by which the expropriators would be expropriated. Lenin similarly believed that huge enterprises had brought the mass production technique to its highest level of development, and that socialism is simply capitalist monopoly applied for the benefit of all the people. Belief in the superiority of size has also been evident even more recently in the West, as can be seen in Galbraith's (1967) notion of the new industrial state, and in the application of France's indicative planning, which assumes the superior efficiency of large organizations (Hansen 1968).

At least until the 1930s, the general direction of technological change was toward a larger scale of operations, but since then newer technologies have made possible efficient production with smaller capital outlays, have lowered barriers to entry, and have brought about a major geographic decentralization of production. The early decentralization technologies occurred in the same areas as the improvements associated with the Industrial Revolution, namely, power, machines, and transportation. Steam power was replaced by electrification, the essential prerequisite to industrial decentralization. Independently operated, multipurpose machinery powered by electricity made it possible for the small plant to adapt its output to changes in demand; and because electricity can be transmitted over great distances, industrial use of electric power is feasible in areas lacking adequate supplies of low-cost fuels. The advent of the motor truck tended to transform the inflow of materials and the outflow of finished products from a giant national pattern into smaller regional and local patterns. In addition, mass automobile ownership meant that it was no longer necessary for a plant to be located within a large industrial center in order to be assured of an adequate labor supply.

It is now evident that electricity, the multipurpose machine, and the truck and automobile were merely the precursors of a whole host of new technologies whose effect on economic structures is in the same direction. As Blair (1972, p. 151) has pointed out:

> With plastics, fiberglass, and high-performance composites, providing high-strength and easily processed materials suitable for an infinite variety of applications; with energy provided by such simple and efficient devices as high-energy batteries, fuel cells, turbine engines, and rotary piston engines; with computers providing a means of instantaneously retrieving, sorting, and aggregating vast bodies of information; and with other new electronic devices harnessing the flow of electrons for other uses, there appears to be aborning a second industrial revolution, which, among its other features, contains within itself the seeds of destruction for concentrated industrial structures.

14.5 Adaptation to a changing spatial division of labor

Although newer technologies are making industries more footloose, this does not mean that the relevant decision makers are indifferent with respect to location. For example, when products enter the highly standardized, mass-production phase of the product cycle, competitive pressures make cheap, non-union labor the critical factor in location decisions. At this point, plants are typically established in small towns and rural areas within industrial countries, or, as is increasingly the case, in such newly industrializing places as Hong Kong, Singapore, Taiwan, South Korea, and various Caribbean islands. Or production may be taken over by indigenous firms in the newly industrializing countries. Similar considerations apply to office work. It was once axiomatic that office operations could be carried out by concentrating them spatially. Now the economics of real estate and the revolution in communications have undermined the need for many centralized operations. Sales, accounting, data processing, billing, and other "back office" functions are increasingly being relocated to smaller towns and the countryside. Moreover, given satellite data transmission facilities, the logic behind using inexpensive overseas labor to perform essentially repetitive tasks (e.g., keyboard labor) is just as applicable to office work as to manufacturing.

The new international division of labor does not imply that manufacturing or other decentralizing activities will disappear from older industrial nations, because new products and processes continually arise to replace older ones. Even in the severe recession of 1983, US manufacturing activities employed 20 million persons, about the same number as in 1970. When it was still fashionable to emphasize the advantages of large cities, their internally generated renewal was regarded as virtually guaranteed by the "breadth" provided by sectoral diversification and the "depth" provided by external economies of agglomeration (Thompson 1968, p. 53). Although Boston, New York, and other large cities in the frostbelt have adapted to changing economic circumstances, the decline of other old industrial areas in Europe as well as the United States has demonstrated that adaptability is not an automatic phenomenon. Olson (1982) has argued that the decline of older industrial areas is a consequence of collusive, rent-seeking "distributional coalitions" that retard adjustment to change and reduce economic growth. Tichy (1984) similarly maintains that these areas are the victims of "indigenous blockage" brought about by barriers to entry and to exit, which may include ties to a local raw materials base, excessively high wages, unadaptable infrastructure and worker skills, union labor-hoarding practices, lack of entrepreneurship, and government subsidies. Where such conditions exist, a region is likely to experience a cycle analogous to the product cycle. Thus, even Silicon Valley could eventually become a stangnant old industrial area in the absence of a more diverse industrial structure.

As for small and medium-size cities, they clearly are no longer condemned to be mere "lower order" central places or passive recipients of older technologies that have filtered down from large metropolitan centers of innovation. The development opportunities represented by the new decentralizing technologies are there to be seized, though this requires sufficient indigenous adaptability. For example, in central and northeast Italy – in the vicinity of Bologna, Florence, Ancona, and Venice – a decentralized network of small firms located in small and medium-size cities has managed to innovate and develop products that compete successfully with those of northern European producers. The economic dynamism of this Third Italy (in contrast with the old Milan–Turin–Genoa industrial area and the less-developed South) ranges across a wide number of sectors, from shoes and textiles to auto parts and machine tools. The machinery used is both technologically advanced and adapted to small-scale production. In part, the success of the small firms is due to the fact that they are not covered by the restrictive tax and labor legislation that applies to large firms. Also, the hierarchical rigidities that characterize interpersonal relations in large plants have been replaced here by more cooperative interactions among owners, technical personnel, and production workers. Entrepreneurship and effective innovation and development strategies are encouraged by the nature of the information and feedback mechanisms that exist among firms. As each firm grows it finds itself more dependent on the help of other firms with complementary activities. Because each firm realizes that it is likely to need help from others, it in turn extends help to others (Piore & Sabel 1983). The whole process corresponds to a balanced growth strategy wherein all firms benefit from the expansion of external industrial and regional economies. Similar developments are also taking place in "peripheral" areas of Portugal and Tunisia (Aydalot 1983, p. 103). In France, the relatively recent economic vitality of small and medium-size cities has been largely a result of vastly improved transportation and communications networks (Planque 1983), and of adaptable local technical, social, and organizational structures (Perrin 1984).

In conclusion, what are the implications of the foregoing analyses for Canada's Atlantic region? Some have already been given in a report of the Economic Council of Canada (1977, p. 143). It does not seem essential for the Atlantic region's production pattern that over half of its population should be located in rural or semi-urban areas; and, at least in Canada, there is a modest positive association between urban size and per capita income up to a size of about 1.5 million inhabitants. Nevertheless, it should not be assumed that nationally determined regional policies can automatically change the degree of urbanization and the urban structure of a region. To alter these patterns "would require changes in the occupational and industrial structure of the region resulting from such factors as an improvement in labor quality, an increase in capital per worker, and a larger share of regional investment decisions taken locally."

Recent US and European experience suggests that in an age of decentralizing technologies, peripheral areas are no longer condemned to economic stagnation and may even have advantages over old industrial areas. But genuine long term regional development cannot be based on a model of diffusion from above. What is required is a model of internal dynamism based on regional social, technical, organizational, and industrial structures and their adaptation to a changing national and international division of labor.

References

Aydalot, P. 1983. Crise économique, crise de l'espace, crise de la pensée spatiale. In *Le développement décentralisé*, B. Planque (ed.), 87–106. Paris: Litec.
Aydalot, P. 1984. A la recherche des nouveaux dynamismes spatiaux. In *Crise et espace*, P. Aydalot (ed.), 38–59. Paris: Economica.
Berg, L. V. D. et al. 1982. *Urban Europe: a study of growth and decline*. New York: Pergamon.

Berry, B. J. L. 1978. The counterurbanization process: how general? In *Human settlement systems*, N. Hansen (ed.), 25–50. Cambridge, Mass.: Ballinger.
Blair, J. M. 1972. *Economic concentration*, New York: Harcourt Brace Jovanovich.
Boventer, E. Von 1973. City size systems: theoretical issues, empirical regularities, and planning guides. *Urban Studies* 10(1), 145–62.
Christaller, W. 1933. *Die Zentralen Orge in Suddeutschland*. Translated as *Central places in southern Germany*, C. W. Baskin (trans.), 1966. Englewood Cliffs, N.J.: Prentice Hall.
Economic Council of Canada 1977. *Living together: a study of regional disparities*. Ottawa.
Galbraith, J. K. 1967. *The new industrial state*. Boston: Houghton Mifflin.
Hall, P. & D. Hay 1980. *Growth centres in the European urban system*. Berkeley: University of California Press.
Hansen, N. 1968. America's challenge and Europe's response. *Journal of Economic Issues* 11(2), 157–65.
Hoch, I. 1976. City size effects, trends, and policies. *Science* 193, 856–62.
Korcelli, P. 1982. Patterns of urban change. *Options* 14(7). Laxenburg, Austria: International Institute for Applied Systems Analysis.
Moomaw, R. L. 1981. Productivity and city size. *Quarterly Journal of Economics* 96(4), 675–88.
Olson, M. 1982. *The rise and decline of nations*. New Haven: Yale University Press.
Perrin, J.-C. 1984. La reconversion du bassin industriel d'Alès: contribution à une théorie de la dynamique locale. *Revue d'économie régionale et urbaine* 25(2), 237–56.
Piore, M. & C. Sabel 1983. Italian small business development: lessons for U. S. industrial policy. In *Collapse and survival: industrial strategies in a changing world*, R. H. Ballance & S. W. Sinclair (eds.), 391–421. London: Allen and Unwin.
Planque, B. 1983. Une nouvelle organisation spatiale du développement. In *Le développement décentralisé*, B. Planque (ed.), 5–26. Paris: Litec.
Pred, A. 1977. *City systems in advanced economies*. New York: John Wiley.
Segal, D. 1976. Are there returns to scale in city size? *Review of Economics and Statistics* 58(3), 339–50.
Sveikauskas, L. A. 1975. The productivity of cities. *Quarterly Journal of Economics* 89(3), 392–413.
Thompson, W. R. 1968. Internal and external factors in the development of urban economies. In *Issues in Urban Economics*, H. S. Perloff & L. Wingo, Jr. (eds.), 43–62. Baltimore: Johns Hopkins Press.
Tichy, G. 1984. A sketch of a probabalistic modification of the product cycle hypothesis to explain the problems of old industrial areas. Paper presented at the Symposium on Regional Development Processes/Policies and the Changing International Division of Labor, UNIDO, Vienna, Austria.
Vining, D. R. & R. Pallone 1982. Migration between core and peripheral regions. *Geoforum* 13(4), 339–410.

15

Evaluating capital grants for regional development

KINGSLEY E. HAYNES & TONY DIGNAN

A Introduction

Several nation-states have developed programs which attempt to influence the location choice behavior of mobile capital.[1] The policy instruments employed for this purpose are many and varied. One source of variation in location policies concerns the ways in which they affect a firm's production function. For example, the British government's Regional Employment Premium (REP) policy reduced the labor costs associated with a particular project, whereas the capital grants employed by the Irish Republic have a direct impact on the fixed asset investment costs of establishing a new enterprise. A second source of variation concerns the spatial scale at which policies operate. For example, the British government's Industrial Development Certificate (IDC) policy was designed to affect the interregional distribution of British industry. The same government's REP policy operates not just at the regional level but also at the international level since it would, in theory at least, have influenced mobile capital in choosing between Britain and competing nations.

A third source of variation concerns the objectives underlying policy instruments. For example, the IDC policy pursued in Britain sought to reduce "congestion" in areas such as the Midlands and Greater London, as well as redistributing employment opportunities and capital investment away from these areas and to such problem areas as the Northeast of England. The capital grants program initiated by the Irish government was aimed at attracting new investment, and the associated employment opportunities, from foreign-based companies to Ireland. The same program, by the regionally differentiated nature of the grants available, has the objective of diverting projects to disadvantaged areas and thus "balancing out" the interregional distribution of employment opportunities in Ireland.

Regardless of the type of instrument employed, any framework for evaluating the efficiency of such policies must contain at least two basic elements. On the one hand, an instrument must be evaluated in terms of how it affects the location choice behavior of individual firms, i.e., an instrument must be evaluated in terms of its "microlevel effectiveness" (Yannopoulos & Dunning 1976). A second and ultimately more important level concerns the efficacy of an instrument in meeting the objective(s) prescribed by the government which formulated and funds the instrument. A convenient term, given Yannopoulos and Dunning's characterization of the relation between the policy instrument and the individual firm, might be "macrolevel effectiveness." However, policy instruments are usually underlain by regional as well as national policy objectives. It would therefore be convenient to distinguish the "mesolevel effectiveness" of a policy, which relates to the middle ground or specifically regional objectives, which are distinguishable from the "macrolevel effectiveness" of national policy objectives. Models for the evaluation of an instrument at its different levels of effectiveness would, of course, need to be interrelated.

The objective of this paper is to provide a framework for evaluating regional policies for industrial development. This is pursued by specifying the kinds of variables which must be considered, as well as their interrelations at various levels.

15.1 Microlevel effectiveness of regional policies

"Microlevel effectiveness" of regional policies refers to the impact of a policy or set of policies on a firm's "location choice behavior." For the purposes of this analysis, "location choice behavior" is taken to encompass not only the choice of a location (regional or urban) but also a firm's behavior with respect to its employment of input combinations and output levels. Moses's (1958) integration of production theory with traditional location theory shows that, regardless of the form of the firm's production function, a firm's cost function varies across locations in the presence of spatially differentiated delivered factor prices, and hence the optimal combination of inputs also varies across locations. In other words, as long as factor prices exhibit some variation over space, the cost-minimizing firm will employ factors in different proportions at different locations. This result has important implications with respect to inferring the level (macro/meso/micro) of regional effectiveness of policies for industrial location since the choice of a set of inputs by a firm affects, inter alia, its employment of labor, an important variable underlying the objectives of most regional policies for industrial location. Also affected by the firm's choice of an input combination is its employment of material inputs, which has ramifications for the nature of backward linkages a firm can be expected to generate.

A second consideration in evaluating the effectiveness of regional policies, particularly at the microlevel, concerns the economic conditions underlying a firm's production activity. Issues of importance here would include the nature of the firm's output markets, the kind of technology employed by the firm, its degree of access to output markets, new products, and new technologies, and also the status of the firm itself, such as branch-plant or independent.

These issues are not unrelated. A branch plant operation may, at least in the short run, face more predictable output markets (in terms of output demands and prices) than independent operations. It may also have greater access to new technologies and products. A priori, such factors would be of importance in determining a plant's ability to expand operations or its propensity to close. Such factors would also be expected to affect a firm's location choice behavior. For example, there may be less uncertainty in anticipated output levels, production technology, and input prices in the case of a branch plant operation than in the case of an independent operation.

In evaluating the microlevel effectiveness of a policy measure, therefore, it is necessary to model the firm's behavior with respect to location choice. Variations in the economic conditions facing different classes of firms obviously mitigate against an all-encompassing model. However, were it possible to do so, the necessary outputs from such a model for purposes of evaluating meso- and macrolevel impacts of a policy would include: the firm's location; its input combinations at the chosen location, by sources of input; and its output levels, by final destination.

In a world of perfect data availability, the above outputs could be aggregated across firms in similar industrial sectors and inserted into an interregional input–output table for the purpose of evaluating meso-and macrolevel impacts on such variables as employment, income, investment, exports, and the like.

For analytical purposes, and to facilitate evaluation of alternative regional policies, assume that a firm seeks a location for a production plant within a particular nation-state (i.e., assume that the firm has made a choice between competing nation states). Further, assume that the firm produces one transportable output from a combination of capital (K), labor (L), and one transportable input (M). Also, the firm operates in a perfectly competitive environment where input and output prices are taken as given and factor prices do not vary across locations except as a function of transport costs. Finally, asume that the firm faces no uncertainty in determining the costs of alternative locations, so that transport cost structures are known; and that the firm employs the criterion of profit maximization in choosing between alternative locations.[2] Given the above assumptions, the firm's problem is to find a location, u, which maximizes profits, Z:

$$\max_{\langle x,u \rangle} Z(x,u) = [p_o - c_o(u)] f(x) - [w + c(u)]'x \qquad (15.1)$$

such that $u \in s, x_i \geq 0$

where: S is the set of feasible locations;
P_o is the price at which output sells;
$c_o(u), c(u)$, are transport cost functions for each u in S;
x is a vector of inputs;
w is a vector of factor prices;
$f(x) = f(K,L,M)$ is the firm's production function; and
f is strictly concave in the region of optimality.

Following Moses (1958), it can be deduced that the firm can determine, for each u, an optimal combination of inputs so that, at each u, the first-order conditions are met, i.e.:

$$[P_o - c_o(u)] f_K(x(u)) - w_K = 0 \qquad (15.2a)$$

$$[p_o - c_o(u)] f_L(x(u)) - w_L = 0 \qquad (15.2b)$$

$$[p_o - c_o(u)] f_M(x(u)) - (w_M + c_M(u)) = 0 \qquad (15.2c)$$

where:

the subscript on f denotes partial differentiation; and
$x(u) = x(p_o, c_o, w, c(u))$, is the profit maximizing combination of inputs for a location at u.

That is, $x(u)$ is a vector of location specific input demand functions, $f(x(u))$ is then the optimal supply function, or level of output in this instance, at each u.

Evaluating capital grants

Thus, for each location, u, the firm can determine the profit-maximizing combination of inputs and choose a location by solving:

$$\max_{\langle u \rangle} Z(u) = [P_o - c_o(u)] f(\mathbf{x}(u)) - [\mathbf{w} + \mathbf{c}(u)]' \mathbf{x}(u) \tag{15.3}$$

such that $u \varepsilon S$

Obviously, since the only source of variation in relative factor prices across locations is due to variations in the cost of transporting M to the plant, the problem in Equation 15.3 is essentially one of minimizing transport costs, which implies that the location most accessible with respect to transporting M and the output will be chosen as the production site.

Now, suppose that the national government partitions the set of feasible locations, S, into two subsets S_A and S_B, where the former set encompasses locations within a relatively disadvantaged region with poor growth prospects, high unemployment and out-migration rates, and low per capita income, relative to region B. The government formulates a policy designed to attract industry to region A and uses as an instrument, for example, direct capital grants which reduce the cost of capital in region A by a factor of k. Thus, there now exists a spatial differential in factor prices other than the differential due to transport costs for M, so that:

$$w_{K,A} = (1 - k) w_{K,B} \tag{15.4}$$

The subsidy will have the effect of changing the firm's optimal location choice if:

$$Z(u_A) + dZ(u_A) > Z(u_B) \tag{15.5}$$

where: $Z(u_A) = \max_{\langle u \varepsilon A \rangle} Z(u)$

$Z(u_B) = \max Z(u)$, assumed $> Z(u_A)$

$\langle u \varepsilon B \rangle$

$dZ(u_A)$ is the change in $Z(u_A)$ due to a change in the price of capital.

The envelope property suggests that, for an infinitesimal change in w_K, the effect on the profit function at u_A will be:

$$\frac{dZ(u_A)}{dw_K} = Z_{wK}(u_A) \tag{15.6}$$

where Z_{wK} is the partial derivative of the profit function w.r.t. w_K.

From Hotelling's lemma, the partial derivative is:

$$Z_{wK}(u_A) = -K(u_A) \tag{15.7}$$

where $K(u_A)$ is the demand for capital at location u_A which yields the optimum level of profit at that location.

Combining Equations 15.6 and 15.7,

$$dZ(u_A) = -K(u_A)\, d_{wK} \tag{15.8}$$

In the event of a subsidy to capital, $d_{wK} < 0$, and so Equation 15.8 would be a positive quantity. Hence, the marginal impact of a subsidy to capital on the maximum profit obtainable at u_A depends on the firm's level of demand for capital at that location – the greater the firm's utilization of capital, the greater the impact of a capital-based subsidy on the relative levels of profit obtainable at alternative locations, and hence the greater the likelihood of a capital subsidy inducing a change in the firm's choice of a location for production.

Suppose a subsidy is sufficient to induce a firm to choose u_A rather then u_B, i.e., the subsidy "works" in terms of affecting the spatial distribution of manufacturing firms. There are two effects to consider with respect to the impact of the subsidy on factor demands. First, the subsidy will induce a change in factor demands at u_A from the optimal presubsidy factor demands. The requisite tool for evaluating the change in factor demands at u_A, i.e., $dx(u_A)/dw_K$, is the substitution matrix which gives the rate of change in factor i if the price of factor j changes.

The matrix can be defined as:

$$Dx(u) = (P_o - c_o(u))\, D^2 f(x(u))^{-1} \tag{15.9}$$

where $Dx(u)$ has elements $\{dx_i/d(w_j + c_j)\}$, $i,j = 1,3$.

Obviously, to exactly specify the elements of the substitution matrix it would be necessary to assume a particular production technology and a set of factor prices. However, some general points can be made. First, if the price of the factor goes down, then utilization of that factor will increase – since $D\mathbf{x}(u)$ must be negative semi-definite, its diagonal elements must be negative. If the elements of $D\mathbf{x}(u)$ are all negative, utilization of the other factors will also increase, depending on the firm's production technology and the relative factor prices. However, since factors will vary in terms of productivity and price, the rate of increase in the utilization will be different for each factor. In other words, the firm will change its optimal mix of factor proportions at u_A in response to a subsidy. For the example above, the greater the productivity of capital in a firm's production function, the greater will be the shift towards capital in the firm's optimal mix of factor proportions.

The second effect which needs to be considered is the relation between the factor demands at u_A in the presence of a subsidy and the "displaced" factor demands at u_B, i.e., will a subsidy-induced shift in the location of the firm result in reduced levels of demand for the various factors. In the model used here, this possibility arises since a shift from u_B to u_A involves a change in two other parameters besides capital, i.e., c_o and c_M. That is, will a subsidy result in:

$$x^*_i(u_A) < x_i(u_B), i=1,n. \tag{15.10}$$

where
$x^*_i(u_A)$ is the optimizing demand function for factor i in the presence of a subsidy to capital.

The answer to this question depends on how the firm adjusts factor demands to changes in the net output price and the cost of transporting M. Obviously, an increase in c_M will result in reduced factor demands. So also will an increase in c_o, since factor demands are functions of output prices as well as input prices. The net effect is indeterminate, however, without knowledge of the firm's production technology and how the parameters c_o and c_M change with location.

The final issue to be considered is the effect of a subsidy on output, since,

$$y(u) = f(\mathbf{x}(u)) \tag{15.11}$$

where $y(u)$ is the profit-maximizing output at u.

Thus, a change in the relative factor prices affects output through the change in factor demands subsequent to a subsidy. This is the "output effect":

$$y^*(u_A) > y(u_A) \tag{15.12}$$

Again, however, it is not possible to determine whether the new optimal output at u_A will be greater than or less than $y(u_B)$, since a switch from u_A to u_B would involve change in $c_o(u)$ and $c_M(u)$.

To summarize, given the profit-maximizing model specified above, if the price of a factor is changed due to a subsidy which discriminates in favor of one region, then:

(a) Whether or not the firm's choice of a location is affected depends on the importance of the subsidized factor in the firm's production function, i.e., the level of the firm's demand for the factor.
(b) Demand for the factor at the subsidized location will increase above the level demand in the unsubsidized case.
(c) The optimal mix of factors at the subsidized location will change (assuming substitutability in the production process).
(d) Output will increase at the subsidized location relative to the unsubsidized output at that location.
(e) Whether or not factor demands and output at the subsidized location represent an increase over the demands at the optimum location in the unsubsidized case depends on how the displacement affects the relative factor prices through transport costs.

More specifically, the microlevel effectiveness of a policy depends on (a) its ability to affect the choice of u; and (b) its impact on $x(u)$ and $y(u)$.

A policy which affects a firm's choice of a location can have either a positive or a negative impact with respect to $x(u)$ and $y(u)$. A policy which does not affect location choice cannot affect the input and output variables. Of course, the effect of a policy in these respects will vary across firms, depending on production technologies and conditions.

The preceding discussion is based on a profit-maximizing approach to location behavior. The analysis can be reformulated in a number of different ways. For example, it could be assumed that the firm employs a cost-minimizing objective function, subject to an output constraint. This would modify the above analysis by predicting increased demand for capital at u_A and decreased demand for other factors.

The production function could also be reformulated. Specifically, the demand for materials might be related to the level of utilization of fixed asset capital. Baumol's (1977) definition suggests that the production function might be restructured so that,

$$M = g(K), \, dM/dK > 0 \qquad (15.13)$$

and

$y = f(K, L, g(K))$

This allows a separation of fixed assets and "flow" assets while maintaining a relation between the two.

Finally, the preceding analysis assumed the vector **w** to be locationally invariant in the presubsidized case. It may be more appropriate to model wage rates for labor as regionally variant, or, the productivity of labor may vary as between the regions (see Keeble 1976).

15.2 Macrolevel effectiveness

The macrolevel effectiveness of a regionally-differentiated capital subsidy depends inter alia, on how the subsidized firm contributes to national income, employment, and output relative to how it would have contributed in the absence of a regional subsidy. An appropriate framework, in principle at least, for analyzing the macrolevel impact is that of an input–output table.

A firm's contribution to employment and income depends on the firm's demand for labor and wages paid. There are, however, indirect effects on employment and income via backward linkages. Assuming that a new entrant to the labor market employs previously unemployed labor, then:

$$dE_i(u) = L_i(u) + dL_j(M_i(u) \cdot b_M, K_i(u), b_K) \quad (15.14)$$

where dE_i is the additional labor generated by a new firm's production activities;

$L_i(u)$ is the firm's optimizing demand for labor;

$dL_j(.)$ is a function giving the additional employment generated in the jth industrial sector, and is a function of the firm's domestic purchases of capital and materials;

b_K, b_M, are the proportions of capital goods and raw materials demanded by i which are supplied by the domestic economy; and

$j=1,J$, are the J industrial goods producing sectors of the domestic economy.

Thus, $dL_j(.)$ denotes the labor impact of the firm's backward linkages with the domestic economy. The income effect of i's activity can be defined as:

$$dY_i(u) = [L_i(u) \cdot w_i L + dL_j(.) \cdot w_j L] (1 + m) \quad (15.15)$$

where: w_L is a wage rate; and
m is an income multiplier.

Using Equations 15.14 and 15.15, the macrolevel effectiveness of a subsidy to a set of firms can be gauged by considering:

$$dE_i(u^*) - dE_i(u) \tag{15.16a}$$

$$dY_i(u^*) - dY_i(u) \tag{15.16b}$$

where u^* is the firm's optimal location choice in the absence of a subsidy.

Thus, if Equations 15.16a and 15.16b are both negative, then the regional policy can be judged ineffective in terms of its impact on national income and employment growth. If Equations 15.16a and 15.16b could be estimated this would provide a measure of the "loss" entailed by a regional policy aimed at deflecting location choices to less advantaged regions. The gains against which such a loss would be traded off depends on the regional objectives articulated and the extent to which these are accomplished.

15.3 Mesolevel effectiveness

The employment and income effects at the regional level can be estimated by replacing b_M, b_K, and m in Equations 15.14 and 15.15 with b_{Mr}, b_{Kr}, m_r where r subscripts the regions, $r=1, R$. Thus, given the appropriate data, dE_{ir} and dY_{ir} could be computed for each firm and aggregated to give estimates for employment and income generation.

As noted above, the mesolevel effectiveness of a policy depends on the objective(s) underlying the use of a particular instrument. A wide variety of objectives can be pursued, though the reduction of regional per capita income and unemployment rate differentials are "standard" objectives. Restoring demographic balance by stemming out-migration is another consideration which appears in the justification of regional policy. Thus, for example, if a regional policy aims at reducing per capita income differences, then the "gain" from employing location-deflecting incentives might be written as the contribution of incentive-leveraged employment to reducing the variance in regional per capita incomes:

$$\text{Var}(Y_r/P_r) - \text{Var}(Y_{r,t+n}/P_{r,t+n}) \tag{15.17}$$

where: Y_{rt} is total regional income at time t;
$Y_{r,t+n}$ is total regional income after n years of the operation of a subsidy scheme;
$Y_{r,t+n}$ is a function of, inter alia, dY_r. A similar type of function could be defined for regional unemployment rates and migration rates.

Obviously, the objective of a regional policy with respect to Equation 15.17 would be to maximize the value of the difference in the variances. Conversely, the national government, in resorting to a regional policy, would seek to minimize the differences, Equations 15.16a and 15.16b. This suggests that consideration of macro- and mesolevel effects of an incentives policy can be integrated by means of a programming function which treats the macrolevel "losses" and the mesolevel "gains." The difficulties of this task would reside in the noncommensurability of elements of the objective function (compare Equations 15.16b and 15.17) and also in obtaining the requisite data.

Table 15.1 Main regional incentives in EEC countries.

Country	Incentive name	Incentive type[a]				
		CG	IRS	TC	DA	L
Belgium	interest subsidy		×			
	capital grant		×[b]			
	accelerated depreciation				×	
Denmark	company soft loan		×			
	municipality soft loan		×			
	investment grant	×				
France	regional-development grant	×				
	local business tax concession			×		
Germany	investment allowance	×				
	investment grant	×				
	ERP soft loan		×			
	special depreciation				×	
Ireland	capital grant (new)	×				
	capital grant (re-equipment)	×				
	export-profit tax relief			×		
Italy	capital grant	×				
	national soft loan		×			
	social security concession					×
	tax concessions			×		
Luxembourg	capital grant	×		×		
	tax concession					
Netherlands	investment premium	×				
United Kingdom	regional development grant	×				
	soft loan		×			
	interest relief grant		×[b]			

[a]: Abbreviations: CG, capital grant; IRS, interest related subsidy; TC, tax concession; DA, depreciation allowance; LS, labor subsidy.
[b]: These incentives are calculated in terms of the interest concessions which would have been awarded had a soft-loan award been made. Because of this, they have been allocated to the interest related subsidy column although they are in effect capital grants.
Source: Yuill et al (1980), Table 11.3.

Table 15.2 Maximum levels of assistance in the EEC countries.

Country	Problem region	Maximum aid as a net grant equivalent percentage of initial investment		Maximum aid in European units of account (EUA) per job created by initial investment
(1) Ireland	whole country			
Italy	Mezzorgiorno			
UK	Northern Ireland	75%	or	13,000 EUA
Germany	Berlin (West)			
France	Overseas Departments			
(2) France	Regional-development Grant Areas			
Italy	aided center–north	30%	or	5,500 EUA (up to 50%)
UK	Development Areas			
(3) Germany	Zonal Border Area			
Denmark	Special Development Regions	25%	or	4,500 EUA (up to 30%)
(4) All other community regions[a]		20%	or	3,500 EUA (up to 25%)

[a]: Excluding Greenland, where there are no aid ceilings.
Source: Yuill et al (1980), Table 11.2. Original source: Commission on the European Communities, COM (78) 636 final, Brussels, 21 December 1978.

Investment incentives of various forms are widely used in a number of developed and developing countries. Tables 15.1 and 15.2 show, respectively, the types of regional investment incentives and the maximum assistance levels of the incentives in the countries of the EEC. Canada provides an example of a country outside Europe which has made use of investment incentives such as direct capital grants (Hewings 1977). The most popular form of subsidy would appear to be direct capital grants whereby the national government contributes some proportion of the capital costs associated with a new development. Other forms of assistance to capital include accelerated depreciation allowances and low interest loans or interest rate subsidies. More recently, equity participation has been used as a means of attracting new investment (e.g., the Irish Industrial Development Authority, and the Welsh and Scottish Development Boards). The extent of coverage of regional policy programs in terms of impacted population in the EEC countries is illustrated in Table 15.3.

The reasons underlying the formation of regional policy objectives and the national economic conditions underlying the application of policy instruments vary widely between different countries. In accounting for the use of investment incentives in the EEC countries Yuill et al. (1980) provide a good illustration of how different sets of forces operate in different countries to shape the form of regional policy. However, a

Table 15.3 Proportion of total population in assisted areas, EEC countries.

Country	Designated problem regions[a]	Regional population as % of national total
Belgium	Development Zones	42
Denmark	Development Regions	27
France	Regional development grant Award Zones	35
Germany	GA[b] areas	36
Ireland	Designated Areas	33
Italy	Mezzogiorno	35
Luxembourg	no designated areas	
Netherlands	investment premium areas	17
United Kingdom	assisted areas plus Northern Ireland	45

[a]: Detailed descriptions of the individual regions can be found in Yuill et al (1980).
[b]: Gemeinschaftsaufgabengebiete.
Source: Yuill et al (1980), Table 11.1.

number of reasons can be identified as underlying the use of capital-based incentives, which are the primary forms of incentive used in the EEC countries. First, investment subsidies can be expected to stimulate output and thus divert resources from consumption into capital formation, particularly if the marginal propensity to consume is high. A related benefit on the output side is that the activity of export-oriented investment projects can have favorable balance-of-payments effects. Second, leveraged investment stimulates the creation of employment opportunities in two ways: directly in terms of the demand for labor on the part of assisted projects, and indirectly in terms of the increased demand for material inputs resulting from investment activity. Third, investment based subsidies may stimulate the adoption of up-to-date and competitive technologies since the cost of capital is reduced. Regional differentials are utilized when an economy faces imbalances in the attractiveness of different regions.

Regional imbalances can be due to a number of factors. A region may possess an outmoded industrial structure which is overbalanced with slow-growth of stagnating industries. Alternatively, a region may lack an industrial base and be overly dependent on the agricultural sector. In either instance, the use of investment subsidies, through their output and employment creating effects and stimulation of the adoption of new technologies, can be justified on the ground of redressing imbalances in the distribution of employment opportunities. An efficiency argument in favor of regionally differentiated subsidies is that diversion of investment to struggling regions results in the utilization of resources which might otherwise remain underemployed, particularly surplus labor which may suffer problems of mobility. An illustration of these situations and the consequent policy response is provided by an overview of the practice of investment incentives in the United Kingdom and the Republic of Ireland. The regional problem in the former country has developed to a large degree from the outmoded industrial structure of the assisted areas, while in the Irish case the regional problem has been exacerbated by an overdependence on the declining agricultural sector and lack of an industrial base.

B Regional policy: dual perspectives

15.4   The United Kingdom

Evolutionary perspective

Regional policy in the United Kingdom dates from the enactment of the Distribution of Industry Act in 1945.[3] The Act was essentially concerned with relieving high unemployment in the so-called Development Areas (DAs), including Glasgow, Cardiff, Swansea, and Newcastle, and also with restraining and redistributing industrial development in the Southeast and the Midlands due to fears of overconcentration and congestion in the urban centers of the "core," as Keeble (1976) refers to the Southeast and Midlands. Thus, the primary concern of the Act was the internal distribution of British industry. The Act adopted what might be called a "carrot-and-stick" approach. The Board of Trade (BOT) was empowered, inter alia, to purchase land and build factories within the DAs, as well as to make grants and loans to DA manufacturing firms. With respect to the more prosperous regions of the core, the BOT exercised control over industry through a building license system established for rationing purposes during World War II. The regulatory "stick" component of regional policy was considerably strengthened in 1948 with the creation of the Industrial Development Certificate (IDC) system under the powers of the 1947 Town and Country Planning Act. Under the IDC system, any development in excess of 5000 sq. ft. required the permission of the BOT. The express purpose of the system was to redirect some proportion of developments and expansions proposed for the core area to the peripheral DAs. That is, the hope was that if a development was refused permission in the core it would transfer the proposed development, and its associated investment and employment, to the periphery.

The next major change in British regional policy came in 1960 with the repeal of the 1945 Act and the passing of the Local Employment Act. Under this new Act, the DAs were replaced with smaller Development Districts (DDs), identified as areas suffering persistently high unemployment. The act strengthened the existing financial incentives by making it easier for the BOT's Advisory Commission to make loans and grants toward the purchase of new machinery. The Act also introduced building grants for new investments located in the DDs which opted to build their own unit rather than renting from the BOT.

Subsequent to the 1960 Act, government expenditure on factory building, loans, and grants increased significantly (Keeble 1976). Further, IDC controls were applied with greater stringency. For example, in the Southeast and Midlands, the expected employment associated with all refused development, taken as a percentage of total employment generated by approved developments plus employment associated with refusals, rose from 13.7% in 1959 to 29.9% in 1966 (Moore & Rhodes 1976).

The 1963 Employment Act was important in two ways. First, the financial incentives were strengthened. Second, the incentives were clarified and standardized – 25% towards the cost of factory construction in a DD and a 10% cash grant towards the cost of new plant and equipment.

A third important piece of legislation was the Finance Act of 1963 under which the system of incentives was extended by providing for a form of accelerated depreciation, called "free depreciation." Specifically, industrialists could choose a write-off rate for tax refund purposes and depreciate new equipment to the point where their tax liability was zero until such time as costs were recovered. The measure amounted to an interest free loan since tax due was not reduced but delayed until equipment had been fully depreciated.

In 1966, subsequent to the election of a Labour government, the Industrial Development Act was passed. This Act abolished the DDs and replaced them with a new and enlarged set of DAs. The 10% grant and free depreciation were both revoked and replaced with more substantial standard grants of 40% towards equipment costs within DAs and 20% outside the DAs. The 25% building grant within DAs was retained, as also was accelerated depreciation in the form of initial (first-year) allowances for DA investments, though the amount of capital costs allowable for depreciation against tax was taken net of any cash grants.

In 1967 the system of regional incentives was further extended with the introduction of Regional Employment Premiums (REPs) and Special Development Areas (SDAs). The former was the first direct subsidy to labor and comprised a payroll subsidy of £1.50 per week for men employed in DA manufacturing establishments, £0.75 for women, and £0.475 for girls. These subsidies averaged out to about 7% of labor costs when introduced but were eroded over time by inflation (Moody & Smith 1975). The SDAs were a response to particularly high unemployment in some former coal-mining regions within the DAs. More extensive benefits were accorded industrialists locating in the SDAs.

In 1970 the patchwork of assisted areas was added to by the creation of Intermediate Areas (IAs). These were recommended by the Hunt Report (1969) as a mechanism for dealing with areas such as Yorkshire and Humberside where low unemployment rates concealed major problems such as high levels of out-migration and structural unemployment. IAs, however, did not become the focus of significant attention and only a small number of areas were designated.

The period 1970 to 1972 has been characterized by Keeble (1976) as one of "anti-policy." The incoming Conservative government greatly narrowed the interregional differentials in assistance which had been developed during the 1960s and also lowered the overall levels of assistance to industry. Capital grants were abolished and replaced with a form of accelerated depreciation – first-year allowances of 100% in DAs and 80% in NDAs. Also, the IDC controls were substantially relaxed.

The 1971/2 recession prompted a return to the system of incentives developed during the 1960s. The 1972 Industry Act restored the investment grants, as well as the free (accelerated) depreciation which had proven very popular during its first lifetime. Capital costs, for tax purposes, were taken gross of investment costs. An unstandardized form of assistance was also introduced by giving the Secretary of State for Industry discretionary permission to apply selective regional assistance (loans, grants, etc.) to modernization schemes as well as to job-creation activities.

A measure of the Conservative government's shift on regional policy is that the Labour government which acceded to power in 1974 made only one major adjustment to the 1972 system: REPs were doubled rather than being phased out as intended by the Conservatives. The Labour government also reduced the IDC thresholds, thus strengthening the system's regulatory control, and extended DA status to a number of areas such as Merseyside.

The early 1970s also saw significant institutional change, with the creation of Regional Development Boards, and particularly the Scottish and Welsh Development Agencies. The Development Agencies were charged with re-structuring their regional economies through infrastructure development (e.g., advance factory building), support of indigenous industry, and so on.

The latter half of the 1970s witnessed significant retrenchment in the area of regional policy as public expenditure cuts by the national government took their toll. The REP scheme was abolished in 1976, and grant payments were withdrawn from mining and construction. The coming to power of the Conservative government in 1979 heralded even more radical changes. Aiming for cost-effectiveness, greater concentration on the most distressed areas, and reduced levels of total expenditure, the government reduced the spatial extent of the assisted areas. The capital grant allowance was reduced from 20 to 15% of costs for DA investments and was removed altogether from the IAs. The criteria for grant eligibility were also considerably tightened. Yuill et al. (1980) suggest that the changes would have had the effect of reducing the number of successful applicants, with grant awards being biased toward investments with a genuine choice of location and against small projects and minor extensions. Both the factory building program and the IDC system were retained. However, the frequency of IDC refusals, in the face of lower investment activity and slack labor markets in both assisted and non-assisted areas, has been greatly reduced.

The system of incentives

British regional policy from 1945 to the present has exhibited a number of important features. First, the rationale for regional policy has primarily been drawn from a concern with the spatial distribution of domestic industry and related employment opportunities. In particular, incentives have been most strongly developed for areas suffering high unemployment and experiencing difficulty in generating growth due to their particular industrial structures. The assisted areas have been primarily focused on areas where the industrial structure was created in the nineteenth century and which ossified and stagnated during the twentieth century: the Northeast, Glasgow, South Wales, and so on. Thus, British regional policy has been largely concerned with *restoring* areas suffering outmoded industrial structures rather than stimulating industrial development from scratch. However, some of the assisted areas did comprise relatively unindustrialized regions, such as Devon and Cornwall and the Scottish Highlands, so that there are curious variations in the location characteristics of the various assisted areas. That is, the British "periphery" arguably consists of two portions, the "rural periphery", as Spooner (1972) refers to Devon and Cornwall, and the "urban-industrial periphery".

Second, the national government has employed a wide mix of policy instruments. These include "coercive" measures such as the IDCs which have been mixed with subsidies to capital (grants and accelerated depreciation) and labor (the now-defunct REP), and also various forms of "indirect" leverage such as the preparation of industrial estates. Further, the commitment of the national government to regional policy has varied over time. Moody and Smith (1975) have attempted to evaluate the level of subsidy to new investments for different subsidy regimes and spatial areas. The time period covered by Moody and Smith (1975) is 1966 to 1974, when three different subsidy regimes were successively in operation: the 1966 Development of Industry Act system (1966–70, Moody & Smith's Period 1); the "anti-policy" years between 1970 and

1972 (Period 2); and the system introduced in 1972 (Period 3). Moody and Smith discuss two methods for evaluating the subsidy contribution to capital costs for a "representative" firm. The first, the "grant equivalent method", which is used by the EEC Commission and the BOT, takes the grant equivalent of a capital investment subsidy to be "the discounted present value of the anticipated stream of future receipts to the enterprise" (ibid., p. 274). The second method, proposed by Moody and Smith, is the "unit rental" approach. The concept refers to the "annual charge required to maintain and service each unit of the capital stock existing at a particular point in time" (ibid, p. 279). In an unsubsidized and untaxed situation, the rent per unit of capital is:

$$c = r + d \qquad (15.18)$$

where: r is interest charges per annum for borrowed funds invested in the capital stock; and
d is the cost of replacing a given proportion of a unit of the stock.

The "borrowed funds" against which r is charged refer to any source of capital financing, including retained earnings. Thus, if investment is funded entirely out of retained earnings then r is the required rate of return.

In the presence of a tax rate, t, the rate or return which must be achieved to service c at rate r, is:

$$r = r^* - (r^* t) \qquad (15.19)$$

or,

$$r^* = \frac{r}{(1-t)}$$

where r^* is the rate of return needed to service c at rate r.

If the government contributes a capital grant at a rate g per unit of capital, then the effect is to reduce the rate of return needed to return r on the capital invested so that:

$$r^* = \frac{r(1-g)}{(1-t)} \qquad (15.20)$$

The cost of replacement, d, is simiarly affected, so that in the presence of a cash grant subsidy to capital at rate g the cost per unit of capital is:

$$c = \frac{r(1-g) + d(1-g)}{(1-t)} \qquad (15.21)$$

This basic procedure is developed by Moody and Smith to estimate the unit rental cost of capital for each of the three periods noted above. Their results are presented in Table 15.4, where the neutral row gives the unit cost in the absence of any form of subsidy. The table is useful in clarifying the extent of the regional differential in each period, and also the variation in levels of subsidy and differentials for each period. Table 15.5, also from Moody and Smith, compares capital subsidy percentages using the "grant equivalent", or NPV, and unit rental methods. The unit rental percentages are computed as the percentage of neutral cost comprised by the subsidized cost. The figures in the table are interpretable as the subsidy contribution per pound of capital invested. As can be seen, the two methods are not perfectly correlated. The unit rental approach gives an estimate which is consistently higher than the NPV approach. Further, the two methods do not, in all cases, predict an equivalent direction of change in the subsidy component in the event of a change in policy. The lack of perfect correlation derives from what Moody and Smith refer to as the "discounting" and "depreciation" effects. The former effect arises because NPV involves discounting over a period of time, while unit rental is time invariant. The depreciation effect relates to the treatment of how a cash grant affects future gross profits needed to cover replacement costs under different depreciation regimes. Despite these variations, Table 15.5 provides a good indication of the extent to which a new investment can benefit from subsidies and how the level of subsidy varied across the major regions.

Table 15.4 Annual rental cost per £100 of capital stock.

	Plant	Buildings	Plant and buildings combined (4:1)[a]
Period 1			
Development areas	12.4	12.2	12.4
Nondevelopment areas	16.6	18.1	16.9
Period 2			
Development areas	14.4	8.8	13.3
Nondevelopment areas	15.5	16.4	15.7
Period 3			
Development areas	8.6	9.8	8.8
Nondevelopment areas	14.4	15.3	14.6
"Neutral"[b]	20.7	19.7	20.5

Assumptions: $r = 0.10$; $d = 0.05$ (plant); $d = 0.04$ (buildings).
[a]: Plant and building costs were combined in a ratio of 4 to 1.
[b]: The "neutral" row gives rental cost in the absence of a grant and an accelerated depreciation allowance.
Source: Moody & Smith (1975), Table III.A.

Table 15.5 A comparison of capital subsidy percentages.

	Plant		Buildings		Combined plant/buildings	
	NPV	Unit rent	NPV	Unit rent	NPV	Unit rent
Period 1						
Development areas	38.89	40.1	36.2	38.1	35.95	39.7
Nondevelopment areas	18.36	19.8	10.2	8.1	16.75	17.5
Period 2						
Development areas	15.58	30.4	43.8	55.3	21.22	35.4
Nondevelopment areas	13.02	25.1	10.2	16.8	12.46	23.4
Period 3						
Development areas	39.84	58.4	35.3	50.2	38.93	56.8
Nondevelopment areas	15.58	30.4	13.4	22.3	15.14	28.8

Source: Moody & Smith (1975), Table IV.

Empirical analyses of micro- and macrolevel effectiveness

A number of studies have attempted to estimate the impact of subsidies on job creation in the assisted areas. Keeble (1976), in a regression analysis of percentage changes in manufacturing employment within the British sub regions (counties and conurbations), found the coefficient on an assisted area status dummy variable to be insignificant for the period 1958–66, but positive and significant for the period 1966–71. It should be noted that the subsidy system for most of the latter period was the relatively strong one created by the 1966 Industrial Development Act, so that the result certainly suggests that policy had some kind of an impact, though the form of the impact cannot be gauged due to the type of variable used by Keeble. A study by Henderson (1980) found the level of employment generated by immigrant firms to be positively related to the availability of sites and factories, as well as to advance factory building, both of which are functions of central government policy and its variation, which would reflect the spatial priorities of the central government. Rich (1980) has also suggested that regional policy was important in diverting firms to Scotland, an assisted area.

Moore and Rhodes (1976) developed a regression model which attempts to explain moves to DAs by manufacturing industry over the period 1945 to 1974 as a function of the pressure of aggregate demand and a number of policy instruments. The equation estimated (t−ratios in brackets) was:

$$\text{MDA}_t = 29.67 - 7.97\text{MU}_t + 2.01\text{II}_{t-1} + 2.05\text{IDC}_{t-1} + 52.67\text{REP}_{t-1} + u_t$$
$$(4.29)\quad (1.81)\quad\quad (5.52)\quad\quad (5.76)\quad\quad\quad (4.79)\quad\quad (15.22)$$

$$u_t = 0.49u_{t-1} - 0.71u_{t-2} + v_t$$

MDA_t = number of moves to DAs originating outside the DAs in time t;
MU = male unemployment rate, a proxy for the pressure of aggregate demand;
II = discounted present value of the regionally differentiated investment incentives per £1,000 of capital expenditure;
IDC = index of stringency of application of IDC controls;
REP = an index number reflecting the value of the Regional Employment Premium in real terms; and,
u, v, are disturbances.

The significance of the negative coefficient for MU suggests that, when aggregate demand is slack, so that unemployment rises, firms outside the DAs are reluctant to expand their operations, and thus the DAs' ability to attract new movers is reduced. The significance of each of the policy variables suggests that the strength of regional policy was important in generating new manufacturing activity in the DAs. The relationship between regional policy and the movement of firms to the DAs was also examined by MacKay (1979).

Moore and Rhodes's study is also useful in that it attempted to estimate the employment-creating effects of the policy instruments for 1960–71. Their estimates are reproduced as Table 15.6. As can be seen, the model estimated by Moore and Rhodes suggests that the IDC controls were the most important factor in generating employment (an estimated 8,325 jobs per year). It should be noted here that these figures give approximate estimates of the mesolevel job-creation effectiveness of the instruments and ignore the macrolevel impact which would include a measure of the effect of policy on job creation in the non-DAs.

The effects of the policy instruments on job creation as estimated by

Table 15.6 Estimated employment creation induced in Development Areas by regional policy (United Kingdom).

Policy	Annual average	Total 1960–71
Industrial Development Certificate	8,325	100,000
investment incentives (8 years)	5,875	47,000
Regional Employment Premium (4 years)	3,500–5,250	14,000–21,000
special development areas (4 years)	0–2,500	0–10,000
Total		161,000–168,000

Source: Moore & Rhodes (1976), Table 3.

Moore and Rhodes related only to new manufacturing employment due to immigrant industry. Estimates of the *total* effect of the regional policies vary considerably. An earlier paper by Moore and Rhodes (1973) estimates that, between 1960 and 1972, 250,000 to 300,000 additional jobs were created in the DAs due to regional policy. This broad order of magnitude is supported by Brown (1972). For the latter part of the 1960s, Brown (1972) estimates that manufacturing employment grew by about 30,000 per annum in excess of the amount that could have been expected in the absence of policy. Brown also estimated an extra 29,000 "spin-off" jobs in the service sector due to multiplier effects. Ashcroft and Taylor (1977, 1979), however, suggest that the DA employment effects were much lower during the 1960s. Their study estimates an additional 9,000 jobs per annum, based on an estimate of about 40% of moves to DAs deriving from regional policy. The Ashcroft and Taylor study differs from Moore and Rhodes in that the former focus on investment demand rather than the pressure of aggregate demand appears as the key national level variable affecting the number of moves susceptible to regional policy. MacKay (1979), using an approach based on factory building activity, suggests an employment impact which is less than Moore and Rhodes's estimate but greater than Ashcroft and Taylor's.

An analysis by Massey (1979) argues that the kinds of jobs which have been created in the DAs, regardless of their magnitude, have been primarily unskilled and semi-skilled with a greater dependence on cheaper female labor than in the core areas. She also suggests that the more highly skilled occupations and key functions such as research and development continue to be located in the core areas. The precise role of regional policy in this de-skilling of direct DA labor is unclear, though arguably investment-based incentives provide an incentive to locate routinized processes in the DAs both to lower capital costs and to take advantage of the abundance of labor in the DAs. To the extent that incentives leverage de-skilled production processes, the direct and indirect income effects for the assisted region are reduced.

Lund and Gleed (1979), in a reformulation and extension of Brown's (1972) work, have examined the DA share of new manufacturing investment. They suggest that regional policy, and specifically capital grants, have positively affected the DA share, though the evidence is rather sparse due in part to data constraints.

The role of regional policy in the UK

The papers cited above, for the most part, suggest that the various regional policy tools have been instrumental in diverting employment, firms, and investment to the DA. Thus, the microlevel effectiveness of the various regional policies is strongly supported.

Table 15.7 Factors cited in the choice of Devon and Cornwall by new industry.

Factor	Factories citing as main factor (%)	Factories mentioning (%)
attractive area to key workers and management	29.5	49
availability of labour supply	22.5	65
other labour advantages	3.5	24
access to Devon and Cornwall's market and raw materials	9.0	15
proximity to other factories and regions	12.0	24
availability premises or site	4.0	17
local authority co-operation	4.5	15
Board of Trade influence	3.0	15
other	6.0	19
unknown	6.0	—

Source: Spooner (1972), Table 3.

However, other locational factors were at work during the 1960s which were also redistributing industry. Keeble (1976) suggests that, up to about 1960, the spatial processes underlying the distribution of British industry could be summarized as having a centralizing effect with new investment strongly attracted to the core where access to domestic markets could be maximised. Subsequently, according to Keeble, diseconomies of agglomeration at the core have induced significant centripetal forces in the distribution of industry and fostered decentralization. The precise role of regional policy in the decentralization of British industry during the 1960s is unclear. It is unclear whether policies merely supported the tendency for new investment to decentralize or played a leading role in the decentralization process. Spooner's (1972) analysis of movements to Devon and Cornwall during the 1960s is suggestive of the former conjecture. His survey results are reproduced as Table 15.7. The interesting aspect of this table is the minor role played by the BOT, which was concerned with allocating assistance during the period covered. Devon and Cornwall, during this period, contained both assisted and nonassisted areas. Spooner notes that grants to industry within the DAs are standardized, so that the relative importance of the factors cited may reflect reasons for choosing Devon and Cornwall as opposed to other assisted areas rather than the rest of the United Kingdom in its entirety. The importance of the labor force factor is noteworthy in this respect.

Apart from the precise role played by regional policy as a decentralizing force, the impacts of the particular forms which regional policy instruments have taken has generated much discussion. In particular, the hypothesis that capital-based subsidies are most attractive to capital-intensive industry has received attention (Brown 1972, Lund & Gleed

1979, Buck & Atkins 1976, Chisholm 1970). The policy concern associated with this hypothesis is that capital-based subsidies may induce substitution of capital for labor. According to Buck and Atkins, "investment subsidies always [in the absence of perfect factor complimentarity] involve a substitution effect with respect to labor, and, in some cases, this may exceed the output effect, resulting in a net reduction in the demand for labor" (ibid., p. 216). Buck and Atkins estimated the following equation for 77 British industries from 1968 census data:

$$\ln(V/L) = \ln a + b \ln(W/L) + u \qquad (15.23)$$

where: V is value added in money terms;
L is total employees;
W is wages and salaries in money terms;
$a, b,$ are parameters; and
u is a random disturbance.

The parameter b represents the elasticity of substitution of capital for labor. For a standard Cobb–Douglas production function, b would be estimated as 1.0 (i.e., a 1% increase in wages per employee results in a 1% increase in the capital-to-labor ratio). If a Harrod–Domar assumption of perfect factor complementarity holds, $b = 0$. The estimates of b suggested the Cobb–Douglas condition for 38% of the industries, the Harrod–Domar assumption for 57% (i.e., b not significantly different from zero), and $b > 1$ for the remaining 5%. These finding suggest that significant substitution effects are possible in a large proportion of British industries. In exploring how this substitution effect may interact with capital-based subsidies to new investment, Buck and Atkins utilize additional employees per 1,000 sq. ft. of floor space as a (rough) proxy measure for capital intensity. The DA ratio and the ratio for the rest of Britain tended to move in tandem, but at different levels, over the period 1961 to about 1966. This suggested to Chisholm (1970) that capital-based subsidies were not inducing substitution for labor at a more significant rate in the DAs than in the rest of Britain. However, subsequent to 1966, the data show a very different rate of change in the DA ratio than in the ratio for the rest of Britain, the direction of which supports Buck and Atkins' contention that subsidies to capital induce greater capital intensity and labor substitution. Survey evidence produced by the Department of Industry (1974) is also used by Buck and Atkins to substantiate their proposition. The survey found that labor supply considerations and financial incentives were major determinants of industrial location (cited by 40% and 27%, respectively, of the firms surveyed). Since labor was in abundant supply in the DAs, Buck and

Atkins suggest that the increasing intensity of investment could not have been achieved without a substantial substitution effect, underpinned by capital-based subsidies, against labor.

15.5 Irish industrial policy for regional development

Evolutionary perspective

During the period spanning the 1930s up until the publication of the first Programme for Economic Expansion in 1958, Irish national industrial policy was based around protectionism, with the objective being to stimulate economic independence and self-sufficiency through import substitution. One outcome of this policy was that it provided a powerful incentive for industry to concentrate in locations with good access to the major population centers and thus led to polarization of industrial employment growth from a regional perspective (Ross 1978). In particular, the Dublin region and the Northeast attracted the major share of industrial development, with counties along the Atlantic seaboard failing to develop a significant industrial base. National industrialization policy was turned completely around during the 1950s. During that period, the government initiated formal economic planning built around the preparation of plans aimed at developing industrial employment opportunities as a means of enhancing income growth and attaining full employment. The government thus took steps to assist and promote export-oriented industrial development and also to attract foreign-based firms. It was felt that the nation lacked native capital as well as the technology necessary for industrialization and for making the transition from an agriculture-based economy. Over the next two decades, the tariff barriers underpinning protectionism were gradually removed. The Anglo-Irish Free Trade Agreement (AIFTA), signed in 1965, was the first major step in this regard, with accession to the EEC in 1970 marking a second major step.

Legislative development

The legislative history of Irish regional policy for industrial development dates from the passing of the Undeveloped Areas Act in 1952. This Act initiated a programme of state incentives designed to attract new industry to the poorer parts of the country, most notably counties west of the Shannon river, Donegal, Kerry, and West Cork. The justification of the incentives lay in the perception that industries locating in these "undeveloped areas" were likely to suffer cost disadvantages due to such factors as inadequate access to the major centers of population and underdeveloped infrastructural facilities. The "welfare" rationale for the Act was that the undeveloped areas were those which were most lacking in an industrial base which could provide employment opportunities to compensate for the ongoing decline of agriculture (the economic "base" of the underdeveloped areas) as a source of employment. These economic problems were manifested in very high rates of out-migration and, relative to the national average, low levels of per capita income and high levels of unemployment. A measure of the extent of uneven development characteristic of the Irish space economy can be gauged by considering that, over the period 1966–71, net emigration for the province of Connaught (which includes counties west of the Shannon) was 10 per 1,000, compared to a national average of 3.7 per 1,000. In 1969, per capita income in Connaught was £320, compared with £551 for Dublin. The unemployment rate for North Connaught in 1972 was 12.2%, compared with 8.1% for the nation. Table 15.8 gives a number of indicators for the Irish regions.

The primary incentive introduced by the Act comprised non-repayable cash grants, with statutory limits of 50% and 100% towards, respectively, the cost of machinery/equipment, and land and buildings. Other forms of assistance included grants for labor training and infrastructural assistance.

Industrial assistance was extended to all parts of the country with the passing of the Industrial Grants Act in 1956. This Act applied to those areas of the country not covered by the 1952 Act, and was intended to stimulate manufacturing employment and import substitution. However, the regional differential was maintained by offering assistance only towards the cost of buildings, with a statutory limit of 67% and a grant limit of £50,000. This regional differential was eroded by successive amendments to the basic Acts over the period 1959 to 1969. The 1959 Industrial Grants Act raised the grant ceiling for projects located outside the Undeveloped Areas to £250,000, and also provided for cash grants of up to one-third of the cost of machinery and equipment while maintaining the statutory limit for assistance towards building costs. The rationale for this step was the heightening of competition with other European countries for foreign direct investment. The regional differential was further eroded by the 1963 amendments to the Industrial Grants and Undeveloped Areas Acts. These amendments broadened the range of incentives available to industry, primarily through the introduction of adaptation grants of up to 25% of costs. Further, the regional grant differential was abolished for grants in excess of £250,000 and diluted for grants less than that amount. For example, grants of up to two-thirds of

Table 15.8 Selected indicators for the regions of Ireland.

Region[b]	Per capita income £ 1973[a]	% real increase 1960–1973	Annual average % increase in population 1971–7	1975–7	Manufacturing as % of labor force 1978
Donegal	426	95	0.3	2.1	14.5
North West	444	97	0.3	2.1	15.7
West	459	100	0.3	1.2	13.2
Mid West	535	94	1.5	1.9	18.2
South West	551	91	1.1	0.2	18.6
South East	529	93	1.3	1.1	21.4
East	653	79	1.8	1.9	17.0
North East	508	98	0.7	1.4	22.9
Midlands	463	91	0.3	0.6	18.7

[a] 1969 Prices.
[b] The Designated Areas include Donegal, the Northwest, the West, and parts of the Northeast, the Midwest, and the Southwest.

Source: IDA Industrial Plan 1978–82 (1979), Chart 5.4.

the cost of land and buildings could be made in "exceptional circumstances" outside the Undeveloped Areas. These steps were taken in response to prompting from such organizations as the Council for Industrial Organization (CIO) and the National Economic and Social Council (NESC), which argued that maximizing national employment growth should be the overriding consideration in formulating industrial policy instruments, particularly in a free-trade environment.

In 1969, the Industrial Development Act was passed and both the Undeveloped Areas and Industrial Grants Acts were repealed. Under the 1969 Act, the country was divided into the Designated Areas (DAs) and the Non-Designated Areas (NDAs). The former region roughly corresponds to the former Undeveloped Areas. The primary purposes of the Act were to update and clarify the incentives available to industry, as well as to integrate the process of allocating grants with the promotional aspects of the so-called New Industry Programme. Thus, all areas of the country were, for the purposes of industrial development assistance, subject to a single legislative instrument. Further, the plethora of incentives to be made available was articulated in a very structured fashion. The basic cash-grant system was streamlined and the regional differential was strengthened. The standard grants were set at up to 40% of the cost of fixed assets invested for the DAs and up to 25% for the NDAs, with an additional 20% payable under "exceptional" circumstances such as, for example, in the case of a particularly favorable new industry, such as one with high growth potential. No limit was set on the level of grant which could be approved, but grants in excess of £350,000 required the consent of the government. The Act also included provisions for re-equipment grants (up to 35% in DAs, 25% elsewhere) designed to assist existing industry in adapting to new technologies and competition circumstances; grants to aid research and development (up to £150,000 or 50% of costs, whichever is less); and also assistance towards interest payments on loans and factory rents.

The above list does not complete the range of incentives available, which stretch to labor training assistance, equity participation, provision of advance factories, and infrastructural assistance. However, the regional development core of the industrial development program, particularly with respect to the attraction of new investments, remains the system of non-repayable cash grants. This system remained fundamentally unchanged during the 1970s, though there were important modifications and adjustments. The conditions underlying the allocation of grants were modified in 1970 by linking the level of grant to employment generation. Thus, for a DA location, a firm could receive up to 50% of the cost of fixed asset investment as long as the grant cost per job created did not exceed £5,000. For counties in the NDAs outside Dublin, the standard limit was set at 35% of eligible costs, subject to a limit of £4,000 per job.

For Dublin, the limits were set at 25% and £3,000. The 60% limit for "exceptional circumstances" was, however, retained. The administrative limit for Dublin-based projects was increased in 1977 to the level obtaining in the remainder of the NDAs in response to the severe employment losses suffered by the Dublin region in the wake of the 1974–6 recession.

The above outline of legislative developments relates to what is currently called the New Industry Programme (NIP). However, other Acts and policies of regional interest have been enacted and formulated over the period from 1952. In particular, there was the creation of the Shannon Free Airport Development Company (SFADCo), under an Act of 1959, which was charged with the economic development of the Shannon airport zone. SFADCo was given the power to offer standard grants of up to 50% of the cost of land, machinery, and buildings, as well as more favorable export tax relief than could be obtained in the remainder of the country. The Gaeltacht Industries Act of 1957 focuses on Irish-speaking areas, principally located along the Atlantic seaboard. The Gaeltacht Authority set up under this Act was given power to award cash grants and take out equity in new projects under a 1965 amendment, but its orientation is primarily towards craft industries of a small scale.

Important extensions of industrial policy during the 1970s included the initiation of a Small Industries Programme designed to supplement the employment-creating efforts of the NIP. There is some evidence that this program is assuming increasing importance (Boylan & Cuddy 1984), particularly in light of the Telesis Report (1982) which stressed the need to develop firms which could act as suppliers of inputs to NIP firms. Another extension of the development program initiated in the 1970s was a scheme to assist in the creation of service industries, such as engineering consultancies and so on. These programs have not received the amount of attention and research devoted to the NIP.

Institutional developments

With respect to the regional dimension of industrial development policy in Ireland the most important institution is undoubtedly the Industrial Development Authority (IDA). The IDA was established in 1949 and given the task of promoting the growth of manufacturing industry in Ireland. For the period 1952 to 1969 the IDA worked in tandem with the grant-giving authority, An Foras Tionscail, with respect to incentives under the Undeveloped Areas and Industrial Grants Acts. The 1969 Industrial Development Act abolished An Foras Tionscail and vested both the promotional and the grant-giving function with the IDA. Under the 1969

Act, the IDA was also empowered to prepare plans for industrial development and to include in its plans employment targets for the nine physical planning regions of Ireland established under the 1963 Local Government (Planning and Development) Act. (This Act is modeled after the Town and Country Planning Act enacted in the United Kingdom in 1947.) While the IDA's regional plans for industrial development are formulated in consultation with local and regional bodies, it is nonetheless the IDA's function to prepare employment targets for each region. Further, it is the IDA which negotiates projects under the NIP.

The IDA performs promotional functions both within Ireland and abroad. With respect to the latter, the IDA maintains offices in a variety of different international locations, including New York, Chicago, London, Frankfurt, Tokyo, and others. Its agents at these offices actively solicit new investment from carefully selected firms within selected industrial sectors. For example, during the mid- to late 1970s, the IDA focused a lot of attention on attracting "high-technology" firms in sectors with above-average growth potential in terms of participation in world markets, such as firms in the computer and electronics industry. All grants offered by the IDA are negotiable, so that the statutory limits are rarely reached. The IDA's assistance to firms does not stop at allocating grants. For example, although firms are free to choose a location anywhere in the country, the IDA does assist firms in obtaining a suitable site. It can offer factory floor space in a variety of industrial estates which are constructed under contract to the IDA. It also helps new projects to obtain planning permission for new developments. The IDA also plays a role in establishing relations between new industries and trade unions. The IDA maintains "branch offices" in each of the planning regions which can perform such functions, among others. The IDA also maintains contact with firms after they have been established at a location, essentially to encourage expansions and to ward off closures.

Objectives and strategies for regional development

The policy objectives underlying the 1952 Undeveloped Areas Act were related to the perceived need to rectify the severe economic imbalances in industrial employment opportunities then existing between the DAs and the NDAs; that is, providing employment opportunities for residents of the Undeveloped Areas, stemming out-migration and stimulating population growth, and raising per capita income levels. The problem of migration has historically been most severely felt by the Underdeveloped Areas and has been comprised of two main flows: one, internal, and primarily oriented to the Dublin region; the other, external, and directed toward the United Kingdom and the United States. Since the average migrant tends to be fairly young, out-migration has had a strong negative impact on population growth in the western countries through its effect on the rate of natural increase (Kennedy and Bruton 1975). Between 1966 and 1971, the rate of natural increase in Connaught was 4.4 per 1,000 population as against 10.1 for the nation (an average substantially affected by the rate for Leinster – which contains the counties along the Eastern seaboard, including Dublin – of 13.2).

As alluded to in the foregoing review of legislative developments, the importance attached to the regional problems in industrial development policy was consistently reduced during the 1960s as the economy struggled to adapt free trade and international competition for foreign direct investment. Concurrently, however, there was much debate during that period and into the 1970s on appropriate spatial strategies for industrial development. Essentially, the debate centered on whether or not efforts should be concentrated on a few carefully selected growth poles, at least until the economy had adapted to free-trade conditions and its products could compete effectively in world markets, or, alternatively, whether growth should be dispersed so that development could be diffused to all regions. The impetus for this debate came from a number of studies of the Irish planning regions conducted during the 1960s. In particular, the Buchanan Report (1968) suggested that available resources be concentrated in a selected set of urban growth centers – the major national centers of Dublin, Cork, and Limerick, with a second tier consisting of Waterford, Dundalk, Drogheda. In support of a growth center strategy, O'Neill (1971, 1973) suggested that the process of industrial development in Ireland over the period 1926 to 1966 could be characterized as exhibiting a strong tendency toward clustering of economic activity. Further O'Neill suggested that the more clustered an industry, the lower the failure rate of establishments located within a cluster. She also suggested that growth rates of new establishments tended to be higher where clustering occurred. O'Neill's study has been subjected to strong criticism from O'Farrell (1974) on the basis of its methodological and conceptual shortcomings, e.g., the lack of statistical tests of the various hypotheses.

The government has considered the question of a spatial strategy for industrial development in a number of documents. In 1958, concern was expressed regarding the viability of a policy of decentralization, and whether or not the concentration of industries close to the large centers of population might not be the most appropriate means of approaching economic development (First Programme 1958). By contrast, the 1965 Report of the Committee on Development Centres and Industrial Estates advocated a policy which would include dispersion of estates over wide areas of the North and West. In 1965, the government issued a statement on regional policy in which it suggested the dispersal of industrial activity yields important social advantages and should be facilitated where such is economically feasible. A further statement issued in 1969 explicitly rejected the growth center options spelled out in Buchanan (1968) on the basis that this would preempt development in areas outside the designated centers. The second statement concerned with regional policy also spelled out some specific policy objectives. In particular, the statement suggested that growth in Dublin be limited to its natural increase. This objective received concrete expression in the 1969 Industrial Development Act which set the standard grant limit for Dublin at a level below that of any other location. The statement also specified that employment opportunities should be broadly based, within the constraint of achieving a faster national growth rate and achieving full employment, in order that "involuntary population dislocation" be minimized.

A further statement issued in 1972, in response to regional plans put forward by the IDA, suggested that the government was prepared to accept some reduction in growth in exchange for a more even spread of employment opportunities. Indeed, the period covered by the aforementioned IDA plans, 1972-7, would seem to be the period in which the commitment to a broadly based regional strategy was most fully articulated in the production of industrial development plans. In effect, the government was assuming that the Dublin region and, to a lesser extent, the traditional industrial centers of Dundalk and Drogheda in the Northeast were capable of self-sustained industrial growth. However, these were precisely the regions which had benefited the most from the earlier protectionist policies, and whose industrial structures were biased toward the traditional industries, such as clothing and textiles, which were the least equipped to withstand the 1973-6 recession. The East region, dominated by Dublin, is estimated to have lost 25,560 manufacturing jobs over the period 1973-7 as against gains of only 14,600 for a net loss of 11,050 (see Table 15.9). The Northeast also suffered a net loss, of 1,000. These were the only regions to suffer net losses of employment during the period 1973-7 (IDA 1979). Accordingly, in 1977 the 25% limit on grants applicable to Dublin was raised to 35%, in line with the rest of the NDAs. The IDA also began to focus on the creation of small industries in Dublin city center.

In summary, a detailed and explicit spatial strategy for industrial development has not been articulated in the sense of a program setting out the relations between urban areas and different levels of the urban hierarchy and how these relations can best be taken advantage of in terms of new industry development. There has developed a spatial strategy of sorts, insofar as the IDA produces plans which set out job

Table 15.9 Employment gains and losses in manufacturing industry for the Irish planning regions, 1973–7.

Region[a]	Gross job target 1973–7	Gains	Losses	Net change
Donegal	2,800	2,300	1,500	800
North west	1,700	1,800	700	1,100
West	5,300	7,350	2,200	5,150
Mid west	5,400	5,300	5,390	—
South west	9,400	9,100	8,100	1,000
South east	4,700	7,200	4,450	2,750
East	17,000	14,600	25,650	−11,050
North east	5,300	4,500	5,500	−1,000
Midlands	3,400	5,350	2,200	3,150
Total	55,000	57,500	55,600	1,900

[a] See note b, Table 15.8.
Source: IDA Industrial Plan 1978–82 (1979), Chart 5.3.

targets for different regions and town groups within each region. Indeed, the IDA targets are highly disaggregated at the urban level – about 300 towns were allocated targets in the 1973–7 plan. The basic philosophy underlying regional industry policy has been to decentralize employment, within the constraint of maximizing national employment opportunities. Thus, NIP projects have been dispersed throughout the country rather than concentrated in a selected set of growth centers. It can be suggested that the type of foreign-based NIP project which the IDA has succeeded in attracting to the country lends itself, in many ways, to a policy of decentralization (see Perrons 1983).

In the next section, some salient characteristics of NIP projects are examined. It will be seen that the "typical" project exports a very high proportion of its output (so that its dependence on the domestic market and access to that market is relatively slight, either in terms of serving final demand or in terms of forward linkages to other producers), and also imports a very high proportion of its material inputs (so that its dependence on domestic subsuppliers, and level of domestic backward linkages, tends to be relatively low).

Characteristics of NIP projects

The most detailed study of the characteristics of NIP projects, in terms of characteristics such as employment, inputs, and so on, is that conducted by McAleese (1977), who surveyed 431 establishments that received grant assistance between 1960 and 1973. Though the study is somewhat dated, recent evidence, while lacking the detail of McAleese's study, suggests that the salient characteristics of NIP projects have not altered dramatically (Telesis 1982). The following tables summarize some of the more important results of McAleese's study for firms classified by nationality and industry.

From Tables 15.10–13, which classify firms by nationality, it can be seen that:

Table 15.10 Characteristics of Irish New Industry projects receiving grant assistance between 1960 and 1973.

Corporate nationality	% of all new projects ($N = 431$)	Mean Employment	Employment share (%)	Share of exports in 1974 total sales (%)
North American	18.1	178	23.0	95.2
United Kingdom	16.5	100	11.8	81.9
German	12.8	86	7.9	82.3
other EEC	7.2	227[a]	11.7	67.4[b]
other European	4.9	113	3.9	97.4
Far East	0	0	0	0
other foreign	0	0	0	0
Irish	38.1	147	40.1	54.4[c]
all	97.4[d]	140	98.5[e]	86.3[f]

[a] 14 Dutch firms employed an average of 395 people.
[b] Dutch firms only exported 63.6%.
[c] Figure refers to 1973.
[d] 2.6% were joint ventures.
[e] Remainder due to joint ventures.
[f] Some grant assisted overseas firms agreed to refrain from the development of home market sales in direct competition with domestic suppliers. Other factors explaining high ratios: (a) small size of the Irish Market; and (b) high level of product specialization (McAleese 1977).

Source: McAleese, (1977), Tables 3.3 and 4.3 and Figure 3.2.

Table 15.11 Destination shares of 1974 exports by Irish New Industry projects which received grant assistance between 1960 and 1973 (%).

Corporate nationality of project	Destination					All areas
	US	UK	EEC	EFTA	Other areas	
North American	20.1	21.4	29.9	6.3	22.4	100.1
United Kingdom	3.3	77.9	6.3	1.1	11.7	100.3
EEC[a]	19.5	33.9	33.6	6.2	6.8	100.0
other European	24.9	37.6	12.7	3.2	21.7	100.1
other foreign	15.9	55.5	1.2	1.2	26.4	100.2
Irish	8.2	52.3	18.3	3.9	17.3	100.0
all	13.5	43.5	21.5	4.4	17.1	100.0

[a] Seven countries.

Source: McAleese (1977), Table 4.7.

Table 15.12 Import/export structure of Irish New Industry projects in 1974.

Corporate nationality	% Trading with affiliates	Sales to affiliates as % of exports	Purchases from affiliates as % of imports	Import content (%) of expenditures on:	
				All inputs	Raw materials
North American	85.0	77.0	46.0	n.a.	n.a.
United Kingdom	69.0	39.0	38.0	n.a.	n.a.
EEC	63.0	29.0	32.0	n.a.	n.a.
other foreign	65.0	41.0	13.0	n.a.	n.a.
all foreign	74.0	55.0	29.0	58.1	88.8
Irish	n.a.	n.a.	n.a.	48.1	77.8
all projects	n.a.	n.a.	n.a.	55.3	85.3

n.a. Not available.
Source: McAleese (1977), Tables 4.9 and 5.4.

Table 15.13 Source of new products by corporate nationality of grant assisted New Industry projects locating in Ireland between 1960 and 1973.[a]

Corporate nationality	New product source:					All
	(1) Irish R&D	(2) Parent Firm R&D	(3) Other (Licensing, etc.)	(4) Both (2) & (3)	(5) combination of (1), (2) & (3)	
North American	7.5	62.3	5.7	7.5	17.0	100 (N = 53)
United Kingdom	15.0	52.5	17.5	2.5	12.5	100 (N = 40)
German	17.2	55.2	6.9	3.4	17.2	99.9 (N = 29)
other foreign	13.2	68.4	7.9	2.6	7.9	100 (N = 38)
all foreign	12.5	60.0	9.4	4.4	13.8	100.1 (N = 160)

[a] Figures based on 160 useable replies from a sample of 173.
Source: McAleese (1977), Table 6.6.

(1) Exports account for the bulk of sales by NIP projects – 86.3% on average (Table 15.10). For all corporate nationalities, the largest proportion of these exports, 70.6%, are to European Community (EEC) countries (Table 15.11). Further, for foreign-based firms, a high percentage of export sales are to affiliates (Table 15.12). This is particularly true for North American firms: 77% of export sales by such firms were to affiliates. Thus, on the average, forward linkages of foreign-based projects lie outside the domestic economy.

(2) The import content of total expenditures on inputs was, on average, 55.3% (Table 15.12). For raw materials, the import content was, on average, 85.3% (Table 15.12). Thus, on the average, the bulk of backward linkages were also located outside the local economy.

(3) Foreign-based firms tended to depend on nonlocal sources for new products, particularly R&D by the parent company (Table 15.13).

In combination, the above findings suggest that, for the period covered by McAleese, foreign-based NIP projects did not develop significant linkages with the domestic economy, with respect to inputs, outputs or product development. The major locally demanded input has been labor (19.5% of expenditures by the surveyed firms). Localization and urbanization economies would seem to have been weak. Under these circumstances, a policy of decentralization of employment is feasible, but possibly at the cost of sacrificing stronger domestic links. On the output side, it was a requirement of policy during the period covered by

McAleese that grants be offered to firms whose products would, for the most part, be exported and which would not compete directly with existing Irish firms on the domestic market. A recent study, however, has suggested that NIP firms would not have been averse to developing localized backward linkages, since importing inputs incurs transport costs which increase with distance from the major ports of Dublin, Cork, Waterford, and Limerick, and also increases the possibility of delays and so on (Telesis 1982).

Several observations can be made with respect to the data on firms classified by industrial sector (Tables 15.14 and 15.15):

(1) Table 15.14 shows that NIP projects represent a significant proportion of employment, exports, and gross output for a number of industries, particularly metals and engineering, structural clay/cement/glass, and other (principally consumer goods such as toys).
(2) Output per employee (in £000's) of NIP projects is quite variable, ranging from 4.3 to 26.3 with a mean of 10.1 (Table 15.14). However, for most industries output per employee in NIP projects exceeded the national average. However, in most industries, wages and salaries represented a lower proportion of gross output for NIP projects as compared with the national average (Table 15.14).
(3) The importance of raw materials as a percentage of total expenditures by the surveyed firms was also quite variable, ranging from 23.9% to 84.5% with a mean of 69.4% (Table 15.15). Labor costs are also quite variable, ranging from 7% to 44.1%.
(4) The mean grant as a percentage of fixed asset investment was 37.3% for Irish firms and 39.5% for Overseas firms (Table 15.15).

These data suggest that there is a good deal of heterogeneity in the behavior of different industrial sectors, and this would need to be considered in any locational analysis. However, in terms of grant allocations as a percentage of fixed asset investment, there does not seem to have been any particular bias in favor of any one industrial sector.

Location patterns of New Industry projects

The most striking feature of the location pattern of grant-assisted New Industry in Ireland is the extent to which it has been dispersed throughout the country. Table 15.16 shows the distribution of New Industry projects and employment over the nine planning regions for the period 1960–73. The dispersal pattern continued into the 1970s, as indicated by the employment estimates shown in Table 15.9. Further,

Table 15.14 Selected characteristics of grant-assisted New Industry projects by industrial group in 1974.

Industry	New industry[a] share of:			Output per employee ('000s)		Exports as % of total sales	Materials, etc., as % of gross output	Wages & salaries as % of net output	
	Employment	Exports	Gross output	New industry	National average			New industry	National average
food	20.1	55.5	32.3	26.3	16.4	69.5	85	6	10
drink & tobacco									
textiles	18.8	41.4	23.4	8.1	6.5	74.0	50	6	13
clothing & footwear	39.5	84.0	45.8	4.3	3.7	65.8	64	16	21
wood & furniture	17.5	42.2	19.8	6.3	5.6	25.2	50	23	28
paper & printing	9.7	37.5	12.1	7.2	5.8	58.0	50	24	23
chemicals	20.7	60.0	32.7	21.5	13.7	92.1	37	23	30
structural clay/cement/glass	31.3	58.8	21.5	4.6	6.8	53.7	38	8	14
metals & engineering	42.5	93.3	41.4	6.8	7.0	74.4	44	38	27
other	35.6	63.6	24.0	9.0	13.3	86.9	55	21	23
all manufacturing	28.7	62.1	30.5	10.1	9.5	73.6	47	16	15
							62	14	17

[a] The term "New Industry" refers to the set of projects which received financial assistance under the New Industry Programme (NIP).
Source: McAleese (1977), Tables 3.1, 4.1, and 5.1.

Table 15.15 New Industry[a] expenditure by category and industry group as percentage of total expenditures, 1974.

industry	Raw materials	Packaging industry, transport, materials for repairs	Royalties, licenses, interest	Labor	Fuel & electricity	Total (m.)	Import content	Capital grants as % of fixed assets	
								Irish	Foreign
food, drink, & tobacco	84.5	5.2	1.3	7.0	1.9	99.9 (276.6)	5.6	38.1	36.5
textiles	69.1	5.2	3.8	18.9	3.3	100.3 (42.4)	68.1	43.0	49.9
clothing & footwear	56.1	5.0	1.0	34.5	1.7	98.3 (30.1)	37.0	35.5	40.3
wood & furniture	46.4	10.3	6.2	32.0	5.2	100.1 (9.7)	31.3	36.8	41.2
paper & printing	48.0	5.9	2.0	36.3	6.9	99.1 (10.2)	34.0	38.5	39.0
chemicals	60.1	8.9	8.2	18.4	5.1	100.7 (31.6)	65.4	33.8	37.5
structural clay/cement/glass	23.9	12.2	6.1	44.1	13.1	99.4 (21.3)	17.3	29.8	40.8
metals & engineering	60.9	6.3	2.9	27.1	1.2	98.4 (153.4)	59.1	38.0	37.9
other	59.4	8.4	4.9	23.9	2.5	99.1 (76.1)	59.3	41.1	37.2
all manufacturing	69.4	6.3	2.9	18.5	2.9	100.0 (651.4)	34.2 39.0	37.3	39.5

[a] See note a, Table 15.14.
Source: McAleese (1977), Tables 5.3 and 7.5.

Table 15.16 Distribution of New Industry[a] sponsored projects locating in Ireland between 1960 and 1973 and employment in 1973.

Region[b]	Projects		Employment[c]		Population, 1971, %
	Number	%	Number	%	
Donegal	23	5.5	1,564	3.5	3.6
Northwest	13	3.1	1,137	2.5	2.6
West	38	9.1	2,228	5.0	8.7
Midwest	59	14.1	6,709	15.0	9.0
Southwest	90	21.5	10,997	24.5	15.6
Southeast	44	10.5	5,180	11.6	11.0
East	78	18.7	10,778	24.0	35.7
Northeast	45	10.8	4,182	9.3	5.8
Midlands	28	6.7	2,047	4.6	7.8
Total	418	100.0	44,822	100.0	100.0

[a] See note *a*, Table 15.14.
[b] See note *b*, Table 15.8.
[c] Relates to successful establishments only, i.e., those operational at June 1973.
Source: O'Farrell (1975), Tables 1 and 5.

Table 15.17 Distribution by town size group of new industry[a] projects locating in Ireland between 1960 and 1973.

Town-size group	N of projects	Firms per town
Less than 1500	105	0.28
1,500–5,000	132	1.81
5,000–10,000	52	2.36
10,000–25,000	42	3.82
25,000–150,000	51	12.75
Dublin	36	36.00

[a] See note *a*, Table 15.14.
Source: O'Farrell (1975), Table 12.

New Industry activity has been dispersed to all levels of the urban hierarchy, as Table 15.17 indicates, though the IDA has experienced difficulty in attracting new overseas investment to urban areas of less than 1,500 population. These locational patterns reflect the spatial strategy underlying the practice of Irish regional policy, particularly as it was practiced and articulated during the 1970s. In this respect, the following quotation taken from the IDA's Industrial Plan 1978–82 is instructive:

> Much of the discussion on location strategy in Ireland has focussed on the issue of "growth centres" and whether or not a growth centre

strategy is appropriate for our needs. The IDA experience has demonstrated the feasibility of locating industry outside, as well as within, the main growth centres. In the period to 1982, IDA's location strategy will continue to be based on bringing 'jobs to the people' and will benefit from the operational experience in the past. Rapid growth in manufacturing employment is scheduled for the main urban centres but, in addition, the nucleus of industrial development will be further encouraged in the smaller centres. (p. 45).

Thus, the overall objective is to spread employment opportunities throughout the country. There are variations in the operational objectives established vis-à-vis the regions. The 1978–82 Plans, formulated in the wake of a recession which had a particularly severe impact on the most industrialized regions of the East and Northeast (see Table 15.9), specified three different operational objectives with regard to the planning region. Thus, for the East region, "surgery" was seen as required to mend the impact of redundancies occurring during the recession; for the four less developed regions (Donegal, Northwest, West, and Midlands), higher than average growth rates were targeted to continue the establishment of an industrial base; and for the remaining regions containing established industry, "adaptation" assistance was prescribed to modernize and maintain "sufficient expansion to achieve a moderate growth in employment" (IDA, p. 45). While these objectives reflected the economic conditions of the period, they were nonetheless underlain by a desire to achieve regional convergence, as witnessed by the higher target growth rates for the less developed regions.

Table 15.18 New industry manufacturing establishments locating in Ireland between 1960 and 1973 classified by grants as a percentage of fixed assets.

Location[a]	Under 20%	20–29.9%	30–39.9%	over 40%	All
Designated areas	21	13	38	136	208
Nondesignated areas	20	53	82	55	210

[a] See note b, Table 15.8.
Source: O'Farrell (1978), Table 4.3.

O'Farrell's (1975, 1978) research suggests that the dispersal of industry in the pursuit of convergence was underpinned by the system of regionally differentiated grants. Table 15.18 shows the distribution of capital grants as a percentage of fixed asset investment between DA and NDA projects for 1960–73. Grants in excess of 40% of fixed asset investment were made to 6% of the DA Projects, compared to 29% of the NDA projects. As O'Farrell notes, these data do not reveal whether the

Table 15.19 Selected characteristics by regional location of grant-assisted New Industry projects located in Ireland between 1960 and 1973.

	Location[a]	
	Designated areas	Nondesignated areas
No. of firms[b]	169	183
Employment		
total	14,113	30,709
(% of total)	(31.5%)	(68.5%)
per firm	84	167
Grants		
mean per firm	171,500	271,400
mean per job	2,516	1,865
Fixed assets		
mean per firm	450,000	809,000
mean per employee	5,357	4,847
employment per £1,000 fixed assets	1.9	2.1

[a] See note *b*, Table 15.8.
[b] The total no. of firms receiving assistance from 1960 to 1973 was 418, with 208 located in the Designated Areas and 210 located in the Nondesignated Areas. The following data refer to the subset of firms which received assistance and which had not closed by 1973. No data is available on the firms which closed before 1973.

Source: Data reported in O'Farrell (1975) was used in computing the above means.

capital grant differential is cause or effect of the location decision. That is, did the differential make a significant difference to firms in their choice between alternative locations; or did firms settle on a particular DA location for reasons other than the grant and then qualify for the higher DA grant simply by dint of their location choice? The answer to this question would be revealing in terms of the effectiveness of a regional differential. If the relationship is from the grant to the location, then the differential is effective at the microlevel in terms of location choice. Conversely, if the relationship is, so to speak, from the location to qualification for higher grant, then the differential is extraneous to the location decision and therefore unnecessary. The extent to which the relationship varies by type of firm (capital vs. labor-intensive; domestic vs. export market oriented; small vs. large; and so on) also provides fruitful grounds for further research. Nonetheless, the data in Table 15.18 certainly suggest that the dispersed pattern of firms came at a price since assistance to DA firms seems to have been much higher than that for NDA firms, on the average.

Table 15.19 presents a summary of the differences between DAs and NDAs in the economic behavior of grant-assisted new projects. As can be seen, DA firms, on average, tended to be smaller than NDA firms. However, the variance in the size distribution of DA firms was reflected in a lower level of mean grant per firm in the DAs as compared with the NDAs. The grant per job created was considerably larger in the DAs than in the NDAs for the period covered. Finally, the smaller mean size of firms in the DAs is also reflected in a smaller mean fixed asset investment by DA firms, though the fixed assets per employee was larger for DA firms than for NDA firms. Thus, the data in Table 15.19 indicate that the location choice behavior of firms varied across DA and NDA locations. The data do not reveal anything concerning the dimensions underlying the observed variations, though there is some indication that, if employment per £1,000 of fixed assets can be used as a proxy for capital intensity, DA firms tended to utilize capital more intensively than NDA firms, at least on the average.

In summary, these two examples, the United Kingdom and Ireland, indicate that interaction between micro/meso/macro level regional development issues within the context of capital grant programs is essential to any evaluation or assessment process. Further, this multilevel approach may also be critical for any development of formal evaluation strategies in regional policy.

Notes

1 "Mobile capital" is used here to refer to investment capital which is not restricted in its location behavior to a particular place or set of places. One problem with the use of this phrase is that an investment project which might be considered "mobile" at one spatial scale is not necessarily "mobile" at another spatial scale. For example, a project which must ultimately be located in a deep-water harbor facility may well be considered "mobile" from the point of view of competing nation-states. However, within a particular chosen nation-state, such a project would undoubtedly face a very restricted set of locational opportunities.
2 This criterion is not the only plausible motive a firm could employ. For example, a firm's behavior could be underlain by strategic considerations related to market access. This type of behavior is relevant to firms operating in an oligopolistic market. However, if the domestic market of the chosen nation-state is sufficiently small so that the firm's output markets are primarily external, then profit-maximizing behavior would seem plausible for a location within the chosen nation-state.
3 The Special Areas (Development and Improvement) Act, aimed at areas particularly ravaged by the Depression of the '30s, does pre-date the 1945 Act.

The scope of the 1936 Act, in terms of policy instruments and geographical coverage, however, seems fairly limited even though $5m. was advanced to industrialists locating in the Special Areas between 1934 and 1939. Also, the building of advance factories and industrial estates, a policy which survives to the present day, was initiated with the 1936 Act. However, the 1945 Act was underpinned by the Barlow Report (1940) which explicitly articulated the British regional problem for the first time, and, as Keeble (1976) notes, was important in crystallising public opinion and generating commitment to regional concerns.

References

Ashcroft, B. and J. Taylor 1979. The effect of regional policy on the movement of industry in Great Britain in *Regional policy: past experience and new directions*, D. MacLennan and J. B. Parr (eds.), pp. 43–64. Oxford: Martin Robertson.

Ashcroft, B. and J. Taylor 1977. The movement of manufacturing industry and the effect of regional policy. *Oxford Economic Papers* **29**, 84–101.

Barlow Report 1940. *Report of the Royal Commission on the Distribution of the Industrial Population*. Cmnd 6153. London: HMSO.

Baumol, W. J. 1977. *Economic theory and operations analysis*, 4th ed. Englewood Cliffs, N.J.: Prentice Hall.

Boylan, T. A. and M. P. Cuddy 1984. Regional industrial policy: performance and challenge. *Administration* **32**, 255–70.

Brown, A. J. 1972. *The framework of regional economics in the United Kingdom*. Cambridge University Press.

Buchanan, C. and Partners 1968. *Regional studies in Ireland*. Dublin: An Foras Forbartha.

Buck, T. W. and M. H. Atkins 1976. Capital subsidies and unemployed labour, a regional production function approach. *Regional Studies* **10**, 215–22.

Chisholm, M. 1970. On the making of a myth? How capital-intensive is industry investing in the Development Areas? *Urban Studies* **7**, 289–93.

Department of Economic Affairs 1969. *The Intermediate Areas: report of a committee under the chairmanship of Sir Jospeh Hunt*. Cmnd 3998. London: HMSO.

Department of Industry 1974. Inquiry into Locational Attitudes. Published in *Minutes of Evidence taken before the Trade and Industry Sub-committee of the 1973/4 Expenditure Committee on Regional Development Incentives*, HC 85-1.

Henderson, R. A. 1980. The location of immigrant industry within a U.K. assisted area: the Scottish experience. *Progress in Planning* **14**, 104–226.

Hewings, G. J. D. 1977. *Regional industrial analysis and development*. New York: St. Martin's Press.

Hughes, J. G. 1975. *Regional policy in Ireland: a review*. Dublin: N.E.S.C. Report no. 4. Prl 4147.

Industrial Development Authority 1979. *Industrial Plan, 1978–82*. Dublin: Industrial Development Authority.

Keeble, D. 1976. *Industrial location and planning in the United Kingdom*. London: Methuen.

Kennedy, K. A. and R. Bruton 1975. *The Irish Economy.* Brussels: Commission of the European Communities, Studies, Economic and Financial Series No. 10.

Lund, P. J. and R. H. Gleed 1979. The Development Area share of manufacturing industry investment 1966–69. *Regional Studies* **13**, 61–72.

MacKay, R. 1979. The death of regional policy – or resurrection squared? *Regional Studies* **13**, 281–95.

Massey, D. 1979. In what sense a regional problem? *Regional Studies* **13**, 233–43.

McAleese, D. 1977. *A profile of grant-aided industry in Ireland.* Dublin: Industrial Development Authority.

Moody, T. and K. G. D. Smith 1975. Some problems in the evaluation of subsidies to British manufacturing industry. *Oxford Economic Papers* **27**, 274–94.

Moore, B. and J. Rhodes 1976. Regional economic policy and the movement of manufacturing firms to Development Areas. *Economica* **43**, 17–31.

Moore, B. and J. Rhodes 1973. Evaluating the effects of British regional policy. *Economic Journal* **83**, 87–110.

Moses, L., 1958. Location and the theory of production. *Quarterly Journal of Economics* **73**, 259–73.

O'Farrell, P. N. 1975. *Regional Industrial Development Trends in Ireland 1960–1973.* Dublin: Industrial Development Authority.

O'Farrell, P. N. 1974. Regional planning in Ireland – the case for concentration: a re-appraisal. *Economic and Social Review* **5**, 499–514.

O'Farrell, P. N. 1978. An analysis of new industry location: the Irish case. *Progress in Planning* **9**, 129–229.

O'Neill, H. B. 1973. Regional planning in Ireland – the case for concentration. *Irish Banking Review*, Sept., 9–20.

O'Neill, H. B. 1971. *Spatial planning in the small economy: a case study of Ireland.* New York: Praeger.

Perrons, D. C. 1981. The role of Ireland in the new international division of labour: a proposed framework for regional analysis. *Regional Studies* **15**, 81–100.

Programme for Economic Expansion (First) 1958. Dublin: Stationery Office, Prl. 7239.

Report of the Committee on Development Centres and Industrial Estates 1958. Dublin: Stationery Office, Prl. 8461.

Rich, D. C. 1980. Locational disadvantage and the regional problem: manufacturing industry in Scotland, 1961–1971. *Regional Studies* **14**, 399–417.

Ross, M. 1978. Comprehensiveness in regional policy. In *Irish Economic Policy: A Review of Major Issues*, B. R. Dowling and J. Durkan (eds.), pp. 297–334. Dublin: E.S.R.I.

Spooner, D. J. 1972. Industrial movement and the rural periphery: the case of Devon and Cornwall. *Regional Studies* **6**, 197–215.

Telesis Consultancy Group 1982. *A review of industrial policy.* Dublin: NESC Report no. 64.

Yannopoulos, G. N. and J. H. Dunning 1976. Multinational enterprises and regional development: an exploratory paper. *Regional Studies* **10**, 389–99.

Yuill, D., K. Allen and C. Hull 1980. *Regional policy in the European community: the role of regional incentives.* New York: St. Martin's Press.

Conclusions

BENJAMIN HIGGINS and DONALD J. SAVOIE

In this final chapter, we attempt to distill the information, analysis, and wisdom provided by the workshop into conclusions regarding regional development policy. In doing so, it is inevitable that the ideas of the editors themselves should weigh more heavily than those of the other authors of this volume, if only because no attempt was made during the workshop to reach a consensus. The chapter, in other words, is not meant to be a *summary* of the discussion. Rather, it reflects the impact of *all* of the discussion, in the workshop as well as in the volume, on the *editors'* views as to how regional development policy should evolve during the next decade or so. It does not commit other participants in the conference in any way.

The present volume reflects the current yeasty, transitional state of regional analysis, policy, and planning. The professional skill, the scientific integrity, and the concern for social welfare of the participants are well established. The various papers reflect broad and deep experience, as well as training, tools, and analytical ability. Yet the questions posed in the introduction have not all been answered. Doubts and disagreement remain. No one could agree with all the participants on every issue without sinking into a quagmire of self-contradiction. But in the aggregate the papers demonstrate how scientific progress is made in the social sciences, and point out the path by which ultimate agreement is reached.

The most formidable barrier to the achievement of instant unanimity is that various participants in the seminar view differently the very field of regional development, its scope and method, its status and role within the social sciences, and in economic and social policy. For some the devotion of time and energy to regional analysis is justified on pragmatic grounds. Urban and regional planning is an established profession and an honest one. There are courses to be taught, seminars to be conducted, textbooks to be written, consulting assignments to be undertaken. Those who pursue the profession competently will find it rewarding, intellectually and materially. Some, not necessarily different, members of the group would maintain that regional analysis is a recognized component of economics and of other social sciences, and that it can be handled with appropriate adaptation of familiar techniques. For them the existing whole of any one discipline is considerably greater than its regional part. But for a few, regional analysis is a new and superior *method* of tackling the whole field of economics (or other disciplines) while broadening its scope by studying actors on the spot and by dealing effectively with space as well as time, and integrating the two. With this concept, regional analysis is greater than the existing whole of mainstream economics (or other discipline). This latter view seems to be the one held by François Perroux, John Friedmann, Benjamin Higgins, and perhaps, although less clearly, by William Alonso. The other participants seem to cling to some combination of the first and second views.

The division with respect to the usefulness of neoclassical economics in resolving policy issues at the regional level corresponds quite closely to the division with respect to scope and method, which is natural enough. Those who think that neoclassical economics works well will be less eager to try something new. There were, to be sure, no advocates of strict laissez-faire in the seminar; at the very least intervention is needed to remove, offset, or improve existing policies and programs in the field of regional development. Beyond that "the market" has imperfections and needs "patching." No one argued for maintenance of the status quo. On the other hand, those who were least satisfied with the results of operation of a "free market" recognized that one can utilize neoclassical tools and techniques to find ways of improving its performance. There was general agreement, indeed, that in the hands of master craftsmen like Thomas Courchene and James Melvin, the neoclassical tools can be effective instruments for tackling some kinds of policy questions. But a fundamental split remained, based more on differing appraisals of the same set of facts than upon diverse ideological starting points. Some saw the market as the best available instrument for achieving social and economic goals, perhaps with a bit of patching. Others – again, essentially Perroux, Friedmann, Higgins, and Alonso – felt that no amount of patching could render any possible real world market capable of "maximizing social welfare"; tailor-made policies at the regional level and multilevel planning would be necessary to do that.

It should be noted that retaining, enlarging, and improving the neoclassical system, while at the same time exploring the frontiers of a broader system, more biological or thermodynamic in approach, are not totally incompatible. Atomic physics did not replace Newtonian mechanics, it added to it. In Sri Lanka both the Ministry of Public Health and the World Health Organization favor the maintenance of the traditional vedetic medicine while introducing and expanding the practice of modern Western medicine, because both systems work.

The main difficulty is that not all the facts are clear-cut, and even when "opaque facts" exist there is room for differing interpretations of them. One would think that the nature of interactions between interregional migration and regional disparities would be easy enough to establish. Yet in the seminar were representatives of two schools of thought on this question. One group expected migration to reduce regional gaps, and deplored policies that tend to retard migration from poorer, more stagnant regions to richer, more dynamic ones. The other group regarded "cumulative causation" as the rule, and argued that migration tends to make rich regions richer and poor regions poorer. It is interesting that John Vanderkamp, using all the data he could muster and analyzing them with sophisticated econometric techniques, arrived at no very clear answer for Canada regarding migration and regional gaps.

With regard to regional disparities as such, there is evidence of a change of attitude. No one in the seminar made an impassioned plea for the elimination of regional gaps, let alone suggesting effective policies for doing so. Indeed here is one area where participants at opposite ends of the spectrum with regard to the basic conflict of views tended to converge. Courchene and Melvin spoke of "a natural level of regional disparities," and Perroux of "optimal regional differences." Are these two concepts the same? Again we are confronted with questions of fact. The "natural" level of regional disparities, like Milton Friedman's "natural" rate of unemployment which assures price stability, could in some circumstances be very high indeed, perhaps so high as to enter the category of Perroux's "unbearable disequilibrium." When "regions" have distinct social and political meaning, as they do in Canada, it may make sense to use regional policy to tackle problems which are not really regional in origin, but which reflect problems attached rather to particular sectors, industries, occupations, or social groups. Yet it was noteworthy that no one in the seminar thought of "regional development" primarily in the sense of eliminating regional disparities. The emphasis was rather on making full and efficient use of resources, natural and human, in every region.

Growth poles

In a conference organized in honor of François Perroux with Perroux himself participating, there was naturally a good deal of discussion of growth poles. There was general agreement that growth poles are not dead, and they not only exist but are alive and well, and still living mainly in Paris. But the concept that is alive and well is very different from the one that has usually been applied by governments that have announced a growth pole strategy. Several of the participants expressed disillusionment with growth poles in the guise of a simple operational tool. Yet perhaps this conference has served to remind us that the growth pole concept as Perroux originally conceived it was considerably more than that. Perroux's two papers in this volume probably constitute the most complete and systematic statement yet published of his own concept; here, growth poles appear as one component of a much broader general theory. This theory, with growth poles as sets of basic activities in a system of interactions in space and irreversible time, is far more complex than the simple idea of a selected urban center generating spread effects to its immediately surrounding geographic region. Even understanding Perroux's system is difficult enough. Not only are the terms and concepts unfamiliar, the whole approach is unfamiliar, perhaps more so than those of Keynes's *General Theory* when it first appeared. Applying *these* concepts to policy and planning will be no easy task. Here the neoclassical economists and their critics converge; both groups agree that true development poles cannot be created at just any old place that some government chooses.[1] For a development pole to be successful certain conditions must be met. There are complex yet systematic sets of interactions in space and time, and these must be understood if the functioning of national and international economies as a whole are to be understood. They must be pinned down and applied if regional policy-making and planning are to be complete and effective. It is not an easy task, but given the sophistication of today's analytical and quantitative techniques, it is not an impossible task either.

Especially important, perhaps, is further research on spatial interactions in terms of flows of information and innovation – until recently a sadly neglected subject. The world is in a state of flux where factors determining location of economic activity are concerned, with access to advanced technology and information becoming ever more important. But it is not quite clear what changes in urban structures can be expected as a result. Niles Hansen's paper and the discussion around it showed that something is happening to urban hierarchies in industrialized countries, although it is not altogether sure what. New patterns of regional development are appearing in almost all advanced countries. It seems that hierarchies of cities in terms of size need no longer be matched by a parallel hierarchy in terms of quality of economic activity and style of living. Increasingly, small and middle-sized cities are showing themselves capable of developing or attracting sophisticated enterprises and a high quality of life. During the 1970s there seemed to be a tendency for high-tech industry and sophisticated services to flee the largest metropolitan centers, leading some observers to speak of deindustrialization, deurbanization, and "polarization reversal." But in the 1980s in some industrialized countries there has been a tendency for the largest metropolitan centers to resume rapid growth. It is too early to say whether a trend towards long-run "polarization reversal reversal" has set in; here is an area where further research is needed.

It seems that today's "propulsive enterprises" have become so mobile and so flexible as to scale that almost anything can happen, including a renewed trend towards agglomeration in existing metropolitan centers. Instead of throwing away "pôles de croissance" with a sigh of relief, we shall be obliged to study them more carefully than ever, including, as Perroux has so often stressed, the transmission lines and the receptors at the other end as well as the generators.

Perhaps the participants could have been brought to agree with Perroux on the following propositions regarding growth poles:

(a) Development involves polarization.
(b) Growth poles are accordingly a "good thing", a source of dynamism in the economy, which generate spread effects *somewhere*, but not necessarily in their own peripheral geographic region.
(c) The principal role of growth poles is as a source and a diffuser of innovations.
(d) Therefore growth poles should be encouraged to form and to play this role, even if it involves some degree of domination/dependence relationship.
(e) A policy of selected decentralization, or creation of "pôles d'équilibre," is not in conflict with this Perroux-style growth pole policy.
(f) Since investment decisions in propulsive industries are risky and discontinuous, temporary subsidization can be justified in the same way that protection of "infant industries" is justified. Growth pole strategy might be regarded as infant industry strategy set in space and time, and should involve nurturing healthy infants for strictly limited periods, together with refusal to run life-support systems for doddering geriatrics.
(g) There may be cases when small and middle-sized cities can serve as growth poles.
(h) What is excluded from a Perroux-style growth pole strategy is pushing and pulling enterprises at random into retarded and disadvantaged regions when the conditions for generation of spread effects are not present – in other words, the kind of growth pole strategy that was in fact pursued in many countries during the 1960s and 1970s.

Optimal size of cities

There was not a great deal of discussion as to whether polarization of economic activity in large cities is a "good thing" or a "bad thing." For Perroux the concentration of economic activity and progress in a few poles is simply the way that capitalistic development takes place, just as for Schumpeter monopolies are the price of progress, not even necessary evils, but not evils at all. For the most part this view was not seriously challenged, although John Friedmann's preference for settlement in smaller centers was evident. The discussion of "optimum size of city" that took place some years ago seemed to lead to the conclusion that there is no such thing as *the* optimal size, and interest in the subject waned. But this loss of interest may have been premature. The range of choice of city size without loss of "efficiency" may be wider than was once thought, and more study is necessary if planning is to include a concept of optimal urban *structure*. It is no longer so certain as it once seemed that there are thresholds of city size where various types of economic and social activity can be expected to appear. Perhaps the more sophisticated education- and technology-intensive (and satisfying) activities need not be concentrated in large cities while the less skilled, more routine and more boring activities are concentrated in small ones. On the other hand, it is less obvious than it once seemed that as it grows, every city must reach a point where it becomes inefficient and unpleasant. Even if such a point exists for every city, it need not be the same for all of them. There is some evidence that small towns that attract high-tech industry and sophisticated services tend to be close enough to large metropolitan centers to be able to "borrow size" from them, but even this "law" is open to question and needs further study. In any case, we are confronted with a need to redirect our energies for analysis, policy formulation, and planning away from individual cities of various sizes to entire urban hierarchies, their interactions, and their impacts on the pattern of regional development within a national and international economy.

Regional disparities and government intervention

The neoclassicists in the group presented some persuasive arguments on the side of greatly reduced government intervention. The question was forcefully put to the group as to whether regional "disparities" are not simply regional "differences," in human and natural resources, in structures of employment and output, in preferences, and the like. Why should governments attempt to remove or offset such differences? Put another way, what is it that governments are trying to accomplish when they mount regional development programs? If there is a particular region with low wages and high unemployment, then surely, they insist, we ought to treat the problem as one pertaining to individuals and social groups, not to a "region." We should not take the view that we are concerned with the region as such, or as one neoclassicist put it, "the patch." The individual is what matters.

This view was of course challenged. John Friedmann made the point that within the narrow limits of neoclassical economics, neoclassicists can build invulnerable fortresses by employing sophisticated economic models. But, he pleaded, we are not dealing with atoms swirling around in space at random; rather, we are dealing with social structures populated by people. People identify with these social structures, with their communities and with regions. If the neoclassical apparatus cannot deal with this crucial fact, he suggested, then it ought to be too bad for the apparatus, not for the region.

The debate raged on, and it seemed that the deliberations served only to strengthen the resolve of both groups. But those supporting government intervention were somewhat on the defensive. Somehow, they had to explain the lack of success of costly government programs for regional development over the past 20 years. Neoclassicists, meanwhile, could sit back and declare "we were right then and we are still right." Governments should not intervene to prop up the region, or the "patch."

Thus, there were in the seminar two competing approaches to regional development, the same two basic approaches we have had since regional development first surfaced as a field of study and government activity. In many ways, the influence of each paradigm has waxed or waned more in tune with general economic circumstances and prevalent political mood of the country than on its own merits. It seems that in times of growth, and when governments place priority on redistributive policies, government measures for promoting regional development are favored. When governments retrench on redistributive policies, regional development programs tend to be cut back, and observers invariably point to the neoclassical approach as the way ahead for regional policy.

This debate has been of little assistance to government officials charged with planning regional development initiatives. Elected politicians, particularly those from slow-growth regions, are committed to government-sponsored regional development initiatives, and will remain so notwithstanding the persuasive logic of the neoclassicists. The same can be said for bureaucrats in regional development agencies. Other theories of regional development advanced have also been of little help. Neo-Marxist theory is an example. The theory suggests that it is convenient for capitalists to maintain regional disparities so that a pool of cheap labor in lagging regions can be utilized by developed regions when needed, and then dismissed whenever economic circumstances make labor redundant (see, e.g., Mandel 1973). To the workaday regional planner, the neo-Marxist dependency theory exudes an air of otherworldliness evading the problems with which he has to grapple, and so provides little guidance for policy decisions.

That we should have competing theories or approaches to the study of regional development should come as a surprise to no one. Economists and public policy analysts are well known for presenting contradictory approaches to a particular problem. What is different in this context is that senior researchers in the field admit that considerable uncertainty still exists. With very few exceptions, even the staunchest supporters of any one theory will readily admit that it explains only part of the situation and that it needs to be complemented by another theory, or that more work is required on the theory itself. In uncharacteristic fashion, the Economic Council of Canada (1977) summed up the situation this way: "Doctors used to try to cure syphilis with mercury and emetics. We now know that mercury works but emetics do not and, moreover, that penicillin is best of all. We suspect that the regional disparity disease is presently being treated with both mercury- and emetic-type remedies, but we do not know which is which. Perhaps one day an economic penicillin will be found" (Higgins (1983) made this point in much the same words.)

No one questions that we have not yet found a general theory of regional development. Yet it is in this framework of imperfect and incomplete knowledge that regional development policies and initiatives have been defined and updated during the past three decades. Practitioners of regional development in Europe, North America, Australasia, and developing countries have had very little in the way of a widely accepted theoretical framework from which initiatives could be formulated. Participants at the conference attempted to deal with this reality and to explore avenues that may hold promise. "Back to the laboratory," remarked one participant at one point. Before returning to the laboratory, however, it is wise to pause and reflect on the things we have learned thus far about regional development.

The first thing is that many of us overestimated the ability of government to influence the pace and location of economic activity. The war on regional disparities was no more easily won than the war on poverty. Second, no panacea for regional development was discovered nor is one likely to be, at least in the near future. The first step in making progress may be to admit that *there is no general theory* which would enable us to deal with all cases and all objectives of regional development, and that it is unlikely that one will surface.

In the light of this deficiency, one participant urged that we adopt a clinical approach. Only on the basis of a thorough diagnosis of each case, can we decide what the major problems are, establish priorities for dealing with them, and, on the basis of our knowledge of the anatomy, biochemistry, and physiology of the "patient," together with knowledge of other case histories, prescribe treatment. But we had better keep our eye on the patient as treatment proceeds and be prepared to change it if it appears not to work. We must reconcile ourselves to the fact that there are no "wonder drugs" in development. What is required for a policy of checking growth of the largest metropolitan centers may not be the same treatment that is required for alleviating poverty in a retarded region, or for achieving general improvements in the distribution of welfare among regions and social groups. In some circumstances, accelerating growth of the national economy may require still other measures. And we must be prepared to find that achieving some of these goals may require more continuous and more drastic treatment than seems necessary at first.

The point was also made that in future, regional development efforts should not be presented primarily as a means of reducing gaps in per capita income among regions, although it could have that effect as a by-product. Rather, it should be presented as a program to exploit opportunities to utilize labor, natural resources, and capital more fully and more efficiently. It should be focused on areas where output and incomes are lower than they could and should be, because the labor force, the natural resource endowment, or the capital stock is under-utilized or badly utilized. These areas would include not only those where unemployment and the incidence of relative poverty are high, but also resource frontier areas which need some kind of government intervention or support to realize their full potential.

Others suggested that in seeking answers to regional development problems one ought to look to the massive economic restructuring which is currently taking place. The economic development process is changing, and we must weigh carefully several important emerging forces. These include the changeover to a global market system, to a new international division of labor, the growing role of global cities and global economic cooperation, and new ways of integrating local economies into the international economy. These are the big questions that should guide future attempts at defining a new approach to regional development.

One participant maintained that additional research should be undertaken on the relationship between the individual and political institutions. Individuals, it was argued, are losing faith in institutional structures. In the opinion of some conference participants, the dialogue between units – whether between individuals and community, community and regions, or regions and national institutions – is breaking down, or at least it is not as strong as it once was. Individuals seem to be withdrawing from national and even regional institutions and moving towards the community level. This phenomenon should be explored, even though to some the notion of trust and institutional dialogue may not appear to be part of economic measures or of an economic development strategy. But this dialogue can drive the willingness of people to accept the legitimacy of government decision-making. More important, it is of vital importance in the search for setting the appropriate trade-offs between regional equity and national growth. If regional disparities are inevitable, then institutions must have the legitimacy to impress upon individuals living in slow-growth areas that they, and the national community, will have to accommodate a certain level of disparities. Failing this perception, the stress and strain on national political institutions and the national economy resulting from interregional conflicts may well prevent government from implementing its economic strategy, however well conceived.

Note

1 In his paper Perroux chides "his friend Ben Higgins" for daring to ask "Do development poles exist?" I should like to take this opportunity to reiterate that in the article under that title I never questioned that the phenomenon of polarization exists. I was raising the question of whether we can always count on the generation of significant spread effects to the surrounding geographic region in which the pole exists.

References

Economic Council of Canada 1977. *Living together*. Ottawa: Ministry of Supply and Services.
Higgins, B. 1983. From growth poles to systems of interactions in space. *Growth and Change* 14(4).
Mandel, E. 1973. *Capitalism and regional disparities*. Toronto: New Hogtown Press.

Appendix: The main publications of François Perroux

Books

Economic matters

1926   *The problem of profit*. Paris: Marcel Giard.
1930   *The techniques of capitalism*. Paris: Jean Lesfauries.
1933   *The wages of civil servants in France*. Paris: Sirey (a contribution for France to the inquiry of the Verein für Social Politik).
1935   *The economic thought of Joseph Schumpeter: a pure theory of capitalist dynamics*. Paris: Dalloz (new enlarged edn 1965. Geneva: Droz).
1938   *Capitalism and the labour community*. Paris: Sirey.
1943   *Autarchy and expansion*. Paris: Librairie de Médicis.
          The value. Paris: PUF.
1947   *The national income, its calculation and its significance*. Paris: PUF.
1948   *The Marshall Plan, or Europe necessary to the world*. Paris: Librairie de Médicis.
          Capitalism. Que sais-je Collection. Paris: PUF (7th edn 1969). Translations: Japanese 1951, Spanish 1952, Italian 1960, Portuguese (Brazil) 1961, Catalan (Barcelona) 1964, Hebrew (Tel Aviv) 1964, Arabic (Beirut).
1949   *The social book-keeping of the nation*. Pragma Collection. Paris: PUF.
1954   *Europe unbounded by the seas*. Paris: PUF.
1956   *A general theory of economic development: the measurement of economic developments and the concept of progressive economy*. Publications of the I.S.E.A. Series I, fasc. 1, Translated into Greek.
1957   *A general theory of economic progress. I. Components: 1. Creation.* Publications of the I.S.E.A. Series 1, fasc. 2.
          A general theory of economic progress. I. Components: 2. Propagation; A. Micro-economic models. Publications of the I.S.E.A. Series I, fasc. 3.
          The economic problems of "coexistence" and the growth of a worldwide economy. I. The conflict beyond systems. Publications of the I.S.E.A. – also published in *The pacific coexistence* (1958).
          The economic problems of "coexistence" and the growth of a worldwide economy. 2. Development poles and foreign trade. Publications of the I.S.E.A. Series G, fasc. 5.

1958	*The pacific coexistence.* 3 vols. Paris: PUF. Translations: Spanish (Mexico) 1960, Italian (Turin) 1961, German (Stuttgart) 1961, Japanese 1963–4.
1960	*Economy and society, the constraint, the commercial exchange, the gift.* Initiation Philosophique Collection. Paris: PUF (2nd edn 1964). Translations: German (Stuttgart) 1961, Italian (Milan) 1961, Japanese (Tokyo) 1962, Portuguese (Lisbon) 1962, Spanish (Barcelona) 1963, Arabic (Damascus) 1983.
1961	*The economy of the 20th century.* Paris: PUF (3rd enlarged edn 1969). Translations: Spanish, Italian, German (2nd edn), Portuguese.
1962	*The Fourth French Plan (1962–65).* Que sais-je Collection. Paris: PUF (2nd edn 1963). Translations: Portuguese 1962, German 1964, English 1965.
	The economy of young nations. Paris: PUF. Translation: Portuguese 1964.
1963	Dialectics and socialization. Preface to *The works of Karl Marx* (M. Rubel). La Pleiade Collection. Paris: Gallimard.
1964	*Industry and collective creation.* Vol. I: *The Saint-Simonism of the 20th century and collective creation.* Paris: PUF. Translations: Spanish (Buenos Aires) 1964, Spanish (Barcelona) 1965, Portuguese 1965.
1965	*The quantitative techniques of planning.* Paris: PUF. Translations: Greek (Athens) 1968, Rumanian (Bucharest) 1969, Spanish (Barcelona) 1969.
1969	*Research and economic activity* (collective book). Paris: Armand Colin.
	The "independence" of the nation and the interdependence of the nations. Paris: Aubier–Montaigne.
1970	*Industry and collective creation.* Vol. II: *The images of the new man and collective techniques.* Paris: PUF.
	Alienation and the industrial society. Paris: Gallimard.
1971	*The independence of the nation.* Paris: "10–18". Translations: Hungarian (Budapest) 1972.
	Inflation, the dollar, the Euro-dollar (with J. Denizet & H. Bourguinat). Idées Collection. Paris: Gallimard.
1973	*Power and economy.* Etudes Collection. Paris: Bordas. Translations: Italian (Milan) 1978, German (Stuttgart: Haupt) 1983.
1975	*The active units and new mathematics: a revision of the general economic equilibrium theory.* Paris: Dunod.
1980	*The new international economic order.* Encyclopedia Universalis, supplement.
	The transnational firms and the new international economic order. Lyon: *Croissance des Jeunes Nations.*
1981	*A new concept of development.* Paris: Aubier, UNESCO. Translations: English, Spanish.
1982	*A dialogue between monopolies and nations.* Grenoble: Presses Universitaires de Grenoble.

Social matters

1936	*The Hitlerian myths.* Lyon. Translation: Spanish (Rio de Janeiro, São Paulo) 1937.
1937	*Why French?* Paris: Ed. du Cerf.
1939	*Trade-unionism and capitalism.* Paris: Librairie Générale.

1940 *From the Hitlerian myths to German Europe.* Paris: Librairie Générale de Droit et de Jurisprudence.
1942 *Community.* Paris: PUF. Translations: German, Spanish.
1968 *Bread and the word.* Paris: Ed. du Cerf.
1969 *Questions of François Perroux to Herbert Marcuse, who answers.* Paris: Aubier–Montaigne.
1970 *Alienation and the industrial society.* Idées Collection. Paris: Gallimard. Translation: Spanish (Lima) 1970.
1972 *Mass and class.* Mutations–Orientations Collection. Paris: Casterman/Poche.

Roneo books

Economic matters

1935 *The agrarian reforms in Europe.* Paris: Domat–Montchrestien.
1941 *Neo-marginalism.* Paris: Domat–Montchrestien (a lecture delivered at the Ecole Pratique des Hautes Etudes de la Sorbonne, 2nd edn 1945).
1947 *A course of lectures on political economy.* Vol. 1 (5th edn): *Economic systems and structures, the historical formation of capitalism, techniques, organization and the spirit of capitalism.* Paris: Centre de Documentation Universitaire.
The national income and the quantitative political economy. Paris: Centre de Documentation Universitaire (a doctorate course at the Faculty of Law of Paris).
A history of contemporary economic doctrine, J.M. Keynes. Paris: Centre de Documentation Universitaire (a course of lectures at the Institute of Political Sciences).
1949 *A course of lectures on political economy.* Vol. 2 (5th edn): *The firm and capitalism. The growth and the intensity of the capitalist firm. The production and the exchange of goods. The formation and the distribution of credit. Concentration and capitalism.* Paris: Centre de Documentation Universitaire.
1955 *Matters for an analysis of economic growth.* Publications of the I.S.E.A. Series D, no. 8.
Three methods of analysis for the study of under-development. In *Levels of development and growth policy.* Publications of the I.S.E.A. Series F, no. 1.
1961 *Information and industrialization.* A lecture at the Round Table on the Social Premises of Industrialization, Conseil International des Sciences Sociales, 12–15 September, I.E.D.E.S.

Social matters

1944 *The meaning of the new work law.* Paris: Domat–Montchrestien.

Appendix

Brochures and articles

Economic theory

1927   *The problem of profit.* Lyon (brochure).
1935   I concetti de statica et dinamica secondo Giuseppe Schumpeter. *Revista Internationale di Scienze Sociali.*
1938   About the word "capitalism": meaning and misunderstanding. *Esprit.*
1939   The notion of industrial group. *Political Economy Review.*
        Preface to *Initiation into economic theory* (A. Murat). Théoria Collection. Paris: PUF.
1943   The combination of the value of money theory with the value of goods theory. *Contemporary Economy,* December.
        Money in an organized international economy. *Contemporary Economy,* December.
1945   The part played by the apparatus of modern theory in Albert Aftalion's work. In *The scientific work of Albert Aftalion.* Paris: Domat–Montchrestien, February.
1947   The connection of abstract rigor with concrete knowledge in a "positive" economy: a lesson drawn from the work of Gaëtan Pirou. *Political Economy Review,* July–August.
1948   The choices of the producing state and of the consumer. *Econometrica* 16 (January), p. 68 (a summary of the lecture delivered at the Washington Congress in September 1947).
        The outline of a dominant economy theory. *Applied Economy, Records of the I.S.E.A.* nos 2/3 (April–September). Translations: German (Springer–Verlag) 1950–51, English (*Social Research* no. 2) June 1950, Polish (Warsaw) 1960.
1949   Harmonized growth according to Colin Clark. *Banque.*
        The dominance effect in economic relationships. *Hommes et Techniques,* January.
        The generalization of the general theory. University of Istanbul brochure, July (review of the Economic Sciences Department of the University of Istanbul).
        Macrodecisions. *Applied Economy* nos 2/3. Lecture delivered at the Cambridge Congress, England, September. Translations: Italian (*Giornale degli Economisti a Annali di Economia*) September/October 1949, German (Vienna) 1950.
1950   A general interpretation of the general theory. *Banque.*
        Economic spaces, theory and applications. *Quarterly Journal of Economics* LXIV, no. 1. Republished 1965 in *Readings in regional development* (J. Friedman). Cambridge, Mass.: MIT Press.
        Economic spaces. *Applied Economy* no. 1.
        The generalization of the interest theory by Keynes. *Banque,* March.
        A note on the dynamics of dominance. *Applied Economy* no. 2.
1951   J. M. Keynes: Man and the problems of his time. *Contemporary Economy,* January.
        The three analyses of evolution and of the quest for a total dynamics. In Schumpeter's work, *Applied Economy* no. 2.
1952   *The dynamism of human psychism* (Jubilee of Dean Dagenfeld). Schonburg, Wirtschaftliche Entwiclung und Sociale Ordnung. Vienna: Herold.

A notion of competition and the dominance effect. *Banque*, May.

About the notion of economic structure. Preface to *The formation of capital and French reconstruction* (Byais). Centre d'Etudes Economiques.

The cost of man: from the avarice of nations to an economy devoted to the human race. A report of the lectures delivered at Dijon and Lyon at "La semaine sociale" (October) and "La vie intellectuelle" (November).

The future of Europe and the psychosis of location. A synthesis, Brussels, October.

1953 *The economic "leadership" of the USA and a modern analysis of foreign exchanges* (in German, French and Italian). Vienna: Europ (Kreditanstalt-Bankverein).

A general theory of economic activity: the monopolistic competition theory. Preface to the French translation of *Monopolistic competition* (E. H. Chamberlin). Theoria Collection. Paris: PUF.

Etienne Antonelli and the scientific analysis of economic phenomena. *Economic and Social History Review* no. 4.

1954 The gift. Its economic meaning in contemporary capitalism. *Diogène Review*, April.

1955 A note on the notion of growth pole. *Applied Economy* nos 1 & 2.

The theory of monopolistic competition – a general theory of economic activity. *The Indian Economic Review*, February. Translation of the preface to the French translation of *Monopolistic competition* (E. H. Chamberlin). Theoria Collection. Paris: PUF.

1956 *Financial stability and the equilibrium of the balance of payment.* Paris: Public Finance International Institute. A lecture delivered at the Curibita Congress on Public Finance, Brazil, September 1954.

An inaugural lecture at the College of France (5 December 1955). Published by the College of France, May–June.

functions of profit. Preface to *The economy of popular democracies, studies and documents.* I.S.E.A. Series G, no. 1.

1957 The propagation of economic information in modern society. A symposium in honour of Professor Ugo Papi. *L'Industria*, March.

The distinction between economic improvements and the concept of progressive economy, a few American instances. A symposium in honour of Professor Gini, Institute of Statistics, Rome.

Information as a factor of economic development in 20th century societies. Reports and publications of the Sciences, Arts and Literature Society of Hainaut, Mons, French edition 1958, *Diogène Review* no. 1. American edition *Diogène*, spring 1958.

Structural inflation and the economic function of wages: the French example. In *The theory of wage determination* (proceedings of a conference held by the International Economics Association), pp. 251–63. London: Macmillan.

Profit and the economic improvements. *Action Populaire Review*, November.

The development poles and international economy. Symposium: The Challenge of Development. Jerusalem.

1958 The quest for stability: the real factors. *Applied Economy* nos 1 & 2 (a contribution to the Economic Sciences International Association Congress, Rome, September). Translations: English (in *Stability and progress in the world economy*, pp. 105–26. London: Macmillan)

1958; German (Das Streben nach Stabilität: Die realen Factoren. *Zeitschrift für National Okönomie* nos 1/2, pp. 102–34) 1958.

Economic anticipation and harmonized growth. A lecture delivered at the International Congress of the CEGOS, Brussels, June.

On the specificity of a scientifically checked economic power. In *Researches and philosophical and economic dialogues*. Publications of the I.S.E.A. Series M, no. 2.

1959 Indici dei progressi economici e l'idea di economia collectiva. *Studi economia*, translation no. 3 (January–April), Naples.

The development poles and the international economy. In *Foreign affairs* (Trotabas). Paris: PUF.

A note for the French reader about the article of Professor Scitowski, Balanced or not balanced growth? *Applied Economy* nos 1 & 2 (January–July).

A useful distinction for the policy of countries with delayed growth: development points and centers of progress (Morocco and Tunisia). Publications of the I.S.E.A. Series F, no. 12.

Economic structures. Publications of the I.S.E.A. Series M, no. 6.

1960 The specific projects and development plans in the countries with delayed growth. *Encyclopédie Française.* Vol. IX: *The social and economic world.*

Economic experience and economic science. *Encyclopédie Française.* Vol. IX: *The social and economic world.*

The idea of improvement and the contemporary economic science. *Encyclopédie Française.* Vol. IX: *The social and economic world* (lectures at the College of France 1959–60). Translations: Polish (Paris) 1961, Portuguese (Universidade Tecnica de Lisboa) 1963. Also published by I.S.E.A. 1961 (see below).

On economic science. Review of *L'Enseignement superieur* no. 2.

For a necessary renewal: the analysis of innovation and of growth. A participation in the International Congress on Technological Improvement and Italian Society, Milan, June–July. Translation: Italian (Milan, Padua) 1961. See also Innovation and growth, 1961.

On setting up a coupling model between a polarized area and another one. A participation in the Colloquium on Regional Economies, Institute of Economic Science of the University of Liège, April.

The distinction between economic improvements and the concept of progressive economy, a few American instances. An extract from Vol. 1 of *Studi in Onore di Corrado Gini*, Institute of Statistics, Rome.

Polish translations in *Theoria i polityka handlumiedzyparodowego w kapitalismio.* Warsaw: Polskie Wydawnictuwa Gospodarcze:
The dominant economy theory;
The problem of connected growths.

1961 *The idea of improvement and the contemporary economic science.* Publications of the I.S.E.A. Series M, no. 9.

Innovation and growth. A few suggestions for a necessary renewal (in French). In *Il Progresso technologico e la Societa Italiana.* Milan: Guiffre (publication of the acts of the Vienna Congress).

What is development? *Les Etudes*, January.

A lecture, at the Commission des Comptes et des Budgets Economiques de la Nation, the Labour Mass, May.

The criticism of the welfare economy and the quest for a collective advantage. *Arguments*, 2nd term, Liège.

A note on aspiration and expectation. *Economic Science Review* September, Liège.

The economic progress and its meaning. Publications of the I.S.E.A. Series M, nos 11 & 12.

A few considerations and precisions with a view to conversing with Gilles Granger. Publications of the I.S.E.A. Series M, nos 11–12.

Polish translations in *Ekonomia Wobec Potrzeb Ludzkich*. Paris: Ksiergarnia Polska w Paryzu:
The method of generalized economy and the economy of mankind;
The concept of progress facing contemporary economic science;
The industrialization of the 20th century and the chances of a generalized economy;
The hostile coexistence and the advent of the world-wide powers;

1962 Economic structures. In *The meanings and the uses of the term "structure"*. Holland: Mouton.

Indicative planning in France. Proceedings of the Colloquium on Planning, Institut de Sociologie de l'Université Libre de Bruxelles.

The Fourth French Plan (1962–1965). What does our indicative planning consist of? *Applied Economy*, January–June.

1963 The propulsive firms and the growth of a national economy. *Applied Economy*, no. 2.

The propulsive firms and the growth of a national economy. The acts of the French-Canadian Colloquium, November.

The innovation investment for a two sectors model: a sector with fast growth and a sector with slow growth. *Applied Economy* no. 4.

1964 *The propulsive firms and the growth of a national economy.* A report from the Association des Ingénieurs de la Faculté Polytechnique de Mons, February.

The propulsive firms and the growth of a national economy. Institut d'Economie Appliquée, Ecole des hautes Etudes Commerciales, Montréal.

The propulsive firms and the growth of a national economy. Publications in honour of Professor Oscar Lange, Warsaw.

Las industrias Motrices y la Planificacion del Crecimiento de una Economia Nacional de Cordoba, Argentina.

1965 *Las Funciones de Produccion.*
1967 The Euler–Wicksteed Theorem. *Tiers-Monde*, April.

A note on the production function. *Tiers-Monde* **VIII**, no. 31 (July–September).

La Empreza Motriz en una region y la Region Motriz. *De Economia* **XX**, no. 97.

Theory of economic growth. *Waseda Journal of Political Science and Economics*, April.

On the degree of generality of the general equilibrium theory. *Economies and Societies* no. 9, p. 227.

Preface to *Private costs and social costs* (C. Jessua). Paris: PUF.

1970 The implicitly normative concepts and the limits of the modelization of economy (a colloquium at the Institut d'Histoire des Sciences de l'Université de Paris.) In *Economies and societies*. Publications of the I.S.E.A. no. 12.

El Crecimiento, el Desarollo, los Progresos, el Progreso. *De Economia* no. 114, pp. 563–94.

1971 The Heckscher–Ohlin–Samuelson Theorum, the International Trade Theory and the unequal development. *Mondes en développement* no. 1. Translations: Turkish (*Alti Ayda Bir Cikai*), Hungarian (*Acta Oeconomica Academia Scientiarum Hungarica* 5(4), p. 325), Spanish (*Los Cuardernos Franco-Españoles de Economica* no. 1) 1971.

A presentation of the M.A.L. Model and the renewal of the economic exchange models. In *Economies and societies*. Publications of the I.S.E.A. V, no. 10.

Equilibrium by Von Neuman: a first attempt of evaluation. In *Economies and Societies*. Publications of the I.S.E.A. V, no. 10.

1972 *Mathematical structures and real structures in economy*. Fundamental references. Honoris Causa Doctorate, Barcelona University, 15–18 March.

The "unknown parameters" of growth. *L'Expansion*, July.

The mathematization of economic phenomena and including theory. A few stages. In *Economies and societies*. Publications of the I.S.E.A. no. 8.

Macht und Economische Gesetzmässigkeit. Conference Gesellschaft für Wirtschafts und Sozialwissenschaften. Verein für Socialpolitik, Bonn, September.

The necessity of taking into account the concept of power in economic science. The centenary of the Verein für Sozialpolitik.

Preface to *Systems and economic structures* (E. Teilhac). R.E.S. Coll. Paris: Aubier-Montaigne.

Preface to *Foreign trade and the development of the small nation* (A. Basile). Geneva-Paris: Droz.

1972–3 The rational communication between sciences and its impact upon economic science. *Nouvelle Ecole* nos 21–2.

1973 The scientific theory of economy and its application to mathematics. *Elan Review*. Publications of the I.C.S., no. 1 (January).

Towards an "including" theory of profit. *Applied Economy* no. 1.

The propulsive effect: from the analysis to a quantitative marking. *Applied Economy* nos 2–4.

The economic agent (actor), equilibrium and the choice of formalisations. *Applied Economy* nos 2–4.

Economic structure. Der Moderne Strukturbegriff, Wissenschaftliche Buchgesellschaft, Darmstadt.

The scientific theory of political theory. *El Dia Review* (Mexico), 22 April.

The scientific theory of economy and its renovated mathematical formalisation. *Elan Review*, Cahiers I.C.S. no. 1 (January), Strasbourg.

1974 An economic system based on the full development of human energy. *Mondes en développement* no. 7.

A notion of equilibrium and present mathematics, an interpretation. *Mondes en développement* no. 8.

1975 Transnational units and the renovation of the General (closed and open economy) Equilibrium Theory. *Mondes en développement* no. 12. Translation: German (Berlin) 1976.

The "Active" Units in the 20th century and the new mathematical appliances of the general equilibrium. *Economie Appliquée* no. 4.

Economic rationality and statistical rationality. *Revue Statistique.* Bulletin de la Société Statistique de Paris.

1976 *The structures and the dynamics of systems, pluridisciplinary, multidisciplinary, interdisciplinary and all that.* Interdisciplinary Seminars of the College of France, Maloine, Paris.

For a renewal of the theory of the inner and external economic equilibrium. *Mondes en développement* no. 16.

The concept of equilibrium and the current forms of the mathematical presentation. *Economie Appliquée* no. 2.

A notion of equilibrium, present mathematics and the thermodynamics of Ilya Prigogine. Table Ronde du Centre National de la Recherche Scientifique Sadi-Carnot. Paris: C.N.R.S. Editions.

A criticism of the economic rationality and the statistical rationality. In homage to His Eminence Henri Van Camp. Editions du Cinquantenaire de l'Ecole des Sciences Philosophiques et Religieuses, Brussels.

1977 *The renewal of the theory of the general economic equilibrium (equilibrations, dissipating structures, entropies).* Colloquium on The Idea of Regulation in Sciences, Interdisciplinary Researches, directed by P. Delattre. Interdisciplinary Seminars of the College of France, Maloine, Paris.

1978 *The mathematics of Walras and Pareto and the "Active Unit"*, in Honour of Dean Teixera Ribeiro, Coimbra, Portugal.

A policy of sciences and an analysis of innovation and of its propagation. *Chroniques de la S.E.D.E.I.S.*, October.

1979 An outline of a theory of the Dominant Economy. In *Transnational corporations and world order* (G. Modelski, ed.). Readings in international political economy, Washington DC: Seattle University.

1984 The surmounted crisis: struggling monopolies or monopolies backing up the system. *Courrier de l'UNESCO*, January.

Unstable financing and big innovations. A collective publication entitled Finance, production and the lacks of balance in the world-wide economy. *Economies et sociétés* no. 5 (May).

Applied economy

1928 Notes on the national debts distribution in case of a nation's breaking up. *Revue de Science et de Législation Financière*.

The notion of normal profit and the law of 3 December 1926. *Questions Politiques*.

The fascist doctrine and the concept of firm leader. *Revue d'Economie Politique*.

1929 The judicial organization of trusts in the USA. *Revue Politique et Parlementaire*.

1930–5 The French railways and other means of conveyance. *Revue d'Economie Politique*.

1931 Gold and the policy of the Bank of France. *Revue Economique Internationale*. Translation: German (*Goldzufluss nach Frankreich*, Frankfurt am Main). 1931.

Appendix

1932   The German-French economic relations. *Revue de l'Université de Lyon.*
1933   The fascist finances, 1922–1932. *Finanzarchiv.*
       The mixed economy society and the capitalist system. *Revue d'Economie Politique.*
       The French Railways Crisis. *Revue Economique Internationale.*
       The corporative economic system and the capitalist system. *Revue d'Economie Politique.*
1936   Corporations and capitalism (a brochure and a preface to *The evolvement of German trade-unions since the War* (R. Goetz)). Paris.
       The political reorganization in Germany (a study published as a preface to *Agrarian property in Italy* (A. Murat)). Lyon.
1938   *Handicraft in a capitalist system.* Paris: Jean Lesfauries.
       Technics in a modern capitalist system. Paris: Jean Lesfauries.
       For or against the Labour community. Reports of *Philosophie du Droit* nos 3–4.
1940   The central banks and the State. *Revue d'Economie Politique,* July.
1943   The connection between economic and social matters. *Le Droit Social,* March.
1944   The central banks and the State. *Revue d'Economie Politique* nos 4–6 (November).
1945   The Bretton-Woods Agreements. *La Vie Intellectuelle,* April. (Republished in November by Domat–Montchrestien, Paris.)
       The Bretton-Woods International Money and the French Effort. *La Tribune économique* nos 3–4 (May).
       The Bretton-Woods Bank and the international investment. *Revue économique et sociale* no. 18 (August).
       For a policy of prices. Brochure of the Groupes Travail, August.
       Nationalizations. Brochure of the Groupes Travail, September.
       Organized economy and socialized economy. Brochure of the Groupes Travail.
       What is a plan? La Vie Intellectuelle, September.
       Money and foreign trade after the war (a brochure, Centre des Jeunes Patrons. Echanges Internationaux, September).
1946   Both aspects of the English–French economic cooperation. *Courrier Diplomatique* no. 1 (February).
       The Washington Agreements and the future of the French economy. *Productions Françaises,* July.
       The firm leader in the 20th century economy. *Productions Françaises,* September.
       The national income and the economic policy. *L'Actualité Economique et Financière,* June.
       Liberalism or interventionism. (An enquiry of the Revue Economique Franco-Suisse de la Chambre de Commerce Franco-Suisse, September).
1947   The fundamental choices of our foreign policy and the future of our economy. *Productions Françaises,* June.
       The United States and the responsibilities of an internationally dominant economy. Bulletin d'Information des Anciens Elèves du Centre de Perfectionnement dans l'Administration des Affaires (B.I.C.P.A.), December.
       The social book-keeping of our reconstruction. *Productions Françaises,* October.

1948	The indefiniteness of "Checking up global quantities". *Economie Appliquée* no. 1.
	The Marshall Plan. The classical doctrine of investment and the economic reconstruction of Europe. *Les Cahiers du Monde Nouveau* (R. P. Chaillet).
	Nationalizations and national book-keeping. Congrès de la comptabilité, 10–14 May. (Republished in 1949 in *Economie Appliquée* no. 1.)
	The Marshall Plan (a report from the Institut des Hautes Etudes Americaines, brochures VIII–IX).
	Classical tenet and historical accident, the International Investment, the Bretton-Woods bank and the Marshall Plan. *Banque*, June.
	The national accounts and the national capital (an introduction). *L'Actualité économique et financière*, July.
1949	The connections between private book-keeping and national and social book-keeping. (An account to the Conseil Economique et Social, 2 February, reproduced in *Experta* nos 22–3 (March/April)).
	Wages and the balance of under-employment. *Banque*, August.
	The economic co-operation in Europe. A conference held in Munich, 21 September. Published by the Institut für Wirtschaftsforschung.
1950	The Monnet Plan and the economic future of Europe. *Banque*, April.
	Liberal Interventionism and the particular contribution of J. M. Keynes. *L'Actualité économique*, April/June.
	The indefiniteness of full employment. *Banque*, April.
	What about the Schumann Plan? *L'Exportateur Français*, 15 October.
	The coal and steel pool, illusions and realities. *Fédération*, November.
	Re-armament and inflationist pressure. *L'Exportateur Français*, 15 December.
1951	One aspect of the co-ordination of investments in Europe. *L'Exportateur Français*, 15 May.
1952	The Anglo-Iranian Co. and the dominance effects. *Economie Appliquée* no. 1.
	A report on the economic book-keeping of the nation, at the Conseil Supérieur de la Comptabilité (spring 1951). *Bulletin d'information du Conseil Supérieur de la Comptabilité* no. 6.
	A note on the costs of man. *Economie Appliquée* no. 1.
1953	A report at the Commission des Comptes et des Budgets Economiques de la Nation. *Imprimerie Nationale*, March.
	The liberal interventionism. *Cahiers d'information économique*, Paris.
	Present debates on convertibility and the inferences which we should draw from them. *L'Exportateur Français*, 15 May.
	Topics for an analysis of the increase of private wealth in France (1820–1914) (a report at the Congress of the International Association for Research in Income and Wealth (I.A.R.I.W.), Castelgandolfo, 1–6 September).
	The "prescription" of J. M. Keynes and the under-developed countries. Bulletin de l'Union des Exploitations Electriques en Belgique no. 3 (July).
	The industrial public area and the conditions of "coherence". *Economie et Humanisme* no. 8 (September/October).
1954	*The obliteration of the economic function of wages and structural inflation*. Round Table on Wage Determination, I.E.A., Seelesberg, Switzerland, September. (Also published by Macmillan, London 1957).

Appendix

1955 The new meaning of the 20th century credit policy. *Revue de la Conserve*, October.

On the full employment policy, documents and comments. *Cahiers du Centre Français du Patronat Chrétien*, October.

On the full employment policy. *Economie Appliquée* nos 1–2.

1956 Points of view on the growth of the French economy. *Etudes statistiques*. London: I.A.R.I.W. Series 5.

The analysis of economic growth and its application upon French economy 1820–1914. Congress of Poitiers, July 1954. *Association Français pour l'Avancement de la Science*.

The virtues of dialogue – the chances and the risks of a new economy – researches and debates. *Cahiers du Centre Catholique Français* no. 14 (January).

Labour and Civilization. *Esprit*, October.

1957 The crisis of the political power and Big Capitalism. *L'Action Populaire*, January.

The concept of Development Pole and the industrial groups in Africa. *Sentier d'Europe* no. 1 (Bulletin de l'Association des élèves et anciens élèves de l'Institut Universitaire d'Etudes Européennes de Turin).

Development Poles and Eastern Policy. *Politique Etrangère* (special number), Economic development and international co-operation no. 3.

The crisis of the Middle East, the rebellions in Eastern Europe and the struggle for a world-wide economy, for world-wide institutions. Bulletin du Conseil Français pour l'Assemblée Constituante des Peuples no. 16 (January & February).

Two Reports given at the Accounts and Economic Budget National Commission: *I. Accounts 1 and 2 of the economic budget of 1957; II. The actual improvements and the desirable improvements in the setting up of the Social Accountancy of France*.

Are the 20th century big firms making their own revolutions? (a report from the Société Belge d'Etudes et d'Expansion, Liège, not published).

Notes on the quantitative techniques of information and the economic policy. *Revue de l'Institut de Sociologie Solvay* no. 3.

My conception of European Integration. *Revue de la Politique Internationale*, September, Belgrade.

The problems of the Sterling area (lecture, Conseil Economique, 7 November).

1958 The different forms of competition in the Common Market. *Revue d'Economie Politique* no. 1.

The Common Market and the Free Exchange Area. *L'Année Politique et Economique* no. 141 (January–March).

The Common Market and the Free Exchange Area. *Tribune des Nations*, 14 February.

The method of Generalized Economy and the economy of mankind. *Economie et Humanisme*. Translations: Polish (Methode ekonomii Uogolnionej i Ekonomia Ozowieka. *Ekonomia Wobec Potrzeb Ludzkich*, Paris) 1961; Spanish (*De Economia* no. 62, Madrid) 1959.

The Common Market, a danger for the French economy. *Journal des Finances*, 7 March.

1959	Wie kann Frankreich wirtschaftlich gesunden? *Der Volkswirtschaft-und-Finanz-zeitung*, 28 February.
	A developing nation: the Republic of Guinea. *L'Action Populaire Review* no. 129 (June).
	The developing nation and the industrial powers. *Les Cahiers de la République*, July–August.
	The different forms of competition in the Common Market. Session at the Société Royale d'Economie Politique de Belgique, 10 November. Translations: Portuguese (*Analise Economica* nos 7–8 (February), Lisbon) 1959.
	Present trend of financial recovery (in Hebrew). *Law and Economics*, June (Tel Aviv).
	The opposition between the East and the West is temporary. *Fortune Française*, 1 September.
	A dialogue with different authors of studies on the peaceful coexistence. Commentaries. *Arguments*, 3rd quarter (Paris).
1960	*A presentation of the Liège Colloquium on Regional Economy.* Bulletin du Grand Liège no. 36 (March).
	The normalized competition between the East and the West. *Renovation Démocratique* no. 19 (March) (conclusion of the article *The developing nations: from the Quasi-Nation to the Civilized Nation.* Rénovation Démocratique, no. 19 (March).
	The hostile coexistence and the rise of world-wide powers. Bulletin des Communautaires de la Vie Nouvelle no. 4 (reproduction of an article published in *Présence Africaine*, Summer 1958).
	The stabilization of basic products and harmonized growth. *L'Action Populaire Review* no. 139 (June).
	Under-development, the developing nation and the means of a collective economy. A second selection of studies on political and social economy offered to Edgard Milhaud. *L'Economie Collective* (Liège).
	A world-wide market? *Economie Appliquée* no. 2.
	The propulsive firm inside a region and the propulsive area. (a Report at the Liège Congress, presented at the Naples Congress, September). Publications: Italian (in *Rassegna Economica* no. 3) 1960; Belgian (in *Regional expansion theory and policy*, Brussels: Librairie Encyclopédique) 1961; French (in *Cahiers de L'I.S.E.A.* Series AD, suppl. 111) March 1961. Translations: Portuguese (in *Revista Brasileira di Ciencias sociales*), Spanish (in *Cuadernos de la Sociedad Venezolania de Planification*, Caracas) June–July 1963.
1961	Big firms and small nations. *Présence Africaine* no. 38, 3rd quarter.
	Information and industrialization. A meeting at the Round Table on the Social Premises of Industrialization. Conseil International des Sciences Sociales, 12–15 September, I.E.D.E.S.
	The contradictions and difficulties of the 20th Century Plan. *Notre République*, 15 November.
	The blocking factors of growth and development (extracts from a course at the College of France).
1962	Preface to *The economic process of development* (Gannage). Paris: PUF.
	Economy devoted to men of the 20th century. *Afrique documents* no. 62 (March–April), Dakar.

Consideraçoes en torno da noçao de polo de crescimento. *Revista Basileira de Estudios Politicos*. Belo-Horizonte, Universidad de Minas Gerais, January. Translation: Spanish (in *Cuadernos de la Sociedad Venezolania de Planificacion*, Caracas) June and July 1963.

An efficient method of economic policy. *Le Courrier du Parlement*, 11 March.

The future belongs to Europe unbounded by the seas. *La Croix*, 3–5 March.

On the urgency of defining an income policy. *Notre République*, 21 June.

Preface to The origin of the South American common market (V. L. Urquidi). *Tiers-Monde*.

1963 To rescue under-developed countries. *Le Coopérateur de France*, 9 March.

South America and Europe. *Notre République* no. 64 (31 May).

Die Europaische Wirtschaftsgeneimschaft und die Assozierung der Aüssereuropaïschen Länder. Berlin: Dunker and Humblot (a participation in the French–German colloquium organized by Professors Neumark and Marczewski, May 1962).

The young nations of Africa. *Notre République*, 7 June.

Big firms and small nations. A supplement to the Jeannerey Report, July.

South America between the Eagle and the Bear. *Notre République*, 19 July.

National moneys, the European money and the world-wide lack of balance. Choeur des Experts. *Notre République*, 25 October.

Monetary imperialisms or a monetary order? *Notre République*, 15 November.

The predominant part played by the Agricultural Common Policy in the future of Europe. *Notre République*, 20 December.

The economy of the USA: a difficult leadership. *Tiers-Monde*, October–December.

Preface to *The problems of New Algeria*. Paris: PUF.

South America and European Europe. *Notre République*, February.

Towards the liberation of prices. *Notre République*, February.

1964 Europe and the "Kennedy Round". *Notre République*, 7 February.

Tomorrow, South America. *L'Information*, September (about the book of G. Gozard).

The Common Market and South America. Revista de la Faculdad de Ciencias Economicas y de Administracion, Montevideo, June.

The techniques of information (extracted from a lecture at the College of France, 1964–65).

Collective techniques (extracted from a lecture at the College of France, 1964–65).

The French economy. In *France today*, a collective book. Paris: Librairie Hatier.

1965 The outerspace conquest and its peaceful applications. *Aviation Magazine*, June (Paris).

Self-financing. *Notre République* no. 203 (February).

Economic integration: who integrates? For whose benefit? Cordoba Colloquium, Argentina, 26–31 July.

Adjustments of the aerospace industry to disarmament and the role of observation in peacekeeping. International Conference, Oslo, 29 August–1 September.

The integration of South America. (An introduction to the review of *Tiers-Monde*, 9 October).

The Plan, a preferential tool of our economic development. Libres Opinions. *Le Monde*, 14 October.

The integration of the Economic Plan with the Economic and Social Development Plan. UNESCO, 28 December.

Outer space conquest and national sovereignty. *Coopération technique* no. 41, pp. 42–3.

The firm and the 20th century economy (the directors of the firm, profit and productivity, a few fundamental concepts), Vol. III. (co-author Bloch-Laine).

The multiplicator of investment in under-developed countries. *Tiers-Monde*, July–September.

Integracion Economica. *Banco Inter-Americano*, 1 February (a lecture held at the Economic Congress of Cordoba, 21 July 1965).

Frenos y bloqueos del desarollo, Conceptos. *De Economia* no. 93, Ano XIX (July–September).

1967 Preface to Pedagogics applied to economy (Salles). *Technique, Art, Science*, 28 June.

Disarmament and its economic consequences for the atomic and aerospace industries. In *Disarmament and world economic interdependence*. Oslo.

From popularization to development. Colloque des conseillers Agricoles de Vichy, July.

Preface to *The explanation of a text dealing with economy* (Salles). Paris: Dunod.

Quien integra? En beneficio de quien se realiza la integracion? *Banco Inter-Americano de Desarrollo* no. 1 (November).

The economic progress. *Economies et Sociétés* no. 7. Also, *Economies et Sociétés* no. 10 (1968). Translation: Portuguese (São Paulo, Brazil).

1968 *Nuevas estructuras del pensamiento economico.* A lecture at the University of Chile, Santiago, January.

La integracion y el fracaso de la teoria de los intercambios exteriores, Africa, January.

The part played by public and private multinational investments in the development and the integration of South America, Bogotá, April.

The multinational investments and the analysis of the development poles and of the integration poles. *Tiers-Monde* no. 34 (June).

Las inversiones multinacionales y el analysis de los polos de desarrollo y de los polos de integracion. *De Economia* no. 100 (February–March).

Agro-industrial Europe. *La vie Française*, April, p. 3.

Economic spaces, growth poles and propulsive units in agriculture. Angers Colloquium, April.

Economic spaces – big firms – small nations – development – the Anglo-Iranian Company and the Dominance Effects. *Economies et sociétés* II, no. 9 (September).

Integration and the failure of the foreign trade theory. *Economie Appliquée* **21**, no. 2.

Propulsive units in agriculture. *Economie Rurale* no. 78 (December).

El Mercado comun y America Latina. *Revista de la Faculdad de Ciencias Economicas* no. 23 (June; Montevideo, Uruguay).

Multinational investment and the analysis of development and integration poles: remarks. *Inter-American Development Bank*, April (Bogotà, Columbia).

1969   The developing nations: from the quasi-Nation to the Civilized Nation. Semaine Sociale d'Angers, 4 July 1959. In The rise of nations in the human community. *Chronique Sociale*, 4th quarter (Lyon).

Preface to the Rumanian edition of *Quantitative techniques of planning*.

Profit? Its origin and its function. *Office Universitaire de Recherche socialiste (O.U.R.S.)* no. 4 (October).

The dialectics of the innovation of the Market and of the Plan. A conference at the Ecole Nationale des Services du Tresor, Conservatoire des Arts et Metiers, Paris, October.

1970   Growth, development and progress. *Grand Larousse Encyclopédique*, May.

The community of the regions of north-west Europe and the tunnel under the Channel. *Revue du Marché Commun*, November.

Una interpretacion critica del proceso europeo de integracion et desarrollo. Integracion politica y economica. Editorial Universitaria, Santiago, Chile.

Innovation and the "Full Innovation" economic system. *Economie Appliquée* **23** (nos 2–3).

To create ... in order to survive. *Le Coopérateur*, November.

1971   *Europe and the industry-agriculture cooperation. Contemporary Europe* (a summary of lectures at the College of France 1971–72). Paris: Union Européenne d'Editions.

La Pareja industria-agricultura en la integracion europea. Madrid Conference, March.

A face to face with François Perroux. *L'Expansion* no. 37 (January), *El Equilibrio de von Neuman – Ensayo de evaluacion* (The von Neuman Equilibrium, an attempt of evaluation). Madrid Conference, March.

For a peaceful economy. *La Revue Nouvelle*, March.

The firm facing growth. Paris: E.S.S.E.C.

Structuralism, economic models, economic structures. Colloquium of the Institut Collègial Européen, Saclay, September 1970. *Economie Appliquée* **24** (no. 3). Translation: Spanish, March 1971.

Inflation and the resignation of western nations. *Les informations* no. 1357 (May).

The inflation of the sixties (a lecture, Société de Comptabilité de France). *Economie Appliquée* **24** (no. 3). Translation: Italian (Cassa di Risparmio di Roma), June 1972.

Walras or the spirit of creation and independence. *La Gazette de Lausanne,* 4–5 June.

Direct investments and multinational firms in Europe (an interview between François Perroux and Jean Denizet). *La Nation*, 18 January.

Monetary inflation and sectorial structure. *Le Monde*, 7 September.

1972   A liberating economy devoted to mankind (interview). *Cité Nouvelle*, March.

The answer to the demand, activism through supplying. *Essor*, special number, March.

Leadership, dollar, stagflation and all that .... *Dirigeant Review*, June–July.

The Mediterranean system. *Revue du Marché Commun*, July–August.

Developing the human energy. *Nouvel observateur*, 2 October.

Profit and "the part of innovation". *Economie Appliquée* no. 4.

1973 The propagating phenomena and inflation. *L'actualité Chimique* no. 2.

The lessons of European integration and their possible applications to the case of South America. Congress organized by the Instituto de Sociologia y Desarrollo del Area Iberica, Bogota, Columbia, 9 July.

The problem of integration in South America Conference at the Diplomatic Academy of Lima, Peru.

Harmonized growth and the difficulties of integration in the heterogeneous economic spaces. Conference at the CORDIPLAN, Caracas, 27 July.

Balance and structure in the exchanges called "Inter-National". Lecture delivered at the Colloque Franco-Latino-Américain d'Economistes, Tours.

The growth of the French economy, 1946–1970, a first assessment. *Economie Appliquée* nos 2–4.

François Perroux answers to the questions of "Nouvelle Ecole". *Nouvelle Ecole* no. 23 (autumn).

1974 *El Dollar, divisa singular y la reforma de la moneda internacional*. Conference at the Trade and Industry House of Madrid, 1 April.

Diferencia entre polos de desarrollo y desarrollo de los polos, el analisis de los polos de desarrollo: polos, areas y ejes de desarrollo. A lecture delivered at the Trade and Industry House of Cordoba, Spain, 5 April.

The anxiety of Creation and Struggle Strategy. Let us read again Pierre Massé. *Revue de la Défense Nationale*, January.

Late 20th century Europe. *Revue Exil* no. 2 (winter).

Multinational investments. Swedish translation, June.

The dollar and the monetary reformation: I. The "second" 20th century. *Le Monde*, 8 June.

The dollar and the monetary reformation: II. Correcting the Western asymmetry. *Le Monde*, 9–10 June.

A Colloquio con gli economisti europei: François Perroux: la combinazione delle crisi. *L'UNITA*, 16 May, Rome.

1975 Making Israel necessary to world-wide development. *France–Israel informations*, April.

The development policy and the blanks of social accounting. *Mondes en développement* no. 10.

1976 The new international order. *Revue des Etudes Coopératives* no. 185.

The rights and the duties of states in the fields of money and finance. *Economic International Justice*. Paris: Gallimard.

1977 The good use of science, the spirit of renovation and the concept of a lively nation. *L'Appel*, July–August.

The nation and the concept of economic orthodoxy. *L'Appel*, December.

The new international order. *Mondes en développement* no. 19.

Economy and power. *Mondes en développement* no. 17.

The very unequal conditions of international exchanges (an answer to President Lopez Portillo). *Le Monde Diplomatique*, May.

1978 The transnational firms and South America. *Revue de la Défense Nationale*, April.

The equilibrium of passive units and the general "equilibrium" of active units. *Economie Appliquée* nos 3–4.

The possibilities of a wider resort to the means on capital markets to meet the wants of development. *Mondes en développement* no. 20. Translation: English (in *Proceedings of the World Scientific Banking Meeting*, Belgrade, Yugoslavia) 1978.

Transnational firms and development poles. *Forum du Développement* no. 49 (November). United Nations, Geneva, Switzerland.

Development, counter-development, co-development. *Journal Rhône-Alpes*, June.

1979 Considering a fusion. Preface to *"A wedding in Basel"* a history of the *CIBA–GEIGY fusion*, P. Erni. Zurich.

The fusion, the work and the economist. An interview to *Scope* (CIBA–GEIGY), April.

Strategy and economic war. *Revue Africaine de Stratégie*, January.

The notion of *"Strategic expense"* and the *"Active Unit"*. Publications of the A.F.E.D.E., April.

The idea of an endogenous and integrated global development (D.G.E.I.). A document intended for a meeting of experts on the concept of integrated development, Quito, 27–31 August. UNESCO.

The policy of science, the analysis of innovation and of its propagation. *Economies et Sociétés* nos 11–12, Series H.S., no. 23.

1980 Getting over the crisis. *Choisir*, February (Geneva, Switzerland).

The world-wide economy and its new spaces. *Chroniques d'Actualité de la S.E.D.E.I.S.*, 1 March.

What does being competitive mean? I.S.M.E.A. Colloquium, 10–14 March, Senat, Paris.

The peregrinations of an economist and the choice of his route. *Banco Nazionale de Lavaro* no. 130 (June).

A new development requires a new financing. International Conference on Development Financing, Dubrovnik, Yugoslavia, 26–31 August.

The coupling of industries and agricultures in the dynamics of a multidimensional development. *Mondes en développement* no. 30.

An international monetary reform through regionalization. *Le Monde*, 12 August.

1981 Economy with a scientific purpose and the thermodynamic inspiration. Académie Royale des Sciences, des Lettres et des Beaux Arts, Brussels, Belgium. *Chroniques d'actualité de la S.E.D.E.I.S.*, 15 January.

The Cancun Meeting: a new chance anyway. *Le Monde*, 20 October.

Cancun: what is the meaning of the North-South Conference? *France Catholique – Ecclésia*, 22 October.

Structure and the exchange called "International". The reconsidered general equilibrium. *Rivista Internazionale di scienze Economiche e Commerciali* no. 1 (December).

1982 The "inner" market and its conquerors. A dialogue with G. Blardone, in the *Chroniques d'Actualité de la S.E.D.E.I.S.* XXVI, no. 5 (1 March). Translation: Italian (*Rassegua Economica* no. 2) March–April 1982.

Economic competitions and collective competitions. In *Dialogue des monopoles et des nations*. Translation: Italian (*Rivista di Politica* VII) 1982.

1984 Beyond the welfare state. *Economie Appliquée* no. 1 (also to be published by the University of Padua in association with the International Jacques Maritain Institute, Rome).

Social matters

1928   *Georges Sorel and the General Strike.* Revue de l'Université de Lyon.
Fascist syndicalism. *Revue d'Economie Politique.* The dictatorship of the prolateriate among Marxists, *Questions Pratiques.*

1930   The evolution of the notion of defence of professional interests in agricultural trade unions. *Revue d'Economie Politique.*

1936   "Paternalism" against the human being. *Esprit.*
Labour law and the worker. *Esprit.*
Il Socialismo tedesco a proposito dell'ultimo opera di Werner Sombart. *Rivista Italiana di Scienzo Economiche.*
A proposito del "Sicialismo tedesco". *Rivista Internazionale di Scienze Sociali.*

1938   The limit and the enlargement of the notion of class. *Esprit.*
Notes on the use of texts with general contents. *Esprit.*
On Counter-Revolution. *La Vie Intellectuelle* nos 10–11.
The intelligence of the nation. *Esprit.*
Representation as fiction and as a reality. *Esprit* nos 1–2.
The fertility of custom: parliamentary custom, professional custom. *Revue de Synthèse*, December (about the last book of Maxime Leroy).

1941   Towards a community order and a community economy. *Construire.*
Our community. In *The French Community I: community and society.* Paris: PUF.

1942   Our community. In *The French Community.* Paris: PUF.
The Labour Charter, its contents and its spirit. *Rencontres.*
The proletariate within the nation: the proletariate and capitalism, the proletariate and the community (a brochure).
The French community IV: community and economy. Paris: PUF.
The firm and the Labour Community. In *The French Community IV: community and economy.* Paris: PUF.

1943   The "Science" of man and economic science. In *Three essays on the science of man.* Paris: Librairie Médicis.

1945   *Democracy.* Brochure of the Groupes de travail, July.
Liberalism and freedom. (an extract from *Mélanges* by Gonnard).

1946   The ambiguity of federalism. A collection of essays entitled *Nation or Federalism.* Présences collection. Paris: Plion.
Socialism and tradition. *La Vie Intellectuelle*, June.

1949   The everlasting order of agriculture. *Critique* no. 32 (January) (about *The everlasting order of agriculture* (M. R. Maspetiol)).
Fatherhood and brotherhood, the Christian family and the "murder of the father". *Critique*, July.

1950   Don't let us be narrow-minded European people. *La Vie Intellectuelle*, April.

1952   Notes on the economic status of religious communities in the economic life of France nowadays. In *Poverty, a problem of today's religious life* (a collective book). Paris: Ed. du Cerf.

1955   *The world and Europe* (Die Eine Welt und Europa), Dokumente, Offenburg (extracts from *Europe unbounded by the seas.* Paris: PUF.)
The part played by international organizations in the training of new international élites. *Bulletin Mensuel d'Information de L'O.F.I.* no. 2 (an allocution at the Inaugural Meeting on the Orientation to an International Function).

Europe unbounded by the seas. *Recherches et Débats*, special number, May (a lecture delivered on 24 January at the Centre Catholique des Intellectuels Français).

The barbarians and the quest for a new economy. *Informations Catholiques Internationales* no. 13 (1 December).

Mankind has to build its house and its Church. *Combat*, 30–31 July. Translations: Arabic (*Ac chirah*, Beirut); Hebrew (*The co-operative economy*, Tel Aviv) January, 1958; Ecole Estienne, 1959.

1956   *On a few aspects of barbarism in the economic life of peoples, the Church and the civilizations.* Semaine des Intellectuels Catholiques, November. Paris: Publications of C.C.I.F.

A simple question on the freedom of research. *Chronique Sociale* no. 5 (September, Lyon).

Auguste Comte reproved political economy. *Le Monde*, 14 November.

Albert Aftalion, a necrological note. *Economie Appliquée* no. 4.

Preface to *The world-wide agrarian policy and the experiment of Israel* (Professor A. Granott). Paris: PUF.

1958   Introduction to *Cahiers de Marxologie* (Rubel). Paris: Publications of the I.S.E.A.

La Poverta. Vol. III, pp. 205–31. Edizione Paoline.

1959   *Stellung der Arbeitenebmer in der Modernen Wirtschaftspolitik*. Internationale Tagung des Sozialakademie Dortmund (Herausgegeben von Unv. Prof. H. Bayer) Berlin: Dunker & Humblot.

1961   *Christianity and civilization, the aberrations of man*. Paris: Horay (a publication of the lectures delivered in La Semaine des Intellectuels Catholiques, 1960).

A foundation rite (against the death penalty). The execution of a couple (a reproduction of the article published in *L'Actualité Religieuse*, 1 July 1953).

Feeding men, hunger and thirst. The route of silent men. Translations: Spanish (Mexico) 1963, Esperanto (Paris) 1963.

1962   Preface to *Algeria of tomorrow*, a collective book. Paris: Tiers-Monde, PUF.

Against the social life. *Croissance des Jeunes Nations* no. 14 (September).

Collective creation and the economy of the 20th century. *La Croix*, 11–12 November.

The spirit of collective creation in the present economic context (work, creation, contemplation). In *Work and the human condition*. Fayard. (Semaine des Intellectuels Catholiques, November.)

The historical chances of unity. *La Croix*, 12 December.

1963   *Working for peace and competition between economic systems*. Ville d'Avray: Publications of the Mouvement Chrétien pour la Paix.

The mental under-development of the "white man" and the problem of under-developed countries. *Le Cri*, January.

The Fourth Plan and collective creation. *Notre République*, 24 February.

The future of African nations. *La Croix*, 28 February.

Opposing death penalty. *Réforme*, 2 March.

Europe unbounded by the seas. *Notre République*, 1 March.

Dialectics and socialization. Preface to *The Works of Karl Marx*. Vol. 1 (M. Rubel, ed.). La Pleiade Collection. Paris: Gallimard.

Poverty and the word. *Cahiers Universitaires Catholiques*, April (Paris).

Preface to *Feeding men* (Cepede). Brussels: CEP.

Main publications of François Perroux

1964
: The failures of enrichment and efficient poverty. *Croissance des Jeunes Nations*, April (conference held in Strasbourg, 3 January 1964).
: Wealth and poverty in the 20th century: questions asked to Christians. In *The Church invited to be courageous*. Paris: Centurion.
: Humaneness is not a quality of the Marxist class alone. *Notre République*, April.
: The French economy. In *France today*, a collective book. Paris: Librairie Hatier.
: *Alienation and collective creation*. Publications of the I.S.E.A., M 20.
: An economy devoted to any man and to all men. *La Vie Enseignante*, September/October. Translation: Spanish (Lima) 1964.
: The image of the New Man and the collective techniques of the second half of the 20th century. *Tiers-Monde*, October/December.
: Planetary economy. *Tiers-Monde*, October-December.
: Which future for under-developed countries? *Notre République*, October.

1965
: *An opening address at the Académie des Sciences d'Outre-Mer*. A publication of the Académie des Sciences d'Outre-Mer, February.
: Los Creadores Politicos. *Economia Politica*, January and March (Mexico).
: Creation, a vocation of the 20th century. *Notre République*, March.
: *The limits of the integration of young people in the plans of developing countries*. Childhood, Youth and Development Plans Meeting, 19–21 May.
: Social progress and economic progress. *El comercio*, 30 May, Lima.
: The aerospace conquest and its peaceful applications. *Aviation Magazine*, June (Paris).
: The firm today. *Notre République*, 1 October.
: Industry and collective creation. *Humanisme et Entreprise* no. 34 (December).
: Man and the collective creation. *La Pignata*, December.

1966
: The limits of the integration of a childhood and youth policy in a development plan. *Les carnets de l'Enfance* no. 5. UNICEF.
: *Brochures on childhood*. Colloquium, UNICEF, February. Printed in May.

1967
: Towards an economy of the whole man and of all men. *Project* no. 15 (May).
: A note on the town considered as a development pole and as a center of progress. *Tiers-Monde*, May.
: Preface to Pictures and machines. *Coopération Technique*, 14 June.
: Preface to *Poblacion mundial y los medios de subsistancia* (Cepede and Houtart).
: *Las Alienaciones en el Medio Industrial*. Amaru, Revista de Artes y Ciencias Universidad de Ingenieria, Lima, no. 2 (April).
: Industria y creacion colectiva. *De Economia* no. 96, ano XIX (October, Madrid).
: *Social promotion*: the rise of groups and the order of power. The official opening of the Law Faculty of Lyon (November).
: *Firms and societies*. Ecole Alsacienne, Paris, 12 December.
: The image, the machine, the social mechanics. *Technique, Art Science* no. 214 (December).

1968
: The nation and the liberation of masses. *Notre République* no. 31 (June). Translation: Spanish (*El Tiempo*, Bogota) 1968.

La Nacion y las exigencias de la economia del siglo veinte. Anales de la Faculdad de Ciencias Juridicas y sociales, Universidad de la Plata **XXIII**.

1969   *Innovation and the plan.* French–Rumanian Colloquium, Bucharest.

An interview on "Bread and the world". *Croissance des Jeunes Nations*, July.

The diffusion of information through mass techniques. Assemblée de la Presse Etrangère, Paris, October.

Economy and the future of mankind. Rencontre entre Chrétiens, Paris.

1970   A new spirit for a new society. *La nation*, June.

The mass society and the 20th century economy. Association pour la promotion économique et sociale, Le Havre, June.

To connect promotion with participation. *Economies et Sociétés* no. 9.

First remarks on participation. *Economies et Sociétés* no. 9 (August).

1971   Perroux, il Buon Samaritano dello Sviluppo, interview. *Citta Nuova*, 25 October.

1972   Money should be disgraced. *Panorama d'Aujourd'hui*, November.

1973   A second-reading of Saint-Simon: industry and the universalization of culture. *Economies et Sociétés* no. 1.

The rise of masses, interview. *Combat*, 17 April.

The economy of the 20th century and the full development of human energy. A lecture delivered at the Secundas Jornadas Internacionales del Pensamiento Communitario, organized by the Center of Social and Economic Researches for South America, Merida, Venezuela.

1974   *The preference for life.* A lecture delivered at the Colloquium on Abortion and the Crisis of Society, organized by L'Association Française de Prospective Sociale, Tours, 22–23 March.

A recollection of Serge Tchakhotine. *Combat*, 10 January.

An interview with François Perroux. *La Nouvelle Action Française*, 6 March.

1975   From man to man, a common norm to economy and to nature. *Economies et Sociétés*, Series ES2.

1977   The evidence given by the witnesses of freedom. *Le Monde*, 1 October.

The antidote to alienations, a challenge of Henri Bartoli. *Le Monde*, July.

Whom is it by? France is an actor and not an object. *Le Monde*, December.

Where to find money for under-developed countries? *Le Monde*, December.

Money and monetarism. *Le Figaro*, July.

The very unequal conditions of international exchanges (an answer to President Lopez Portillo). *Le Monde Diplomatique*, May.

1978   Social promotion, a warrant for peace and a universal aspiration. *Comprendre* nos 43–4.

Growth, for whom and what for? *Le Monde*, April.

An interview with the economist François Perroux: regions, economy and power. *Action Royaliste*.

The canvas of time, an interview with André Fontaine. *Le Monde*, 28 June.

The crisis of the economic science or the failure of economists. *Journal Rhône-Alpes*, 26 September.

Transnational firms and development poles. *Forum du Développement* no. 49 (November). United Nations, Geneva, Switzerland.

1979	On frugality: Tevoedjre meeting Rousseau. *Choisir*, June (Switzerland).
1980	The present crisis started long before the rise of oil prices of 1973. An interview, *Journal La Meuse*, 5 May (Liège, Belgium).
	The dialogues of Athens, with President Tsatsos and Mrs Tsatsos. On Radio-France.
	The will to be competitive. *Le Monde*, 25 March.
1983	This love which does not lie. *France Catholique* no. 1884 (21 January).
	One may doubt the ability of the State to arbitrate the interests on which one is dependent. *Royaliste* no. 376 (17 February).
	Facing the "Coalition of the Masters" one should first agree on a common language. *T.E.L.*, 3 March.
	Raising the monetary veil. *Le Monde*, 21 May.
	Culture is not an adornment. *Enjeu*, July–August.
1984	Economy with a scientific purpose and the thought of Teilhard de Chardin. *Mondes en Développement* nos 47–8.

Political matters

1933	*The Small Agreement: the conflict between politics and economy in Danubian Europe.* Lyon.
1934	Danubian Europe. *Affaires extérieures*.
1935	The Small Agreement since its origins. *Encyclopédie balkanique*. A new tenet of public law – Portugal and Salazar, an attempt of interpretation. *Affaires Etrangères*.
1938	"Weltanschauung" and policy. *La Vie Intellectuelle*, October.
	La Crisi dell'Europa. *Rassegna di Politica Internazionale* 8, ano XIII.
1945	America and us. *Productions Françaises*, September.
	A preface to peace. *Productions Françaises*, September.
	The Labour Party and the international situation. *Productions Françaises*, December.
1946	The political power and its functions. *Groupe Travail*, March.
	Marxism and political power. *Groupe Travail*, March.
1949	A debate over American aid (an answer to Georges Bataille). *Critique* no. 30 (November).
	Beyond the nation – from the slogan to the analysis. *Fédération* nos 55–6 (November).
	Partisan nations. *Fédération* nos 55–6 (November).
1951–2	*The quest for Europe.* A lecture delivered at the Centre Universitaire Méditérranéen. Published in the reports of this centre, Vol. V.
1952	Hubert Beuve-Méry and the French Independence. *La Vie Intellectuelle*, July.
	The aerospace conquest, socialization, universalization. *Comprendre* nos 23–4. Extract republished in *Bulletin de l'Union Catholique des Scientifiques Français*, September/October 1962.
1958	The hostile coexistence and the advent of world-wide powers. *Présence Africaine* (summer). Also published in *Conflent* no. 1 (May) 1959.
	The hostile coexistence and the planetary economy. *Cahiers Internationaux de Sociologie* XXV.
1959	The tendency to economic integration in the present world. In *L'Encyclopédie Française*. Vol. XX: *The aspects of the present world, 1958*.

The peaceful coexistence. *Rénovation Démocratique* no. 12 (February).
The dialogue between Kruschev and Eisenhower: can the opposition between capitalism and communism be got over? Translation: Italian (*Il Protagore* no. 5, Rome).

1962 The aerospace conquest and the national sovereignty. *Diogène* no. 39 (July/September).

1965 A presentation of "South America and European Europe". *Coopération Technique* nos 38–40.
Egypt 1965. *Notre République* no. 181 (2 July).
An estimation of the septenate of General de Gaulle, the only applicant for the future. Answers to both the questions of *Notre République* no. 196 (26 November).
Liberating by the means of science, techniques and industry. *Notre République*, 22 November.
A new horizon. *Notre République*, 23 December.

1967 *The agrarian problems of Southern Americas*. International Colloquium, C.N.R.S., July.
An intervention at the Academie des sciences d'Outre-Mer. *Japon*, February.
A note on The town considered as a development pole and as a center of progress. Spain at the time of development. *Tiers-Monde* no. 32, p. 1147.

1969 Preface to *Economic and cultural Rumania*. Geneva: Droz.

1970 Economic independence or satellization? *Les Informations*, March.
Cooperation tomorrow. *Les Cooperateurs*, February.
The awakening of the strengths of a nation through a great, clearly defined plan. *La Nation*, June.
Policy begins where violence stops. Mouvement International de la Reconciliation, Mulhouse, May.
Information without formation. Association de la Presse Etrangère. Also published in *Tribune Libre*, 1971.

1971 The dollar: Europe is reasonable. *Le Coopérateur de France* no. 542 (9 October).

1972 Strengths in the world and security in Europe. *Le Monde Diplomatique*, May.

1975 The logic of the Barre Plan and the real problems of inflation. *La Vie Française*, September.

1977 Does the world belong to industrialized nations or do industrialized nations belong to the world? *Le Monde Diplomatique*, May.

1978 Eighteen months of economic policy. An interpretation and perspectives. *Chroniques d'Actualité de la S.E.D.E.I.S.*, March.

1979 Europe unbounded by the seas in 1979. *Chroniques D'Actualité de la S.E.D.E.I.S.*, February.

Philosophical matters

1963 The failure. *La Croix*, 2–3 June.
1965 *Collective creation and 20th century Christianity*. Publications of the I.S.E.A., January.

War or the sharing of bread, the peaceful coexistence. *Vie Enseignante*, June.

The presence of R. P. Lebret. *La Croix*, 21 July. Also published in *Tiers-Monde*, September 1966 and *Economie et Humanisme*, October 1966.

The praise of Professor Couffignal. *Technique Art Science*, October.

1966 The failure of modern economy and the chances of human progress. *Le Saulchoir*, May. Translation: Spanish (Barcelona) June 1967.

1967 The encyclical letter on resurrection and the uses of undue authority of the Great. *La Croix*, 19–21 April.

An interrupted piece of music (Père Maillard). *La Croix*, 21–22 May.

Preface to *Death penalty* (Savey-Casard). Geneva: Droz.

1968 A homage to Mr Henri Laugier. *Biology and development*. Paris: PUF.

1970 *Who is in favour of Jesus Christ? An Answer*. Paris: Editions du Cerf.

Herbert Marcuse and the finality of the occidental society. A lecture at the Institute de France, Académie des Sciences Morales et Politiques, March.

The failure of modern economy and the chances of modern progress. *Faim et soif des hommes* no. 4.

The intellectual crisis of French catholicism. *La Nation* (about the book of Jean Lacroix).

To connect promotion with participation. *Economies et Sociétés* no. 9 (August).

First remarks: "Participation". *Economies et Sociétés* no. 9 (August).

Herbert Marcuse and the finality of contemporary society. Institut de France, Académie des Sciences Morales et Politiques, November.

Questions of François Perroux to Herbert Marcuse, who answers. A debate. Marseilles: Sup de Co.

Questions of François Perroux to Herbert Marcuse. Editorial, *Nova Terra*, Barcelona, Tamarit.

1971 Participation is a liberation. *Le Télégramme de Paris* no. 44 (January).

The damned part and silence. *L'Arc*, 12 March (a conference on Georges Bataille, Orleans).

El Recurso Humano (Human energy). A conference in Malaga, March.

The alienation of industrial societies and the liberation of man. A conference at the C.F.T.C. of Rouen, March.

Philosophy and critical theory of society (Italian translation). Rome: Citta Nuova Editrice.

Industry and the universalization of culture (Spanish translation). Madrid.

1972 An evidence in the book *Points of view*, dedicated to Pierre Lebrun. Paris.

1972–3 The human energy. *Communion* no. 103.

1973 *The economic agent (mathematical structures and the structures of the real)*. A lecture delivered at the Advanced School of Management, Bogota, Columbia, 12 July.

Power and economy. A conference held at the Center of Advanced Military Studies, Lima, Peru, 17 July.

The mathematization of the agent. A lecture delivered at the Academy of Sciences of Peru, Lima, 18 July.

1974 *El Equilibrio General restructurado por las unidades activas*. A lecture delivered at the Second French–Spanish Colloquium, Madrid, 2–4 April.

The economic agent: mathematization and reality. A conference held at the Colegio Universitario de Estudios Financieros, Madrid, 3 April.

The analysis of inner and outer commercial exchanges: its unification through resorting to topological spaces. A lecture delivered at the French–Polish Colloquium, Paris, 27 May.

The topological theory of the Including Equilibrium and the thermodynamics of Ilya Prigogine. A lecture delivered at the colloquium on Sadi Carnot and the rise of Thermodynamics, Ecole Polytechnique, Paris, 13 June.

The economic agent, mathematization and reality. Varied studies offered to André Carrigou-Lagrance.

1975   In the name of law. *La Croix*, 6–7 July.

1983   *The text of the intervention at the International Colloquium on Teilhard de Chardin.* UNESCO, Philosophy Series B, October.

Index

Aftalion, Albert 77
aid, international: urban and regional development 300–1
Alonso, William 15, 315, 376; on population factor 16–17, 131–41
altruism 201, 203
Amin, S.: dependency theory 103; on Third World 107
Amoroso, Luigi 80
analysis techniques 17–18, 142–68; choice of 142; evaluation of 142; economic base models 143; input-output models 144–5; shift-share analysis 146–7; gravity models 147–8; cost-benefit analysis 148–9; structural econometric models 149–51; time-series forecasting models 151–2; vector autoregression model 151–2; demoeconomic models 152–4; multi-regional models 154–6; qualitative impact models 156–7; growth poles 157–9
Antonelli, Etienne 77
Appalachia Regional Commission 6
Arrow, Kenneth J.: Perroux on 34, 84
Atlantic Development Board 4–5
atomism 117–18
Australian Arbitration Commission 200

Baran, Paul: on Third World 97
Bocage, Ducarmel: on Perroux 46
Boudeville, Jacques 49, 117; revision of growth pole theory 44–5, 105
Boulding, Kenneth: *The Economics of Love and Fear* 34
Breton, Albert: competitive federalism 228
Buchanan Report (Ireland) 360
bureaucracy training 301–3

Canada: regional policies 4, 7, 20–4, 225–43; Department of Regional Economic Expansion 7; Special Area Agreements 7; comparative advantage approach 10; subsidies 10; regional disparity 197–8; trade-off curves 206–7, 212–21; federalism 225–43; unemployment 230, 256–61; regional expenditure 231; *see also* Quebec
capital grant: policy 26; evaluation of 330–74
capitalism: and regional planning 118

cargo cult 138, 139
Chamberlin, Edward 81
China: enterprise zones 139
city *see* urban development
classical economics 116–19; *see also* neoclassical economics
Clavel, Pierre 119; opposition planning 124
community indifference curve 179–80
comparative advantage 9–10
consumer 171–7
Corragio, J. L.: on growth poles 95, 96, 97
cost-benefit analysis 148–9
Courchene, Thomas J. 15; neo-classicist 1, 12, 169–89, 376; on factor mobility 18; on interregional disparity 186–8
Cournot, A. 84
cumulative causation concept: Myrdal's 24, 43, 198

Davin, L. E.: on growth poles 102
Debreu, G. 84
decentralization 319–20, 360–1; and technology 324–6
demoeconomic models 152–4
demometrics 132–5
Department of Regional Economic Expansion (Canada) 7
dependency theory 97–100; and linkages 103–4
developing countries: and transnational firms 61–6; industrial structure 68; dependency theory 97–9; and technical progress 105; and New International Economic Order 106–7; and World Bank 299–317
development areas 71
development axes 55, 71
development poles 48, 49–50, 70; and present-day dynamics 51–4; and economic policy 54–8; criticisms answered 58–60; effects of 71–2; *see also* growth pole
Dignan, Anthony: on capital grants 26, 330–74
disparity, regional 24, 105–6, 126, 198, 269–95, 377, 380–1; natural level of 18, 186–8; United States 197; Myrdal on 198; and national development 204–6; and trade-off curves 206–8, 210–21;

411

unemployment 229–31, 269, 271–2; income 231–6, 269–72; and migration 270–96
distribution: growth pole theory 104–6; incentives 330–74
Distribution of Industry Act (UK) 343
Domar, Evsey: on cumulative causation 198
domination 14, 82, 94, 96–100
Duquesne de la Villele, Marjolin 48

earnings: disparity 234–6, 269–70
economic base models 143
Economic Commission for Latin America 98
Economic Development Administration (USA) 7, 45
economic policy: and poles of development 54–8
efficiency 194–5
endowment difference model 182–6
enterprise zones 139
entrepreneurship: Schumpeter on 38–9; Perroux on 40; and population 139–41
environment policy 73
equilibrium theory 13, 34, 36, 50, 51; Perroux and 80, 83, 84
European Economic Community: regional policy 5; regional incentives 340; maximum assistance levels 341; assisted areas 342
export push development 75
Eyrault, M. 77

factor mobility 18, 186
federalism 4; and regional development 225–43; political process 225–9; heterogeneous preferences 225–6; production and trade 226–7; intergovernmental trading 227–9; competitive 228
fiscal equalization program: Canada 4
fiscal transfers 229–40
fluctuation, regional 209–10
forecasting techniques 142; see also analysis techniques; models
Forest, Yvon: on politics of place 16, 115–30
France 8; urban development 324, 328
Frank, A. G.: on NIEO 106–7
Friedman, Milton 196; on natural rate of unemployment 208, 377
Friedmann, John 15, 49, 376; on politics of place 16, 115–30; on city size 380; on neoclassical economics 381
fundamentalism, economic 135–8

Gaile, G. L.: on growth poles 105
Gaitskell, Hugh 79

Galbraith, John Kenneth: on power 199; on new industrial state 325
Gini, Corrado 80
Gonnard, René 77
government: intervention 1–2; 380–1; and wage determination 200; federalism 225–43; decision-making process 227; *see also* federalism
gravity models 147–8
growth: growth-inducing units 67; growth-inducing industries 67–9
growth poles vii, 6–9, 40, 41–6, 48–50, 61, 70, 198, 377–9; theory and strategy 91–111; historical context 92–5; alternatives compared 95–107; Perroux's theory 96–7, 378; and domination 96–100; and linkages 100–4; and distribution 104–6; and inequalities 105–6; analysis 157–9; *see also* development poles

Haberler, Gottfried von 78
Haddad, Gaston 219–20
Hansen, Niles M. 49; on cities 25–6, 314–15, 318–29, 378
Harrod, Sir Roy 81; growth theory 43; cumulative causation 198
Hayek, Friedrich von 78, 81
Haynes, Kingsley: on capital grants 25, 26, 330–74
heterogeneous preferences 225–6
Hicks, Sir John R. 81; on welfare 33; trade cycle model 209
Higgins, Benjamin 66, 375–84; on United States 5; on regional development and national economy 21, 193–224; on Perroux 31–47; on Europe 93; on growth pole strategy 105; on macro-regions 148
Hirschmann, Albert 117; on linkages 101

incentives: investment 341–2; regional 330–74; United Kingdom 346–9
income disparity 231–6, 269–70
Industrial Development Act (Ireland) 357, 358, 361; (UK) 344
Industrial Development Authority (Ireland) 358–9
Industrial Development Certificate (UK) 330, 343
Industrial Grants Act (Ireland) 355–7
industrialization 68–9
industry, growth-inducing 67–9
inequality *see* disparity
inflation: Canada 218–21
infrastructure projects 7
innovation 378; as economic driving force 38–9, 40, 42; Perroux's innovation effect 67, 94; and population 135–41

Index

input-output models 144–5
institutional learning 301–3
integration pole 70–1
interdependence 82–3
investment: and linkages 102; incentives 341–2
Ireland 26; capital grants program 330–1; regional development 354–72; Anglo-Irish Free Trade Agreement 354; Undeveloped Areas Act 354–5, 359; Industrial Grants Act 355–7; indicators 360; Industrial Development Act 357, 358, 361; New Industry Program 358, 362–71; Industrial Development Authority 358–9; migration 359–60; location patterns 366–71
Isard, Walter 81, 117; and regional science 6; general equilibrium theory 50
Italy: decentralization of labor 327

Japan: Technopolis Plan 8; growth poles 45

Keynes, John Maynard 33, 80; general theory 13, 37–8, 81, 117; unemployment paradigm 247–8
Kindelberger, Charles: on dominance 36

labor: migration of 24, 133–4, 135, 152–4, 270; labor force participation rates 134; social cost of 244–68; defined 245–6; spatial division of 326–8
Lajugie, Joseph 49
land policy 73
Leontief, W.: on developing countries 105–6
Lévesque, René 123
linkages, economic 14, 100–4; Perroux on 101, 103; dependency theory view 103–4
Lipsey, R.: trade-off curves 208
Local Employment Act (UK) 343–4

Machlup, Fritz 78
MacNamara, Robert 306
market: new economic fundamentalism 135–8; failure 195–6; mechanism of 196–201; omissions 201–2
Martin, Fernand: on unemployment insurance benefits 23–4, 244–68
Marxism 39, 94, 103, 198; neo-Marxist theory 198–9, 302; on industrialization 325
Mathur-Rosen econometric model 143
Mauritania: growth poles 45
Mayer, Hans 78
Melvin, James 15; neoclassical theory 18, 169–89, 376; on interregional disparity 186–8, 377
migration 24, 133–4, 135–8, 270–1, 377; and

policy analysis 152–4; and amenities 270–1; and disparity 270–96; cities 322; Ireland 359–60
Milner, H.: on Quebec 123
Mises, Ludwig von 78, 79
models: economic base 143; input-output 144–5; shift-share 146–7; gravity 147–8; cost-benefit 148–9; structural econometric 149–51; time-series 151–2; demo-economic 152–4; multiregional 154–6; qualitative impact 156–7; growth pole analysis 157–9
monopoly 115, 199–200; Schumpeter on 39; Perroux on 95
Moore, B., and Rhodes, J.: shift-share analysis 146
Moore, C. L.: on minimum requirements 143
Moore, C. W.: on growth poles 102
Morgenstern, Otto 13, 78, 83, 170
multiregional models 154–6
Myrdal, Gunnar 80, 117; cumulative causation 24, 43, 198; on regional disparity 204; on migration 271

national development: and regional planning 118; and regional economy 193–224; and regional disparity 204–6
Neminov, Professor: on growth poles 48
neoclassical economics 43, 169–89, 194, 197, 376; philosophical assumptions 202–4; unemployment paradigm 247–8
Neumark, Fritz 80
New Industry Program 358, 362–71
New International Economic Order 106–7
Nijkamp, P.: qualitative impact analysis 156–7
Nugent, J. B.: on linkages 101–2

Organization of Petroleum Exporting Countries (OPEC) 107

Paelinck, J.: on growth poles 102
Pareto, Vilfredo 83; Pareto optimum 202
Perroux, François 12–15, 19, 31–47, 48–90, 171, 376; growth poles vii, 6, 9, 40, 41–6, 48–50, 61, 92–111, 198, 378, 379; "Au delà du Welfare State" 33–7; on welfare economics 33–7, 203; and Keynes 37–8; and Schumpeter 38–41; theory of space 40; general theory of development 48–76; in Vienna 78–80; in Rome 80; in Paris 80; in England 81; theory of interdependence 82–3; and linkages 101; and regional planning 117; on neo-classical economics 169–70, 188–9; on interregional disparity 171, 187, 226, 377;

publications 385–410
philosophy: of welfare economics 202–4
Pigou, A. C.: economic policy maxims 88
place, politics of 16, 115–28; in Quebec 120–4; and planning 127–8
planning: economic 94, 115; regional 115–28; and politics of place 127–8
Pleven, René 81
polarization *see* development poles; growth poles
Polenske, Karen R.: on growth poles 14, 41, 91–111
policy analysis *see* analysis techniques
population factor 17, 131–41; migration 133–4, 135; labor force participation rates 134; forecasting models 152–4
Prebisch, Raul 106
Prebisch-Singer thesis 97
preference differences 172–3; traditional model 177–80; international model 180–2
production technology 226–7
Public Works and Economic Development Act (USA) 7–8

qualitative impact analysis 156–7
Quebec 16, 17; and politics of place 120–4; and innovation 141; economic fluctuations 210

Rao, V. S. 172
Raynauld, André: on federalism 22–3, 225–43
recession 211
Regional Employment Premium (UK) 330, 344
regional planning 155–28
regional policy: microlevel effectiveness 331–8; macrolevel 338–9; mesolevel 339–43; UK 351–4; Ireland 354–72
regionalism: Quebec 120–4
Rhodes, J.: shift-share analysis 146
Richardson, Harry W. 15; on tools of regional analysis 17–18, 142–68; on USA 197
Robertson, Sir Dennis 81
Robinson, Joan 81
Rodwin, Lloyd: on World Bank 25, 299–317
Rogers, Andrei: demometric models 132
Rostow, W. W.: stages of economic growth theory 117
Rousseau, Jean-Jacques 35
Royal Commission on the Economic Union and Development Prospects for Canada 2

Sakashita, N.: on cost-benefit analysis 148

Samuelson, Paul 81; *Economics* 94; Stolper-Samuelson theorem 172, 177, 178, 179
Savoie, Donald J. 375–84; on government intervention 2
Schmitt, Carlo 80
Schofield, J. A.: cost-benefit analysis 148
Schumpeter, Joseph 14, 33, 37, 38–41, 78, 81; influence on Perroux 94
Scitovsky, Tibor 34
Seers, D.: on Third World 105
Sen, Amartya: on altruism 203
shift-share analysis 146–7
Smith, Neil: neo-Marxism 199
social aspects 131–41
Solow, Robert: on market failure 195
Sombart, Werner 79
space, economic theory of 40, 81, 93
Spain 8
Spann, Othmar 78
Special Area Agreements (Canada) 7
Spiegel, Henry W.: on Perroux 46
statism 118
Stolper-Samuelson theorem 172, 177, 178, 179
Streeten, Paul 81; on Perroux vii, 32
Strigl, R. von 78
structural econometric models 149–51
structuralists 98
subsidies 10–11
Szentes, T.: on dependency relations 103–4

tariff policy 19–20, 179; and inter-regional trade 180–2, 185; and factor mobility 182
technology 378; and decentralization 324–6
Technopolis Plan (Japan) 8
Tennessee Valley Authority 5–6
Third World *see* developing countries
time-series forecasting models 151–2
Tinbergen, Jan: on distribution 105–6
trade: theory 9; neoclassical model 172–6; tariffs 176, 179, 180–2; preference differences 177–80; interregional 180–6; and national market 227
trade-off curves: and regional disparity 206–8, 210–21
transfers: regional 229–40, 271; personal 274
transnational firms: and developing countries 61–6
transportation 55
trends, regional 209–10

Undeveloped Areas Act (Ireland) 354–5, 359
unemployment 208; disparity 229–31, 269, 271–2; types of 247–8; Canada 220, 256–61; and wages 271–2
unemployment insurance benefits 244–68;

and unemployment rate 248–54, 256–9; welfare implications 254–6

United Kingdom 8; subsidies 10; capital grant policy 26; Regional Employment Premium 330, 344; Industrial Development Certificate 330, 343; investment incentives 341; regional policy 343–54; Distribution of Industry Act 343; Local Employment Act 343–4; Finance Act (1963) 344; Industrial Development Act 344

United Nations: Economic Commission for Latin America (ECLA) 106; Conference on Trade and Development (UNCTAD) 106

United States of America: regional policy 5; Economic Development Administration 7, 45; Public Works and Economic Development Act (1965) 7–8; growth poles 45; and world trade 82; regional disparity 197; regional development 205; cities 321

urban development 318–29, 378–9; World Bank 299, 303–6; patterns of change 323–4; decentralization 324–6; optimal size 380

urban disamenities 136

Uri, Pierre 80

Vanderkamp, John: on disparity 24, 269–95, 377

vector autoregression model 151–2

Vienna school of economics 78–80

wages: determination of 200; disparity 271, 290; and unemployment 271–2

Walras, Léon 77; equilibrium theory 13, 34, 50, 51, 80

Walton, J.: on internal dependency 98

Weaver, Clyde: *Territory and Function* 49

Weber, Alfred 140

Weber, Max 33, 139, 140

welfare economics 202; Perroux on 33–4; philosophical assumptions 202–4; implications of unemployment insurance benefits 254–6

Wicksell, Knut 80

Williams, Raymond: on capital restructuring 119

Williamson, Jeffrey: on regional disparity 205

World Bank 25, 299–317; bureaucracy training 301–3; urban and regional programs 303–6

Yotopoulos, P. A., and Nugent, J. B.: on linkages 101–2